Contents

Preface
to the First Edition

When lawyers present their cases before the courts, they often engage in debate. Another word for debate, when applied to the judicial process, is forensics (L. *forensis*, market, or forum). Over the years, the increasing application of scientific principles to difficult court cases has given rise to the general field of *forensic science*, or science as applied to law. Forensic science includes all areas of scientific endeavor, such as medicine, psychiatry, psychology, geology, physics, chemistry, and biology. That particular area of forensic science which describes the services normally provided by crime laboratories is known as *criminalistics*.

The one statement that perhaps most clearly epitomizes the pursuits of the criminalist is that made by Edmund Locard, who said, "Every contact leaves a trace." Many years ago such a statement was merely a dream, but modern technology now permits many contacts to be detected, and the future holds the promise of more to come. Even Locard would be amazed by the fact that it is now possible to take fingerprints from the throat of a strangled person, determine a smoker's blood type from the remains of a cigarette butt, and, by the use of holography, to measure the size of an invisible shoeprint left on a carpet. Certainly every contact leaves a trace; it is up to us to detect it. The following experiments show how a number of contacts are detected. We hope that you find them interesting, gaining a better appreciation of what a criminalist does, while exciting your ingenuity so that in the future you may well discover how to detect a new contact.

It must be clearly understood that this set of experiments is intended as an introduction to the analyses performed in a forensic laboratory. They are an attempt to acquaint a non-science student with the investigation of physical evidence through the use of scientific procedures. They are written at an introductory level, using terms that can be understood by the nonscience student. The experiments are actual procedures, modified to fit the background of the student.

Advanced-level experiments are also included for the science-oriented student. Those experiments are designed to familiarize these students with basic criminalistic techniques, such as the application of electrophoresis, the typing of bloodstains, and the determination of the index of the refraction of glass specimens through use of the Becke line technique.

The specific objectives of this set of laboratory experiments are as follows:

1. To provide a first set of laboratory experiments for criminal justice and general science students who have had little or no previous science laboratory experience.

2. To show beginning students in criminal justice and general science the significance of physical evidence at the scene of a crime.

3. To demonstrate what happens to physical evidence when it is sent to the laboratory so that students will know what is needed, how much is needed, and how to prepare it.

4. To educate the student in basic laboratory practices so that they can ask and/or answer questions more intelligently in a court of law.

5. And probably most important, to educate students so that they will not unintentionally destroy physical evidence at a crime scene, and will in fact try to preserve it for the trained forensic scientist.

It must be pointed out, and strongly emphasized, that these experiments, while being actual laboratory analyses, are designed to provide the students with an overview of what can be done, not to make them polished forensic scientists.

The views expressed in this manual are those of the authors.

PREFACE TO THIS EDITION

A few changes have been made to this edition. Experiment 40 has been updated using newer methods and improved reagents. This has allowed for this experiment to be completed in less time and with improved accuracy. A new chapter utilizing PCR amplification has been added to the Manual (Experiment 41).

A student once made the following comment. "I have learned a lot in this class, but since I'm not going to be a police officer, I have no idea how I might use it." The answer was, "In your lifetime you might be the first one at the scene of a crime. Now that you know what constitutes physical evidence and how important it is to obtain it in its original state, you can keep the crowd of onlookers away from it until the police arrive. This can be an invaluable service."

We continue to include selected references from the literature. Every now and then a student wants to know more and the teachers need to know more to make their lectures and discussions more accurate. We limit our suggestions from two main forensic journals most likely to be in libraries: the *Journal of Forensic Science* (American), and the *Journal of the Forensic Science Society* (British). This journal was renamed *Science and Justice* in 1995. The web page address for the Journal of Forensic Science is http://journalsip. astm.org/JOURNALS/FORENSCI/jofs_home.html

Remember—this is an introductory course, the students taking it have had very little science background.

Acknowledgments

We wish to thank the following people and organizations for providing technical information for the writing of these laboratory experiments for this and the previous editions.

Mr. James Rhodes, Supervisor of the Laboratory of the Minnesota Bureau of Criminal Apprehension.

Mr. Leslie Loch, Crime Investigator based in St. Cloud, Minnesota.

Captain Richard Witschen, St. Cloud Police Department.

Corporal Mike Lofgren, Minnesota Highway Patrol, expert on automobile lamp glass fragmentation and speed determination.

Mr. Ronald Jones and Mr. Robert Olsen, the Kansas Bureau of Investigation Criminalistics Laboratory at Topeka, Kansas.

Lt. Patrick B. Glynn, Wichita, Kansas Criminalistics Laboratory.

Lt. Al Riniker, Riley Co. Kansas Police Department.

Chief Kenneth Dickinson, Waite Park Police Department, Waite Park Minnesota.

Dr. Jeffrey Payne, 3M Co., Minneapolis Minnesota.

Laura Anne Roselli, Biotechnology Department, Burlington County College, Mt. Laurel, New Jersey.

Miss Nikki James for the final exams.

Annina Carter, Adirondack Community College for reviewing the manual.

The *Journal of Forensic Science*, *Forensic Science*, and the *Journal of Forensic Science Society* were consulted at great length to determine updated criminalistics procedures, particularly those which were at a level that could be understood by non-science majors.

Richard James
Clifton Meloan
Richard Saferstein

The Metric System

The **metric system** of units is used in most scientific work, and a list of commonly used units follows. You should familiarize yourself thoroughly with these units, and with the relationship of these units to common units of the English system.

The fundamental unit of **linear** measurement is the **meter**, (m).

The fundamental unit of **mass** measurement is the **gram**, (g).

The fundamental unit of **volume** measurement is the **liter**, (L).

Commonly used prefixes of the foregoing fundamental units are

deci-	(d)	1/10 or 0.1
centi-	(c)	1/100 or 0.01
milli-	(m)	1/1000 or 0.001
deka-	(dk)	10
hecto-	(h)	100
kilo-	(k)	1000

Thus, 1,000 meters (m) is 1 kilometer (km), 0.1 gram (g) is 1 decigram (dg), 0.001 liter (L), is 1 milliliter (mL), and so on.

Some of the common English units and their approximate metric equivalents are

1 inch	= 2.54 centimeters	1 meter	= 39.37 inches
1 foot	= 30.5 centimeters	1 liter	= 1.06 quarts
1 pound	= 453.6 grams	1 kilogram	= 2.2 pounds
1 ounce	= 28.35 grams	1 quart	= 0.94 liters
1 fluid ounce	= 29.6 mL		

1.0 mL of water weighs 1.0 g.   1.0 liter (L) of water weighs 1.0 kg.

FACTOR LABEL SYSTEM FOR MAKING CONVERSIONS

A convenient method for converting from one set of units to another without getting mixed up is to use a **numerical factor** followed by a **units label**; the **factor-label method**. A pattern that can be followed is:

What you have $\times$ Leave a space $=$ What you want
plus its units   for factors   plus its units

The **factor** should be written so a unit on the top (numerator) will cancel a unit on the bottom (denominator).

EXAMPLES:

1. A shoe imprint found at a scene was found to be 13.0 inches long. How many centimeters long is this shoe?

$$\frac{13.0 \text{ inches}}{1} \times \frac{2.54 \text{ cm}}{1.0 \text{ inch}} = 33.02 \text{ cm}$$

Notice that the factor is arranged so that the numerator (top) of one set of units will cancel the denominator (bottom) of another set of units. You use as many factors as you need until the units on the left side of the equation equal the units on the right side of the equation.

2. I am 74 inches tall. How many meters tall am I?

$$\frac{74 \text{ inches}}{1} \times \frac{2.54 \text{ cm}}{1.0 \text{ inch}} \times \frac{1 \text{ meter}}{100 \text{ cm}} = 1.88 \text{ meters}$$

3. A bullet slug weighs 0.62 ounces. How many milligrams does it weigh?

$$\frac{0.62 \text{ ounces}}{1} \times \frac{28.35 \text{ grams}}{1.0 \text{ ounce}} \times \frac{1,000 \text{ mg}}{1.0 \text{ grams}} = 17,577 \text{ mg}$$

4. A room is 12 ft wide and 15 ft long. How many square meters (m^2) is the floor in this room? Follow the same pattern, just use the factors more than once if you need to.

$$\frac{12 \text{ ft}}{1} \times \frac{15 \text{ ft}}{1} \times \frac{30.5 \text{ cm}}{1.0 \text{ ft}} \times \frac{30.5 \text{ cm}}{1.0 \text{ ft}} \times \frac{1.0 \text{ m}}{100 \text{ cm}} \times \frac{1.0 \text{ m}}{100 \text{ cm}} = 16.7 \text{ m}^2$$

For practice in evaluating units of the metric system, do the following exercises.

EXERCISES

1. Add: 3.45 g, 0.06 kg, 0.67 g, 690 mg, 2 dg.

2. Add: 3.28 g, 8,604 mg, 6.20 dg, 0.780 kg, 5.62 g, 0.08 dg.

3. Add: 5.2 L, 5,300 mL, 0.44 L, 50 mL.

4. Add: 0.30 m, 450 cm, 4.2 m, 600 mm, 2.8 cm, 4 dm, 60 mm.

5. Add: 78 cm, 567 mm, 14 dm, 1.2 m, 0.023 km, 75 mm.

6. How many liters are contained in a 1.00 cubic meter container, and what would it weigh if it were filled with water? Ignore the weight of the container (hint: 1 L of water weighs 1 kg).

7. Fill in the blanks.
   a.   1 centimeter (cm) = _____ inch (in)

   b.   1 pound (lb) = _____ kilogram (kg)

   c.   1 quart (qt) = _____ liter (L)

   d.   1 ounce (oz) = _____ grams (g)

   e.   2 ounces (oz) = _____ milliliters (mL)

   f.   100 meters (m) = _____ yards (yd)

   g.   1 mile (mi) = _____ kilometers (km)

   h.   1 gallon (gal) = _____ milliliters (mL)

   i.   1 square inch (in^2) = _____ square centimeters (cm^2)

   j.   1 cubic decimeter (dm^3) = _____ cubic centimeters (cc) or (cm^3)

Practice in Making Laboratory Measurements

This is an introductory laboratory exercise intended to prepare you for Experiment 3, which deals with the analysis of glass fragments. You will become more familiar with measurements using the metric system and learn to use a laboratory balance. In this exercise you will determine the density of several objects by various methods. Do the parts of this exercise slowly and carefully so that you fully understand what is required and what the results indicate.

Density is a physical property of matter, which is specific to the sample being measured and which may be used as a means of identification or comparison, whichever is required. The equation for density is:

$$\text{Density} = \frac{\text{mass of object}}{\text{volume of object}} \quad \text{expressed either as } \frac{g}{cm^3} \text{ or } \frac{lb}{ft^3} \qquad (2\text{–}1)$$

The utility of this type of determination may be made more clear to you by the following example. Suppose that a man has a body volume of 3 cubic feet and weighs 198 lb. What is his density? The calculation would be done by application of equation 2–1.

$$\text{Density} = \frac{\text{weight}}{\text{volume}}$$

$$= \frac{198 \text{ lb.}}{3 \text{ ft}^3} = 66 \text{ lb/ft}^3$$

Water weighs 62.4 lb/ft^3. Therefore, if the man jumps into a lake or swimming pool, he will sink unless he knows how to swim or to keep himself afloat holding air in his lungs. In other words, an object placed in a fluid sinks if its density is greater than that of the surrounding fluid and floats if its density is less than that of the surrounding fluid.

THE TRIPLE-BEAM BALANCE

The **triple-beam balance** is the least sensitive balance commonly found in the chemistry laboratory. Figure 2–1 shows one such type of balance. It consists of a single pan on the left side of the beam. The right side of the beam is divided into three arms, each of which holds a rider. The two arms containing the larger riders are notched. With the pan empty, the point should come to rest midway on the scale at the extreme right. The object to be weighed is placed on the pan. The heaviest rider (10 g in this case) is moved to successive notches until the pointer drops to the bottom of scale. The rider is then moved back one notch. The same procedure is then followed for the 1-g rider. The 0.01-g rider is carefully moved along the arm until the pointer is midway on the scale. The weight of the object is then the total of the values on each of the arms.

EQUIPMENT

1 Balance, triple-beam (capable of an accuracy to ±0.01 g, with a support arm for immersion measurements)
1 Beaker, 250-mL
   Cylindrical solids (wooden rods)
1 pr Goggles, safety

1 Graduated cylinder (1000-mL is best)
   Irregular metal objects
1 Meter stick or metric ruler
   Rectangular metal solids
1 pr Scissors
   String, 60–90 cm long

METHOD

PART A: DENSITY OF RECTANGULAR SOLIDS

In this part of the exercise you will determine the density of an object by applying the relationship

$$\text{Density} = \frac{\text{mass of object (g)}}{\text{volume of object (cm}^3)}$$

See Table 2-1 for the density of various common materials.

1. Obtain a rectangular solid from the sample supply.

2. Measure the three dimensions of the object with a ruler, using the centimeter as the unit of measurement, and record the values on the data sheet.

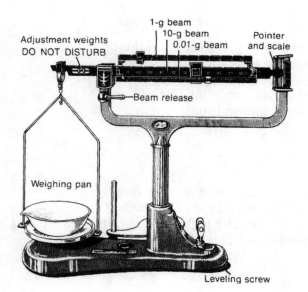

FIGURE 2–1   A triple-beam balance.

TABLE 2–1	Densities of Various Common Materials (g/cm³)		
Material	**Density**	**Material**	**Density**
Cork	0.22–0.26	Glass, flint	2.9–5.9
Bone	1.7–2.0	Iron	7.86
Glass, window	2.47–2.56	Brass, yellow	8.44–8.70
Flint	2.63	Lead	11.34
Aluminum	2.70	Gold	19.3

3. Determine the volume by applying the formula

    V = length × width × height. (2–2)

    The volume will then be derived in units of cubic centimeters.

4. Determine the mass of the object by use of the laboratory balance.

5. Measure the mass of the object to the nearest 0.01 g, and record the mass on the data sheet for this exercise.

6. Determine the density of the object by applying the formula given at the beginning of this section, and record the value on the data sheet.

PART B: DENSITIES OF CYLINDRICAL SOLIDS

1. Obtain a cylindrical solid from the sample supply, measure its mass in the same manner as done previously, and record the value. Since this object is not of the same shape as the rectangular solid, you will have to determine its volume by use of a different mathematical relationship. The formula to be used in this case is

    Volume = $\pi r^2 h$ (2–3)
    where π = 3.14
              r = radius
              h = height or length of the object

    The height and radius of a cylinder are shown in Figure 2-2.

2. Measure the diameter in cm, and divide by 2 to obtain the radius.

3. Measure the height or length of the object in centimeters.

4. Record these values, and determine the volume of the object.

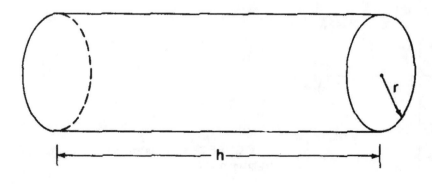

FIGURE 2–2 Diagram of a cylinder showing the measurements needed.

5. Enter this value on the data sheet.

6. Determine the value for the density of the object by using the relationship

    D = M/V

    and record this value.

PART C: DENSITIES OF IRREGULARLY SHAPED SOLIDS

1. Obtain an irregularly shaped solid from the sample supply. Since it would be very difficult to obtain the volume of this object by measurement, we will approach this determination in a different manner.

2. Measure the mass of the object by using the balance as you did before.

3. Obtain a graduated cylinder from the equipment supply and fill it with water to one of the graduations. The volume of water is read by noting the position of the bottom of the curve (meniscus) of the liquid level, as shown in Figure 2-3.

4. Record this value.

5. Tie a piece of string around the object. Gently lower the irregular object, and lower it into the graduated cylinder so that it is entirely immersed (submerged) below the water level. Note that the water level has risen in the graduated cylinder. (This method would not be used for an object that would absorb water or dissolve in it.)

6. Read the level of the meniscus and record it.

7. Subtract the first value from the second value for the water level, and you have the volume of the object by a method known as **water displacement**. Record this value also.

You may now find the density of the object by applying the following reasoning. The volume of the object has been indirectly determined and is expressed in milliliters of water, its equivalent volume. A relationship exists in the metric system between units of volume of liquids and units of volume of solids. This relationship is

$$1 \text{ mL} = 1 \text{ cm}^3 \tag{2-4}$$

Thus, all that is necessary to express the volume in milliliters is the volume in cubic centimeters.

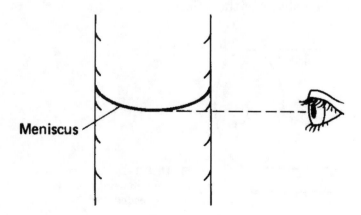

Meniscus

FIGURE 2-3 Illustrating a meniscus and proper eye level.

8. Determine the density by applying the equation in step B-6. Record this value.

9. Repeat the steps in Part C using the rectangular or cylindrical solid sample, and record the values for the mass, volume, and density of this object.

PART D: CLEANUP, CALCULATIONS, AND QUESTIONS

Dry all glassware, return all materials to the place from which you obtained them, and clean up your work area. Complete the data sheet, answer the questions, and hand your completed papers to your laboratory instructor.

EXPERIMENT 2   Name _____

DATA SHEET   Date _____

PRACTICE IN MAKING LABORATORY MEASUREMENTS

Part A: Density of Rectangular Solids   **Calculations:**

Mass

Volume

Density

Part B: Density of Cylindrical Solids   **Calculations:**

Mass

Volume

Density

Part C: Density of Irregularly Shaped Solids   **Calculations:**

   1. Irregular solid

     Mass

     Volume of water with solid immersed

     Volume of water initially

     Volume of solid

     Density

2. Rectangular or cylindrical solid   Calculations:

Mass

Volume of water with solid immersed

Volume of water initially

Volume of solid

Density

Questions

1. Compare the density of a single solid object by various methods. Which methods do you think give the most accurate values? Why?

2. Could you have used the method in Part C for determining the volume of any wooden solid object? What would you have to change in the apparatus to permit the value for the volume to be more accurately obtained?

Density of Glass Fragments

This experiment will allow you to become still more familiar with the metric system and, at the same time, determine the density of some glass samples. By this means you will attempt to establish the possibility of two glass fragments having a common origin.

The procedure in Experiment 6 is more commonly used to compare the density of two pieces of glass (scene and suspect) to show that they have a common origin. However, if only one piece of glass is available (scene or suspect), a density measurement might well provide some direction regarding what type of glass to look for in order to make a comparison. The important point, however, is that this technique is not limited to glass, and it is for this reason that this experiment is included. For example, one of the authors (Meloan) was involved in a trial in which the density of the rubber covering of a truck power-steering hose was the deciding factor. The density was determined using the technique described below, with the exception that a correction for the supporting wire was made.

The density of objects is determined by measurement of the mass, volume, or loss of weight in water of the object, and then applying a mathematical relationship to arrive at a value for this property. The method for the determination of volume used in this exercise is based on a physics relationship known as **Archimedes's principle**. This principle states that an object immersed in a fluid displaces a volume of fluid equal to its volume. For example, a 1 cm cube of glass placed in water will "push aside" 1 cubic centimeter of water. Another statement of this principle is: **an object immersed in a fluid (water in this instance) is buoyed up by a force equal to the weight of the displaced fluid**. In other words, if we **assume** that a 1 cm cube of glass weighs about 2.5 g while a 1 cm cube of water weighs 1 g, when the glass cube is placed in water it will weigh 2.5 g minus 1 g, or 1.5 g. Since 1 cubic centimeter of water is equal to 1 g of water, we now have the volume of the glass.

CRIME SCENE

During a burglary, a glass object has fallen off of a table onto the floor. The floor has no carpet covering and the glass object has shattered. If the burglar was near the object when it shattered, perhaps small fragments of glass can be found lodged in his clothing, especially in the lower trouser leg areas or the soles of his shoes. A suspect is apprehended and his living quarters searched. A pair of trousers is found which does indeed have glass fragments in the fibers, and a few fragments of glass are removed from one pair of his shoes. Density determinations are to be done and an attempt made to link the pieces of glass in the trousers and shoes to the fragment collected at the scene. This, along with other physical evidence obtained, may serve to place the suspect at the scene of the burglary.

Glass from various sources, such as windowpanes, automobile headlights, bottles, and plate glass doors, all have slightly different densities. This makes it possible in some cases to help place a suspect at the scene of the crime if they have broken a glass object and if small fragments have become lodged in their clothing. The density of the glass may be only very slightly different, but careful analysis will make these differences apparent.

Forensic laboratories can analyze glass fragments as small as 1 mm wide by 3 or 4 mm long and determine their densities. Actually, for pieces that small, we suggest the procedures set forth in Experiment 7. This exercise will deal with much larger pieces of glass in order that the measuring device will require less technique. The principles are the same in both cases however, and technique is still very important. Table 3-1 gives the density for several types of glass and similar materials.

EQUIPMENT

1 Balance (±0.01 g or better) with support rack provision
8 Beakers, 250 mL (for knowns and unknowns)
1 pr Goggles, safety

1 pr Scissors
Small pieces of various types of glass
1 m String

METHOD

Obtain glass fragments from both the beakers labeled "unknown" and those labeled "known." The unknowns are numbered 1, 2, 3, and 4. The knowns are lettered A, B, C, and D. The object is to determine whether the numbered and lettered fragments have similar densities.

PART A: DENSITY MEASUREMENTS—TRIPLE BEAM BALANCE

1. Obtain a balance, a piece of string, and a 250 mL beaker.

2. Tie the string around the glass fragment, and suspend it from the pan support hook.

3. Weigh the glass fragment in air to the nearest 0.01 g, and record this value.

TABLE 3–1	Densities of Various Common Materials (g/cm³)		
Material	**Density**	**Material**	**Density**
Amber	1.06–1.11	Mica	2.6–3.2
Celluloid	1.4	Quartz	2.65
Bone	1.7–2.0	Beryl	2.69–2.70
Porcelain	2.3–2.5	Glass, flint	2.9–5.0
Glass, window	2.47–2.56	Diamond	3.01–3.52
Glass, headlight	2.47–2.63		

4. Place a 250 mL beaker nearly filled with water (tap water is fine) on the beaker support, and suspend the glass in the water. Adjust the glass height in the water so that it does not touch the walls of the beaker.

    Weigh the glass fragment suspended in water to the nearest 0.01 g, and record this value.

5. The density of the glass fragment is determined by the following relationship:

$$\text{Density of object} \ = \ \frac{\text{mass of object in the air}}{\text{loss of mass of object in water}}$$

6. Repeat this process for the other glass fragments you have chosen to work with.

7. Record the density of each fragment on the data sheet.

PART B: DENSITY MEASUREMENTS—ELECTRONIC BALANCE

When using an electronic balance, the glass sample is suspended over the balance rather than suspended from the balance as is the case with the triple beam balance. Consequently, the use of the electronic balance requires a small change in the calculations for this experiment.

1. Obtain a balance, a piece of fine string, and a 250 mL beaker.

2. Add a suspension support to the pan and zero the balance.

3. Weigh the glass fragment in air to the nearest 0.001 g and record this value.

4. Add the beaker support as in Step 4 of the triple beam experiment.

5. Place a 250 mL beaker nearly filled with water on the beaker support, tie the string around the glass fragment and suspend the glass in the water. Adjust the glass height in the water so that it does not touch the walls of the glass beaker.

6. Weigh the glass fragment suspended in water to the nearest 0.001 g and record this value. Convert this value to milliliters. (Recall that 1g of water has a volume of 1 mL.) This is the volume of the glass sample.

7. The density of the glass fragment is determined by the following relationship:

$$\text{Density of object} \ = \ \frac{\text{mass of object in the air (g)}}{\text{volume of the glass sample (mL)}}$$

8. Repeat this process for the other glass fragments you have chosen to work with.

9. Record the density of each fragment on the data sheet.

PART C: CLEANUP, CALCULATIONS, AND QUESTIONS

1. Return all materials to the place where you obtained them.

2. Be sure that everything is clean and dry.

3. Complete the determination by following the instructions in the data sheet and reporting your results.

SELECTED SOURCES FOR ADDITIONAL INFORMATION

Bajic, Stanley J., Aeschliman, D.B., Saevelt, N., Baldwin, D.P., and Houk, R.S., "Analysis of glass fragments by laser ablation-inductively coupled plasma-mass spectrometry and principal component analysis," *J. Forens. Sci.,* 50 (5), (2005), 1123.

Bottrell, M., and Webb, J.B., "Review of: Forensic Interpretation of Glass Evidence," *J. Forensic. Sci.,* 47 (4), (2002), 926.

Brewster, F., Thrope, J.W., Gettinby, G., and Caddy, B., "The retention of glass particles on woven fabrics," *J. Forens. Sci. Soc.,* 30 (1985), 798.

Collins, Peter, Coumbaros, L., Horsley, G., Lynch, B., Kirkbride, K.P., Skinner, W., and Klass G., "Glass containing gunshot residue particles: A new type of highly characteristic particle?" *J. Forens. Sci.,* 48 (3), (2003), 538.

Coulson, S.A., Buckleton, J.S., Gummer, A.B., and Triggs, C.M., "Glass on clothing and shoes of members of the general population and people suspected of breaking crimes," *Sci. & Just.,* 41 (1), (2001), 39.

Hicks, T., Vanina, R., and Margot, P., "Transfer and persistence of glass fragments on garments," *Sci. & Just.,* 36 (2), (1996), 101.

Marcouiler, J.M., "A revised glass annealing method to distinguish glass types," *J. Forens. Sci.,* 35 (3), (1989), 554.

Montero, Shirly, Hobbs, A.L., French, T.A., and Almirall, J.R., "Elemental analysis of glass fragments by ICP-MS as evidence of association: Analysis of a case," *J. Forens. Sci.,* 48 (5), (2003), 1101.

Pounds, C.A., and Smalldon, K.W., "Distribution of glass fragments in front of a broken window and the transfer of fragments to individuals standing nearby," *J. Forens. Sci. Soc.,* 18 (1978), 197.

Slater, D.P., and Fong, W., "Density, refractive index, and dispersion in the examination of glass. Their relative worth as proof," *J. Forensic. Sci. Soc.,* 27 (1982), 474.

Underhill, M., "The acquisition of breaking and broken glass," *Sci. & Just.,* 37 (2), (1997), 121.

EXPERIMENT 3

DATA SHEET

Name _____

Date _____

DENSITY OF GLASS FRAGMENTS

Part A: Density Measurements

1. Weight of the glass fragments in air.

   A   1

   B   2

   C   3

   D   4

2. Weight of the glass fragments in water.

   A   1

   B   2

   C   3

   D   4

3. Volume of the glass fragments (air weight minus water weight)

   A   1

   B   2

   C   3

   D   4

4. Density of the glass fragments

A   1

B   2

C   3

D   4

Part B: Cleanup, Calculations, and Questions

1. Based on the results of this experiment, match the fragments lettered A, B, C, and D with fragments 1, 2, 3, and 4.

   A matches _____

   B matches _____

   C matches _____

   D matches _____

2. How certain are you that the fragments you have matched do have a common origin? Give your reasons.

Practice in the Use of the Microscope

The **microscope** is one of the most valuable tools of forensic scientists. They use it to study hair, fibers, seeds, soils, metals, paints, anything and everything involved in a crime. It is believed that engravers used glass globes filled with water as magnifying glasses at least 3,000 years ago. The simplest microscope is called a **magnifying glass**. Optical microscopes magnify because light rays reflected from an object bend (refract) as they pass through one or more lenses.

How big you can make the object depends on the refractive index (bend power) of the glass in the lens. Hand lenses are 3 to 10×. Since the light rays are spread out when an object is magnified, the magnified object is not as bright as the original. To make it as bright as it was originally additional light must be used. This is the purpose of having a mirror under the lens of the microscope. It collects sunlight or light from an auxiliary lamp. The **condenser** focuses the light collected by the mirror onto the sample.

Suppose that you took a small section of a magnified object and placed a second lens over it. This magnified section could then be further magnified and we would have a **compound microscope**. The Dutch spectacle maker, Zacharias Janssen, is credited with discovering this principle and making the first compound microscope in 1590. Since then, there have been many improvements although the basic concept has remained essentially unchanged. Magnification up to about 400× is possible with ordinary illumination. With a substage condenser to focus more light on the object and with better lenses, it is possible to go to 1000× magnification. About the highest magnification that can be obtained with a compound microscope is 2500×.

The quality of a microscope resides in the lenses. Slight imperfections can cause large distortions in the object that is viewed. In addition, various colors refract at different angles, so correcting lenses must be added. Expensive microscopes have excellent correcting lenses, while less expensive microscopes may not even have correcting lenses.

In working with a compound microscope, you will find the following terms useful:

Working distance—the distance between the specimen and the tip of the objective lens. In general, the higher the magnification, the shorter the working distance.

FIGURE 4–1 General structure of a compound microscope.

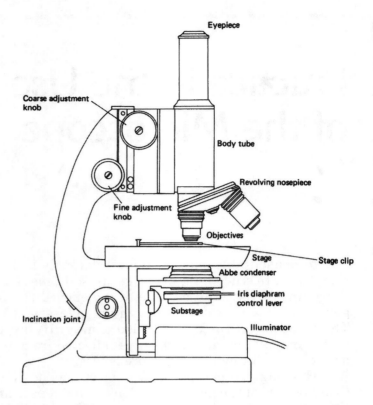

Depth of focus—the thickness of the object that is simultaneously in focus. The higher the power of magnification, the less is the depth of focus.

Field of view—the area or diameter of the specimen that is in view. The higher the power of magnification, the less is the field of view.

Magnification—to determine the magnification of a microscope **multiply the magnification of the eyepiece by the magnification of the nosepiece**.

Figure 4-1 shows the basic parts of a compound microscope.

EQUIPMENT

1 Auxiliary light (for the stereoscopic microscope)	1 Microscope, stereoscopic
1 bx Cover glasses	1 bx Microscope slides
1 pr Forceps	1 Razor blade
1 pr Goggles, safety	1 pr Scissors
1 bx Lens paper	10 Vials, glass, 6 dram, to hold paint chips and matches
1 Medicine dropper	
1 Microscope, compound	1 White card, 7.5 × 10 cm

CHEMICALS

Modeling clay	Paper matches, at least from three different books
Newspaper	Tea
Paint chips from several cars. Get at a salvage yard	Tobacco

PART A: THE COMPOUND MICROSCOPE

1. Obtain an assigned compound microscope from the cabinet, and carry it back to your seat at the lab table.

2. With a piece of lens paper, lightly wipe any dust and grease from all the exposed glass surfaces. Never use anything else to do this job.

3. Spend the next few minutes becoming familiar with the names and locations of the various important parts of the instrument; Figure 4-1 will help.

    Several important rules are to be noted in connection with the foregoing procedures:

    a. To find an object, **always start your examination with the low-power objective, never with the high**. The low-power objective reveals an area of the slide some 20 times greater than the high-power, making it 20 times easier to locate the desired object.

    b. To bring the object into focus, **always focus upward**, with the coarse adjustment. (NOTE: Some microscopes focus by moving the stage up and down rather than the body tube. In such cases the focusing is downward—away from the nonmovable parts.) You want to focus upward because when your eye is at the ocular (eyepiece), it is impossible to determine how far down or up the tip of the objective has traveled. In focusing down, carelessness might result in crushing the specimens.

    c. When the high-power objective is being used, never use the coarse adjustment.

Kohler Illumination

Anyone can eventually adjust a microscope to view an object placed on a slide. However, if you want to do it the best way possible to get the brightest image with the best focus possible, then you should use **Kohler illumination**. This is a method to align the optics and focus all of the components so as to minimize distortion and to obtain uniform brightness. It should be done with every sample, and particularly so if a photomicrograph is to be made. It can be done in less than five minutes once you know how to do it. An uncentered lamp filament will usually not show up until a photomicrograph is taken and then the photo will be unevenly exposed. It has been estimated that 90% of the people who use a microscope do not use Kohler illumination, either because they do not know what it is or do not know how to make the adjustments. Since a microscope is a major component of a criminalistics laboratory and because many photomicrographs are taken, it is desirable that you should know the basics of how to establish Kohler illumination. A comparison can be made between a finely tuned engine and one that needs a tune up. Both will run and both will do the job, but to get the best performance and have the greatest piece of mind, you use the one that is properly tuned.

The components that need to be adjusted are: (a) the **light source**, (b) the **field diaphragm**, (c) the **condenser**, (d) the **objective lens**, and (e) the **iris diaphragm**. While all of these can be adjusted on a high quality microscope, usually only the condenser and the iris diaphragm can be adjusted on student type microscopes. The directions given below are for use with a high quality microscope. Your instructor will tell you how many you can do with your microscope.

1. Place the **fixed objective** lens in place. This is usually a 10× objective lens. Adjust its height to be about 2–3 mm above the stage with the coarse focusing adjustment.

2. Turn on the lamp. If it has an adjustable intensity control, adjust the intensity to be bright, but not cause you to squint. Feel comfortable.

3. If the microscope is binocular (two eyepieces) adjust their separation to fit your eyes.

4. Place a slide, with a specimen on it, on the stage and center it.

5. Open both the field and iris diaphragms completely so the specimen can be viewed. You should have a full field of view with an unfocused specimen close to the center. See Figure 4-2 (A).

6. Bring the specimen into focus by focusing up, first with the coarse adjusting knob, then with the fine adjusting knob. See Figure 4-2 (B).

7. Completely close the field diaphragm (the one just in front of the lamp) or until about all you can see is a fuzzy circle around your specimen. Almost the entire field will be black except for a small white circle of light around your specimen and the separation between the black and white will usually be fuzzy and multi colored. Keep your specimen inside of the light area, or at least so you can see part of it. See Figure 4-2 (C).

8. Move the condenser up or down to focus the edge of the diaphragm. You should now be able to see that the circle is actually a polygon. See Figure 4-2 (D).

9. Your specimen should be in the center of the lighted area. If it is not, and you have condenser controls (usually two adjusting screws with handles on them just under the stage), adjust the condenser so your specimen is in the center of the bright area. See Figure 4-2 (E).

10. You should be able to move any other higher power objective in place and the specimen should still be in the center. If it is not, then there are inset adjusting screws at the base of each objective lens where it fastens onto the turret. These can be adjusted to center the specimen. **Only the instructor should do this if it is necessary.**

11. Open the field iris until the lighted area just fills the circular field. You should be able to see a polygon perfectly inscribed and just touching the outer rim of the field of view.

12. Remove one of the eyepiece oculars so you can look down the body tube.

    If you have a high quality microscope with a lamp adjustment then do step 13. If not, go to step 14. Refer to Figure 4-3.

13. Focus an image of the lamp filament on the objective back focal plane by moving the lamp with its adjusting screws.

14. Open or close the iris diaphragm (right under the stage) until the polygon fills about 70–80% of the field of view (Figure 4-4). This provides for good image contrast, a flatter field, and better depth of field.

15. Replace the eyepiece ocular. You now have Kohler illumination. See Figure 4-2 (F). Unless you did step 10, you should repeat this each time the objective is changed.

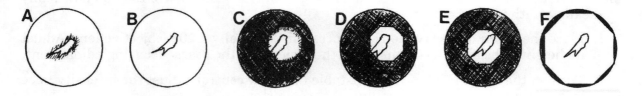

FIGURE 4–2   Selected views for establishing Kohler Illumination.

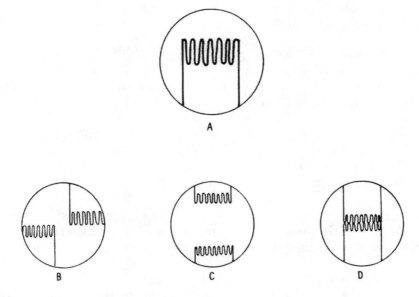

FIGURE 4–3 (A) A diagram of the image of the filament of a quartz-iodine bulb as seen in the plane of the aperture diaphragm of the condenser. (B) One possible appearance when the lamp system is out of adjustment. Two images of the filament (one inverted and produced by the mirror behind the lamp) are not coincident. (C) The filament images have not been aligned. (D) The final correct adjustment when the images are both aligned and made contiguous. *Courtesy of S. Bradbury, "An Introduction to the Optical Microscope," Oxford University Press, (1984).*

METHOD

1. Cut the letter "h" from a newspaper. Place it on a clean slide, and with a medicine dropper, place one drop of water on the letter.

2. Wait a moment before covering it with a cover slide. Hold the cover slide at about a 45° angle to the support slide, and then slowly lower it. A gentle tapping will usually remove any bubbles that may be present.

3. Place the slide on the stage and clamp it down. Move the slide so that the letter is in the middle of the hole in the stage. Make certain that the low-power objective is in place. Viewing the stage from the side, use the coarse adjustment wheel to lower the objective until either the stop is reached or the objective is approximately 2 cm from the cover slide.

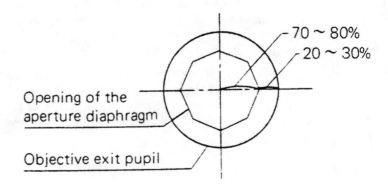

FIGURE 4–4 The final adjustment with the iris diaphragm. *Courtesy of Olympus Optical Co., Ltd., Tokyo, Japan.*

4. Turn on the substage illuminator of your microscope if it has one or the auxiliary lamp if the lighting is separate.

5. Now, looking through the ocular, slowly raise the tube with the coarse adjustment knob until the letter "h" is in focus. If you cannot see the object, center the slide more carefully and repeat the whole procedure. The focus may be made sharper by a slight turn on the fine adjustment knob.

6. Open and close the iris diaphragm by turning the diaphragm handle, which projects laterally from the lower portion of the condenser. The iris diaphragm controls the amount of light reaching the specimen. Adjust it to make the image as sharp as possible (maximum definition).

7. The image is in focus 3 to 4 mm above the eyepiece. **Thus, there is no reason to press one's eye to the ocular.** Some students who wear glasses find it advisable to remove them, others to keep them on, as determined by experience.

8. To change to high power, make sure that you have focused sharply under low power on the object and centered it in the field. Then **carefully** swing the high-power objective into place. The microscopes are **parfocal**. This means that once the image is brought into sharp focus under low power, it will remain in focus when the high-power objective is turned into position. The high-power objective should not strike the slide, though it will come very close. A few turns of the fine adjustment knob, either up or down, should suffice to bring the "h" into sharp focus. If it does not, go back to step 3 and begin again. Once the image has been brought into sharp focus, it may be necessary to readjust the diaphragm opening, as discussed in step 8 in the Kohler Illumination section.

EXERCISES

1. Examine the "h" under the low power objective.
   a. Is the image right side up?
   b. Move the slide to the left: Which way does the image seem to move?

2. Under high power, examine the letter "h."
   a. Note the many clear spaces **within** the letter; these are obviously caused by imperfect contact between the press and paper. The high power lens is able to resolve these imperfections. The microscope then does two things: It enlarges (magnifies) the object, and **resolves** distinctly between closely situated structures in the object (note that magnification and resolution are not the same).
   b. Take particular note of the fibrous texture of the newspaper. When you focus on different levels by turning the fine focus knob, you will notice that some fibers go out of view and others come in view. This is a maneuver for which you will find frequent use and which will enable you to determine whether a particular object is located above, below, or in the same plane as another object.
   c. The total magnification of the image formed by the microscope is determined by multiplying the individual magnifications of the ocular and the objective. The magnifying power of these lenses are clearly marked as 10×, 40×, and so on. What is the magnification of the image at low power?
   d. What is the magnification at high power?

3. Repeat these exercises using the letter "e."

FIGURE 4–5 Zeiss Stereo Microscope STEMI 2000. *Courtesy of VWR Scientific Products, West Chester, PA, www.vwrsp.com.*

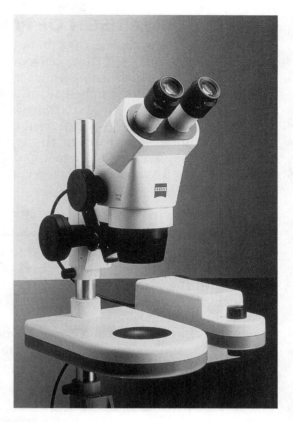

PART B: THE STEREOSCOPIC MICROSCOPE

Obtain an assigned stereoscopic microscope, and carefully carry it back to your desk or bench. Familiarize yourself with the parts of the microscope.

1. Place the previously prepared "h" slide onto the microscope stage. Illuminate the slide from above with an illuminator or any available light source.

2. Set the magnification knob to the highest power (2× or 3×). Look through the right eyepiece and adjust the focusing knob until the letter "e" is sharp.

3. Reset the magnification knob to the lowest power (1× or 0.7×). Without touching the focusing knob, look through the left eyepiece, and, using only the left eye, turn the eyepiece adjusting ring clockwise or counterclockwise until the image is sharp. Make sure that the eyepiece maintains contact with the adjusting ring. The adjusting ring is set in the position that best accommodates each viewer's eyes. Once set, it should not be changed.

4. The magnification knob allows you to change the power continuously to exactly the best magnification for a given specimen. The stereoscopic microscope allows you to scan an object at a lower power and then to concentrate on some particular detail by increasing the power gradually to the desired value.

EXERCISES

1. Examine the previously prepared "h" and "e" slides under the set stereoscopic microscope. Is the image right side up? Move the slide to the left: which way does the image seem to move?

2. Examine tea and/or cigarette tobacco under both low- and high-power magnification.

3. Examine the tips of your fingers under the stereoscopic microscope. Locate the ridges that form a fingerprint. Locate the sweat pores that exist on these ridges.

PART C: COMPARISON OF PAINT CHIPS

There are very few objects that do not have some sort of lacquer, varnish, or paint as a protective coating. When these objects are involved in a crime, the protective coating is often broken loose. A close examination of paint flakes may well be of use. Generally, several layers of paint are applied to an object. The color of an undercoat or primer usually differs from that of the final coats, and if the object has been painted several times, there will then be several layers of different thickness and color. If a paint chip is placed on edge and viewed under a microscope, these layers are readily visible.

Under a stereoscopic microscope, the number of layers, the color, and the relative thickness from a suspect paint chip can be matched with the reference paint.

CRIME SCENE

A hit-and-run accident has occurred in which a parked car has been sideswiped. A witness was able to get only two numbers of the license number. The police have found three cars that fit the general description of auto style, color, and license number. All three are older cars that have many scratches and dents on them, so no definitive conclusion can be drawn. Each driver has denied any responsibility for the accident. The police have obtained a chip of paint from each car and from the vehicle that was hit. These have been given to you, and your job is to see if a match can be made.

METHOD

1. Place a white plate or piece of white cardboard on the stage of the stereoscopic microscope.

2. Obtain a piece of clay about the size of a small marble, and press it into the plate so that it looks like a small pyramid.

3. Using a razor blade, make a small V cut in the top of the clay about half as deep as the paint chip is wide.

4. With forceps, carefully place the paint chip from the victim's car in the V cut so that the edge of the paint chip is up. Press the clay together to hold the chip.

5. Turn on the illuminator, and direct it onto the paint specimen. Using the lowest power on the microscope, focus on the edge of the paint chip. Use your fingers to press the clay to position the paint chip so that the cut edge is horizontal and in focus over as much of its length as possible.

6. Repeat steps 1 through 5 with one of the comparison paint chips.

7. See if you can match the paint chips. Record what you see.

8. Repeat steps 1 through 6 with each of the suspect paint chips to see if you can make a match.

9. Clean up the area, and put the clay back in the package.

PART D: COMPARISON OF PAPER MATCHES

From time to time a forensic laboratory may be asked to see whether a torn-out paper match comes from a partially used book, usually taken from an accused person.

Cursory examination of any matchbook will reveal that it contains two pieces of cardboard secured in the book with a staple. The individual match body is formed by a series of partial cuts in this cardboard; thus each layer of matches was originally a single piece of cardboard.

The obvious first attempt to match a torn-out match to a partially filled match book requires physically fitting the torn edges of the match to the corresponding portion of the torn book. Barring success in this attempt, a forensic examiner will then try to compare the suspect match with matches remaining in the book in order to establish an adjacent relationship.

Such a comparison can be conducted under a stereoscopic microscope. The most significant features to look for in the comparison of paper matches are:

1. Color, width, and thickness.

2. Most matches are made from reprocessed cardboard. Examination of the match edges may reveal inclusions consisting of a large variety of colored fibrous material, aluminum foil, and other contaminants that were involved in the production of the cardboard. A side-by-side examination of matches for comparable inclusions is probably the easiest and most significant feature to look for in match comparisons.

3. Another feature for comparison is the presence of continuous fibers between adjacent matches. These fibers may exist on the upper and lower surfaces of the matches.

CRIME SCENE

A burglary has been committed, and, apparently, in addition to the burglars inside the building, a lookout was posted. The detective at the scene noticed a few cigarette butts by the back door, as well as a few paper matches. He picked these up as possible evidence. A few days later three suspects are apprehended. A search of the clothing in their apartments yields a book of matches in the trouser pocket of one of the suspects. Your job is to see if the match found at the back door is from the book recovered from the suspects.

METHOD

1. You will be given two matches for comparison.
2. Compare the matches' color, width, and thickness.
3. Under the highest power of the stereoscopic microscope, hold the edges of the matches side by side, and compare them for any matching characteristics.
4. Holding the upper surfaces of the matches side by side, compare them for any matching characteristics under the stereoscopic microscope. Repeat this examination for the underside of the matches. Are the matches alike? How certain can you be that they originated from the same book?

SELECTED SOURCES FOR ADDITIONAL INFORMATION

Allen, T.J., "The examination of thin sections of colored paints by light microscopy," *Forens. Sci. Intl.*, 57 (1992), 5.

Allen, T.J., "The removal of paint smears from tools and clothing for microscopical examination and analysis," *Forens. Sci. Intl.*, 52 (1991), 101.

Antonenko, N.E., "Diatom analysis lives on," *Can. Soc. Forens. Sci. J.*, 20 (1987), 101.

Dabdoub, G., and Severin, P., "The identification of domestic and foreign automobile manufacturers through body primer characteristics," *J. Forens. Sci.*, 34 (6), (1989), 1395.

Dixon, K.C., "Positive identification of torn burned matches with emphasis on crosscut and torn fiber comparisons," *J. Forens. Sci.*, 28 (2), (1983), 330.

Elliott, B.R., Goodwin, D.G., Hower, P.S.0, Hayes, P.M., Underhill, M., and Locke, J., 'The microscopic examination of glass surfaces," *J. Forens. Sci. Soc.*, 25 (1985), 459.

Funk, H.J., "Comparison of paper matches," *J. Forens. Sci.*, 13 (1968), 137.

Gerhart, F.J., and Ward, D.C., "Paper match comparisons by submersion," *J. Forens. Sci.*, 31 (4), (1986), 1450.

Grieve, M.C., "New man-made fibers under the microscope-Lyocell fibres and Nylon-6 block co-polymers," *Sci. & Just.*, 36 (2), (1996), 71.

Kohler, A., "Ein neus beleuchtungsverfahren fur mikrophotographische zwecke," *Zeit wiss. Mikroskop.* (1893), 443.

Kopchick, Kristin A., and Bommarito, C. R., "Color analysis of apparently achromatic automotive paints by visible microspectrophotometry," *J. Forens. Sci.*, 51 (2), (2006), 340.

McCrone, W.C., McCrone, L.B. and Delly, J.G., "Polarized Light Microscopy," Ann Arbor, Mich.: *Ann Arbor Science Publishers*, 1978.

McCrone, W.C., "Calibration of the Mettler hot stage," *J. Forens. Sci. Soc.*, 27 (1987), 207.

McDermott, S.D., and Willis, S.M., " A survey of the evidential value of paint transfer evidence," *J. Forens. Sci.*, 42 (6), (1997), 1012.

Nelson, R., "A microscopic comparison of fresh and burned bone," *J. Forens. Sci.*, 37 (4), (1992), 1055.

Platek, S.F., Keisler, M.A., Ranieri, N., Reynolds, T.W., and Crowe, J.B., "A method for the determination of syringe needle punctures in rubber stoppers using stereoscopic light microscopy," *J. Forensic. Sci.*, 47 (5), (2002), 986.

Suzuki, E.M., "Infrared spectra of U.S. automobile original topcoats (1974-1989) V: Identification of organic pigments used in red non-metallic and brown non-metallic and metallic monocoats-DPpredBO and thioindigo Bordeaux," *J. Forens. Sci.*, 44 (2), (1999), 297.

Suzuki, E.M., "Infrared spectra of U.S. automobile original topcoats (1974-1989) VI: Identification and analysis of yellow organic automotive paint pigments-isoindolinone yellow 3R, isoindoline yellow, anthrapyrimidine yellow and miscellaneous yellows," *J. Forens. Sci.*, 44 (6), (1999), 1151.

Suzuki, Edward M., and McDermot, M. X., "Infrared spectra of U.S. automobile original finishes. VII. Extended range FT-IR and XFR analysis of inorganic pigments in situ-nickel titanate and chrome titanate," *J. Forens. Sci.*, 51 (3), (2006), 574.

Van Hoven, H.A and Fraysier, H.D., "The matching of automotive paint chips to surface striations alignment," *J. Forens. Sci.*, 28 (2), (1983), 463.

Wiggins, Kenneth G., Holness, J., and March, B. M., "The importance of thin layer chromatography and UV microspectrophotometry in the analysis of reactive dyes released from wool and cotton fibers," *J. Forens. Sci.*, 50 (2), (2005), 364.

Zieba-Palus, J., " Selected cases of forensic paint analysis," *Sci. & Just.*, 39 (2), (1999), 123.

EXPERIMENT 4   Name _____

DATA SHEET   Date _____

PRACTICE IN THE USE OF THE MICROSCOPE

Part A: The Compound Microscope
   1. Sketch what an "h" looks like when viewed under this microscope.

Part B: The Stereoscopic Microscope
   1. Sketch what an "h" looks like when viewed under this microscope.

Part C: Comparison of Paint Chips
   1. Sketch the edge of the paint chip that you examined.

Part D: Comparison of Paper Matches
   1. Sketch the fiber patterns on two matches when looked at broadside.

   2. Sketch the fiber patterns on two matches when looked at on edge.

Refractive Index (RI) of Glass Fragments*

The analysis of glass chips sometimes involves measurement of the refractive index of the glass. **Refractive index is a measure of the bending of a ray of light as it passes from air into a solid or liquid.** Every material has its own characteristic refractive index. This measurement either provides additional data for the determination of the possible common origin of two glass samples, or helps to disprove this possibility.

IMMERSION METHODS

When a transparent object such as a glass chip is immersed in a liquid, it is seen by the unaided eye or under a microscope as having a dark or colored boundary, a sort of "halo." This is called the **Becke line**. The intensity of this visible boundary around the glass depends on the difference in refractive index between the glass and the liquid. In general, the greater the difference between the refractive index of a specimen and that of a surrounding medium, the more distinct is the Becke line. As the refractive indices of the specimen and liquid approach equality, the Becke line will tend to disappear. Indeed, if the indices of a colorless specimen and the surrounding medium are equal, the specimen will be practically invisible.

A difference in refractive index of ±0.002 between the glass chip and the immersion liquid can be readily observed. With light of one wavelength (monochromatic light), temperature control, and sufficient practice, differences as small as ±0.0001 may be detected. The refractive index of a substance varies considerably with different wavelengths of light. Normally, the value is determined in the presence of sodium light.

A common procedure for determining the refractive index of a glass chip is to immerse the chip in a liquid of about the same refractive index and then observe it through a microscope. The investigator may commence with a series of standardized immersion liquids, or he or she may mix two liquids until the refractive index of the mixture is the same as the glass sample and then determine the refractive index of the mixed liquids with a refractometer. To determine when the refractive index of the

---

*Parts of this experiment were taken from A. S. Curry, ed., *Methods of Forensic Science*, Vol. 4. New York: John Wiley & Sons, Inc., 1965, pp 126–129.

immersion liquid is equal to that of the glass chip, the investigator may observe the Becke line, using normal illumination with monochromatic light. If all of the glass chips examined show minimal contrast and no Becke lines in the same immersion liquid, it can be concluded that they all have comparable refractive indices.

An important advantage of the Becke line is not merely the fact that it indicates a difference between the indices of the glass and liquid, but that it indicates which possesses the higher value. Hence, the BECKE LINE MOVES TOWARD the medium of HIGHER refractive index if the focus of the microscope is RAISED and TOWARD the medium of LOWER refractive index if the focus is LOWERED. This observation allows an examiner to properly select a liquid that most closely matches the refractive index of glass. This is shown in Figure 5-1.

It is well known by people who use microscopes all of the time that when a colorless transparent object is being examined with a microscope by transmitted light, visibility of the object is enhanced as the condenser diaphragm is closed, although resolution is sacrificed. Furthermore, reducing the aperture of the optical system of the microscope enhances visibility by emphasizing the refractive index difference between the transparent object and the mounting medium. Therefore, in examining glass chips for refractive index, a minimum numerical aperture should be used.

STANDARD IMMERSION LIQUIDS

Standard immersion liquids may be prepared from two miscible liquids, one of which has a lower and the other a higher refractive index than the refractive index of the glass samples. A series of mixtures is made to cover the expected range of glasses in steps of 0.001 or 0.002. Although the refractive indices of glasses may vary considerably (Table 5-1), the refractive indices of most glass samples encountered in practice lie between 1.51 and 1.52. Automobile headlight glass generally has a refractive index range of 1.47 to 1.49.

The liquids chosen should be of low volatility, chemically stable, and of congenial smell. Castor oil (1.48) and clove oil (1.54) serve as quite suitable liquids and are readily available. Mixtures of these two liquids are reasonably stable in refractive index. Several other liquids that can be used are shown in Table 5-2.

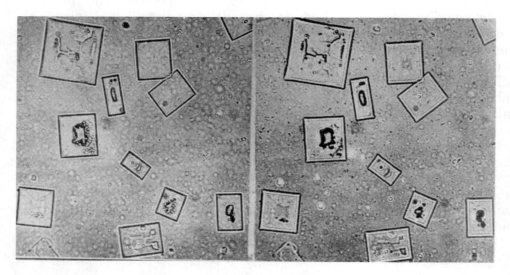

FIGURE 5–1   The Becke Line: Sodium chloride (refractive index = 1.544) in a liquid of refractive index 1.540. Left: On focusing upward slightly. Right: On focusing downward slightly. *Courtesy of Handbook of Chemical Microscopy by E.M. Chamot and C.W. Mason. Copyright © 1951. Reprinted by permission of John Wiley & Sons, Inc.*

TABLE 5–1	*Index of Refraction for Several Glasses*
Glass	**Index of Refraction**
Headlight glass	1.47–1.49
Television glass	1.49–1.51
Window glass	1.51–1.52
Bottles	1.51–1.52
Ophthalmic lenses	1.52–1.53

Many workers prefer to purchase their refractive index liquids from the R. P. Cargille Laboratories (55 Commerce Road, Cedar Grove, New Jersey 57009). The refractive indices are adjusted to within ±0.0002 of the stated values, and each liquid is also labeled with its temperature coefficient and dispersion. If you desire to prepare your own series, the adjustment of each mixture to its desired value is carried out with a refractometer, preferably the **Abbe refractometer**, which enables each mixture to be adjusted to the nearest ±0.0001. The standardized liquids are conveniently stored in 2- or 3-dram screw-capped vials in a rack. Thin glass rods may be used to transfer drops of liquid from the vials to the microscope slide.

EQUIPMENT

2 Cover slips (optional)	1 Refractometer, Abbe or equivalent
1 pk Filter paper	1 Sodium vapor lamp (preferably) or
1 pr Goggles, safety	Ilford spectrum yellow filter
1 bx Kim wipes	11 Stirring rods, glass, 3 mm × 10 cm
4 Medicine droppers	4 Vials, 3 dram, for glass fragments
2 Microscope slides (cavity works best)	11 Vials, glass, 3 dram with screw
1 Microscope (100_ is sufficient)	caps, for liquid samples
1 Mortar and pestle, small,	
to grind glass fragments	

TABLE 5–2	*Liquids for Refractive Index Determination*
Compound	$^{n}D^{20}\,°C$
Methyl alcohol	1.3288
Water	1.3330
Ethyl acetate	1.3727
n-Butyl alcohol	1.4022
Olive oil	1.4667
Cyclohexanol	1.4678
Castor oil	1.4820
Benzene	1.5011
Chlorobenzene	1.5250
Clove oil	1.5430
Nitrobenzene	1.5526
Bromoform	1.5973
Iodobenzene	1.6200

REAGENTS

Bromoform (R.I. = 1.59)
Castor oil (R.I. = 1.48)
Clove oil (R.I. = 1.54)
Ethanol, 95% (for cleaning)
Mixtures of olive oil and clove oil
    in 5:1, 4:2, 3:3, 2:4, and 1:5 ratios

Get headlight glass from an auto
   salvage yard
Olive oil (R.I. = 1.46)
Potassium chloride (KCl) crystals
Small chips of glass samples
Sodium chloride (NaCl) crystals

PART A: THE BECKE LINE CONCEPT

As an exercise in familiarizing yourself with the appearance of the Becke line, you will be asked to estimate the refractive indices of two solids: sodium chloride and potassium chloride. In order to accomplish this you will be supplied with the following three liquids: castor oil, clove oil, and bromoform.

1. Place a few crystals of sodium chloride on a microscope slide, add 1 drop of castor oil to the crystals, and cover them with a cover slip.

2. Turn on the sodium vapor lamp, and adjust the microscope. If a sodium lamp is not available, an Ilford spectrum yellow filter, which has a maximum transmission of 590 nm, may be used to provide an appropriate equivalent of sodium light (589 nm). (Note: The nanometer is used as a measure of the wavelength of radiation. It is 1×10^{-9} m in length and is abbreviated nm.)

3. Most microscopes have a 16 mm (2/3-in.) objective which should be used to view the crystals. Bring the crystals into focus.

4. Observe the bright border or "halo" that surrounds one of the larger crystals. If the halo seems indistinct, it may be made more pronounced by closing down the condenser diaphragm.

5. Turning the coarse adjustment, slowly focus upward. Observe whether the bright line (Becke line) moves away from the crystal (toward the castor oil) or toward the crystal. Next, slowly lower the objective, and note the direction in which the Becke line moves. The Becke line moves toward the medium or lower refractive index if the focus is lowered. Does castor oil have a higher or lower refractive index than sodium chloride?

6. Repeat steps 1 through 5 for sodium chloride immersed in clove oil. Does sodium chloride have a lower or higher refractive index compared with clove oil?

7. Repeat steps 1 through 5 for sodium chloride immersed in bromoform. Does sodium chloride have a lower or higher refractive index compared to bromoform?

8. To which of the three liquids does sodium chloride's refractive index come the closest? Why?

9. Repeat steps 1 through 5 for each of the three liquids immersed in potassium chloride. Which liquid has the closest refractive index to potassium chloride?

PART B: REFRACTIVE INDEX OF AUTOMOTIVE GLASS (ADVANCED)

CRIME SCENE

A hit-and-run accident has occurred. The officer at the scene recovers a few pieces of glass which she believes came from the vehicle in question. The next morning the police visit all the garages and service stations in town, and they find that eight headlights have been changed since the accident, three of which were broken at the time they were changed. The police recover these three headlights and send them to you. Your job is to measure the refractive index of the glass found at the scene and that of the three headlights to see if a match is possible.

METHOD

You will prepare a series of solutions ranging from either pure olive oil or castor oil, to pure clove oil. The indices of refraction of the solutions composed of mixtures of the two liquids chosen are determined by use of the refractometer. Six or eight mixtures having refractive indices between 1.46 and 1.53 are usually sufficient and are easily made by the use of medicine droppers. These solutions are then stored in properly labeled small screw-cap glass bottles. Proceed as follows.

1. Turn on the sodium vapor lamp, and adjust the microscope.

2. The crime scene glass fragment is placed on a microscope slide in 1 drop of one of the standard liquids, and covered with a small cover glass. The cover glass ensures that the chip is completely immersed and minimizes any spurious lens effects from the surface of the drop. As noted earlier, maximum sensitivity is obtained by having the minimum aperture in the optical system. Most microscopes have a 16 mm (2/3-in.) objective, which should be used with an eyepiece of 10× magnification. Lower powered objectives with stronger eyepieces may be preferred by some workers.

3. Observe the Becke line and then focus upward and downward to determine whether the glass fragment or the solution has the higher refractive index. When the refractive index of the glass and the immersion liquid are the same, the chip will become almost invisible, and it may be difficult to find and bring into focus the edges of the chip. If a white light is used, the glass chip may be found both by observing the color fringes—blue outside the chip and reddish on the inside—due to the dispersion difference between the glass and the liquid (Christiansen effect), and by noting the difference between the colorless glass chip and the (frequently) yellow immersion liquid. When the edge of the chip has been brought into focus, sodium light is substituted for the white light.

   By focusing up or down and following the Becke line (Figure 5-1), the investigator will be able to ascertain whether the reactive index of the fragment is the same as the liquid, or, if there is a difference, to make an approximate assessment by which the next immersion liquid may be selected.

4. The first liquid may be removed with filter paper and the next liquid flowed under the cover slip; any surplus can be absorbed by the filter paper. It is easier, however, to use a fresh chip, particularly if the larger of the two glass samples (scene or suspect) is examined first. With a little experience, the investigator should obtain the refractive index of the average glass sample after trying three or four immersion liquids.

5. Repeat this process until the refractive index of the glass is between the closest two immersion mixtures.

6. Record the refractive index range for this piece of glass.

7. Repeat the entire process for the remaining samples.

8. Turn off the sodium vapor lamp.

9. Clean out all the vials.

10. Clean up the area.

SELECTED SOURCES FOR ADDITIONAL INFORMATION

Almirall, J.R., Cole, M.D., Gettingby, G., and Furton, K.G., "Discrimination of glass sources using elemental composition and refractive index: development of predictive models," *Sci. & Just.*, 38 (2), (1998), 93.

Bates, J.W. and Lambert, J.A., "Use of the hypergeometric distribution for sampling in forensic glass comparison," *J. Forens. Sci. Soc.*, 31 (4), (1991), 449.

Crockett, J.S., and Taylor, M.E., "Physical properties of safety glass," *J. Forens. Sci. Soc.*, 9 (1969), 119.

Dabbs, M.D.G., "Density distribution of two glass populations," *J. Forens. Sci. Soc.*, 8 (1968), 71.

Espinoza, E.O., and Thornton, J.I., "Three dimensional presentation of glass density versus refractive index data," *J. Forens. Sci.*, 31 (2), (1986), 687.

Evett, I.W., and Buckleton, J., "The interpretation of glass evidence," *J. Forens. Sci. Soc.*, 30 (4), (1990), 215.

Evett, I.W. and Lambert, J.A., "Further observations on glass evidence interpretation," *Sci. & Just.*, 35 (4), (1995), 283.

Heideman, D.H., "Glass comparisons using a computerized refractive index data base," *J. Forens. Sci.*, 20 (1975), 103.

Jousimaa, K., and Rautavuori, H., "Preparation of glass fragments for analysis," *J. Forens. Sci.*, 27 (3), (1982), 471.

Koons, R.D., and Buscaglia, J., "The forensic significance of glass composition and refractive index measurements," *J. Forens. Sci.*, 44 (3), (1999), 496.

Lentini, J.J., "Behavior of glass at elevated temperatures," *J. Forens. Sci.*, 37 (5), (1992), 1358.

Locke, J. and Unikowski, J.A., "Breaking of flat glass—Part 1: Size and distribution of particles from plain glass windows," *Forens. Sci. Intl.*, 51 (1991), 251.

Locke, J. and Unikowski, J.A., "Breaking of flat glass - Part 2: Effect of pane parameters on particle distribution," *Forens. Sci. Intl.*, 56 (1992), 95.

Locke, J. and Scaranage, J.K., "Breaking of flat glass - Part 3: Surface particles from windows," *Forens. Sci. Intl.*, 57 (1992), 73.

Marcouiller, J.M., "A revised glass annealing method to distinguish glass types," *J. Forens. Sci.*, 35 (2), (1990), 554.

Ojena, S.M., and Deforest, P.R., "Precise refractive index determination by the immersion method using phase contrast microscopy and the Mettler hot stage," *J. Forens. Sci. Soc.*, 12 (1972), 315.

Ojena, S.M., and Deforest, P.R., "A study of the refractive index variations within and between sealed beam headlights using a precise method," *J. Forens. Sci.*, 17 (1972), 409.

Pitts, S.J., and Kratochvil, B., "Statistical discrimination of float glass fragments by instrumental neutron activation analysis: Methods for forensic science applications," *J. Forens. Sci.*, 36 (1), (1991), 122.

Rees, P.O., "The determination and the comparison of the refractive index of glass fragments by means of a temperature control method," *J. Forens. Sci. Soc.*, 8 (1968), 25.

Smalldon, K.W., and Brown, C., "The discriminating power of density and refractive index for window glass," *J. Forens. Sci. Soc.*, 13 (1973), 307.

Thornton, J.I., and Crim, D., "The use of k values in the interpretation of glass density and refractive index data," *J. Forens. Sci.*, 34 (6), (1989), 1323.

Underhill, M., "Multiple refractive index in float glass," *J. Forens. Sci. Soc.*, 20 (1980), 111.

Walsh, K.A.J., Buckleton, J.S., and Triggs, C.M., "A practical example of the interpretation of glass evidence," *Sci. & Just.*, 36 (4), (1996), 213.

Welch, A.E., Richard, R. and Underhill, M., "The observation of banding in glass fragments and its forensic significance," *J. Forens. Sci. Soc.*, 29 (1), (1989), 5.

Zeichner, A., and Feingold, G., " Improved sample holder for refractive index measurements of small, single, glass fragments," *J. Forens. Sci.*, 34 (4), (1989), 1003.

EXPERIMENT 5

DATA SHEET

Name _____

Date _____

REFRACTIVE INDEX OF GLASS FRAGMENTS

Part A: The Becke Line Concept

1. Sodium chloride crystals

   Observations:

   Castor oil   Clove oil   Bromoform

   Conclusions:

2. Potassium chloride crystals

   Observations:

   Castor oil   Clove oil   Bromoform

   Conclusions:

Part B: Refractive Index of Automobile Glass (Advanced)

a. Index of refraction of standard solutions and proportions used in making the standards.

	Index of refraction	Drops of Castor oil	Drops of Clove oil
1.			
2.			
3.			
4.			
5.			
6.			
7.			
8.			
9.			
10.			
11.			

b. Index of refraction of glass samples

   A. Suspect 1:_____

   B. Suspect 2: _____

   C. Suspect 3:_____

   D. Scene: _____

c. Matches of glass fragments based on the index of refraction.

How certain are you that the fragments you have matched do have a common origin? Give your reasons.

Density of Glass by Flotation and Density Gradient Columns

The objective of glass comparison is to associate one glass fragment with another while minimizing or eliminating the possible existence of other sources. Glass will have its greatest evidential value when it can be individualized to one source. Such a determination, however, can only be made when the suspect and crime-scene fragments are assembled and physically pieced together (a physical match). The possibility that two pieces of glass originating from different sources will fit exactly together is so unlikely as to exclude all other sources from practical consideration. If this effort fails, the forensic examiner will compare the glasses to determine whether they have or do not have the same densities and refractive indices. This experiment will allow you to become familiar with laboratory techniques employed for comparing the densities of glass. The purpose of such an analysis is to establish the possibility or impossibility of any glass fragments having a common origin.

The simplest comparative-density technique is known as **flotation** (not floatation). It is based on the observation that a solid particle will float in a liquid medium of greater density, sink in a liquid of lower density, or remain suspended in a liquid of equal density. A second comparative-density technique is the **density gradient** method. A standard density gradient tube is made up of layers of two liquids mixed in varying proportions so that each layer has a different density value. When completed, a density gradient tube will usually have 6 to 10 original layers, in which the bottom layer has the heaviest density and the top layer the lightest density. After standing for 24 hours these layers will diffuse into one continuous gradient. A solid particle added to the tube will sink until its density is the same as the surrounding liquid and then remain suspended at that level. Furthermore, if absolute density values are desired, the gradient tube can be calibrated by adding to it solids of known densities. Densities for glass and similar materials are listed in Table 3-1.

CRIME SCENE

During a mugging the attacker drops his glasses and one lens breaks. He picks up the pieces and flees. The victim, however, observes this incident and when the police officer arrives, describes it to him. The officer, upon careful searching, finds a few very small pieces of glass. These have been given to you. Once the suspect is apprehended, you try to match the glass fragments.

EQUIPMENT

8	Beakers, 250-mL (for knowns and unknowns)	2	Glass tubes, 30 × 1 cm (closed at one end)
1	Brush, test tube	1 pr	Goggles, safety
1	Buret holder	1	Medicine dropper
4	Rubber stoppers, small	1	Micrometer, optional
1	Forceps	1	Mortar and pestle, small
1	Funnel, glass, 35 mm	1	Pencil, grease
1	Pipet bulb	1 pr	Scissors
1	Pipet, Mohr, 5 mL	1	Spatula
1	Rack, test tube	1	Stirring rod, glass, 4 m × 15 cm
1	Ring stand	5	Test tubes, 10 cm
1	Ruler (metric)	21	Vials, to hold compounds from Table 6-1
	Samples of small glass fragments, eyeglass, window pane, headlight.		

REAGENTS

Bromobenzene (d = 1.52)   Bromoform (d = 2.89)
Several small crystals of a few of the
  compounds listed in Table 6-1

METHOD

Obtain a glass fragment from each of four beakers labeled "unknown" and those labeled "known." The unknowns are numbered 1, 2, 3, and 4. The knowns are lettered A, B, C, and D. The object is to determine whether the numbered and lettered fragments have a common origin. In some instances, this cannot be done with absolute certainty. Do the very best you can.

PART A: PHYSICAL MATCHING

Try to obtain a physical match between fragments if possible. That is, match letters, if present, on two fragments by fitting together any scratches on the fragments, or by some other piecing together of the fragments. Such a fracture match—a physical match of two fractures—is conclusive proof that they were once the same piece of glass. Record any physical match on the data sheet.

PART B: EDGE THICKNESS

Compare the fragments by measurement of the thickness of the edges of the fragments. Truly accurate measurement requires a micrometer. However, a visual comparison of pieces of glass placed side by side is fairly reliable. Although the results may not be conclusive in themselves, they may help the decision-making process later. Record any similarity in edge thickness on the data sheet. Use the metric scale on a ruler for better comparison of edge measurement.

TABLE 6–1	Crystals of Different Densities (g/cm³)		
Compound	Density	Compound	Density
$KC_2H_3O_2$	1.57	KF	2.48
$Na_2B_4O_7.1OH_2O$	1.73	$NaC1O_3$	2.49
$Na_2C_4H_4.2H_2O$	1.82	$KClO_4$	2.52
$K_3Fe(CN)_6$	1.85	$CuC1_2.2H_2O$	2.54
KNO_2	1.91	NaF	2.56
KC1	1.98	$MgSO_4$	2.66
KNO_3	2.10	$K_2Cr_2O_7$	2.67
NaCl	2.16	$KMnO_4$	2.70
$NaNO_3$	2.26	Na_2CrO_4	2.72
$KC1O_3$	2.32	$AgClO_4$	2.80

PART C: DENSITY COMPARISON BY FLOTATION

1. Before adding the glass fragments to the test tube, it is important that each piece of glass be carefully examined and briefly sketched. This will allow the examiner to identify each fragment when placed in the mixture of bromoform and bromobenzene.

2. A cleaned and dried sample of an unknown glass particle is placed in a test tube containing 1–2 mL of bromoform. The glass will float on the liquid's surface. This indicates that the density of the liquid is greater than that of the glass. Slowly add a less dense liquid (bromobenzene) dropwise, with stirring, until the particle is exactly suspended. If too much bromobenzene is added, so that the glass particle begins to sink, gradually add more of the heavier liquid.

3. Add a similarly sized, cleaned, and dried sample of the known glass. If the two glasses are similar in density, each will remain suspended in the liquid. Otherwise, one particle will tend to rise or sink relative to the other.

4. Systematically compare all the unknown glasses to the known glasses, attempting to match up a lettered fragment with a numbered glass.

PART D: DENSITY COMPARISON BY DENSITY GRADIENT TUBES (ADVANCED)

An alternative technique of comparing the densities of glass particles is to use density gradient tubes. In this experiment we not only compare glass, but show you an easy way to calibrate the density column so that a fairly accurate estimate of density can be made. This is done by adding to the density column small crystals of ionic salts whose densities are known, but which are insoluble in the organic liquid.

METHOD

You will prepare three identical density columns, add a few crystals of known density to each column to calibrate them, and then add the small fragments of glass. You should be able to measure the density and determine if the suspect glass matches that found at the scene.

1. Place five test tubes in a test tube rack.

2. Prepare the following mixtures (b–f) by pipetting into the test tubes the ratios listed:
   a. Pure bromoform
   b. 0.5 mL of bromobenzene, 2.5 mL of bromoform
   c. 1.0 mL of bromobenzene, 2.0 mL of bromoform
   d. 1.5 mL of bromobenzene, 1.5 mL of bromoform
   e. 2.0 mL of bromobenzene, 1.0 mL of bromoform
   f. 2.5 mL of bromobenzene, 0.5 mL of bromoform
   g. Pure bromobenzene

3. Place a buret holder on a ring stand.

4. Mark off seven equal spaces along each of three glass tubes.

5. Place the columns in the buret holder, being sure the bottoms are securely closed, with waxed-in or taped-in rubber stoppers if necessary.

6. Carefully add the solutions in the order listed in step 2 (bromoform, the bottom).

7. With a forceps, carefully select one of the more dense crystals listed in Table 6–1 and add it to one of the columns. Repeat this process until you have added at least seven different crystals to each column. Record which ones you use.

8. Allow the crystals to settle for about 10 minutes and measure their height from the bottom of the tube with a metric ruler.

9. Carefully add a few of the glass fragments (suspect and scene) found to match in Part C to their respective columns, and allow the columns to stand overnight.

10. Record the height of the marker crystals in each column.

11. Plot density versus height for the marker crystals in each column.

12. Determine the height of the glass in each column.

13. From the graph plotted in step 11, determine the density of the glass in each column.

14. Clean out the columns, and pour the solutions into the recycle bottle.

SELECTED SOURCES FOR ADDITIONAL INFORMATION

Brown, G.A., "Factors affecting the refractive index distribution of window glass," *J. Forens. Sci.*, 30 (3), (1985), 806.

Cobb, P.G.W., "A survey of the variations in the physical properties of glass," *J. Forens. Sci. Soc.*, 8 (1968), 29.

Curran, J.M., Triggs, C.M., Buckleton, J.S., Walsh, K.A.J., and Hicks, T., "The interpretation of elemental composition measurements from forensic glass evidence, I," *Sci. & Just.*, 37 (4), (1997), 241.

Curran, J.M., Triggs, C.M., Buckleton, J.S., Walsh, K.A.J., and Hicks, T. "The interpretation of elemental composition measurements from forensic glass evidence, II," *Sci. & Just.*, 37 (4), (1997), 245.

Curran, J.M., Triggs, C.M., Buckleton, J.S., Walsh, K.A.J., and Hicks, T., "Assessing transfer probabilities in a Bayesian interpretation of forensic glass evidence," *Sci. & Just.*, 38 (1), (1998), 15.

Dabbs, M.D.G., and Pearson, E.F., "Some physical properties of a large number of window glass specimens." *J. Forens. Sci. Soc.*, 17 (1972), 70.

Dabbs, M.D.G., and Pearson, E.F., 'The variation in refractive index and density across two sheets of window glass." *J. Forens. Sci. Soc.*, 10 (1970), 139.

Dolan, D.N., "Vehicle lights and their use as evidence," *J. Forens. Sci.*, 11 (1), (1971), 69.

Fong, W., "Value of glass as evidence." *J. Forens. Sci. Soc.*, 18 (1973), 398.

Heye, C.L., Rios, F.G., and Thornton, J.I., "Density characterization of armor piercing ammunition," *J. Forens. Sci.*, 40 (3), (1995), 401.

Hicks, T., Vanina, R., and Margot, P., "Transfer and persistence of glass fragments on garments," *Sci. & Just.*, 36 (2), (1996) 101.

Kahane, D., Thornton, J.I., and Crim, D., "Estimation of the absolute density of glass following the sink float technique," *J. Forens. Sci.*, 32 (1), (1987), 87.

Lambert, J.A., Satterthwaite, M.J. and Harrison, P.H., "A survey of glass fragments from clothing of persons suspected of involvement in crime," *Sci. & Just.*, 35 (4), (1995), 273.

McCrone, W.C., and Hudson, W., "The analytical use of density gradient separations," *J. Forens. Sci. Soc.*, 14 (1969), 370.

McJenkins, S.P., and Thornton, J.I., "Glass fracture analysis," *J. Forens. Sci. Soc.*, 2 (1973), 1.

McQuillan, J., and Edgar, K., "A summary of the distribution of glass on clothing," *J. Forens. Sci. Soc.*, 32 (4), (1992), 333.

Miller, E.T., "Forensic glass comparisons," in *Forensic Science Handbook*, R. Saferstein Ed., Prentice-Hall, Englewood Cliffs, N.J. (1982).

Smalldon, K.W., and Brown, "The discriminating power of density and refractive index for window glass," *J. Forens. Sci. Soc.*, 13 (1973), 307.

Thornton, J.I., Crim, D., Hauser, L., and Kahane, D., "Correlation of glass density and refractive index-implications to density gradient construction," *J. Forens. Sci.*, 29 (3), (1984), 711.

EXPERIMENT 6   Name _____

DATA SHEET   Date _____

DENSITY OF GLASS BY FLOTATION AND DENSITY GRADIENT COLUMNS

Part A: Physical Matching
Set No._____

Part B: Edge Thickness
1. Measurement of the edges of the fragments (thickness)

    A   1

    B   2

    C   3

    D   4

2. Tentative comparisons

Part C: Density Comparison by Flotation

      A. _____

      B. _____

      C. _____

      D. _____

Part D: Density Comparison by Density Gradient Tubes (Advanced)

a. Record the crystals used for calibration here.

	Column 1				Column 2				Column 3		
	Crystal	Init ht	Final ht		Crystal	Init ht	Final ht		Crystal	Init ht	Final ht
1.											
2.											
3.											
4.											
5.											
6.											
7.											
8.											
9.											
10.											

b. Plot density versus height for each column on the graph paper provided.

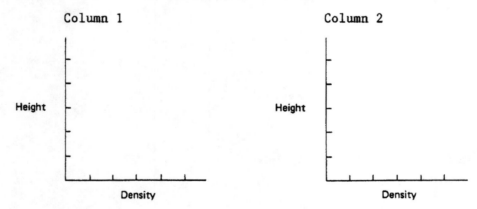

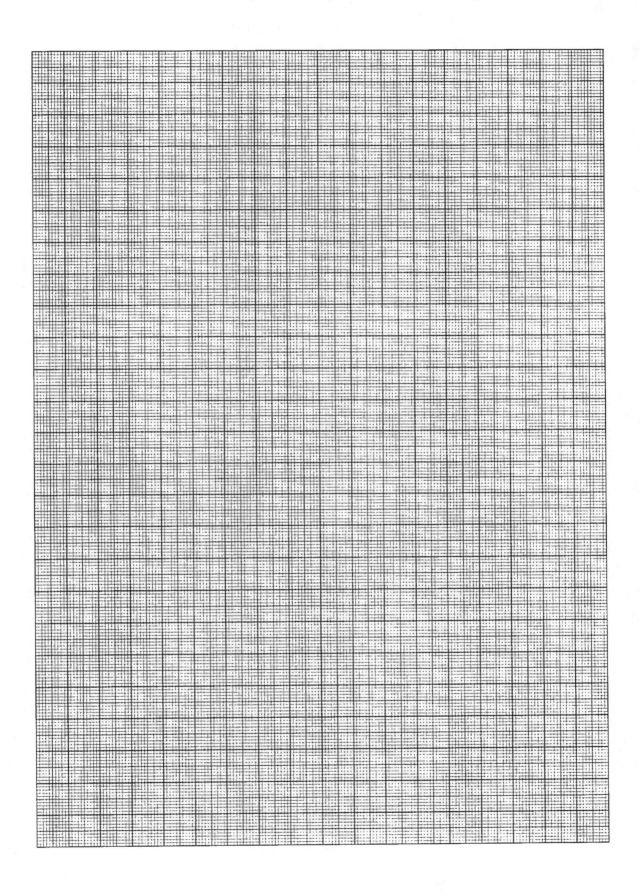

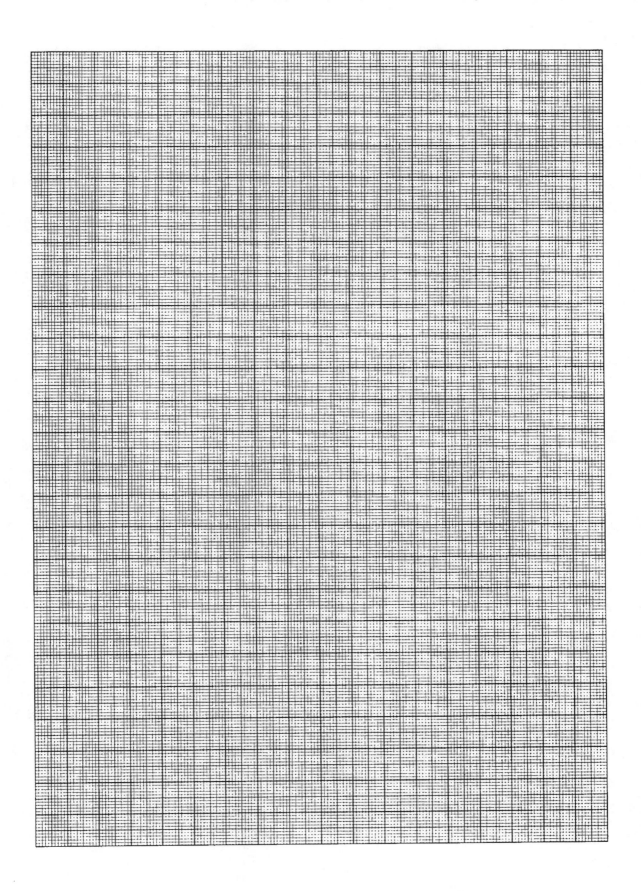

c. Indicate on the graphs in step 1 where the glass particles are.

d. What are your conclusions? Which glass samples match, if any?

Questions

1. If your density profiles are not the same, what would you do the next time that you make this type of column?

2. Now that you know the density of glass fairly well, you could make a density gradient column covering 0.1 density units from the top to the bottom of the column. What mixtures of bromoform and bromobenzene would you use to make such a column?

3. How certain are you that the fragments you have matched do have a common origin? Give your reasons.

Soil Analysis

Soil is a common form of physical evidence found at the scene of such crimes as hit-and-run accidents, automobile collisions, rapes, and burglaries. Soil from the crime scene may be picked up by an automobile, thus providing a valuable link between the car and the crime. Similarly, soil or mud found adhering to clothing or shoes may provide the clue that can link a suspect to a particular crime site.

The two methods that we shall use in the analysis of soil samples to determine whether or not the samples have a common origin, are easily performed, take little time, and yield data that may be useful. These methods are (1) a density profile, and (2) a settling-rate curve. (Exhaustive methods, such as geological examinations, will not be undertaken in this experiment.)

About three hundred years ago Galileo found that a ball of wax, placed between a layer of salt water and a layer of fresh water, would float. That is, he observed that objects float at the level of their density. Therefore, if you drop an object into a column of several liquids of different densities, the object will sink to the place where its density just equals the density of the surrounding liquid.

Figure 7-1 shows a density gradient column for determining a soil profile, made by mixing various proportions of xylene (d = 0.88) with bromoform (d = 2.89). In 1904, George Popp, a German forensic chemist, presented soil evidence at the trial of Karl Laubach, believed to be the first time that this type of evidence was used in court. Laubach was convicted because the soil on his trousers matched the soil on a head scarf used to strangle Eva Disch.

For our experiment a soil sample is dried at 100° C for 1 hour and then sieved; a small amount of the 30 to 45 mesh fraction is placed on the top of the column. Dense particles will settle to their level in a few minutes, but less dense particles may take a few hours to stop moving. (Note: The size of a particle does not change its density, only how fast it will settle. Why?) The soil profile at the scene is then compared with the soil profile from the suspect.

The same technique can be used to determine the density of very small glass fragments, as in Experiment 6. However, in Experiment 6 the density gradient column is made from solutions of bromoform (d = 2.89) and bromobenzene (d = 1.52).

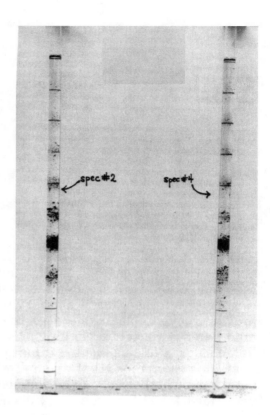

FIGURE 7-1   Soil density profile. *Courtesy of New Jersey State Police*

CRIME SCENE

A woman has been beaten and sexually assaulted in a park while walking back to her apartment from work. The crime took place at approximately 11:00 P.M. The investigating officers have obtained a description of the assailant and placed into custody three young men answering to the description. The assault took place in an area where the ground was damp, and the officers investigating the scene noticed that the soil was compressed in one area, as if the assailant's knee had gouged into a soft place in the earth. The victim has picked one of the three men out of the lineup, stating that he was her attacker. The officers assigned to the case have searched the accused man's apartment and found a pair of trousers with soil particles lodged in the fabric of the knee area. The laboratory analyst's task is to attempt to determine whether the soil in the trouser fabric and the soil from the compressed area at the scene do indeed have a common origin. You are the analyst. Remember, one can get dirt on the knees of a pair of trousers in many ways. You may determine that the accused is innocent also. This is only one piece of evidence, not conclusive in itself, even if positive.

EQUIPMENT

1 Balance capable of measuring ±0.01 g or more
1 Beaker (graduated), 100 mL
1 Brush, test tube, small diameter
1 Buret holder
4 Rubber stoppers, small
3 Glass tubes, 30 cm × 10 mm
    (closed at one end)
1 pr Goggles, safety

1 Ring stand
1 Ruler, metric
20 Sample bottles, 2 oz, for known
    and unknown soil samples
1 Funnel, glass, 35 mm
1 Set of sieves, ranging in size
    from 25 to 80 mesh
1 Spatula

1 Graph paper, cm or 0.1 inch ruling
7 Medicine droppers
1 Mortar and pestle
1 Motor-driven sieve shaker (optional)
1 Pencil, grease
2 Pipets, 5 mL
1 Rack, test tube

1 Spectrophotometer, Bausch
   & Lomb Spectronic 20*
   or equivalent
7 Tubes, test, 10 cm
7 Vials, 4-dram
  Weighing paper
  Cuvettes

REAGENTS

Soil samples of differing composition (gravel, peat, loam, fine sand)
Bromoform
Xylene

METHODS

PART A: SAMPLE PREPARATION

The first step in soil analysis is to obtain a sample composed of uniformly sized particles. This is done by sieving the gross sample obtained from the crime scene or from the possessions of the suspect.

1. Arrange the set of sieves in numerical order with the smallest number at the top and the largest at the bottom (the smaller the number, the larger the mesh of the wire screen in the sieve).

2. Place the sieves on the shaker (if available), and pour your sample into the top sieve.

3. Place the cover on the upper sieve, fasten the binding straps, and turn on the power switch of the shaker. (If a power shaker is not available the shaking of the sieves can be done manually.) Allow the shaker to operate for 5 minutes. The time is not particularly crucial; only the proper separation of particles is really important.

4. Turn off the shaker and release the binding straps.

5. Remove the sieve cover, and separate the sieves. The only portion of sample to be used in the analysis is one taken from a sieve with a screen mesh in the middle range (45 mesh works well). The other portions should be recombined and saved for possible future needs. Be certain to label them.

PART B: DENSITY GRADIENT TUBE

This analysis depends upon the principle that an object will be suspended in a liquid whose density matches its own. It will sink in a liquid that is less dense and float in a liquid that is more dense.

1. Prepare the tube in the following manner. Obtain bromoform and xylene and make mixtures of the two liquids in the proportions listed below (3 mL of each solution):

   a. Pure bromoform (density 2.89)   b. 0.5 mL xylene, 2.5 mL bromoform

   c. 1.0 mL xylene, 2.0 mL bromoform   d. 1.5 mL xylene, 1.5 mL bromoform

e. 2.0 mL xylene, 1.0 mL bromoform   f. 2.5 mL xylene, 0.5 mL bromoform
g. Pure xylene (density [0.88])

2. Mark off seven equal increments on the 30 cm glass tubes. A tube that has a solid glass seal on one end is preferred. However, the end can be closed with a rubber stopper, but the **rubber stopper must be either taped or waxed in, or it will often fall out.**

3. Carefully pour each of the solutions in the order listed in step 1 into each tube. Begin with the bromoform, the most dense liquid.

4. Close the top of the column with a small rubber stopper to prevent evaporation and place the tube in a buret holder.

5. Repeat the above, filling a second and third tube, and place them in a holder also.

6. Place a small amount (0.1 g) of the suspect sample soil into each of the tubes and an equal amount of soil found at the scene into the third tube. Be certain to label each tube. Most particles will reach their depth within a few minutes, but allow the tubes to stand for 24 hours for minor adjustments, and then compare the levels at which the soil particles have become suspended. If they are the same, the scene and suspect soils have the same density distribution. If they are found at different levels, the soils are probably not the same.

7. Clean up—dispose of the xylene-bromoform mixture in an appropriate waste container.

NOTE: if you get a definite layer or layers of particles after 24 hours at the boundaries where you added the different solutions, then the column has not reached density equilibrium and should be allowed to set for a while longer.

PART C: RATE OF SETTLING OF SOIL PARTICLES

This is a very lengthy experiment if there is clay in the sample.

This method of comparison of two soil samples is rapid (unless clay is involved), simple, and gives some idea of the composition of the soil sample. If the soil sample contains much lightweight material, such as clay, the rate of settling will be slow. If it contains a large amount of heavy material from gravel, such as quartz, settling will be quite rapid. The analysis must be repeated for each sample being investigated. This procedure will make use of a visible spectrophotometer, such as the Bausch & Lomb Spectronic 20 or its equivalent.

The controls of the spectrophotometer are shown in Figure 7-2, and the light's path through the instrument is illustrated in Figure 7-3.

Directions

NOTE: A flashing display indicates that the reading is out of range. Dilute the sample.

1. Turn on the instrument by rotating the Power Switch/Zero Control clockwise until you hear a click. Allow the instrument to warm up for 15–20 minutes to stabilize the source and detector.

2. Adjust the wavelength to 450 nm.

3. Set the display mode to Transmittance by pressing the Mode control key until the LED beside "transmittance" is lit.

FIGURE 7–2 Spectronic 20D. *Courtesy of VWR Scientific Products, West Chester, PA, www. vwrsp.com.*

4. Adjust the 0% T with the Power Switch/Zero Control. Make sure the sample compartment is empty and the cover is closed.

5. Place some water in a cell or 4-inch test tube, and insert it all the way down into the sample compartment. Align the guide mark on the cell with the mark on the instrument. Make a mark on the tube if necessary.

6. Adjust the display to 100% T with the Transmittance/Absorbance Control. Remove the cell from the sample compartment and empty the water.

7. Recheck the 0 (step 4) and 100% T settings, steps 5 and 6.

8. Weigh 0.5 g of your homogenous soil sample onto a weighing paper.

9. Fill a clean cuvette about two-thirds full of water.

10. Add the 0.5 g sample of soil, and shake the tube vigorously for approximately 1 minute.

11. Immediately insert the tube into the sample compartment, close the cover, and record the percent transmittance from the scale.

12. Continue to take readings every 30 seconds for the first few minutes, then at longer intervals until the percent transmittance reaches a stable value or until 10 minutes of recording values has been reached.

13. Repeat for each soil sample you are investigating.

14. Record all observations on the data sheet, and using linear graph paper, make plots of time versus percent transmittance for each sample. More than one plot can be made on a sheet of paper.

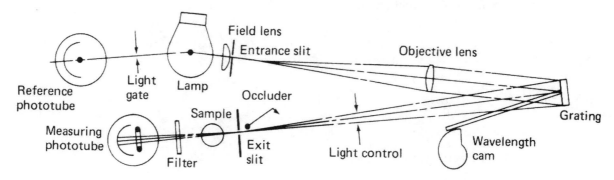

FIGURE 7–3 An optical and component diagram of a Spectronic 20. *Courtesy Bausch and Lomb Optical Company, Rochester, NY.*

15. Compare the rates of settling for the soil samples, and draw conclusions as to the similarities or differences between them. The shape of the plot is important, not the actual values for the percent transmittance.

16. Wash all glassware, and return it to the location from which you obtained it.

17. Turn off the spectrophotometer, and replace the cover.

SELECTED SOURCES FOR ADDITIONAL INFORMATION

Antoci, P.R., and Petraco, N., "A technique for comparing soil colors in the forensic laboratory," *J. Forens. Sci.*, 38 (2), (1993), 437.

Bresee, R.R., "Density gradient analysis of single polyester fibers," *J. Forens. Sci.*, 25 (3), (1980), 564.

Chaperlin, K., and Howarth, P.S., "Soil comparison by the density gradient method—A review and evaluation," *Forens. Sci. Intl.*, 23 (1983), 161.

Dudley, R.J., "The use of color in the discrimination between soils," *J. Forens. Sci. Soc.*, 15 (1975), 209.

Dudley, R.J., "The use of density gradient columns in the forensic comparison of soils," *Med. Sci. Law*, 19 (1979), 39.

Hiraoka, Y., "A possible approach to soil discrimination using x-ray fluorescence analysis," *J. Forens. Sci.*, 39 (6), (1994), 1381.

Horswell, J., Cordiner, S.S., Maas, E.W., Martin, T.M., Sutherland, K.B.W., Speir, T.W., Nogales, B., and Osborn, A.M., "Forensic comparison of soils by bacterial community DNA profiling," *J. Forens. Sci.*, 47 (2), (2002), 350.

Junger, E.P., "Assessing the unique characteristics of close proximity soil samples: just how useful is soil evidence?" *J. Forens. Sci.*, 41 (1), (1996), 27.

Murray, R.C., and J.C.F. Tedrow, *Forensic Geology.* New Brunswick, N.J., Rutgers University Press, 1975.

Nute, H. D., "An improved density gradient system for forensic science soil studies," *J. Forens. Sci.*, 20 (4), (1975), 668.

Petraco, N., and Kubic, T., " A density gradient technique for use in forensic soil analysis," *J. Forens. Sci.*, 45 (4), (2000), 872.

Siegel, J.A., "A review of "Forensic Geology," *J. Forens. Sci.*, 39 (1), (1994), 289.

Vass, A.A., Bass, W.M., Wolt, J.D., Foss, J.E., and Ammons, J.T., "Time since death determination of human cadavers using soil solution," *J. Forens. Sci.*, 37 (5), (1992), 1236.

Wanogho, S., Gettinby, G., Caddy, B., and Robertson, J., "Determination of particle size distribution of soils in forensic science using classical and modern instrumental methods," *J. Forens. Sci.*, 34 (4), (1989), 823.

EXPERIMENT 7

DATA SHEET

Name _____

Date _____

SOIL ANALYSIS

1. Comparison of samples by density gradient tube (diagram the distribution by measurement from the top of the column)

   Suspect A   Scene   Suspect B

2. Data from rate-of-settling determination

Time				% T				Time				% T		
A	S	B		A	S	B		A	S	B		A	S	B

3. Plots of time versus rate of settling (on graph paper); attach to this report.

4. Conclusions as to similarities or differences of samples and possibility of common origin (use the back of the page).

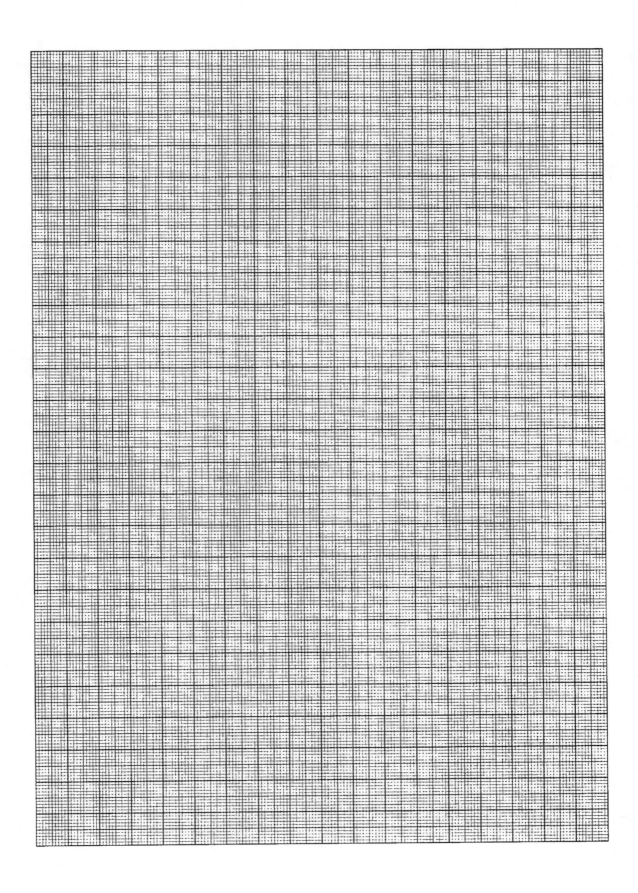

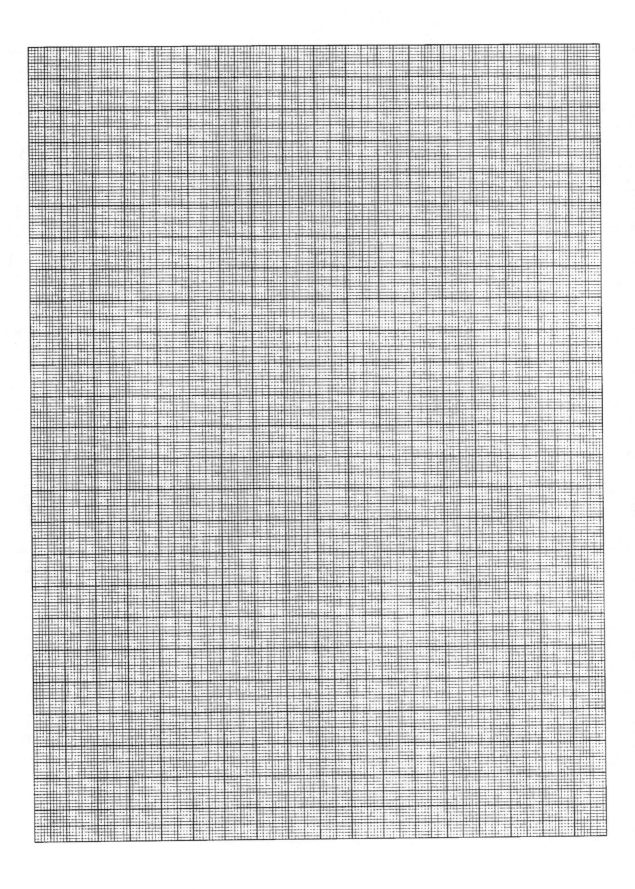

Powder Residues on Fabrics

It is not uncommon for law enforcement officers to encounter the use of firearms in criminal investigations. Among other things, investigators often need to know the distance a firearm was held from the victim at the time of discharge. Determination of the distance from a target at which a weapon is fired can only be made by comparing the powder residue pattern around a bullet hole to patterns made by the suspect weapon fired at varying distances from a test target. If the suspect weapon is not available, the examiner will try to estimate the muzzle-to-target distance by examining the bullet hole(s) present on the target. Such factors as the presence of tearing, singeing, or melting of the fabric; the presence of carbonaceous smoke around the hole (unburned and partially burned gunpowder on the fabric); and the presence of metal particles are used in estimating the muzzle-to-target distance.

Smokeless powders are comprised of nitrocellulose obtained from cotton or wood fibers which have been treated with a mixture of concentrated nitric acid and sulfuric acid. Smokeless powder is therefore rich in what are chemically referred to as **nitrates**. When smokeless powder burns or partially burns, as when a cartridge is fired, it will decompose to form what are called **nitrites**.

The presence of nitrites on a fabric can be very helpful to a criminalist who is interested in determining whether a hole in question was made by the passage of a bullet through the fabric. By establishing the presence of nitrites on the fabric, the criminalist can chemically show that the hole was made by a bullet. Furthermore, if a suspect weapon is available, comparing the developed nitrite distribution pattern to patterns obtained from firing the weapon at known distances can be a useful technique for determining the shooting distance from the target. Such information will help investigators decide whether a shooting case was possibly homicide, suicide, or an accident. The technique discussed is of particular value when the cloth is colored or a mix of colors and the gray powder patterns are not visible.

In Part A of this experiment* the firing of a bullet on a target will be simulated by placing the chemical sodium nitrite on a cloth or paper unless actual cloth with test firings has been prepared. The nitrite particles are

---

*Part A of this experiment is based on material obtained from Maiti 1973; see the selected sources at the end of this experiment.

then transferred from the surface onto a chemically treated photographic paper which contains a mixture of p-nitroaniline, 2-naphthol, and magnesium sulfate. In the presence of these chemicals, the nitrite particles will react to form a red colored dye.

CRIME SCENE

A hunter has found the body of a deceased male in a woods. The first examination indicates that he probably died of a heart attack. However, the coroner notices a few small holes in the victim's shirt which could have been made by a small caliber slug; or it may be just a circular tear from a 1imb punching through the material. The wound hole from a small caliber weapon sometimes closes over, and unless extreme care is taken, it may well be overlooked. Your job is to determine if any of the holes in the shirt are bullet holes.

EQUIPMENT

2	Forceps		Photographic paper (glossy), 8 sheets
1	Funnel, short stem	1	Sprayer, aerosol
1 pr	Goggles, safety	2	Towels, cloth, about 45 cm × 45 cm
1	Iron, electric		Towels, paper
1	Pencil, grease	2	Trays, photographic

Cloth containing a bullet hole and a hole not made by a bullet. These should be about 30 cm × 30 cm of colored, striped, or multicolor fabric.

Cloths containing bullet holes at 1, 2, and 4 ft. These should be white cloth about 30 cm × 30 cm for the knowns so the student can see the powder pattern other than the nitrite particles.

Cloth containing a bullet hole made at an unknown distance (the instructor may wish to use cloths treated with sodium nitrite in place of actual bullet holes).

REAGENTS

Acetic acid, 10% (v/v)

Buffer (1.9 g of sodium bitartrate and 1.5 g of tartaric acid in 100 mL of H_2O, pH 2. 8)

Hydrochloric acid (HCl), 5% (v/v)

Lead salt solution, 0.01% (w/v)

Photographic hypo ($Na_2S_2O_3.5H_2O$) 227 g/L

Sodium hydroxide, 10% (v/v)

Sodium nitrite, (0.6 g in 100 mL of water)

Solution containing p-nitroaniline, 2-naphthol, and magnesium sulfate (0.25% each in 1:1 aqueous alcohol)

Sodium rhodizonate. A fresh, saturated, aqueous solution must be prepared daily.

PART A: BULLET HOLES IN FABRIC

1. Ordinary glossy photographic paper is completely desensitized by placing it in a hypo bath for 5 minutes (four sheets will be necessary).

2. Wash off the hypo and dry the paper by placing it between paper towels.

3. Soak the photographic paper in a solution containing p-nitroaniline, 2-naphthol, and magnesium sulfate.

4. Dry the paper.

5. Place a clean cloth towel on a flat surface.

6. Place the photographic paper on the cloth, emulsion side up.

7. Place the test fabric (face down) on this paper.

8. Place another towel, moistened with 10% acetic acid, on top of this.

9. Cover with a dry towel.

10. This entire pack is then pressed for 5 to 10 minutes with a warm electric iron.

The prepared photographic paper, when examined, is found to have a number of red spots, which correspond to the position of the partially burned powder grains (nitrites).

This test is sensitive to burned and partially burned black and smokeless powder. A permanent representation of the powder residue is produced without altering or destroying the fabric of the bullet hole. If the garment is bloodstained, the photographic paper should be moistened with 10% sodium hydroxide, using a cotton swab. The nitrite particles will now appear as blue spots on a pale yellow background and will not be mistaken for blood.

PART B: SODIUM RHODIZONATE TEST FOR LEAD RESIDUES

The firing of the weapon will not only propel gun powder residues toward the target, but primer residues also leave the muzzle as a cloud of finely dispersed particles. These primer residues generally contain lead, barium, and antimony. These particles are capable of traveling for long distances (up to 10 ft). When they strike the target, they may adhere, becoming part of the visible residue pattern, or they may bounce off, leaving behind an invisible trace of primer residues. In addition to the primer residues, lead and antimony, removed from the bullet surface by the bore of the weapon, may be deposited on the target. Lead and antimony may also originate from the base of the bullet when it is pushed toward the target by the expanding gases in the barrel.

The sodium rhodizonate test is a sensitive test for many types of metals. By spraying the sodium rhodizonate solution around the area of a suspect bullet hole, a firearms examiner can detect the presence or absence of lead. At the present time, firearms examiners are experimenting with the possibility of using lead distribution patterns around a bullet hole as a means of determining the distance from which the bullet was fired. The colors developed with sodium rhodizonate are entirely dependent upon the metal present and the degree of acidity. At a pH of 3, a pink color is obtained with lead. The test can be made more specific by spraying with 5% hydrochloric acid. The hydrochloric acid spray changes the color of the product of the reaction of sodium rhodizonate and lead (lead rhodizonate) to blue. Apparently, this blue color is caused by the formation of a complex between lead rhodizonate and hydrochloric acid.

CRIME SCENE

A man has been found shot to death, with a gun in his hand. He had talked about suicide for several weeks, but was also a feisty fellow known to have more than one enemy. If he committed suicide, the powder pattern should show a firing distance of less than 2 feet. A murder might also show a distance of less than 2 feet, but if it is more, suicide is ruled out. Your job is to test his shirt for the powder pattern.

You will be given three pieces of fabric with bullet holes on them from distances of 1, 2, and 4 feet. You are to determine their powder patterns, compare these with the suspect's shirt, and make your own conclusions.

METHOD

A number of the test materials used in the experiment described in Part A have either been treated with a lead-containing solution or are actual bullet holes in cloth.

1. Repeat steps 1 through 10 from Part A. Spray each of the cloth samples with sodium rhodizonate solution.

2. Overspray each target with the buffer. What color develops?

3. Overspray each target with 5% hydrochloric acid. What color develops?

SOME SOURCES FOR ADDITIONAL INFORMATION

Andrasko, J., and Pettersson, S., "A simple method for collection of gunshot residues from clothing," *J. Forens. Sci. Soc.*, 31 (3), (1991), 321.

Andrasko, J., "Characterization of smokeless powder flakes from fired cartridge cases and from discharge patterns on clothing," *J. Forens. Sci.*, 37 (4,) (1992), 1030.

Basu, S., Boone, C.E., Denio, D.J., and Miazaga, R.A., "Fundamental studies of gunshot residue deposition by glue-lift," *J. Forens. Sci.*, 42 (4), (1997), 571. (Na- rhodizonate)

Bhattacharyya, C.N., "Dispersion of firing discharge residues using a Maxwellian model," *Forens. Sci. Intl.*, 42 (1989), 271.

Beiser, R., "Experiences with zincon, a useful reagent for the determination of firing range with respect to lead free ammunition," *J. Forens. Sci.*, 39 (4), (1994), 981.

Brazeau, J., and Wong, R., "Analysis of gunshot residues on human tissues and clothing by x-ray microfluorescence," *J. Forens. Sci.*, 42 (3), (1997), 424.

DeGaetano, D., and Siegel, J.A., "Survey of gunshot residue analysis in forensic science laboratories," *J. Forens. Sci.*, 35 (5), (1990), 1087.

Glattstein, B., Vinokurov, A., Levin, N., and Zeichner, A., Improved method for shooting estimation-part I: Bullet holes in clothing items," *J. Forens. Sci.*, 45 (4), (2000), 801.

Glattstein, B., Zeichner, A., Vinokurov, A., and Shoshani, E., "Improved method for shooting distance determination-part II: Bullet holes in objects that cannot be processed in the laboratory," *J. Forens. Sci.*, 45 (5), (2000), 1000.

Havekost, D.G., Peters, G.A., and Koons, R.D., "Barium and antimony distributions on the hands of non-shooters," *J. Forens. Sci.*, 35 (5), (1990), 1096.

Leckstrom, J.A., and Koons, R.D., "Copper and nickel detection on gunshot targets by dithiooxamide test," *J. Forens. Sci.*, 31 (4), (1986), 1283.

Maiti, P.C., "Powder patterns around bullet holes in blood stained articles," *J. Forens. Sci. Soc.*, 13 (1973), 197.

Missliwetz, J., Denk, W., and Wieser, I., "Shots fired with silencers—A report of four cases and experimental testing," *J. Forens. Sci.*, 36 (5), (1991), 1387.

Schwartz, R.H., and Zona, C.A., "A recovery method for airborne gunshot residue retained in human nasal mucus," *J. Forens. Sci.*, 49 (4), (1995), 659.

Singer, R.L., Davis, D., and Houck, M.M., "A survey of gunshot residue analysis methods," *J. Forens. Sci.*, 41 (2), (1996), 195.

Steinberg, M., Lewt, Y., and Tasu, M., "A new field kit for bullet hole identification," *J. Forens. Sci.*, 29 (1), (1984), 169.

Tschirhart, D.L., Noguchi, T.T., and Klatt, E.C., "A simple histochemical technique for the identification of gunshot residue," *J. Forens. Sci.*, 36 (2), (1991), 543.

Walker, J.T., "Bullet holes and chemical residues in shooting cases," *J. Crim. Law Criminol.*, 31 (1940), 513.

Zeichner, A., and Levin, N., "Collection efficiency of gunshot residue (GSR) particles from hair using double-side adhesive tape," *J. Forens. Sci.*, 38 (3), (1993), 571.

Zeicher, A., Levin, N. and Dvorachek, M., "Gunshot residue particles formed by using ammunitions that have mercury fulminate based primers," *J. Forens. Sci.*, 37 (6), (1992), 1567.

EXPERIMENT 8   Name _____

DATA SHEET   Date _____

POWDER RESIDUE ON FABRICS

Part A: Bullet Holes in Fabric

1. Attach your patterns to this sheet of paper.

2. What is your conclusion and what is your reasoning?

Part B: Sodium Rhodizonate Test for Lead Residues

1. Attach your patterns to this sheet of paper.

2. Based on your test patterns, what do you think the limits of such a test would be with respect to firing distance.

Blood Identification and Typing

A common form of physical evidence found at the scene of crimes involving physical violence is that of blood. Blood may be present in the form of pools, splatters, or stains. Blood should be looked for in burglaries as well. It is difficult for a burglar to break a window or force a door without getting scratched and thereby leaving a small amount of blood at the scene. The first analysis performed on this evidence is the determination of whether or not the stains are blood, and if so, whether they are of human origin. If of nonhuman origin, it may be useful to know from what animal the blood originates. If the stains are of human origin, the analysis is then extended to the determination of blood group and other blood factors that can associate the blood with a particular person.

The fact that there is such a thing as a blood type was discovered in 1900 by Karl Landsteiner, who found that blood from one person would not always mix freely with blood from another person, but would sometimes clump or **agglutinate**.

He identified four types, which he named O, A, B, and AB. It has since been found that approximately 43% of the population has O-type blood, 42% A, 12% B, and 3% AB. If a drop of blood is found at the scene of the crime, identification of its type may serve to screen out several suspects. Leone Lattes was the first to make use of blood groups in the courts of Italy in 1916. It was used in England in 1922 and in the United States in the early 1930s.

In 1927, another system was discovered, the MN system. In this system approximately 30% of the population is M, 22% N, and 48% MN.

In 1940, Alexander Weiner, working with rhesus monkeys, discovered a third system in which 85% of the population had a factor called Rh+; the 15% who did not have the factor were called Rh-. Since that time, other Rh factors have been discovered and divided into six groups, D, d, C, c, E, e. This allows for a further 27 combinations. However, at the time of this writing, we do not yet have an antiserum for d, so there are only 18 usable combinations.

In recent times, many other substances have been found in blood which are becoming increasingly important for the individualization of blood stains; several of these are listed below.

1. Phosphoglucomutase (PGM): PGM-1, 58%; PGM-2, 6%; PCM 2-1, 36%

2. Adenylate kinase (AK): AK 1, 93% ; AK 2-1, 7%

3. Adenosine deaminase (ADA): 1, 90%; 2-1, 10%; 2, 0.2%

4. Glucose-6-phosphate dehydrogenase (G-6-PD): B, 62%; BA, 25%; A, 12%

5. 6-phosphogluconate dehydrogenase (6-PGD): A, 92%; AC, 8%; C, 0.2%

6. Erthrocytic acid phosphate (MAP): A, 13%; B, 35%; C, 0.2%; BA, 43%; CA, 3%

7. Esterase D (EsD): 1, 79%; 2-1, 19%; 2, 2%

8. Polymorphic proteins—Group Specific Component (Gc) and haptoglobins (H_p): H_p1, 14%; H_p2-1, 53%; H_p2, 32%

Let us see what value these factors can have for the forensic chemist. Before 1900, blood was just that—blood; and other than the fact that you could tell from an analysis of the blood spatter design that the attacker was wounded and perhaps where, blood could not be used to narrow the list of suspects. That has now changed dramatically.

Suppose that a blood stain was found to be A, N, Hp-1, Rh-, PGM-2, and EAP-BA. What are the chances that a suspect would have this type?

$$1\,per = \frac{100}{42} \times \frac{100}{22} \times \frac{100}{14} \times \frac{100}{15} \times \frac{100}{6} \times \frac{100}{43} = 1\,per\,19{,}975$$

This can free a lot of innocent people and corroborate the guilt of a suspect.

If a few drops of fresh blood are available along with the apparatus and expertise to test the blood for all of the systems now known, it is possible to narrow the list of suspects to about 1 in 7,000,000. With the recently discovered DNA, probe technique (discussed in part in a later experiment), which many laboratories are capable of doing at the moment, it is possible to theoretically, at least, identify 1 out of 10,000,000,000 people. Since there are only about 5,500,000,000 in the world, this makes modern blood typing an individual technique.

As noted above, many systems of blood grouping can be used, but the one that we shall use in this exercise is the **ABO** system, and possibly the **Rh** system. Our purpose will be to determine whether a particular stain is blood or not, and if so, to type that blood by the ABO system. (The Rh factor will be determined at the option of the instructor.)

This exercise is performed on liquid blood, as the volume of sample will make it easier for you to do the determination. A later experiment deals with stains and will be easier to do after having gained experience from this one.

EQUIPMENT

1	Brush, test tube	1	Microscope (100×)
2	Bulbs for disposable pipets		Microscope slides
	Cover glasses	1	Pencil, grease
	Filter paper squares, 2 cm × 2 cm		Pipets, disposable
1 pr	Gloves, rubber or plastic	1	Rack, test tube, for 10 cm test tubes
1 pr	Goggles, safety		Wood splints (toothpicks serve well)
	Microlance, sterile, disposable		
	(buy individually prepackaged)		

REAGENTS

Bleach such as Clorox   Distilled water

Denatured alcohol   Hematest tablets (from any drug store)

Unknown blood samples (from students or from a hospital blood bank)

Known A, B, O, and AB blood samples (get outdated blood either from a hospital or the closest Red Cross blood bank; keep refrigerated)

Pieces of cloth stained with various red to brown materials (e.g., paint, shoe polish, ketchup)

Anti-A antiserum (get outdated material from a hospital)

Anti-B antiserum (get outdated material from a hospital)

Anti-D antiserum (get outdated material from a hospital) (for Rh+ or Rh−)

DEFINITIONS

Agglutination—the clumping together of blood cells.

Agglutinin—an antibody in plasma that promotes agglutination.

Agglutinogen—a substance in red blood cells that acts as an antigen and incites the production of agglutinin.

Antibody—a substance in blood that reacts with a specific antigen, causing blood cells to clump together.

Antigen—a substance that incites the formation of antibodies.

Hemoglobin—the oxygen carrying coloring matter of red blood cells.

Plasma—the colorless fluid of the blood.

Serum—the clear yellowish liquid part of blood after the fibrin and corpuscles have been removed.

PART A: IS IT REALLY BLOOD?

NOTE: To be on the safe side, please wear disposable gloves when working with blood samples and place them in the trash barrel when the lab is over. Everyone worries about AIDS, but hepatitis B is far more communicable.

To identify a stain as blood, we must know what kind of reaction is to be expected in a positive test. We do this by means of a Hematest tablet. Hemoglobin catalytically decomposes hydrogen peroxide or sodium peroxide with the liberation of oxygen. In an acid solution, oxygen acts on the o-tolidine found in a Hematest tablet to turn it into a blue-colored derivative. The reagents are all contained within the test tablet, except for the hemoglobin that catalyzes the reaction. This is contained within the blood stain.

1. Place 1 drop of blood on a piece of filter paper and allow it to dry.

2. Obtain a Hematest tablet and break it up into four more or less equal parts.

3. Place one portion of the tablet in the center of the bloodstain. Put 1 drop of distilled water **on the tablet**, wait a few seconds, and place another drop of distilled water **on the tablet**, being certain that the water flows down the sides of the tablet and onto the stain. Within a few seconds you will see a blue-green ring spreading out on the filter paper around the base of the tablet. This is a positive test that the stain is indeed blood. There are some other types of stains that will interfere and produce the same color as will blood, such as dry bleach residues and some plastics; therefore, the test is only presumptive, and a second test should always be made on an adjacent, unstained area to check for background interferences. This concept is called **running a blank** and, as a general rule in criminalistics, should always be done.

4. Now obtain four pieces of cloth that have stains on them, and repeat this test for each of them. The scraps of cloth are numbered. If the test is positive, identify the stain on

the cloth as blood, and include the number of the scrap on the data sheet. If the test is negative, record the stain as being of an origin other than blood, along with its identification number. Be sure to run a blank. Repeat this test for each of the other samples of stain on the cloth. Record all identification numbers and results on the data sheet. This test is often done at the crime scene to determine whether a stain is blood and therefore evidence to be collected.

PART B: INCOMPATIBILITY RELATIONSHIPS IN THE ABO SYSTEM

Table 9-1 shows the relationship between different blood groups in the ABO system. Whole blood can be separated into serum and red blood cells. Mixing serum or whole blood from donors of one blood type with red blood cells or whole blood from an individual of a different type may result in an incompatibility reaction. For instance, when serum or whole blood from a type A individual is mixed with red blood cells or whole blood cells from a type B individual, the red blood cells clump together, or agglutinate. This reaction occurs since type A blood contains anti-B antibodies. These antibodies combine with B antigens on the red blood cells to cause agglutination. This is shown in Figure 9-1.

The agglutination takes place because the type-A serum contains substances known as anti-B antibodies, which react with materials called type-B antigens present on the surface of type-B blood cells. This reaction between antigen and antibody causes the red blood cells to stick to each other, as shown in Figure 9-1. Determinations of blood groups of the ABO system are rapid and simple. The type is readily determined by adding a known commercial antiserum (antibodies) to the blood and looking for the presence or absence of agglutination.

This section deals with the typing of blood by use of the ABO system.

1. Obtain a glass microscope slide and a grease pencil.

2. Mark off the slide into three equal parts, as shown in Figure 9-2.

3. Label the three sections A, B, and D respectively, from left to right (D is for Rh+ or Rh−).

4. Obtain a test tube with a labeled blood sample in it, and record the number of the sample on the data sheet.

5. Place 1 small drop of the blood sample on each of the three sections of the slide by using a disposable pipet.

6. Dispose of the pipet in a waste container filled with 10% bleach solution.

7. Spread out the drop with a wooden splint or tooth pick.

8. Take the small bottles of antisera and add 1 drop of antiserum-A to the drop of blood in the section of the slide labeled A, 1 drop of antiserum B to the section B drop of blood, and 1 drop of antiserum D to the section D drop of blood.

TABLE 9–1	General Summary of Incompatibility Relationships for the Blood Group	
Blood Groups	**Antigens on Red Blood Cells**	**Antibodies in Serums**
A	A	Anti-B
B	B	Anti-A
AB	A and B	Neither anti-A or anti-B
O	Neither A nor B	Anti-A and anti-B

FIGURE 9–1
Schematic diagram
of agglutination.

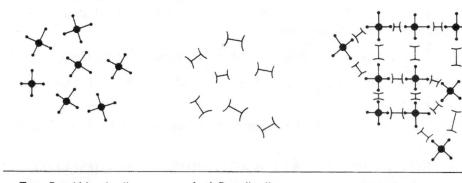

Type B red blood cells   Anti-B antibodies   Agglutination

9. Use a small wood splint to stir and mix the drops, being careful to avoid contaminating one section with the next. Use a clean wood splint for each section.

10. After mixing, look at the drops. If agglutination has occurred, you will see small specks or dots in the drop. If not, it will be clear.

11. Place the slide on the stage of a microscope, and examine each drop for agglutination.

12. Sketch the appearance of agglutinated red blood cells and unagglutinated red blood cells in the labeled circles on the data sheet. It is possible that the blood sample you have selected does not show one or the other of these states. If it does not, complete the sketching when you have observed a drop that does show the other state.

13. Repeat step 12 with three other labeled blood samples, recording all results on the data sheet.

14. Repeat the typing procedure for at least two unknown samples of blood. Be sure to record the identification number for each sample of blood that you work with.

15. Optional: Type your own blood. With a **sterile** hemostat, make a puncture in the tip of your middle finger. (Caution: Always cleanse the tip of your finger with 70% alcohol before and after making the puncture.) Place a drop of blood in each of three sections of a fresh slide. Immediately cover the puncture with a bandage and put on disposable gloves.

16. Perform steps 7 through 11.

17. If you have had your blood typed before, how do your results compare?

18. When you have finished typing the blood samples, record the results and return the tubes, **uncontaminated**, so that someone else may use them.

NOTE: When you clean up the area, rinse with bleach anything that you are going to save that has come in contact with blood. Actually, hepatitis is more communicable than AIDS, so we are taking no chances in either case.

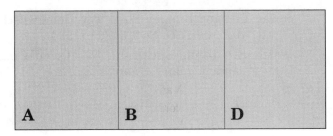

FIGURE 9–2   Preparation for A and B blood
typng.

19. Clean all of the slides you have used, first with denatured alcohol, then with soap and water, then bleach, and, finally, rinse them with distilled water, wipe them dry, and return them to the box.

20. If syringes were used, rinse them with bleach and then with distilled water.

21. Be certain to return all other materials that you have used, and clean up your bench area.

22. Complete the data sheet, answer all questions, and hand them in to your instructor.

SELECTED SOURCES FOR ADDITIONAL INFORMATION

Baird, J.B., "The individuality of blood and bloodstains," *The Canadian Soc. Forens. Sci. J.*, 11 (1978), 83.

Bowen, K.L., and Wickett, S.T., " The facts of fingerprinting techniques on blood grouping," *Can. Soc. Forens. Sci. J.*, 21 (1988), 29.

Cox, M., "A study of the sensitivity and specificity of four presumptive tests for blood," *J. Forens. Sci.*, 36 (5), (1991), 1503.

Espinoza, E.O., Kirms, M.A., and Filipek, M.S., "Identification and quantitation of sources from hemoglobin of blood and blood mixtures by HPLC," *J. Forens. Sci.*, 41 (5), (1996), 804.

Kobilinsky, R., and Sheehan, F.X., "Human blood typing: A forensic science approach, Part I: Background," *J. Chem. Ed.*, 65 (1988), 531.

Hatch, A.L., "A modified reagent for the confirmation of blood," *J. Forens. Sci.*, 38 (6), (1993), 1502.

Hulse-Smith, L., Mehdizadeh, N. Z., and Chandra, S., "Deducing drop size and impact velocity from circular bloodstains," *J. Forens. Sci.*, 50 (1), (2005), 54.

Lee, H.C., Gaensslen, R.E., Carver, H.W., Pagliaro, E.M., and Carroll-Reho, J., "ABH antigen typing in bone tissue," *J. Forens. Sci.*, 34 (1), (1989), 7.

Liechti-Galliti, S., and Neeser, D., "Efficient and reliable PCR-based detection of the ABO blood group alleles: genotyping on stamps and other biological evidence samples," *J. Forens. Sci.*, 41 (4), (1996), 653.

Mizuno, Natsuko, Ohmori, T., Sekiguchi, K., Kato, T., Fujii, T., Fujii, K., Shiraishi, T., Kasai, K., and Sato, H., "Alleles responsible for ABO phenotype-genotype discrepancy and alleles in individuals with a weak expression of A or B antigens." *J. Forens. Sci.*, 49 (1), (2004), 21.

Noda, H., Yokota, M., Tatsumi, s., and Sugiyama, S., "Determination of ABO blood grouping from human oral squamous epithelium by the highly sensitive immune histochemical staining method ENVISION+," *J. Forens. Sci.*, 47 (2), (2002), 350.

Raymond, M.A., Smith, E.R., and Liesegang, J., "The physical properties of blood—forensic considerations," *Sci. & Just.*, 36 (3), (1996), 153.

Roy, R., "Concentration of urine samples by three different procedures: ABO typing from the concentrated urine samples," *J. Forens. Sci.*, 35 (5), (1990), 1133.

Sheehan, F.X., and Kobilinsky, L., "Human blood identification, forensic science approach," *J. Chem. Ed.*, 61 (1984), 542.

Spear, T.F., and Binkley, S.A., "The HemeSelect test: a simple and sensitive forensic species test," *J. Forens. Sci. Soc.*, 34 (1), (1994), 41.

Walsh. K.A.J., and Buckleton, J.S., "Calculating the frequency of occurrence of a blood type for a 'random' man," *J. Forens. Sci. Soc.*, 31 (1) ,(1991), 49.

Westwood, S.A., and Werrett, D.J., " The collaborative study on typing group-specific component in casework bloodstains," *J. Forens. Sci. Soc.*, (30 (1), (1990), 33.

Xingzhi, X., Ji, L., Hao, F., Ming, L., and Zhuyao, L., "ABO blood grouping on dental tissue," *J. Forens. Sci.*, 38 (4), (1993,) 956.

Zhou, B., Guo, J., Wang, C., and Chen, J., "The rapid determination of the ABO group from body fluids (or stains) by dot enzyme linked immunoabsorbent assay (dot ELISA) using enzymes labeled monoclonal anti-bodies," *J. Forens. Sci.*, 35 (5), (1990), 1125.

EXPERIMENT 9   Name _____

DATA SHEET   Date _____

BLOOD IDENTIFICATION AND TYPING

1. Make a sketch of the bloodstained filter paper with a positive reaction to the Hematest tablet.

2. Identification of stains as blood (positive or negative).

	Cloth sample	Test
1.		
2.		
3.		
4.		

3. Blood typing (known samples): + indicates agglutination; − indicates no agglutination.

Blood type	Anti-A	Anti-B	Anti-D

4. Appearance of agglutinated and unagglutinated red blood cells.

Agglutination   Unagglutination

5. Blood sample (unknown)

Antiserum A

Antiserum B

Antiserum D

Blood type

Questions

1. The ABO blood typing was quite easily performed on the volume of blood used in this exercise. Do you feel that it could be done as easily on a very small volume by use of a microscope? What difficulties can you foresee?

2. How do you suppose one would go about typing a dried blood stain?

3. (One to think about): Do animals have different blood types within a certain species (other than humans, who are also of the animal kingdom)?

Typing of Dried Bloodstains (Advanced)

This analysis is an extension of Experiment 9. In that experiment fairly large quantities of blood samples were available for use in blood-group typing. In this analysis you will be working with dried bloodstains, and the procedure demands more care and precision. Perform the steps of the analysis **slowly** and **carefully**, and be sure of your observations. The hardest part is insuring that you get some of the stain to dissolve. If in doubt, repeat your work.

The test procedure that will be used in this experiment is a reverse grouping technique for the identification of naturally occurring antibodies (agglutinins) in dried bloodstains. The test is performed by adding known red blood cells (antigens) to the bloodstain and looking for the presence or absence of agglutination. The best test results will be obtained with stains that are less than 2 weeks old.

CRIME SCENE

During the course of a robbery the victim resists and is beaten severely by the assailant. While lying on the floor, he is kicked about the ribs, head, and face by the robber. A description of the attacker has resulted in a woman being taken into custody. Upon examination of her clothing, what appear to be bloodstains have been found on her blouse. Analysis shows the stains to indeed be blood. The suspect states that she had recently been afflicted with a nosebleed and the blood had spattered on her blouse; she had not yet had time to clean it. The suspect's blood has been typed and found to be of type AB. The victim has blood type 0. The problem now is to type the bloodstains from the suspect's blouse. This will be very useful in helping to link the suspect with the scene of the crime.

EQUIPMENT

3	Beakers, 50 mL	1	Microscope with 100× magnification
1	Bottle, wash, 250 mL	1	Pencil, grease
1	Brush, test tube, small	1	Rack, test tube
1	Dish, petri	1 pr	Scissors or single edge razor blade
1	Filter paper	1	Towel, cloth
1 pr	Goggles, safety	4	Tubes, test, 10 cm
1	Holder, test tube		Corks or rubber stoppers
1	Medicine dropper		Disposable gloves
2	Microscope slides (glass), depression type		

REAGENTS

A red blood cells   Distilled water

B red blood cells   Hematest tablets

Bloodstained cloth samples   Saline (0.9%)

Laboratory Safety: Gloves and goggles should be worn routinely as good laboratory practice.

PART A: TYPING DRIED BLOODSTAINS

1. Obtain a bloodstained piece of cloth, scissors or razor blade, and two depression type microscope slides.

2. Cut the bloodstained areas into pieces approximately 4 to 5 mm^2, and place them into separate wells on the slides.

3. Repeat step 2 with an unstained area next to the bloodstain.

4. Prepare a solution of commercial A and B cells by diluting them to 0.1 with a 0.9% saline solution. Use 10 cm test tubes.

5. Add 1 drop of the appropriate cells to each of the stained and unstained cloths.

6. A moisture chamber is prepared by moistening filter paper with saline and placing it in a petri dish. Place the microscope slides in the moisture chamber for 15 minutes with occasional gentle rotating.

7. Place the slide on the stage of a microscope, and examine it for agglutination.

8. If no agglutination occurs, let it stand for another 15 minutes in the moisture chamber and examine again. Microscopic examination should be repeated every 15 minutes for a period of approximately 2 hours, or until you are convinced that the stain has or has not agglutinated.

9. Record all test results on your data sheet.

PART B: BLOOD TEST SENSITIVITY

In this portion of the laboratory exercise you will try to determine how diluted a bloodstain may be and still give a positive reaction to the Hematest tablet. You performed this test in the previous experiment to show that blood was indeed present. If you are uncertain how you did this, review the explanation of this test.

1. Place 1 drop of blood in a 10 cm test tube.

2. Add distilled water to fill the tube.

3. If a slight reddish tinge in the solution is still evident, take 1 drop of this solution and place it in another test tube.

4. Fill this second tube with distilled water. Seal each tube with a rubber stopper or cork.

5. Shake both test tubes, and test 1 drop of each with a small portion of a Hematest tablet.

6. Record the results of both tests on the data sheet.

7. Roughly calculate the dilution of the blood in each tube as follows. There are approximately 20 drops of water per milliliter. Measure the volume of water in each tube in milliliters and multiply by 20 in each case. The dilution then becomes:

$$\text{Tube 1: } = \text{Dilution}_1 \times \frac{1 \text{ drop of blood}}{\text{total drops of solution}}$$

$$\text{Tube 2: } = \text{Dilution}_2 = \text{dilution}_1 \times \frac{1 \text{ drop of solution}}{\text{total drops of solution}}$$

8. If the test was positive for the second tube, repeat the dilution a third time and test again.

9. If this test is still positive, repeat a fourth time.

10. Calculate each dilution as before, and record these values.

11. What is the final dilution which gives you a positive reaction to the Hematest tablet? Record.

SELECTED SOURCES FOR ADDITIONAL INFORMATION

Andrasko, J., and Rosen, B., "Sensitive identification of hemoglobin in bloodstains from different species by HPLC with combined UV and fluorescence detection," *J. Forens. Sci.*, 39 (4), (1994), 1018.

Boshinshi, J.S., and Davis, J.G., "A simple procedure for ABO, typing of dried bloodstains on fibers by the absorption-elution technique," *J. Forens. Sci. Soc.*, 13 (1973), 217.

Budowle, B., Leggitt, J.L., Defenbaugh, D.A., Keys, K.M., and Malkiewicz, S.F., " The presumptive reagent fluorescein for detection of dilute bloodstains and subsequent STR typing of recovered DNA," *J. Forens. Sci.*, 45 (5), (2000), 1090.

Chisum, W.J., "A rapid method for grouping dried bloodstains," *J. Forens. Sci. Soc.*, 11 (1971), 205.

Cox, M., "Effect of fabric washing on the presumptive identification of bloodstains," *J. Forens. Sci.*, 35 (6), (1990), 1335.

DeForest, G.P.R., "A review of interpretation of bloodstain evidence at crime scenes," *J. Forens. Sci.*, 35 (6), (1990), 1491.

Edelman, G.M., "The structure and function of antibodies," *Sci. Am.*, 223 (1970), 34.

Kimura, H., and Matsuzawa, S., "Lewis blood group determination in bloodstains by planimetric measurement of eluted monoclonal antibodies," *J. Forens. Sci.*, 36 (4), (1991), 999.

Kobilinsky, L., and Sheehan, F. Y., "Human blood typing: A forensic science approach. Part II: Experiments," *J. Chem. Ed.*, 65 (1988), 624.

Lee, H.C., "Identification and grouping of bloodstains," *Forensic Science Handbook*, R. Saferstein, Ed. Prentice-Hall, Englewood Cliffs, N.J. (1982).

Levkov, J.S., "A method for the determination of the MN antigen in dried blood," *J. Forens. Sci.*, 32 (2), (1987), 357.

Lima, S.M., and Newall, P.J., "Km(3) identification by enzyme linked immunoabsorbent assay (ELISA) as an internal control for Km(1) activity—Determined by inhibition in dried bloodstains," *J. Forens. Sci.*, 35 (3), (1990), 537.

Lincoln, P.J., and B.E. Dodd, "An evaluation of factors affecting the elution of antibodies from blood stains," *J. Forens. Sci. Soc.*, 13 (1973), 37.

Matsuzawa, S., Kimura, H., Itoh, Y., Wang, H., and Nakagawa, T., "A rapid dot blot method for species identification of bloodstains," *J. Forens. Sci.*, 38 (2), (1993), 448.

Mudd, J.L., "A microplate method for reverse ABO typing of bloodstains," *J. Forens. Sci.*, 31 (2), (1986), 418.

Pettenati, M.J., Rao, P., Schnell, S., Hayworth-Hodge, R., Lantz, P.E., and Geisinger, K.R., "Gender identification of dried human bloodstains using fluorescence in situ hybridization," *J. Forens. Sci.*, 40 (5), (1995), 885.

EXPERIMENT 10   Name _____

DATA SHEET   Date _____

TYPING OF DRIED BLOODSTAINS (ADVANCED)

Part A: Typing Dried Bloodstains

+ indicates agglutination; − indicates no agglutination

Specimen no.	A blood cells	B blood cells	Blood group

Part B: Blood Test Sensitivity

Dilution	Reaction to Hematest tablet

Questions

1. Assume that there are 20 drops per milliliter and one dilutes 1 drop of blood serially in each of five test tubes, each of which has a volume of 5 mL. What will be the final dilution?

2. If a blood specimen clumps with the addition of A cells, but does not react with B cells, what is its blood group?.

3. If agglutination does not take place upon the addition of A and B blood cells, what is this blood group?

Fingerprinting

Fingerprints are a very common form of physical evidence. It requires considerable expertise in the area of fingerprinting to be able to accurately classify prints and match prints with each other. If a suspect's fingerprints match those found at a crime scene, this is highly conclusive proof of a link between the two.

In this experiment you will not attempt to classify fingerprints. Rather, you will investigate the methods used in developing and lifting latent fingerprints from a number of objects, made of a variety of materials. You will also try to match the prints with inked prints. Chemical methods used to make fingerprints visible will be covered in Experiment 12. **Latent prints** are those invisible prints left on an object by a person. These must be developed through the use of dusting powder or a chemical solution. **Inked prints** are those taken directly from a person's fingers through the use of an ink pad or block.

The origin of the use of fingerprints is lost in history, although it is known that the Chinese knew of and used fingerprints before the birth of Christ. In 1886, a Scottish physician, Henry Fauld, first published the view that fingerprints could be used for identifying individuals. We owe the beginnings of our present system to Sir Francis Galton in the 1880s. Sir Edward Richard Henry developed a simplified system for classifying fingerprints, which was adopted by Scotland Yard in 1901.

There are a number of basic fingerprint patterns (arches, loops, whorls). The fingers on a person's hand may contain a number of patterns. These patterns are shown in Figure 11-1. You should make yourself familiar with the characteristic appearance of each of the patterns, as you will be making comparisons with these patterns later in this exercise.

The tips of a person's fingers have small **friction ridges** on them. Along these ridges are small pores which secrete salt (NaCl), water, and proteins. It is those substances, along with oil that may be picked up by touching the hairy portions of the body, which will be deposited on objects that come in contact with the surface of our fingers.

Usually, burglaries and other crimes are committed during times when a building or room is dark. In feeling his or her way around an unfamiliar setting, the person committing the crime may touch several objects. Clear, latent prints are then left in many places. It requires some time to dust and lift these prints. An experienced person is required for this task, as a very good print may be ruined by a poor dusting technique.

FIGURE 11–1
Fingerprint patterns.

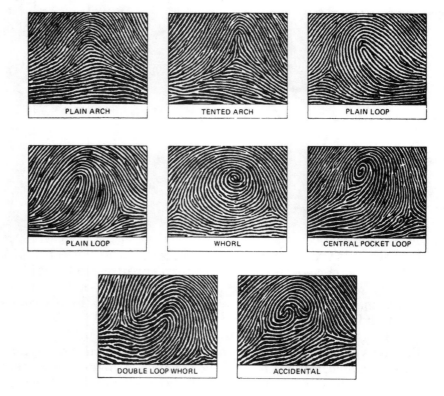

There are a variety of fingerprint dusting powders. The choice of powder color depends to a large extent on the color of the object being investigated for prints. We will make use of two colors of dusting powder: gray for use on dark-colored objects and black for use on light-colored objects, and anthracene for multicolored objects.

One formula for black powder is 88% MnO_2, 14.75% graphite, and 0.2% aluminum. Aluminum is a good sticking agent. Instructions for the use of these powders will be given later.

Latent prints are developed by powders and lifted from the object by use of transparent tape, hinged lifters, rubber lifters, and KromeKote paper. Lifters are available with black, white or transparent backgrounds. One uses black lifters with gray powder and white lifters with black powder. Rubber lifters produce a negative print, that is, the print is the reverse of an inked print from a person's finger. The print on the lifter is photographed, the negative reversed, and a positive print made from it. KromeKote paper has been found useful to lift fingerprints from sweaty or oily surfaces such as skin.

The transparent tape is basically a wide, clear adhesive tape. When pressed against the powder, the print is transferred to the adhesive surface of the tape. The tape is now placed on a paper whose color will provide a suitable contrast with the print. The transparent tape also provides an immediate positive print. You will use both transparent tape and hinge lifters in this experiment.

The hinged lifter consists of a plastic, adhesive-backed sheet attached to a colored cardboard. When the examiner is ready to lift the print, a black or white lifter is selected. (This will be determined by the color of the powder used.) The backing is removed from the plastic sheet, exposing the adhesive. The plastic sheet is now pressed against the developed print, allowing the print to be picked off of the surface. The plastic sheet is then pressed against the colored cardboard. Unlike the rubber lifter, a positive print is immediately obtained.

You may not be able to obtain really clear latent-print development in this exercise, and perhaps this will serve to illustrate to you the importance of technique in this operation. Practice is very important.

You will develop a few of your own latent prints in the beginning of this exercise. If you should find that your skin is quite dry and does not deposit prints very well, this can be remedied. Handling paper dries the skin very quickly. If this is the case, rub your fingers along the side of your nose to pick up some skin oil, or run your fingers through your hair, which will accomplish the same purpose. Good prints will usually result if this is done.

We will not use a crime scene in this experiment. Instead, you will use your own fingerprints in the first portion of your work, and those of other members of the class in the second portion.

EQUIPMENT

	Black backing cards (smooth)		Light-colored glass or ceramic tiles
4	Brushes, fingerprint		Paper, KromeKote, strips 2 cm × 10 cm
	Dark-colored glass or ceramic tiles		(from a local printer)
	Fingerprint cards, FBI type	1	Plate, glass, 15 × 15 × 0.5 cm
1	Forceps	1	Roller, 1.5 cm dia, 10 cm long
1 pr	Goggles, safety	1 pr	Scissors
1	Hand magnifying lens (10× or stronger)	2	Towels, cloth
	Lifters, hinged, 1½′ × 2′ black, white,		Transparent bookbinding tape
	and transparent. Sirchie Laboratories		in a dispenser
	UV (ultraviolet) lamp		White backing cards (smooth)
	(Mineralite works well)		

REAGENTS

Anthracene, powdered

Black fingerprint dusting powder

Gray fingerprint dusting powder

Ink, black, paste, water soluble

Methanol

METHOD

PART A: MAKING A LATENT FINGERPRINT VISIBLE

1. Pick out some glass, metal, or plastic object in the laboratory that has a hard smooth surface and is not multicolored.

2. Place one of your fingers firmly on the object. If your finger is dry, rub it along side of your nose or run your fingers through your hair to pick up some oil.

3. Choose a fingerprint dusting powder of contrasting color.

4. Obtain the brush which is used for that color of powder. (Do not interchange the brushes, as you will obtain poorly developed latent prints owing to the mixture of dusting powers.)

5. Tap the handle of the brush or twirl the brush between the fingers to remove excess powder from the bristles from previous use.

6. Place some of the dusting powder in the lid or on a piece of paper, and dip the tip of the bristles of the brush in the dusting powder. **It is poor technique to have the powder up in the center of the bristles,** as one is unable to control the amount

of powder deposited on the surface to be dusted and can easily ruin very clearly defined latent prints.

7. Using a circular, sweeping motion, and just grazing the surface, brush across the surface until you see the print beginning to appear. Concentrate your brushing on the exposed fingerprint, taking care to continue to brush lightly. If necessary, pick up additional dusting powder, using the same steps as you did before. Once the ridges appear, the motion of the brush should follow the direction of the ridge flow. When the print is clearly developed, stop brushing. Further development may easily destroy the print.

8. Carefully remove any excess powder with a clean brush.

PART B: LIFTING A LATENT PRINT

Three different methods will be done: transparent tape, hinged lifters, and KromeKote paper.

Transparent Tape

1. Pick up the roll of transparent bookbinding tape and with a smooth motion pull off approximately 6–7 cm from the roll. Do not cut the tape from the roll yet.

2. Place the free end of the tape about 6 cm from the top of the developed print. Cover the print with the tape by smoothing the tape over the print with your finger, beginning from the free end and working slowly over the print. **Do not simply lay the tape over the print!** Air bubbles under the tape will partially ruin the lifted fingerprint—hence the necessity for slow, careful smoothing of the tape over the print.

3. After the tape completely covers the print, and extends approximately 1 cm past it, use the roll of tape as a handle and lift the tape with the developed print smoothly from the surface in one continuous, unbroken motion. This will prevent distortion of the print.

4. Place the free end of the tape on a backing card of contrasting color to the dusting powder used. Repeat the laying-down, smoothing operation to eliminate any air bubbles, as you did previously, until the print is taped to the backing card.

5. Cut the tape from the roll, trim any excess tape from the card, and label it for future use. Paste the card onto the data sheet.

6. Record the object from which the print was taken, your initials, and the date on the backing card.

Hinged Lifters

7. Repeat the developing and lifting of prints from one of the objects on the lab bench that has a different color from the one you just did. Make use of the opposite-colored dusting powder. Use a hinged lifter to remove the print from the surface.

8. The following directions are from the Sirchie Laboratories. Open the hinged lifter so that the arrow points to the upper right. Arrow and printing is on the plastic cover.

9. With the thumb and forefinger, peel off the transparent cover, starting at the upper right corner to where the arrow points. The plastic cover with printing and the arrow is then thrown away. The adhesive sheet is now exposed.

10. The tacky side of the lifter is then carefully placed over the latent powdered image or prints. Rub the plastic sheet lightly, then lift off the powdered print. Note that the A is facing you when lifting the latent print.

11. The lifted print is then covered with the hinged cover, and is thus protected from scratches or dirt.

    The best way to cover a latent print after being lifted is to place the lifter on its back (with the adhesive side facing up), then form a curl in the hinged cover and roll on the cover.

12. The lifted print is now permanently sealed. Keep the star facing you or facing up, and the latent print is in its positive position, just as it was found on a surface.

KromeKote Paper

A latent fingerprint impression on the surface of human skin may be lifted prior to being developed by pressing a clean KromeKote card against the skin. The latent impression will transfer to the surface of the KromeKote paper after 2–3 seconds of firm pressure. KromeKote paper comes in 22″ × 28″ sheets and can be purchased from most print shops. Cut it into 2 × 4 cm strips, being careful **not to touch the glossy side**.

13. If you are working in pairs, place your fingers firmly around the wrist of your lab partner; if you are doing this experiment yourself, grab one wrist with your other hand, or have someone else grab you on the wrist.

14. Place the glossy side of a KromeKote card over the area you suspect contains a fingerprint and press firmly for 2–3 seconds.

15. Lift the card carefully to avoid smearing the undeveloped print. It is best to lift one side of the card first, holding the rest of the card in place to prevent slippage, and then continue to lift in a continuous motion until the entire card is free of the skin surface.

16. Place the card on a flat surface, with the glossy side up and carefully tape just the edges of the paper to the surface so the paper won't slide.

17. Dust the print with black dusting powder. To get a proper amount of powder on the fingerprint brush, one should allow the tips of the bristles to touch the powder in the reservoir and rotate the handle between the thumb and forefinger in a back-and-forth motion three or four times. The brush should then be held free of the powder and rotated rapidly an additional three or four times to clear the excess powder from the brush. If white striations appear in the graying background, one is brushing too briskly. The print may be slow to develop, and 5 to 20 seconds of brushing is frequently required to develop a fingerprint.

18. Once developed, the graphite impression may be preserved for analysis and courtroom presentation by placing a strip of cellophane tape over the surface of the KromeKote card.

It should be remembered that the fingerprint obtained will be the mirror image of the standard inked fingerprint impression on file cards. The mirror image can be reversed by photographing the print and using appropriate darkroom techniques. If the print is sent to an outside agency for comparison without reversing the image, an explanation should accompany the print to prevent a technician who is unaware of the circumstances from having difficulty identifying the print.

PART C: FLUORESCENT DUSTING POWDER (ADVANCED)

There are times when you suspect the presence of a print on a multicolored object and the question arises as to what type of dusting powder to use. One approach is to use a fluorescent compound such as anthracene. The latent print is dusted the same as before, but it is observed under ultraviolet radiation which causes the print to produce a purple fluorescence.

Anthracene

1. Place a fingerprint on a multicolored object so that the print covers at least two colors.

2. Dust the print with fine anthracene powder. If the powder does not stick well, it may be mixed with 1% aluminum dust. The powder should go through a 100-mesh screen.

3. Go into a darkroom and expose the print to UV radiation from a Mineral light or other UV source. The print should glow purple.

4. Place a small amount of the anthracene powder on your fingers and look at them under the UV lamp.

5. Wash your hands and repeat the process.

6. What did you observe?

PART D: OBTAINING AN INKED PRINT

You will now obtain inked prints from the hand of another person. Always stand at the subject's left, whether you are rolling his left or right-hand fingers. The subject should stand at forearm's length from the edge of the bench and should be slightly behind you. In rolling the fingers of the right hand, the right thumb should be rolled inward, from right to left and the other four fingers rolled outward, from left to right. This procedure is reversed for the left hand.

1. Obtain a tube of black paste ink, a flat glass plate, an ink roller, fingerprint card, and a classmate. If a fingerprint card is not available use the data sheet.

2. Place about a 1-cm. strip of ink in the center of the glass plate. Roll smooth and even with the roller. **Remember, more prints are ruined from too much ink rather than from too little.**

3. Lay the fingerprint card so that you can easily transfer a print to it.

4. Hold the subject's hand in your left hand, with all of the subjects fingers curled except the one you are inking and recording on the card. Grasp the extended finger of the subject with your right thumb and index finger. Roll the subject's finger on the inked surface, from nail to nail, keeping the finger flat on the plate from the first joint to the tip.

5. Roll the inked finger on the card as previously instructed. Use gentle pressure in rolling the finger, to avoid smearing the ink.

6. Roll the ink on the glass again, or place the next finger on an unused place.

7. Repeat this procedure for all of the subject's fingers on both hands. At the end of a roll, lift the finger upward to prevent smudging of the edge of the print.

8. Have the subject whom you used record the inked prints of your fingers.

9. Clean your fingers by wiping them with a towel moistened with methanol.

10. Referring to Figure 11-1, assign fingerprint patterns to each of your inked prints.

PART E: MATCHING PRINTS

In this exercise you will attempt to match the prints on an object with the prints of a member of the class. There are several glass, metal, and plastic objects on the lab bench. Each is mounted on a piece of masonite or plywood and held in place by a piece of masking tape over the top. This is the way an object should be transported to the laboratory. It allows you to pick up the object without adding additional prints, and the tape over the top touches very little of the object.

What really makes one fingerprint different from another? You must look closely for the fine structure of the ridges or their ridge characteristics and then you will see why it is that no two fingerprints have ever been found that are identical. Figure 11-2 shows some ridge characteristics that you should look for in a fingerprint.

Requirements vary from examiner to examiner, but many require a minimum of 8 to 10 points of similarity between two prints before they will testify that the prints are identical.

In this part of the experiment you will try to match a print with three others. (It would require a great deal of time to match the prints on an object with those of a class member if you had to work with the class as a group.) Your laboratory instructor has collected fingerprints on various objects from members of the chemistry department or this class: these have been divided into groups of three. You will work with the inked prints of the three members of the group to which you are assigned.

1. Develop and lift the fingerprints from the object with dusting powder transparent tape.

2. Fix the tape with the lifted print to the contrasting-color backing card

3. Use a magnifying hand lens to examine the prints carefully, and record any identifying characteristics you may find.

4. Examine the inked prints, and match the sample prints with one of them if you possibly can.

5. Record your results on the data sheet

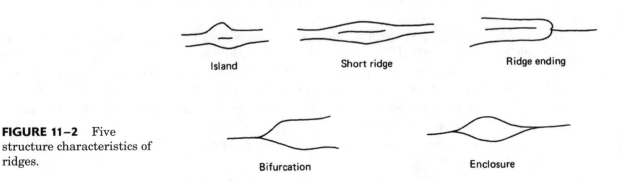

FIGURE 11–2 Five structure characteristics of ridges.

Do you now see why a classification system is necessary? The FBI has about 700,000,000 prints and with the new computer enhanced pattern recognition programs can narrow these down to just a few in less than 15 minutes. You will learn the rudiments of the classification system in your lecture.

6. Referring to the fingerprint pattern chart (Figure 11-1), determine the various patterns of your own prints.

7. Record this information on the data sheet.

8. Look for identifying characteristics common to your own inked prints and the latent prints you have developed from your own fingers.

9. Record these characteristics also.

10. Complete all recorded information required on the data sheet, and tape your developed latent prints and inked prints in the proper spaces. After answering all the questions, give this material to your laboratory instructor.

11. You are finished with the laboratory portion of this exercise. Clean and put away all materials used.

SELECTED SOURCES FOR ADDITIONAL INFORMATION

Allred, C.E., Lin, T., and Menzel, E.R., "Lipid specific latent fingerprint detection: fingerprints on currency," *J. Forens. Sci.*, 42 (6), (1997), 997.

Asano, K.G., Bayne, C.K., Horseman, K.M., and Buckhanan, M.V., "Chemical composition of fingerprints for gender determination," *J. Forens. Sci.*, 47 (4), (2002), 374.

Azoury, Miriam, Cohen, D., Himberg, K., Qvintus-Leino, P., Saari, T., and Almog, J., "Fingerprint detection on counterfeit US$ banknotes: The importance of preliminary paper examination," *J. Forens. Sci.*, 49 (5), (2004), 1015.

Barclay, F., "Friction ridge identification based on pore structure," *RCMP Gazette*, 53 (10), (1991), 18.

Bentson, R.K., Brown, J.K., Dinsmore, A., Harvey, K.K., and Kee, T.G., "Post firing visualization of fingerprints on spent cartridge cases," *Science and Justice*, 36 (1), (1996), 3.

Burt, J. A., and Menzel, E. R., "Laser detection of latent fingerprints: difficult surfaces," *J. Forens. Sci.*, 30 (2), (1985), 364.

Choudhry, M.Y., and Whritenour, R.D., "A new approach to unraveling tangled adhesive tape for potential detection of latent prints and recovery of trace evidence," *J. Forens. Sci.*, 35 (6), (1990), 1373.

Dixon, Kristian, Wu, J., Brennan, R. W., and Goldsmith, P., "Development of a finger printing device for use on a mobile robot," *J. Forens. Sci.*, 49 (2), (2004), 290.

Geller, B., Almog, J., Margot, P., Springer, E., "A chronological review of fingerprint forgery," *J. Forens. Sci.*, 44 (5), (1999), 963.

Geller, B., Almog, J., and Margot, P., "Fingerprint forgery—a survey," *J. Forens. Sci.*, 46 (3), (2001), 731.

Guo, Y., and Xing, L., "Visualization method for fingerprints on skin by impression on a polyethylene terephthalate (PET) semirigid sheet," *J. Forens. Sci.*, 37 (2), (1992), 604.

Hague, F., Westland, A.D., Milligan, J. and Kerr, F.M., "A small particle (iron oxide) suspension for detection of latent fingerprints on smooth surfaces," *Forens. Sci. Intl.*, 41 (1989), 73.

Hazen, R.J., "Significant advances in the science of fingerprints," *Science*, 2nd. Ed., G. Davies, Ed., American Chemical Society, Washington, D.C., 1986.

Howard, S., "Basic fuchsin—a guide to a one step processing technique for black electrical tape," *J. Forens. Sci.*, 38 (6), (1993), 1391.

Kahana, T., Grande, A., Tancredi, D.M., Penaluev, J. and Hiss, J., "Fingerprinting the deceased: traditional and new techniques," *J. Forens. Sci.*, 46 (4), (2001), 908.

Knowles, R., "The new (non-numeric) fingerprint evidence standard," *Sci. & Just.*, 40 (2), (2000), 120.

Laporte, Gerald M., and Ramotowski, R. S., "The effects of latent print processing on questioned documents produced by office machine systems utilizing inkjet technology and toner," *J. Forens. Sci.*, 48 (3), (2003), 658.

Linde, H.G., "Latent fingerprints by a superior ninhydrin method," *J. Forens. Sci. Soc.*, 20 (1975), 581.

Menzel, E.R., "Pretreatment of latent prints for laser development," *Forens. Sci. Rev.*, 1 (1989), 43.

Menzel, E.R., Bartsch, R.A., and Hallman, J.L., "Fluorescent metal-Ruhemann's purple coordination compounds: Application to latent fingerprint detection," *J. Forens. Sci.*, 35 (1), (1990), 25.

Migron, Y., Hocherman, G., Springer, E., Almog, J., and Mandler, D., "Visualization of sebaceous fingerprints on fired cartridge cases: a laboratory study," *J. Forens. Sci.*, 43 (3), (1998), 543.

Moyer, S.W., Meillern, C.P., and Jones, P.F., "The use of o-phthalaldehyde for superior fluorescent visualization of latent fingerprints," *J. Forens. Sci. Soc.*, 18 (1978), 233.

Onstwedder, J., III, and Gamble, T.E., Jr., "Small particle reagent: Developing latent prints on water-soaked firearms and effect on firearm analysis," *J. Forens. Sci.*, 34 (2), (1989), 321.

Pounds, C.A., Grigg, R., and Mongkoiaussavaratana, T., "The use of 1,8-diazafluoren-9-one (DFO) for the fluorescent detection of latent fingerprints on paper—a preliminary evaluation," *J. Forens. Sci.*, 35 (1), (1990), 169.

Schmidt, C.W., Nawrocki, S.P., Williamson, M.A., and Marlin, D.C., "Obtaining fingerprints from mummified fingers: a method for tissue rehydration adopted from the archeological literature," *J. Forens. Sci.*, 45 (4), (2000), 874.

Schwartz, Lothar, and Frerichs, I., "Advanced solvent-free application of Ninhydrin for detection of latent fingerprints on thermal paper and other surfaces," *J. Forens. Sci.*, 47 (6), (2002), 1274.

Steele, Charles A., and Ball, M. S., "Enhancing contrast of fingerprints on plastic tape," *J. Forens. Sci.*, 48 (6), (2003), 1314.

Stucker, M., Geil, M., Kyeck, S., Hoffman, K., Rochling, A., Memmel, U., and Altmeyer, P., "Interpapillary lines—the variable part of the human fingerprint," *J. Forens. Sci.*, 46 (4), (2001), 857.

Trowell, F., "A method for fixing latent fingerprints developed with iodine," *J. Forens. Sci. Soc.*, 15 (1975), 189.

Wen, Che-yen, and Yu, C., "Fingerprint pattern restoration by digital image processing techniques," *J. Forens. Sci.*, 48 (5), (2003), 973.

EXPERIMENT 11   Name _____

DATA SHEET   Date _____

FINGERPRINTING

Part A: Visualizing Fingerprints

1. Describe the surface you used and the results you had.

Part B: Lifting Fingerprints

1. Latent prints lifted with transparent tape.

2. Latent prints lifted with the hinged lifter.

3. Latent prints lifted with KromeKote paper.

Part C: Fluorescent Dusting Powder

1. Describe what you saw when you irradiated the print dusted with anthracene with UV radiation.

2. What was the effect on the fluorescence after you washed your hands?

Part D: Obtaining Inked Fingerprints

Fingerprint patterns of inked prints. Attach the FBI card to this report. Place your fingerprints on the spaces below. Below each print, label it with its general pattern.

1. R. thumb   R. index   R. middle   R. ring   R. little

   L. thumb   L. index   L. middle   L. ring   L. little

2. List the identifying characteristics of your fingerprints.

Federal Bureau of Investigation, United States Department of Justice
Washington, D.C. 20537

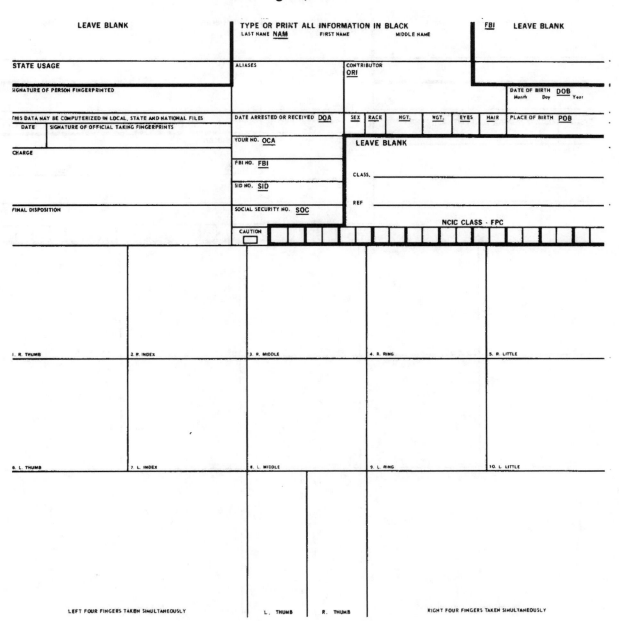

LEAVE BLANK

TYPE OR PRINT ALL INFORMATION IN BLACK
LAST NAME **NAM**   FIRST NAME   MIDDLE NAME

FBI   LEAVE BLANK

STATE USAGE

ALIASES

CONTRIBUTOR
ORI

SIGNATURE OF PERSON FINGERPRINTED

DATE OF BIRTH **DOB**
Month   Day   Year

THIS DATA MAY BE COMPUTERIZED IN LOCAL, STATE AND NATIONAL FILES
DATE   SIGNATURE OF OFFICIAL TAKING FINGERPRINTS

DATE ARRESTED OR RECEIVED **DOA**

SEX | RACE | HGT. | WGT. | EYES | HAIR | PLACE OF BIRTH **POB**

YOUR NO. **OCA**

LEAVE BLANK

CHARGE

FBI NO. **FBI**

CLASS.

SID NO. **SID**

REF

FINAL DISPOSITION

SOCIAL SECURITY NO. **SOC**

NCIC CLASS - FPC

CAUTION

1. R. THUMB   2. R. INDEX   3. R. MIDDLE   4. R. RING   5. R. LITTLE

6. L. THUMB   7. L. INDEX   8. L. MIDDLE   9. L. RING   10. L. LITTLE

LEFT FOUR FINGERS TAKEN SIMULTANEOUSLY   L. THUMB   R. THUMB   RIGHT FOUR FINGERS TAKEN SIMULTANEOUSLY

TYPE OR PRINT ALL INFORMATION IN BLACK

LAST NAME NAM   FIRST NAME   MIDDLE NAME

STATE USAGE

ALIASES

CONTRIBUTOR
ORI

DATE OF BIRTH   DOB
Month   Day   Year

SIGNATURE OF PERSON FINGERPRINTED

THIS DATA MAY BE COMPUTERIZED IN LOCAL, STATE AND NATIONAL FILES

DATE ARRESTED OR RECEIVED   DOA

SEX	RACE	HGT.	WGT.	EYES	HAIR

PLACE OF BIRTH   POB

DATE   SIGNATURE OF OFFICIAL TAKING FINGERPRINTS

YOUR NO. OCA

LEAVE BLANK

CHARGE

FBI NO. FBI

CLASS.

SID NO. SID

FINAL DISPOSITION

SOCIAL SECURITY NO.   SOC

REF

NCIC CLASS - FPC

CAUTION

1. R. THUMB	2. R. INDEX	3. R. MIDDLE	4. R. RING	5. R. LITTLE

6. L. THUMB	7. L. INDEX	8. L. MIDDLE	9. L. RING	10. L. LITTLE

LEFT FOUR FINGERS TAKEN SIMULTANEOUSLY

L. THUMB   R. THUMB

RIGHT FOUR FINGERS TAKEN SIMULTANEOUSLY

FEDERAL BUREAU OF INVESTIGATION, UNITED STATES DEPARTMENT OF JUSTICE
WASHINGTON, D. C. 20537

	YES	NO
PALM PRINTS TAKEN?	☐	☐
PHOTO AVAILABLE?	☐	☐

IF AVAILABLE, PASTE PHOTO OVER INSTRUCTIONS IN DOTTED AREA. (DO NOT USE STAPLES)

SINCE PHOTOGRAPH MAY BECOME DETACHED INDICATE NAME.
DATE TAKEN, FBI NUMBER, CONTRIBUTOR AND ARREST NUMBER
ON REVERSE SIDE. WHETHER ATTACHED TO FINGERPRINT CARD OR
SUBMITTED LATER.

IF ARREST FINGERPRINTS SENT FBI PREVIOUSLY AND FBI NO. UNKNOWN, FURNISH ARREST NO. _____ DATE _____

STATUTE CITATION (SEE INSTRUCTION NO. 9) **CIT**

1.

2.

3.

ARREST DISPOSITION (SEE INSTRUCTION NO. 5) **ADN**

EMPLOYER: IF U. S. GOVERNMENT, INDICATE SPECIFIC AGENCY.
IF MILITARY, LIST BRANCH OF SERVICE AND SERIAL NO.

OCCUPATION

RESIDENCE OF PERSON FINGERPRINTED

SCARS, MARKS, TATTOOS, AND AMPUTATIONS **SMT**

BASIS FOR CAUTION **ICO**

DATE OF OFFENSE **DOO**	SKIN TONE **SKN**

MISC. NO. **MNU**

ADDITIONAL INFORMATION

INSTRUCTIONS

1. UNLESS OTHERWISE PROVIDED BY REGULATION IN YOUR STATE, FINGERPRINTS ARE TO BE SUBMITTED DIRECTLY TO FBI IDENTIFICATION DIVISION. FORWARD IMMEDIATELY FOR MOST EFFECTIVE SERVICE.

2. FINGERPRINTS SHOULD BE SUBMITTED BY ARRESTING AGENCY ONLY (MULTIPLE PRINTS ON SAME CHARGE SHOULD NOT BE SUBMITTED BY OTHER AGENCIES SUCH AS JAILS, RECEIVING AGENCIES, ETC.). REQUEST COPIES OF FBI IDENTIFICATION RECORD FOR ALL OTHER INTERESTED AGENCIES IN BLOCK BELOW. GIVE COMPLETE MAILING ADDRESS, INCLUDING ZIP CODE.

3. TYPE OR PRINT ALL INFORMATION.

4. NOTE AMPUTATIONS IN PROPER FINGER BLOCKS.

5. LIST FINAL DISPOSITION IN BLOCK ON FRONT SIDE. IF NOT NOW AVAILABLE, SUBMIT LATER ON FBI FORM R-84 FOR COMPLETION OF RECORD. IF FINAL DISPOSITION NOT AVAILABLE SHOW PRE-TRIAL OR ARRESTING AGENCY DISPOSITION, e. g., RELEASED, NO FORMAL CHARGE, BAIL, TURNED OVER TO, IN THE ARREST DISPOSITION BLOCK PROVIDED ON THIS SIDE.

6. MAKE CERTAIN ALL IMPRESSIONS ARE LEGIBLE, FULLY ROLLED AND CLASSIFIABLE.

7. CAUTION - CHECK BOX ON FRONT IF CAUTION STATEMENT INDICATED. BASIS FOR CAUTION (ICO) MUST GIVE REASON FOR CAUTION, e. g., ARMED AND DANGEROUS, SUICIDAL, ETC.

8. MISCELLANEOUS NUMBER (MNU) - SHOULD INCLUDE SUCH NUMBERS AS MILITARY SERVICE, PASSPORT AND/OR VETERANS ADMINISTRATION (IDENTIFY TYPE OF NUMBER).

9. PROVIDE STATUTE CITATION, IDENTIFYING SPECIFIC STATUTE (example - PL for PENAL LAW) AND CRIMINAL CODE CITATION INCLUDING ANY SUB-SECTIONS.

10. ALL INFORMATION REQUESTED IS ESSENTIAL.

SEND COPY TO:

REPLY DESIRED?	YES ☐	NO ☐

(REPLY WILL BE SENT IN ALL CASES IF SUBJECT FOUND TO BE WANTED)

IF COLLECT WIRE OR COLLECT TELEPHONE REPLY
DESIRED, INDICATE HERE: (WIRE SENT ON ALL UNKNOWN DECEASED)

WIRE REPLY ☐	TELEPHONE REPLY ☐	TELEPHONE NO. AND AREA CODE _____

LEAVE BLANK

LEAVE BLANK

FEDERAL BUREAU OF INVESTIGATION, UNITED STATES DEPARTMENT OF JUSTICE
WASHINGTON, D. C. 20537

PALM PRINTS TAKEN? YES ☐ NO ☐

PHOTO AVAILABLE? YES ☐ NO ☐

IF AVAILABLE, PASTE PHOTO OVER INSTRUCTIONS
IN DOTTED AREA. (DO NOT USE STAPLES)

SINCE PHOTOGRAPH MAY BECOME DETACHED INDICATE NAME.
DATE TAKEN, FBI NUMBER, CONTRIBUTOR AND ARREST NUMBER
ON REVERSE SIDE. WHETHER ATTACHED TO FINGERPRINT CARD OR
SUBMITTED LATER.

IF ARREST FINGERPRINTS SENT FBI PREVIOUSLY AND FBI NO. UNKNOWN,
FURNISH ARREST NO. _____ DATE _____

STATUTE CITATION (SEE INSTRUCTION NO. 9) <u>CIT</u>

1.

2.

3.

ARREST DISPOSITION (SEE INSTRUCTION NO. 5) <u>ADN</u>

EMPLOYER: IF U. S. GOVERNMENT, INDICATE SPECIFIC AGENCY.
IF MILITARY, LIST BRANCH OF SERVICE AND SERIAL NO.

OCCUPATION

RESIDENCE OF PERSON FINGERPRINTED

SCARS, MARKS, TATTOOS, AND AMPUTATIONS <u>SMT</u>

BASIS FOR CAUTION <u>ICO</u>

DATE OF OFFENSE <u>DOO</u> | SKIN TONE <u>SKN</u>

MISC. NO. <u>MNU</u>

ADDITIONAL INFORMATION

INSTRUCTIONS

1. UNLESS OTHERWISE PROVIDED BY REGULATION IN YOUR STATE, FINGERPRINTS ARE TO BE SUBMITTED DIRECTLY TO FBI IDENTIFICATION DIVISION. FORWARD IMMEDIATELY FOR MOST EFFECTIVE SERVICE.

2. FINGERPRINTS SHOULD BE SUBMITTED BY <u>ARRESTING AGENCY ONLY</u> (MULTIPLE PRINTS ON SAME CHARGE SHOULD <u>NOT</u> BE SUBMITTED BY OTHER AGENCIES SUCH AS JAILS, RECEIVING AGENCIES, ETC.). REQUEST COPIES OF FBI IDENTIFICATION RECORD FOR ALL OTHER INTERESTED AGENCIES IN BLOCK BELOW. GIVE COMPLETE MAILING ADDRESS, INCLUDING ZIP CODE.

3. TYPE OR PRINT ALL INFORMATION.

4. NOTE AMPUTATIONS IN PROPER FINGER BLOCKS.

5. LIST FINAL DISPOSITION IN BLOCK ON FRONT SIDE. IF NOT NOW AVAILABLE, SUBMIT LATER ON FBI FORM R-84 FOR COMPLETION OF RECORD. IF FINAL DISPOSITION NOT AVAILABLE SHOW PRE-TRIAL OR ARRESTING AGENCY DISPOSITION, e. g., RELEASED, NO FORMAL CHARGE, BAIL, TURNED OVER TO, IN THE ARREST DISPOSITION BLOCK PROVIDED ON THIS SIDE.

6. MAKE CERTAIN ALL IMPRESSIONS ARE LEGIBLE, FULLY ROLLED AND CLASSIFIABLE.

7. CAUTION - CHECK BOX ON FRONT IF CAUTION STATEMENT INDICATED. BASIS FOR CAUTION (ICO) MUST GIVE REASON FOR CAUTION, e. g., ARMED AND DANGEROUS, SUICIDAL, ETC.

8. MISCELLANEOUS NUMBER (MNU) - SHOULD INCLUDE SUCH NUMBERS AS MILITARY SERVICE, PASSPORT AND/OR VETERANS ADMINISTRATION (IDENTIFY TYPE OF NUMBER).

9. PROVIDE STATUTE CITATION, IDENTIFYING SPECIFIC STATUTE (example - PL for PENAL LAW) AND CRIMINAL CODE CITATION INCLUDING ANY SUB-SECTIONS.

10. ALL INFORMATION REQUESTED IS ESSENTIAL. -

SEND COPY TO:

REPLY DESIRED? YES ☐ NO ☐

(REPLY WILL BE SENT IN ALL CASES IF SUBJECT FOUND TO BE WANTED)

IF COLLECT WIRE OR COLLECT TELEPHONE REPLY
DESIRED, INDICATE HERE: (WIRE SENT ON ALL UNKNOWN DECEASED)

WIRE REPLY ☐ TELEPHONE REPLY ☐ TELEPHONE NO. AND AREA CODE _____

LEAVE BLANK

LEAVE BLANK

Part E: Matching Prints

1. Identify the object you examined and the procedure you used.

2. Suspect print number _____

    Identity of the suspect to whom the print belongs_____

Fingerprinting (Advanced)

This experiment will be divided into four parts: the use of ninhydrin, silver nitrate, Super-glue, and a fluorescent enhancement of the Super-glue. Your fingers come in continual contact with sweat and body oil. A summary of the components (preparer unknown) in a fingerprint is:

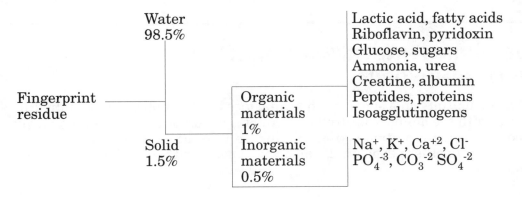

Fingerprint residue

Water 98.5%

Solid 1.5%

Organic materials 1%

Lactic acid, fatty acids
Riboflavin, pyridoxin
Glucose, sugars
Ammonia, urea
Creatine, albumin
Peptides, proteins
Isoagglutinogens

Inorganic materials 0.5%

Na^+, K^+, Ca^{+2}, Cl^-
PO_4^{-3}, CO_3^{-2} SO_4^{-2}

EQUIPMENT

Aluminum foil (tank liner)

1 Bag, plastic, large, Ziplok (alternate)

1 Beaker, 50 mL

1 Beaker, 250 mL

1 Beaker, 1,000 mL

Blank paper checks

2 Brushes, dusting

1 Can, beer, EMPTY

Cotton balls (alternate method)

Dusting powder, black

1 Forceps

1 Funnel, powder, 65 mm

1 pr Gloves, disposable

1 pr Goggles, safety

1 Iron, steam

1 Paper, black, 8½ × 11 inches

2 Racks, wire test tube

2 Sprayers, aerosol

1 Tank, 5-gallon (fish tank will do, but with a glass plastic, or metal cover)

2 Trays, photographic developing

2 Towels, cloth

Towels, paper

1 UV (ultraviolet) lamp (Mineralite works well)

REAGENTS

Acetone

Ninhydrin solution, 5% in acetone

Silver nitrate, 2% in distilled water

Sodium thiosulfate (Hypo) 200 g + 140 g
  of sodium bisulfate/L of water.

Methanol

Rubber cement

Sodium hydroxide, 5% (alternate method)

Super-glue

Fluorescent dye, 5% in methanol (LaPine Scientific Co., Dept. H, 6003 South Knox Ave., Chicago, IL, 60629, Catalog No. 74613H-82, $40/1b)

Zinc chloride solution

Zinc chloride	3 g	Mix the EtOH and HOAc and dissolve the zinc. Then add the
Ethyl alcohol	25 mL	Freon. If 2 layers form, add 1-2 mL of isopropyl alcohol.
Acetic acid	5 mL	
Freon TF	70 mL	(also called Fluorisol, Freon 113, Fluorocarbon solvent 113, or 1, 1, 2-trichloro-1,2,2- trifluoroethane)

METHODS

PART A: OBTAINING FINGERPRINTS FROM PAPER BY MEANS OF NINHYDRIN

You will now develop prints on a separate sheet of paper by the application of ninhydrin. Ninhydrin reacts with the amino acids from the proteins of perspiration. A blue-to-purple color is formed. An acetone solution is used. Ninhydrin is an irritant, so in the interests of safety and comfort to other people in the laboratory, perform this portion of the experiment in a fume hood.

CRIME SCENE

A check has been **kited**, that is, a higher value has been substituted for the one signed for by the owner. The check was then cashed by a forged endorsement. The bank teller became suspicious, did not touch the face of the check, and called security. The police have a suspect and the check. You have been given the check and are to test it for fingerprints. You will first use the ninhydrin technique, then the metal-enhanced ninhydrin technique.

NOTE: Ninhydrin will react with any protein, particularly that **on your fingers**. If you are at all sloppy, you will have purple fingers for over a week. We suggest you wear disposable plastic gloves when doing this experiment.

Have a thief in the dorm? Place a little ninhydrin on a dollar bill or some other object that the thief likes. After the item is taken, look for the one with the purple fingers.

1. Plug in and turn on the steam iron.

2. Touch one or more fingers of one hand to each end of a check.

3. Pour a few milliliters of the ninhydrin solution into a spray bottle; screw the bottle into an aerosol can.

4. Under a hood, lightly spray the paper with ninhydrin solution.

5. Place the sheet of paper in a folded cloth towel.

6. Dry the paper for 3 to 4 minutes, and then cover the paper with a second cloth towel.

7. Iron the upper cloth towel. This will heat the paper without scorching it. Apply heat to the upper towel for a few minutes, then remove the upper towel and observe the developed latent fingerprints. They will be colored a light blue or blue-violet.

8. Cover one end of the check with a piece of paper and spray the other end with 3% zinc chloride. The print should change to orange, which may make it stand out better on some objects. If nickel nitrate is used, the print will turn red. Notice any areas that are not well developed and circle them with pencil.

9. Take the check to a darkroom and examine it under UV radiation from a Mineralite. An argon laser is usually used for this and works much better. (Nickel will not fluoresce). Compare those places on the original fingerprints that you circled and determine if the fluorescence has improved the detection level.

10. Attach this check to the data sheet.

PART B: THE SILVER NITRATE METHOD

One of the components secreted by the pores on the fingertips is sodium chloride (NaCl). Sometimes it is possible to bring out fingerprints on paper by adding a solution of silver nitrate ($AgNO_3$). This solution slowly reacts with the chloride to form silver chloride. Upon exposure to UV radiation, the effect is like that of a photographic film; silver is formed and the ridges turn black on a brown background. Once the print has been developed and photographed, the silver can be removed by either a mercuric nitrate solution or "Hypo."

This technique is sometimes the only one that will work with really old prints because the salt is all that remains. Care must be taken because the black ridges fade away and the brown background gets quite dark. This coloration can be removed by dipping the paper in a 2% solution of mercuric nitrate (CAUTION: this solution is toxic). Silver nitrate stains may be removed with 5 g of mercuric chloride and 5 g of ammonium chloride in 100 mL of distilled water. A newer technique to remove background coloration and stains is to use a mixture of 200 g of sodium thiosulfate and 140 g of sodium bisulfate/liter of water. It takes 10–15 minutes to be effective.

CRIME SCENE

It is suspected that an employee is going through desks that he has no business looking through. The manager noticed some checks had been rearranged on his desk. It is desired to detect the suspect's fingerprints on the checks without leaving any trace so the suspect won't get suspicious. You have been given one of the checks and are to use the silver nitrate method to develop any fingerprints on it. You are to then treat it with a hyposulfate solution to remove the silver so the check can be returned to its original place and as close to its original condition as possible.

1. Place your fingerprints on a check as you did in the ninhydrin experiment.

2. Pour sufficient silver nitrate solution in a tray to cover the paper. Wear disposable gloves. **Do not get silver nitrate solution on your skin.** It will turn black when it becomes exposed to sunlight and will take days to wear off.

3. With the aid of forceps, immerse the paper in the silver nitrate solution, making certain it is covered completely. Allow it to remain in the solution for 4 to 5 minutes.

4. Use the forceps to remove and drain it.

5. Transfer the paper to a folded towel.

6. Allow the paper to dry in a darkened area. Do not expose the paper to direct sunlight.

7. Develop the print by directing the radiation from a UV lamp on the paper. Do this carefully as too much exposure will cause the prints to form and fade very fast. The paper will turn brown, with the print becoming visible as a black or very dark brown color.

8. Dip HALF of the paper (so you can compare to the other half) into a tray containing the hypo and sodium bisulfate and let it stay there until the color fades (from 10–15 minutes).

9. Remove the paper with a forceps, allow the excess liquid to drip away, then place it between the folds of a cloth towel to damp dry.

10. Fold your print (if you get one) in black paper and attach it to your report.

PART C: THE USE OF SUPER-GLUE

In 1976, in Saga prefecture in Japan, Masao Soba, was working with Aron-Alfa, the Japanese version of Super-glue which is in a double container. He noticed white finger-prints on the outside of the inner container and decided to determine how they were formed. In 1978, Noboyuki Otsubo showed Ed German and Paul Norkus of the U.S. Army Crime Lab what the technique was. They brought it to this country and taught it to Frank Kendall. Frank Kendall did experiments to improve the technique and in 1980 published the first English language version of the technique. Since that time, the use of Super-glue to detect fingerprints has become one of the more useful techniques.

Essentially all you need to do is to place the object to be examined in an enclosed chamber (covered fish tank), add a small amount of Super-glue in a small container (bottle cap) and warm it (coffee cup warmer) until it begins to fume. It is thought by many that the fumes are attracted to the fingerprints because the prints are of opposite charge to the fumes. A white image is formed. To the author's knowledge, no one has conclusively determined the chemistry of what is taking place on the ridge surface. It is suspected it involves the salt on the print since the technique works well with old prints that would most likely have lost their oils. If the print is faint, it may be enhanced by dusting it with dusting powder, or it may be sprayed lightly with a fluorescent solution and then examined under UV radiation.

Super-glue is a mixture of 98–99% of either methyl, ethyl, or butyl-2-cyanoacrylate and 1–2% of an inhibitor. The polymerization is easily catalyzed by a base, water being sufficiently basic. The trace moisture on your fingers is the cause of Super-glue sticking your fingers together so quickly.

The moisture in the air is sufficient to initiate polymerization once a drop of the glue is placed on an object. This produces a few long and very strong polymer chains as you have seen demonstrated in TV commercials. If too much moisture is present, a large number of reactions will be started and only weaker short chains will form. While this is poor for glue it works better for fingerprint detection, and many investigators place a small container of water in the developing chamber. Without heat, it takes several hours to form a clear print. With gentle warming, good prints can be obtained in 10–15 minutes.

If sodium hydroxide, a strong base, is used, no heating is necessary to develop fingerprints. A cotton ball is soaked in 0.5 M NaOH solution and dried. This cotton ball is placed in the fuming chamber and when a few drops of Super-glue is added, fumes will form in a few seconds.

This is an excellent method to examine large areas without having to meticulously dust them. For example, the entire inside of a car can be examined in 10–15 minutes.

There are some problems. Fingerprints developed with Super-glue are hard to remove, requiring a mild abrasive and much rubbing which can ruin the surface. While acetone can be used to dissolve the print, it also dissolves paint and may ruin that surface. Therefore, you should not fingerprint an object that may be used again unless you are fairly certain it contains a print. If you fingerprint the inside of a car, the white prints are probably there to stay. Other solvents are nitromethane, dimethylsulfoxide, dimethylformamide, and methylethyl ketone.

The Super-glue technique works well on glass, metal, and plastic. If the item is to be examined for blood, saliva, seminal fluid, fibers, hairs, or anything else, this should be done before fuming with Super-glue because the fuming will usually ruin the examination of other substances. If you are going to do a gun, cork the end of the barrel first.

Super-glue fumes are not particularly toxic, but they will make your nose burn and tears may form at higher concentrations. You will smell it long before these things happen. None the less, it is recommended that the developing chamber be placed in a hood or that you have an exhaust system of some type present.

CRIME SCENE

An empty beer can was found under the seat of an abandoned vehicle suspected of being used in a kidnapping. The owner of the car says that he never drinks that brand of beer. Your job is to determine if there are any prints on this can that do not match the owner's (to check out his story) and to possibly determine those of the kidnapper.

1. Obtain a developing chamber (probably a fish tank), some rubber cement, and a sheet of aluminum foil long enough to cover all but about 10 cm of the inside of the tank.

   In an educational laboratory, a good, inexpensive container is a large plastic container with a sealable cover, easily obtained and inexpensive to replace if necessary. The disadvantage of such a container is the inability to observe the development of prints on the object.

2. Remove any objects from the inside of the developing chamber. Steps 3–5 may be omitted at the discretion of your instructor.

3. If the chamber is glass, wipe off the walls with a cloth dampened with acetone. Do not use acetone on plastic, it will fog up immediately. Use dimethylformamide or one of the other solvents discussed earlier.

4. Place the aluminum foil around the inside of the chamber so that a small opening is located so you can see your object when it is placed on the rack.

5. Place a small amount of rubber cement along the top of the chamber to hold the foil in place. Over a period of time, the walls will become coated with Super-glue polymer, eventually making direct observation impossible.

6. Place a small hot plate inside the chamber and off to one side. A single coffee cup warmer is preferred for this as it produces the right temperature and is constant heat.

7. Place a support rack inside of the chamber. A wire test tube rack is preferred because it is open and lets the fumes penetrate the object from all directions.

8. Your object will be an empty can of beer. For this experiment, wipe it clean of prints, then place several prints on it at various places and over different colors of paint.

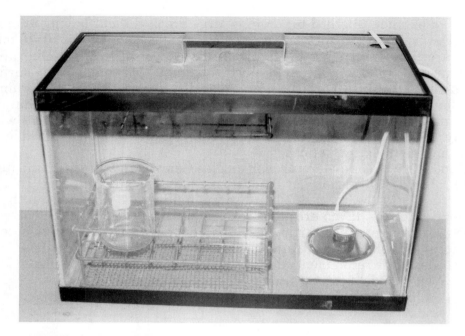

FIGURE 12–1   A typical super-glue fuming cabinet. A 5.5 gallon fish tank.

Now put on plastic gloves on one hand, handle the can, and place it on the rack. Remove the glove (leave it inside out) and place it next to the beer can.

9. Place a **small** metal cup (bottle cap or specimen can) on the hot plate and then add 8–10 drops of Super-glue to it.

10. Place a small beaker of water in the chamber.

11. Place the cover on the chamber and turn on the heater. It normally takes about 2 minutes for the glue to fume. You will be able to smell it. Watch the beer can where you know there is a print as well as the finger tips of the glove. It will usually take about 5 minutes before a clearly visible print is obtained. Let the reaction continue for about 10–12 minutes.

12. Turn off the heater, and, wearing gloves, remove the can. Examine it carefully and write down your observations on the data sheet. Do the same thing with the plastic glove.

13. Proceed to Part D.

PART D: ENHANCEMENT OF SUPER-GLUE FINGERPRINTS BY DUSTING AND FLUORESCENCE (ADVANCED)

Comparisons of various enhancement techniques will be done in this part. You will dust some prints, you will spray some prints, and you will dip some prints. You will do your best to compare the results so that you will know what can be done. There are two schools of thought on the use of fluorescent dyes to enhance the Super-glue imprint. One is to lightly spray the print with a diluted solution of the dye and examine it under UV radiation. The other is to dip the object in a more concentrated solution, leave it there for 1–2 seconds, rinse it off with ethanol, and then examine it with UV radiation. We will let you try both methods.

Please be careful on those steps that involve the use of fluorescent materials. KEEP EVERY ITEM USED WITH FLUORESCENT MATERIALS IN A SEPARATE CON-

TAINER (ZIPLOCK BAG IS GOOD) AND USE A SEPARATE LAB BENCH FOR THIS WORK. DO NOT ALLOW ANY ITEM THAT HAS COME IN CONTACT WITH THESE DYES TO BE USED ON ANYTHING ELSE. Even a small drop will contaminate a bench top and it takes days of washing to completely remove it. Please be careful.

Several fluorescent dyes are commercially available. Rhodamine 6G was made especially to fluoresce at 515 nm so that an argon laser could be used.

1. You will need to locate a poorly developed fingerprint near the end on one side of the can. This will be used for the dipping experiment. You will need to locate two poorly developed fingerprints on the opposite end of the can, one on each side. One will be used for dusting and the other for spraying. Do the same with the glove; only one finger at a time will be used.

   NOTE: Repeat each step with a fingerprint on the plastic glove.

2. Decide which print you want to try to enhance by dusting and examine it closely to see where parts are missing. Carefully dust it with black dusting powder, using the same dusting technique you learned in Part A of Experiment 11. Describe on the data sheet any differences you found.

NOTE: this fingerprint can now be lifted by any of the techniques described earlier.

3. Wrap a paper towel around the end of the can you are going to dip so that spray won't get on the print. Fasten it with tape.

4. Place a few mL of the fluorescent dye in the sprayer and lightly spray (in a hood or spraying chamber) the print you have selected.

5. Allow the dye to thoroughly dry, then view it in a darkened room with a Mineralite (either long or short wavelength). An argon laser may be used if one is available.

6. Place about 100 mL of the dye solution in a 250-mL beaker.

7. Remove the paper towel and dip the end of the can into the dye solution until the print is completely submerged. Let it stay there for 1–2 seconds, then let it drip dry for 10–15 seconds.

8. Hold the can over a 1,000 mL beaker and rinse the surface with a stream of ethanol from a wash bottle.

9. Allow the dye to thoroughly dry, then view it in a darkened room with a Mineralite (either long or short wavelength). An argon laser may be used if one is available.

10. Write your observations and conclusions on the data sheet.

SELECTED SOURCES FOR ADDITIONAL INFORMATION

Almog, J., et al. "5-methylthio ninhydrin and related compounds: A novel class of fluorogenic fingerprint reagents," *J. Forens. Sci.,* 37 (3), (1992), 688.

Almog, J., and Gabay, A., "A modified Super-glue technique-the use of polycyanoacrylate for fingerprint development," *J. Forens. Sci.,* 31 (1), (1986), 250.

Almog, J., "Reagents for chemical development of latent fingerprints: vicinal triketones—their reaction with amino acids and with latent fingerprints on paper," *J. Forens. Sci.,* 32 (6), (1987), 1565.

Almog, J., Hirshfeld, A., Frank, A., Sterling, J., and Leonov, D., "Aminoninhydrin: fingerprint reagents with direct fluorogenic activity—preliminary studies," *J. Forens. Sci.,* 36 (1), (1991,) 104.

Almog, J., Springer, E., Wieser, S., Frank, A., Khodzhaeu, O., Lidor, R., Bahar, E., Varkony, H., Dayans, S., and Rozen, S., "Latent fingerprint visualization by 1,2-indanedione and related compounds: preliminary results," *J. Forens. Sci.,* 44 (1), (1999), 114.

Azoury, Myriam, Gabbay, R., Cohen, D., and Almog, J., "ESDA processing and latent fingerprint development: The humidity effect," *J. Forens. Sci.,* 48 (3), (2003), 564.

Bersellini, C., Garofano, L., Giannetto, M., Lusardi, F., and Mori, G., " Development of latent fingerprints on metallic surfaces using electropolymerization processes," *J. Forens. Sci.,* 46 (4), (2001), 871.

Bramble, S.K., "Separation of latent fingerprint residues by thin layer chromatography," *J. Forens. Sci.,* 40 (6), (1995), 969.

Bramble, S.K., "Fluorescence spectroscopy as an aid to imaging latent fingerprints in the ultraviolet," *J. Forens. Sci.,* 41 (6), (1996), 1038.

Caldwell, J.P., Henderson, W., and Kim, N.D., "ABTS: a safe alternative to DAB for the enhancement of blood fingerprints," *J. Forens. Sci.,* 45 (4), (2000), 785.

Caldwell, J.P., Henderson, W., and Kim, N.D., "Luminescent visualization of latent fingerprints by direct reaction with a lanthanide shift reagent," *J. Forens. Sci.,* 46 (6), (2001), 1303.

Caldwell, J.P., and Kim, N.D., "Extension of the color suite available for chemical enhancement of fingerprints in blood," *J. Forens. Sci.,* 47 (2), (2002), 332.

Cheng, S.G., "ANS (8-anilinonaphthalene-l-sulfonate) a new reagent for detection of fingerprints on cloth," *J. Forens. Sci.,* 33 (2), (1988), 527.

Chesher, B.K., Stone, J.M. and Rowe, W.F., "Use of the Omniprint 1000 alternate light source to produce fluorescence in cyanoacrylate-developed latent fingerprints stained with biological stains and commercial fabric dyes," *Forens. Sci. Intl.,* 38 (1992), 163.

Davies, P.J., Kobus, H.J., Taylor, M.R., and Wainwright, K.P., "Synthesis and structure of the zinc (II) and cadmium (II) complexes produced in the photoluminescent enhancement of ninhydrin developed fingerprints using group 12 metal salts," *J. Forens. Sci.,* 40 (4), (1995), 565.

Elber, R., Frank, A., Almog, J., "Chemical development of latent fingerprints: computational design of ninhydrin analogues," *J. Forens. Sci.,* 45 (4), (2000), 757.

Flynn, Katherine, Maynard, P., Du Pasquier, D., Lennard, C., Stoilovic, M., and Roux, C., "Evaluation of iodine-benzoflavone and ruthenium tetroxide spray reagents for the detection of latent fingermarks at the crime scene," *J. Forens. Sci.,* 49 (4), (2004), 707.

Gardner, Sarah, J., and Hewlett, D.F., "Optimization and initial evaluation of 1,2-indandjone as a reagent for fingerprint detection," *J. Forens. Sci.,* 48 (6), (2003), 1288.

Halahmi, E., Levi, O., Kronik, L., and Boxman, R.L., "Development of latent fingerprints using `a corona discharge," *J. Forens. Sci.,* 42 (50), (1997), 833.

Hauze, D.B., Petrovskia, O., Taylor, B., Joullie, M.M., Ramotowski, B., and Cantu, A.A., "1,2 indanediones: new reagents for visualizating the amino acid components of latent prints," *J. Forens. Sci.,* 43 (4), (1998), 744.

Hewlett, D.F., Winfield, P.G.R., and Clifford, A.A., "The ninhydrin process in supercritical CO_2," *J. Forens. Sci.,* 41 (3), (1996), 487.

Jones, N.E., Davies, L.M., Brennan, J.S. and Bramble, S.K., "Separation of visibly-excited fluorescent components in fingerprint components in fingerprint residue by thin layer chromatography," *J. Forens. Sci.,* 45 (6), (2000), 1286.

Keating, D.M. and Miller, J.J., "A technique for developing and photographing ridge impressions on decomposed water soaked fingers," *J. Forens. Sci.,* 38 (1), (1993), 165.

Kempton, J.B., and Rowe, W.F., "Contrast enhancement of cyanoacrylate-developed latent fingerprints using biological stains and commercial fabric dyes," *J. Forens. Sci.,* 37 (1), (1992), 99.

Kendall, F.G., and Rehn, B.W., "Rapid method of Super-glue fuming application for the development of latent fingerprints," *J. Forens. Sci.,* 28 (3), (1983), 777.

Lennard, C.J., Margot, P.A., Sterns, M., and Warrener, R.N., "Photoluminescent enhancement of ninhydrin developed fingerprints by metal complexation: structural studies of complexes formed between rubemansis purple and group IIb metal salts," *J. Forens. Sci.*, 32 (3), (1987), 597.

Lennard, C.J., Margot, P.A., Stoilovic, M., and Warrener, R.N., "Synthesis and evaluation of ninhydrin analogues as reagents for the development of latent fingerprints on paper surfaces," *J. Forens. Sci.*, Soc., 28 (1988), 3.

Lewis, L.A., Smithwick, R.W., Devault, G.L., Bolinger, B., and Lewis, S.A., "Processes involved in the development of latent fingerprints using the cyanoacrylate fuming method," *J. Forens. Sci.*, 46 (2), (2001), 241.

Lock, E.R.A., Mazzella, W.D., and Margot, P., "A new europium chelate as a fluorescent dye for cyanoacrylate pretreated fingerprints—EuTTAPhen: Europium thenoyltrifluoro acetone ortho phenanthroline," *J. Forens. Sci.*, 40 (4), (1995), 654.

Migron, Y., and Mandler, D., " Development of latent fingerprints on unfired cartridges by palladium deposition—a surface study," *J. Forens. Sci.*, 42 (6), (1997), 986.

Mills, B.W., "A cyanoacrylate vacuum chamber on a budget," RCMP Gazette, 55 (3), (1993) 16. Olenik, J.H., "Super-glue, a modified technique for the development of latent fingerprints," *J. Forens. Sci.*, 29 (3), (1984), 881.

Parkin, B.H., and Hartley, K., "The detection of fingerprints and other marks in body fluids by the use of agar gels," *For. Sci. Intl.*, 35 (1987), 267.

Pounds, C.A., Grigg, R., and Mongkolaussavaratana, T., "The use of 1,8-diazafluoren-9-one (DFO) for the fluorescent detection of latent fingerprints on paper. A prelininary evaluation," *J. Forens. Sci.*, 35 (1), (1990) 169.

Ramminger, U., Nickel, U., and Geide, B., "Enhancement of an insufficient dye-formation in the ninhydrin reaction by a suitable post treatment process," *J. Forens. Sci.*, 46 (2), (2001), 288.

Roux, C., Jones, N., Lennard, C., and Stoilovic, M., "Evaluation of 1,2-indanedione and 5,6-dimethyl-1,2-indanedione for the detection of latent fingerprints on porous surfaces," *J. Forens. Sci.*, 45 (4), (2000), 761.

Schwartz, L., and Frerichs, I., " Advanced solvent free application of ninhydrin for detection of latent fingerprints on thermal paper and other surfaces," *J. Forens. Sci.*, 47 (6), (2002), 1274.

Tissier, P., Didierjean, J.C., Prudhomme, C., Pichard, J., and Crispino, F., "A 'cyanoacrylate case' for developing fingerprints in cars," *Sci. & Just.*, 39 (3) (1999), 163.

Wiesner, S., Springer, E., Sasson, Y., and Almog, J., "Chemical development of latent fingerprints: 1,2-indanedione has come of age," *J. Forens. Sci.*, 46 (5), (2001), 1082.

EXPERIMENT 12

DATA SHEET

Name _____

Date _____

FINGERPRINTING (ADVANCED)

Part A: Ninhydrin

1. Attach your developed prints to this sheet.

2. Do you think the zinc metal treatment was of any value? Explain.

Part B: The Silver Nitrate Technique

1. Attach your developed prints to this sheet.

2. Do you think the clearing solution was effective? Explain.

Part C: Super-glue

1. About how long did it take before you were able to observe some prints?

2. Describe several of the prints that you obtained on the various paint colors.

3. How good were the prints on the glove?

Part D: Fluorescent Enhancement: Techniques (Advanced)

1. Describe the differences you observed between a regular Super-glue print and one that has been dusted.

2. Describe the differences you observed between a regular Super-glue print and one that has been sprayed with a fluorescent solution.

3. Describe the differences you observed between a regular Super-glue print and one that has been dipped into a fluorescent solution.

Comparison of Tool Marks and Casting

In crimes that involve breaking and entering and in safe burglaries, tools are used to effect entry or to open a locked safe. These tools are pointed or have sharp edges which leave identifying marks on the objects upon which they are used.

There are two types of characteristics that relate the tool to the mark it makes on an object: (1) class characteristics, which include such factors as size and general configuration of tools, and (2) individual characteristics, which include structural anomalies that are unique to and distinctive of one specific tool. Individual characteristics are random in nature and result from wear devices used in the manufacture of the tool; from grinding, sharpening; or other finishing procedures, and also from use of the tool.

Examination of a tool mark requires a detailed study of the specific tool and a mapping of its surface structure. A definite distinction must be made between class and individual characteristics in each tool examined. New tools present a problem in this procedure, whereas worn tools are a much simpler case.

NOTE: The terms **mold** and **cast** are often used incorrectly. If you pour Plaster of Paris onto a tire track or footprint, that is called a **cast**. The tire track or footprint indentation acts as the **mold**. If you now use the cast to make a copy in order to obtain something that looks like the original, that is also a cast because now the first cast becomes the mold for the second cast! See why the terms get confused? Suppose you place Plaster of Paris over your face and let it harden. Your face is the mold. When you remove the plaster, you have a cast of your face. If you now fill that cast (which now becomes the mold) with molten bronze and let the bronze harden, when you chip away the plaster, you now have a cast (exact likeness) of your handsome features. Centuries ago, when transportation was slow and embalming techniques not well established, a death mask was made of the deceased's face from wax so that relatives could identify the body at a later date. This was called a **moulage**.

CRIME SCENE

A rear door of a commercial building has been "jimmied." Following the breaking open of the door, the burglar entered the building and removed a large number of items. Investigating officers have made casts of the tool marks on the door jamb, a footprint outside a window, and a tire print in a patch of dirt in the alley. These have been properly marked and sent to the area forensic laboratory. These pieces of physical evidence, along with others, have led to the apprehension of two suspects. Both suspects carry tools in their cars. Screwdrivers and pry bars have been taken from the tools in both cars and sent to the laboratory for comparison with the casts taken at the scene of the crime. You will examine three screwdrivers, catalog the class characteristics and the individual characteristics of each, and attempt to match one of the three screwdrivers with the cast of the tool marks left at the scene.

EQUIPMENT

2	Aluminum strips (approx. 5 × 10 cm)	1	Ruler, metric scale
1	Beaker, 150 mL	1	Spatula
1	Beaker, 1000 mL	1	Stirring rod, large
4	Cardboard, strips (approx. 2 × 30 cm)	1	Tongue depressor or spoon
1	Casserole	3	Toothpicks or wood splints
1	Emery paper	1	Wood block to make tool marks on
1	Forceps	1	Wood or cardboard box, about 10 cm deep
1 pr	Goggles, safety		and large enough for a footprint, filled
1	Hand lens (10×)		with moist dirt so that you can make
1	Lead strip (approx. 5 × 10 cm)		molds and casts inside in rainy weather
1	Microscope, stereoscope		

REAGENTS

Spray can, lacquer

Plaster of Paris

Molds of tool marks from scene

Screwdrivers (samples), 5 of different end types

WD-40 or something similar

Impression plastic (obtain some from a dentist, or order Citricon Bulk Putty Base from Kerr Manufacturing Company, Romulus, Mich. 48174) or liquid silicone rubber compound (obtain from C.R.P., Inc., 206-218 East Hector St., Conshohocken, PA, 19428) or modeling clay.

METHOD

PART A: MAKING A CAST OF A TOOL IMPRINT

Present casting techniques for tool marks use fast-setting silicone plastics such as those used by a dentist to make tooth impressions. Silicone plastic is fast, easy to handle, does not break as easily as other plastics, and gives good impressions of fine detail. Modeling clay can also be used, but be sure it is soft.

You will be given a piece of wood from a window frame that has been pried open. You will make a cast of the pry mark, and determine which of the prying tools on the table was used to open the window.

Whether you use the Citricon putty or the liquid silicone rubber, the technique is the same. The impression material is prepared in about the same way as you make epoxy glue. A catalyst is added and worked in: the material is applied to the mark, allowed to set, and removed.

1. Take one scoop of the silicone-base material (about the size of a ping-pong ball), and add 6 drops of the catalyst from the tube.

2. Work in the catalyst for about 2 minutes, and no longer than 3 minutes, by squeezing the base between your fingers.

3. Press a spatula on one side of the ball to press out any fingerprints, and place this side down on the tool mark.

4. Press the impression material firmly into the tool mark, and allow it to set a few minutes until it hardens.

5. Remove the impression, look at it with the magnifying glass, and then with the stereoscopic microscope, if one is available, record any identifying marks.

6. Determine which tool made the mark, and record your observations.

PART B: INDIVIDUAL CHARACTERISTICS OF TOOL MARKS

1. Obtain one of the suspect screwdrivers, and record the identifying letter on the data sheet.

2. Place a small strip of either lead or aluminum on a flat surface, and use a piece of emery paper to clean and shine the surface (only if needed). Be sure the piece of metal is flat. If it isn't, place a block of wood on it and hit the wood a few times with a hammer to flatten the metal.

3. Hold the sharpened edge of the screwdriver at an angle of 45° to the surface of the lead strip. Exert pressure and draw the blade edge of the screwdriver across the lead strip in one continuous motion. This will leave marks on the plate which are characteristic of that screwdriver and which you will compare with those on your cast. These marks are called **individual** characteristics.

4. Repeat this process a second time, alongside the first trial.

5. Turn the blade of the screwdriver over and repeat the operation to obtain two samples of the scratch marks from this side of the blade. Label this strip of lead with the letter of the screwdriver used to make the marks.

6. Do this for each of the screwdrivers. Be sure to label each mark.

7. Use a hand lens to examine the surface of both sides and edges of the screwdriver blade. A lower-power microscope can also be used.

8. Record all characteristics as class or individual, to the best of your ability. Pay particular attention to the small nicks and wear markings on the blade, as these are the most useful data for comparison with the cast.

9. Repeat the previous steps for the second and third suspect screwdrivers.

10. Be certain that all of the lead or aluminum strips are well labeled for identification.

11. Compare the marks made by the "jimmy" tool that you see in the cast with the marks you have obtained on the lead strip. Also look for nicks and other marks that may be used for comparison.

12. Based on the results of your observations, try to match the suspect tool with the tool marks left at the scene of the crime.

13. Record your result.

This exercise illustrates the difficulty of working with and comparing tool marks as physical evidence in the investigation of crime scenes. In actual laboratory practice, a follow-up of what you have just done is made with a comparison microscope. Its use requires experience and very careful observation. It requires the ability to distinguish between class and individual characteristics of the tool. While class characteristics are not going to do much in the way of relating a tool mark to a single tool, their value lies in ascertaining the type of tool used, and, in some instances, in eliminating certain suspect tools from involvement in a crime. In one year in a Scandanavian country there were 100,000 burglaries. Of these, 10,000 casts were taken and 200 led to convictions.

PART C: PLASTER OF PARIS CASTS OF FOOTPRINTS AND TIRE TREADS

Plaster of Paris (calcium sulfate, $CaSO_4$) is a favorite for making casts because it is inexpensive and readily available. It is not as easy to use correctly as you might expect because it is heavy and tends to crumble the fine structure of the print unless it is poured carefully.

1. Find either a footprint or a tire mark that you want to cast.

2. Carefully surround the impression with a metal or wood strip of not less than 2 cm in height. This will prevent the plaster from flowing beyond the impression area and will allow the rest to be built up to the desired thickness.

3. To help maintain the fine structure, spray the print with lacquer from a spray can. This will hold the particles in place while the Plaster of Paris is poured in. Do not spray directly onto the impression, as you may disturb its fine details.

4. The Plaster of Paris is poured in two steps. First, add enough plaster (7 parts) to water (4 parts) to make an initial pouring 1 cm thick. The mixture should be the consistency of pancake batter. Mix thoroughly, making sure that all the lumps are removed.

5. To prevent any disruption of the impression, the slurry should not be poured directly onto the surface. Instead, the mixture must be poured slowly onto a spoon or tongue depressor held over the impression. Cover the entire impression with approximately 1 cm of Plaster of Paris.

6. Carefully add a few small sticks (tongue depressors) or wire mesh to the surface of the plaster in order to reinforce the cast.

7. Add enough plaster to water to make a second pouring 1 cm thick.

8. Allow the plaster to harden. You can inscribe identifying information on the cast's surface while it is drying. Use straight lines for the lettering.

9. Once you are sure that the cast is firm, clean off the surface by gently brushing away any adhering soil.

10. Carefully examine the cast for any telltale identification marks such as cuts, torn-out places, or imbedded materials.

11. If it is a shoe print, make measurements and compare it with your own shoe. Estimate the shoe size using your shoe as a reference.

12. Label the cast and show it to your instructor.

13. Clean up your area.

PART D: MAKING A CAST FROM A MOLD (ADVANCED)

In part A you made a cast (negative) of a tool-mark impression. We will now use that as a mold to make another cast, but one that is a (positive) of the original impression.

1. Use either a dental-plastic, silicone-rubber, or modeling-clay cast of the impression as the mold for this part.

2. Place about a 2–3-cm diameter ball of moist modeling clay in the bottom of a casserole and flatten it out.

3. Place your impression of the tool mark into the clay and carefully press it down so that the impression is up, and there are no holes under it. This is your mold for the next step, so inspect it carefully to insure that there are no places that will prevent you from removing the casting material later on.

4. Prepare a mixture of Plaster of Paris and water (tap water is fine). Add the plaster to approximately 20 mL of water in a 150 mL beaker. Stir to remove all lumps. The consistency of the mixture should resemble pancake batter. Add water or plaster to make it that consistency.

5. If you want to have a better chance of removing the mold from the cast without breaking it, spray the mold lightly with WD-40 or some other light oil. Too much oil will run into the small indentations and ruin the fine detail.

6. Pour the plaster into or over the mold. Place a piece of wood splint (or a few toothpicks) into the plaster and press them down below the surface. This will add strength to the cast.

7. Allow it to harden. Then tip the casserole upside down and with gentle tapping, remove the cast from the mold (no swearing now).

SELECTED SOURCES FOR ADDITIONAL INFORMATION

Berx, Veerle, and De Kinder, J., "3D measurements on extrusion marks in plastic bags," *J. Forens. Sci.,* 47 (5), (2002), 976.

Bodziak, W.J., "Manufacturing processes for athletic shoe out soles and their significance in the examination of footwear impression evidence," *J. Forens. Sci.,* 31 (1), (1986), 153.

Brown, Sharon, Klein, A. and Chaikovsky, A., "Deciphering indented impressions on plastic," *J. Forens. Sci.,* 48 (4), (2003), 869.

Burd, D. Q., and Gilmore, A.E., "Individual and class characteristics of tools," *J. Forens. Sci. Soc.,* 13 (1968), 390.

Burd, D. Q., and Greene, R.S., "Toolmark examination techniques," *J. Forens. Sci. Soc.,* 2 (1957), 297.

Davis, R.J., "An intelligent approach to footwear marks and tool marks," *J. Forens. Sci. Soc.,* 21 (1981), 183.

Davis, R. J., "A systematic approach to the enhancement of footwear marks," *Can. Soc. Forensic Sci. J.,* 21 (1988), 98.

DeForest, P.R., "A review of tire imprint evidence," *J. Forens. Sci.,* 37 (2), (1992), 663.

DeGruchy, Spencer, and Rogers, T. L. "Identifying chop marks on cremated bones," *J. Forens. Sci.,* 47 (5), (2002), 933.

Flynn, G.M., "Toolmark identification," *J. Forens. Sci.,* 2 (1), (1957), 95.

Geradts, Z., Keijzer, J., and Keerewerr, I., "A new approach to automatic comparison of striation marks," *J. Forens. Sci.,* 39 (4), (1994), 974.

Giles, E., and Vallandigham, P.H., "Height estimation from foot and shoeprint length," *J. Forens. Sci.,* 36 (4), (1991), 1134.

Glattstein, B., Shor, N., Levins, N., and Zeichner, A., "pH indicators as chemical reagents for the enhancement of footwear marks," *J. Forens. Sci.*, 41 (1), (1996), 23.

Gorden, C.C., and Buikraa, J.E., "Linear models for the prediction of stature from foot and boot dimensions," *J. Forens. Sci.*, 37 (3), (1992), 727.

Gunn, N., "New methods of evaluating footprint impressions," *RCMP Gazette*, 53 (9), (1991), 1.

Hall, B.R., and Nolan, A.M., "An improved technique to enable 2-dimensional shoe sole impression evidence to be photographically recorded 'to scale'," *J. Forens. Sci.*, 39 (4), (1994), 1094.

Jay, C.B., and Grubb, M.J., "Defects in polyurethane soled athletic shoes -their importance to the shoe print examiner," *J. Forens. Sci. Soc.*, 25, (1985), 233.

Klees, G.S., "An effective material and method for casting vehicle identification numbers," *J. Forens. Sci. Soc.*, 21, (1981), 347.

Laskowski, G.E., "An improved technique for the visualization of footprint impressions in the insoles of athletic shoes," *J. For. Sci.*, 32 (4), (1987), 1075.

Laskowski, G.E., "Barefoot impressions—a preliminary study of identification characteristics and population frequency of their morphological features," *J. Forens. Sci.*, 33 (2), (1988), 378.

McGraw, A.C., "Casting—another means of identification," *J. Forens. Sci.*, 29 (4), (1984), 1212.

Mikkonen, S., and Astikainen, T., "Databased classification system for shoe sole patterns: Identification of partial footwear impression found at the scene of the crime," *J. Forens. Sci.*, 39 (5), (1994), 1227.

Music, D.J., and Bodziak, W.J., "Evaluation of the air bubbles present in polyurethane shoe out soles as applicable in footwear impression comparisons," *J. Forens. Sci.*, 33 (5), (1988), 1185.

Nichols, R. G., "Firearm and toolmark identification criteria: A review of the literature, Part II," *J. Forens. Sci.*, 48 (2), (2003), 318.

Novoselsky, Y., Glattstein, B., Volkov, N., and Zeichner, A., "Microchemical spot tests in toolmark examination," *J. Forens. Sci.*, 40 (5), (1995), 865.

Ojena, S.M., "A new silicone rubber casting material designed for forensic science application," *J. Forens. Sci.*, 29 (1), (1984), 317.

Ojena, S.M., "A new improved technique for coating impressions in snow," *J. Forens. Sci.*, 29 (1), (1984), 322.

Quatrehomme, G., Garidel, Y., Grevin, G., Liao, Z., Boublenza, A., and Ollier, A., " Facial casting as a method to help identify severely disfigured corpses," *J. Forens. Sci.*, 41 (3), (1996), 518.

Rios, F.G., and Thornton, J.I., "Reduction of specular reflectance on projectiles and toolmarks by ammonium chloride fuming," *J. Forens. Sci.*, 38 (4), (1993), 840.

Robbins, L.M., "Estimating height and weight from size of footprints," *J. Forens. Sci.*, 31 (1). (1986), 143.

Shor, Yaron, Tsach, T., Vinokurov, A., Glattstein, B., Landau, E., and Levin, N., "Lifting shoe prints using gelatin lifters and a hydraulic press," *J. Forens. Sci.*, 48 (2), (2003), 368.

Springer, E., "Toolmark examinations—a review of its development in the literature," *J. Forens. Sci.*, 40 (5), (1995), 885.

Vandiver, J.V., and Wolcott, J.H., "Identification of suitable plaster for crime-scene casting," *J. Forens. Sci. Soc.*, 23, (1978), 607.

Van Hoven, H., "A correlation between shoeprint measurement and actual sneaker size," *J. Forens. Sci.*, 30 (4), (1985), 1233.

Von Bremen, A., "The comparison of brake and accelerator pedals with marks on shoe soles," *J. Forens. Sci.*, 35 (1), (1990), 14.

Zugibe, F.T., Costello, J., and Breithaupt, M., "Identification of a killer by a definitive sneaker pattern and his beating instruments by their distinctive patterns," *J. Forens. Sci.*, 41 (2) (1996), 310.

EXPERIMENT 13   Name _____

DATA SHEET   Date _____

COMPARISON OF TOOL MARKS AND CASTING

Part A: Making a Cast of a Tool Imprint

1. Sketch any identifying marks that you see on the impression.

2. Label your cast and turn it in with this data sheet.

3. What would you do differently if you did it again?

Part B: Individual Characteristics of Tool Marks

Suspect screwdriver   _____

1. Sketch what you believe are the marks that make a comparison possible.

2. List some characteristics of the screwdrivers below.

   Class characteristics   Individual characteristics

Suspect screwdriver   _____
Class characteristics   Individual characteristics

Suspect screwdriver   _____
Class characteristics   Individual characteristics

Cast from tool mark at scene of crime

Class characteristics   Individual characteristics

Results: Which, if any, of the suspect screwdrivers match the tool marks left at the scene of the burglary?

Part C: Plaster of Paris Casts of Footprints and Tire Treads

1. Record any measurements and identifying marks of the footprint.

2. Record any measurements and identifying marks of the tire print.

3. Mark your cast(s) and turn them in with this data sheet.

Part D: Making a Second Cast from a Mold (First Cast) (Advanced)

1. Sketch any identifying marks that you see on this impression that you did not see on the first cast.

2. Label your cast and turn it in with this data sheet.

3. What would you do differently if you did it again?

Questions

1. Based upon your knowledge of the techniques used, is it possible to determine, with any degree of certainty, the class characteristics of a tool from the tool marks left at the scene of a crime?

2. What would be the greatest aid to tool mark comparisons?

3. Would drill bits leave identifying tool marks?

4. Do you believe that the sprayed-on lacquer was of any benefit?

Reproducing Bite Marks

A type of physical evidence which may be encountered in some crime situations is bite marks. These marks may be left on someone's person, as the result of an assault or sexual attack, on a discarded piece of fruit which the perpetrator was eating prior to the criminal act, or on a variety of other items or surfaces. Sometimes the pattern of these bite marks could be very useful in assisting to make an identification. If the bite marks are found on someone's skin, photography is likely the best method of preservation. If on a surface which will degrade quite quickly it may be best to make a cast of the surface, from which a mold is made as a permanent replication of the teeth pattern. If a suspect is found who has the same bite pattern it could be valuable evidence serving to place that person at the scene of the crime.

CRIME SCENE

Police are summoned to the scene of a robbery at a neighborhood grocery. The crime took place during a time when none of the persons who are employed at the place of business were present and therefore there are no eyewitnesses. The crime scene examiners, after having compared fingerprints lifted from various locations around the cash register with elimination prints from store personnel, are left with none that are legible. The robbers, in their haste or ineptitude, bumped against a display of soft drinks packaged in glass bottles. Some of the bottles were broken in the fall and the liquid spilled on the floor. One of the robbers apparently stepped in this liquid and left some visible shoe prints on the tile floor. It is not known how many criminals were involved in this robbery, but someone picked up an apple, took a bite of it and then discarded it before leaving the scene. Perhaps it was a robber. While other crime laboratory personnel are dealing with the shoe prints and other types of evidence present, it is your task, as a forensic analyst in the laboratory, to make a cast of the bite marks in the apple before dehydration and degradation of the apple flesh takes place and destroys the evidence.

EQUIPMENT

1 Electric hot plate, any model, 120 volt
1 Double boiler kettle, 2 quart size is convenient

REAGENTS

FLEXWAX 120® or a similar substance

(NOTE: FLEXWAX 120 is obtainable from AMACO INC, phone 1-800-374-1600. It melts to a clear liquid at 120°F. If maintained at that temperature it will not cause burns to human skin.)

Small soft bristle brushes   Plaster of Paris
Water   Apples

METHOD

1. Your instructor will give you a part of an apple. Being as careful as you can, take a bite of the apple without tearing it. Bite it cleanly so your teeth marks show on the remainder of the apple. (Chew the bite which you have taken thoroughly and swallow it, an exception to the rule of not eating in the lab, or deposit it in the waste basket if you do not like the taste of apples.)

2. Use a soft bristled brush to dip into the melted FLEXWAX and apply a thin coat of wax to the bite mark portion of your apple. Let it cool briefly and then apply a second coat of wax. Repeat this procedure until you have a sturdy coating of wax on your apple, covering the bite mark portion and extending around the apple for a short distance in each direction.

3. Cool the wax thoroughly. This step can be accelerated by holding the wax covered portion of your apple under cold running water over the sink.

4. This step requires some care! Remove the wax cast from the apple, being very careful not to distort the impression of the teeth marks which you have made. The apple should come out of the cast quite easily, but if not, use your spatula as a knife to carefully cut up the apple and remove it without damaging the cast.

5. Support your wax cast in such a way that you can fill it with the Plaster of Paris which you will now prepare.

6. Place about 100 mL of tap water in a 250 mL beaker. Add Plaster of Paris until you have a mixture with a medium batter consistency. Remember, when Plaster of Paris is added to water, hydration takes place and heat is produced which will cause the plaster to "set" quite rapidly. Stir your plaster and water mixture thoroughly and move rapidly through the pouring step. It is necessary to obtain fine detail in your cast in order for it to be forensically useful.

7. Pour the plaster mixture into your mold and agitate it slightly to make certain that it fills all of the impression detail. This will also help to remove air bubbles which sometimes become trapped in the plaster as it hardens.

8. Let the plaster-filled mold rest until the plaster has hardened. If your mixture was prepared properly this will not take more than fifteen minutes or so.

9. Take the mold containing the plaster cast to the kettle of melted FLEXWAX. Peel the wax from the plaster and put it back into the kettle. Be careful not to waste the wax, since it is reusable many times.

10. Compare your cast of your teeth marks with the casts of others in the class.

11. Label your cast with your name and section number, complete the data sheet and questions and be ready to hand them in for grading at the designated time. Be sure to clean up your bench area.

SELECTED SOURCES FOR ADDITIONAL INFORMATION

Bernitz, Herman, Van Heerden, W. F. P., Solheim, T., and Owen, J. H., "Technique to capture, analyze, and quantify anterior teeth rotation for application in court cases involving tooth marks," *J. Forens. Sci.,* 51 (3), (2006), 624.

Holt, J.K., "Identification of bite marks," *J. Forens. Sci. Soc.,* 20, (1980), 243.

James, Helen, and Cirillo, G., "Bite mark or bottle top?," *J. Forens. Sci.,* 49 (1), (2004), 119.

Kennedy, R. B., Pressman, I. S., Chen, S., Peterson, P. H., and Pressman, A. E., "Statistical analysis of barefoot impressions.," *J. Forens. Sci.,* 48 (1), (2003), 55.

Kennedy, Robert B., Chen, S., Pressman, I. S., Yarmashita, A. B., and Pressman, A. E., "A large scale statistical analysis of barefoot impressions," *J. Forens. Sci.,* 50 (5), (2005), 1071.

Kouble, Roland F., and Craig, G. T., "A comparison between direct and indirect methods available for human bite mark analysis," *J. Forens. Sci.,* 49 (1), (2004), 111.

McKinstry, R.E., "Resin dental casts as an aid in bite mark identification," *J. Forens. Sci.,* 40 (2), (1995), 300.

Sperber, N.D., "Lingual markings of anterior teeth as seen in human bite marks," *J. Forens. Sci.,* 35 (4), (1990), 838.

West, M.H., Barsley, R.E., Friar, J., and Seal, M.D., "The use of human skin in the fabrication of a bite mark template: two case reports," *J. Forens. Sci.,* 35 (6), (1990), 1477.

EXPERIMENT 14   Name _____

DATA SHEET   Date _____

REPRODUCING BITE MARKS

Questions

1. Identify the object upon which you found the bite marks.

2. Were the bite marks plainly visible on the object?

3. Could you see enough detail in the bite marks to allow you to make a visual comparison with someone's teeth?

4. Was greater detail in the bite marks visible in the plaster cast which you made? Explain.

5. Did you notice distinct differences between your teeth pattern and those of others in the class with whom you compared casts?

   Would these differences be specific enough to allow you to be identified by the bite pattern of your teeth, given expertise and experience in the use of this method?

6. Describe another crime situation in which this type of reproduction could be useful. (Other than comparison of bite marks.)

If you are interested in further work with FLEXWAX 120 perhaps your instructor will suggest an optional exercise which you could do.

Restoring Serial Numbers on Metals

Most items of commerce are marked in some manner by the manufacturer to identify them. As the value of the item increases, more permanent identifying marks are used. In addition, as the item increases in value, there is a need to give each item its own identifying mark.

Marking is most easily done by stamping a code or serial number on the item in question. When a serial number is stamped into a piece of wood, such as on good-quality furniture, the wood fibers are ruptured to a considerable depth below the visible stamp. If a thief sands off the serial number, it is possible in many cases to treat the surface with dilute sodium hydroxide, which will react faster with broken fibers than with unbroken ones. The serial number will then reappear to some extent, perhaps enough for identification. Trichloroethylene is used in the same way with plastics and hard rubber, and several solutions can be used with the metals. In all cases, the basis of serial-number restoration is that the molecules or crystals under the stamped number are under strain when compared with surrounding areas, so that when a reagent is applied, it will react faster with one area than the other. A great deal of patience is required, and a camera should be handy to record the results as they sometimes fade quickly. If a camera is not available, sketch the lines on a piece of paper as they appear.

Many etching solutions contain acid and metallic ions such as copper. Apparently when iron is under stress, it is more susceptible to electrochemical reaction with copper and hence will dissolve at a faster rate as compared with the surrounding areas of metal. This chemical reaction is as follows:

$$Cu^{+2} + Fe = Cu + Fe^{+2}$$

The copper deposits where the iron has dissolved, thus enhancing the color difference and is the basis for using etching agents to restore obliterated serial numbers.

Experience indicates that a trained person has a reasonably good chance to restore serial numbers on metals, a fair chance on wood and plastic, and a very poor chance on leather goods, although it can and has been done.

The basic technique is as follows:

1. Clean the surface.

2. Smooth the surface with fine emery cloth.

3. Build a dam around the area with clay if irregularly shaped; otherwise, simply swab the area.

4. Add a reagent and watch.

5. Apply a fresh reagent to the dam every 15 to 20 minutes, or swab at 2 to 3 minute intervals.

6. If nothing happens after 1 to 2 hours, change reagents.

7. Be patient and have a camera ready. You may not get a second chance.

CRIME SCENE

After much diligent detective work, the police have located the hideaway of a gang of household thieves. The thieves know something about criminalistics and have removed the serial numbers from everything: typewriters, jewelry, guns, car batteries, bicycles, etc. What is needed is to positively identify an article of this material with a list of the goods reported stolen. Your job is to see if you can restore a serial number on any one of the articles before you.

EQUIPMENT

1 Beaker, 100 mL

1 Block of wood to wrap emery cloth around

1 Camera

   Cotton swabs (like Q-tips)

1 Emery cloth

1 pr Goggles, safety

1 Medicine dropper

Unknowns, small pieces of different types of metal and wood, that have had names or numbers stamped on them are then removed with a grindstone. Do not grind or sand the numbers or letters too deeply, only until they disappear.

REAGENTS

Acetone, in a wash bottle   Modeling clay

Following are some solutions that have been found to work well on the metals listed:

Mild steel: rolled hot, with a black film of slag on it from air oxidation. Prepare a solution of 90 g of $CuCl_2$ + 120 mL of HCl + 100 mL of water.

Stainless steel: rolled cold, and therefore has a shiny appearance. Use 90 g of $CuCl_2$ + 120 mL of HCl + 100 mL of water.

Cast iron: brittle, with a definite graininess on the surface as well as the interior. Use 90 g of $CuCl_2$ + 120 mL of HCl + 100 mL of water.

Brass and copper: Use 25 g of $FeCl_3$ + 25 mL of HCl + 100 mL of water.

Aluminum: Use 25 g of $FeCl_3$ + 25 mL of HCl + 100 mL of water.

Lead: Use a 10% $AgNO_3$ solution; will turn your skin black when exposed to sunlight wherever it touches you unless washed off immediately.

Silver (jewelry): Use 32 mL of HNO_3 plus 290 mL of distilled water. This will turn your skin yellow wherever it touches you unless washed off immediately.

Tin: Use a 10% HCl solution.

METHOD

1. Carefully clean the surface (if a metal) with acetone to dissolve any grease.

2. Normally the area would be photographed. You may do it in this case if you are set up for it.

3. Place a piece of fine emery cloth around a small block of wood and polish the surface (do not use a circular motion) so that it shines and the rough grinding or filing marks disappear. This is done to remove deep scratches that would hold excess solution and to remove the oxide coating on a metal's surface.

4. Again clean the surface with acetone and be careful to avoid getting fingerprints on the surface.

5. If the plate is curved, build a small clay dam around the area to hold the reagent. Be careful to keep the area itself clean.

6. Decide what type of metal you have and get the proper reagent.

7. Pour 30 to 40 mL of the reagent into a 100 mL beaker.

8. If a clay dam is necessary, use a medicine dropper and add the reagent to the metal surface until it is covered, and observe the surface. If no clay dam is used, a cotton swab can be used to apply reagent to the surface. The swab should be moved slowly back and forth over the suspect area.

9. Watch the surface carefully. If numbers or letters begin to appear, sketch them on a piece of paper because some may appear while others disappear.

10. If nothing happens, continue swabbing the suspect area at 2- to 3-minute intervals for at least 30 minutes before quitting.

11. If a good set of numbers appears, photograph them immediately.

12. Clean up the area and turn in your plate to the instructor, along with any sketches you made of partial numbers.

SELECTED SOURCES FOR ADDITIONAL INFORMATION

Bremen, A.V., "The comparison of brake and accelerator pedals with marks on shoe soles," *J. Forens. Sci.*, 35 (1), (1990), 14.

Gorski, Z.M., German, A., and Nowak, E.S., "Examination and analysis of seat belt loading marks," *J. Forens. Sci.*, 35 (1), (1990), 69.

Hunton, R.K., and Puckett, J.T., "Restoring texts of type writer ribbons: a reliability study of the RAW-1 ribbon analysis workstation," *J. Forens. Sci.*, 39 (1), (1994), 21.

Katterwe, H., "The recovery of erased numbers in polymers," *J. Forens. Sci. Soc.*, 34 (1), (1994), 11.

Massiah, E. E., "A compilation of techniques and chemical formulae used in the restoration of obliterated markings," *Assoc. Firearm Tool Mark Examiners J.*, 8 (1976), 26.

Mongan, A.L., "Visualization of a restored serial number using scanning electron microscopy (S.E.M.)," *J. Forens. Sci.*, 41 (6), (1996), 1074.

Polk, D. E., and Giessen, B. C., "Metallurgical aspects of serial number recovery," *Assoc. Firearm Tool Mark Examiners J.*, 7, (1975), 38.

Randich, E., Fickies, T.E., Tulleners, F.A., Andresen, B.D., and Grant, P.M., "Restoration tactics for seriously corroded Cu and Cu-alloy firearms evidence," *J. Forens. Sci.*, 45 (6), (2000), 1316.

Sperry, G.R., "Platen information revealed: a technique for locating latent text on a typewriter (or printer) platens," *J. Forens. Sci.*, 39 (1), (1994), 223.

Srinivasan, G.J., and Thirvnavukkarasu, G., "Decipherment of an obliterated vehicle identification number," *J. Forens. Sci.*, 41 (1), (1996), 163.

Thirvnavukarasu, G., Hemalatha, M., and Kuppuswamy, R., "Restoration of obliterated paint registration number on vehicle.," *J. Forens. Sci.*, 47 (2) (2002), 374.

Turley, D.M., "Restoration of stamp marks on steel components by etching and magnetic techniques," *J. Forens. Sci.*, 32 (3), (1987), 640.

Thornton, J. I., and P. J. Cashman, "The mechanism of the restoration of obliterated serial numbers by acid etching," *J. Forens. Sci. Soc.*, 16, (1976), 69.

EXPERIMENT 15   **Name** _____

DATA SHEET   **Date** _____

RESTORING SERIAL NUMBERS ON METAL

1. State the type of object to be tested.

2. Name the solution used and discuss why you chose it.

3. Record what was observed, with the approximate times involved.

Restoring Bloody Shoe Prints

Processing surfaces that have been contaminated with blood presents problems in the detection of friction ridge skin impressions because the blood prints have different properties than latent print deposits which are made with sweat, fats, or oils. Blood prints on non-porous surfaces can be processed with Coomassie Brilliant Blue or Leucocrystal Violet to detect the faint deposits of friction ridge skin impressions. Coomassie Brilliant Blue and Leucocrystal Violet are dyes that stain proteins present in blood to give a blue-black or bright blue product. The reagents will not detect the normal constituents of latent fingerprints and, therefore, must be used in sequence with other techniques when blood-contaminated latent prints are examined.

Often at the scene of a violent crime there may be blood spots on the floor. If the assailant happens to walk on this blood, it gets on the soles of his/her shoes and can leave partial prints for several steps. After a few steps the visible portion of the bloody print is gone, but their still remains faint traces of the shoe print. By properly applying these dyes to the suspect area it is possible to make an invisible print visible.

The leucocrystal violet requires only one reagent while the Coomassie Blue is the least expensive method for beginners to use. This technique works very well with some pieces of evidence. While it will not provide sufficient ridge detail to identify a fingerprint, if done properly, it is possible to make shoe sole prints, that are normally invisible, visible, on hard to semi-hard surfaces such as paper, cardboard, floor tile, and wood flooring. In favorable cases they can even be made visible on carpeting.

The solutions needed for Coomassie Brilliant Blue and Leucocrystal Violet processing have an indefinite shelf life and may be re-used at the Forensic Scientist's discretion. Storage of the solutions should be in glass bottles which are labeled appropriately.

After mixing, the reagents should be tested by application of the reagent to a prepared latent print that is made with blood or a blood portion. After testing, the reagents can be stored until needed and may be tested prior to use.

ADVANTAGES

Coomassie Brilliant Blue and Leucocrystal Violet are simple, inexpensive processes that may be best for detecting faint, blood-contaminated friction ridge skin impressions on non-porous surfaces.

Leucocrystal Violet may well be the reagent of choice as it is a one-step process that fixes and stains the suspected blood stains. Leucocrystal Violet has very little background staining and should be the reagent of choice for use on any porous or semi-smooth surfaces such as walls.

DISADVANTAGES

Coomassie Brilliant Blue and Leucocrystal Violet will interfere with forensic examinations for body fluids, fibers, hairs, paint, and most other examinations. Care should be taken during the evaluation process so that the impact on other types of examinations is minimized.

Coomassie Brilliant Blue and Leucocrystal Violet will only stain traces of blood present and will not detect the friction ridge skin impressions composed of normal latent print constituents.

PART A: COOMASSIE BLUE PROCESSING

CRIME SCENE

Crime scene investigators were called to the scene of a homicide. The victim was lying in a small pool of blood. It appeared that the assailant stepped in the edge of the pool. A few visible, but smudgy prints were observed leaving the scene and the trail led over a crushed cardboard box and onto a tile floor. Your job is to attempt to develop any residual sole prints on the piece of cardboard box.

EQUIPMENT

2   Atomizer bottles, (like those for thin layer chromatography

1   Balance, ±0.01 g

2   Beakers, 1500 mL

1   Bottle, wash, 250 mL 1/4 students

1 pr   Goggles, safety

1   Graduated cylinder, 100 mL

1   Magnetic stirrer and stir bar

2   Storage bottles (clear or dark)

REAGENTS

Coomassie Brilliant Blue also known as Acid Blue 83

Glacial Acetic Acid   Methanol

Developer solution:

1. Place a 1,500 mL beaker on the magnetic stirrer.

2. Measure out 0.96 grams of Coomassie Brilliant Blue, 84 mL of glacial acetic acid, 410 mL of methanol and 410 mL of distilled water.

3. Combine the pre-measured ingredients in the beaker and stir for approximately thirty minutes or until all of the Coomassie Brilliant Blue is dissolved.

4. Decant the reagent into an appropriately-sized storage bottle or rinse bottle and store until needed.

Rinse solution:

1. Place a 1,500 mL beaker on the magnetic stirrer.

2. Measure out 100 mL of glacial acetic acid, 450 mL of methanol and 450 mL of distilled water.

3. Mix the solution for about thirty seconds and decant into an appropriately sized storage bottle or rinse bottle and store until needed.

Final bath: a water rinse. Distilled water is preferred, but tap water will work if necessary.

METHOD

1. Spray the suspect area with methanol to help fix the print.

2. Spray the fixed suspect area liberally with the Coomassie Brilliant Blue.

3. Allow the developer to remain for 30–90 seconds as needed to make the print visible.

4. Use a wash bottle, and holding the cardboard over the sink, rinse off the developer.

5. The developer and rinse may be applied again and again if necessary until the desired contrast is achieved.

6. When you are satisfied with the development, use a final rinse with distilled water to minimize background staining and improve the contrast.

7. Optional: You may photograph the developed print.

8. Compare your print with those of the suspects.

PART B: LEUCOCRYSTAL VIOLET PROCESSING

This is simpler in that it is a one step process, but the reagent is not as common.

CRIME SCENE

Refer to the crime scene in Part A. This is an alternate method to do the same detection.

EQUIPMENT

    1 Beaker, 500 mL
       Magnetic stirrer
    1 Spray or wash bottle

REAGENTS

Developing solution: Combine in a 500 mL beaker in the order indicated.
(1) S-Sulfosalicylic acid, 10 g; (2) Sodium acetate, 3.7 g; (3) Leucocrystal Violet, 1 g;
(4) Hydrogen peroxide, 3%, 500 mL

Test the reagent by preparing a series of blood prints on a non-porous surface and processing by applying the reagent. Note the development of color and intensity.

Decant the reagent into an appropriately-sized dark storage bottle or rinse bottle and store until needed.

METHOD

When making examinations for latent prints in suspected blood on surfaces, the precautions taken for serological examinations are the same as given previously for Coomassie

Blue although suspected bloodstains revealed with Leucocrystal Violet may be further examined serologically with the PCR technique.

Bloodstains that can be developed with Leucocrystal Violet can be dilute stains as the reagent seems to work well up to a dilution of 1:100.

Leucocrystal Violet uses a one-step application of the reagent onto the suspected blood-bearing surface. The reagent is used as follows:

1. The Leucocrystal reagent is used by spraying or rinsing the suspected blood-bearing surface. Any bloodstains will be colored a purplish-blue.

2. The developed impressions need to be photographed as soon as possible as exposure to light will cause background staining and possible degradation of the developed image.

NOTE: A third reagent, Amido Black, can also be used. However, it is much more involved than the previous methods, but works very well on painted surfaces. The interested investigator may refer to the literature cited below for details.

SELECTED SOURCES FOR ADDITIONAL INFORMATION

Ashe, R., Griffin, R.M.E., and Bradford, B., "The enhancement of latent footwear marks present in grease or oil residues on plastic bags," *Sci. & Just.*, 40 (3), (2000), 183.

British Home Office, Manual of Fingerprint Development Techniques, (1986)

Davis, R.J., and Keeley, A., "Feathering of footwear," *Sci. & Just.*, 40 (4), (2000), 273.

Evett, I.W., Lambert, J.A., and Buckleton, J.S., "A Bayesian approach to interpreting footwear marks in forensic casework," *Sci. & Just.*, 38 (4), (1998), 241.

FBI LFPS Research Team, Federal Bureau of Investigation LFPS Research Memo, (1990).

Fischer, J., Orange County Sheriff's Department Research Memo, (1995).

Fruchtenicht, T.L., Herzig, W.P., and Blackledge, R.D., "The discrimination of two-dimensional military boot impressions based on wear patterns," *Sci. & Just.*, 42 (2), (2002), 97.

Hoogstrate, A.J., Van Den Heuvel, H., and Huyben, E., "Ear identification based on surveillance camera images," *Sci. & Just.*, 41 (3), (2001), 167.

Napler, T.J., "Scene linking using footwear mark databases," *Sci. & Just.*, 42 (1), (2002), 39.

Shor, Y., Vinokurov, A., and Glattstein, B., "The use of an adhesive lifter and pH indicator for the removal and enhancement of shoeprints in dust," *J. Forens. Sci.*, 43 (1), (1998), 182.

Stow, K.M., "Direct lift-enhancement of blood-contaminated shoe marks by leuco malachite green-impregnated membranes," *J. Forens. Sci. Soc.*, 34 (4), (1994), 241.

Wilshire, B., and Hurley, N., "Development of two dimensional footwear impressions using magnetic flake powders," *J. Forens. Sci.*, 38 (2), (1993), 391.

EXPERIMENT 16

DATA SHEET

Name _____

Date _____

RESTORING BLOODY SHOE PRINTS

Part A: Coomassie Blue

1. Attach your developed shoe print to this data sheet.

2. Identify the suspect whose inked shoe print matches your developed bloodstain shoe print.

Part B: Leucocrystal Violet (Optional)

1. Attach your developed shoe print to this data sheet.

2. Identify the suspect whose inked shoe print matches your developed bloodstain shoe print.

Questions

1. Did this method of shoe print development provide good detail?

2. Is this an absolute or comparative analysis?

3. Do you suppose that this method could be used to develop bloody shoe prints on carpeting or upholstered surfaces? If you are interested, ask your instructor to let you try it. (You provide the scrap of carpeting).

Examination of Hair and Textile Fibers by Microscopy

Hair is a very common form of evidence in many cases of homicide, as well is in crimes of sexual assault. It also enters into many cases of burglary. Some of the points that may be proven by the use of hair as physical evidence are as follows:

1. It can link a suspect to the scene of the crime.

2. It can indicate the entrance or exit route of the criminal.

3. It can show contact with the victim.

4. It can serve to identify clothes or shoes, abandoned or denied, by the suspect.

5. It can indicate the contact of a victim in a (hit-and-run) accident with the car of the suspect.

Sometimes the contact itself is not in doubt, but the exact part of the car where the victim was hit plays an important role in the evaluation of the dynamic features of the case.

Hair is only one of many fibers that are analyzed and compared as physical evidence. Fibers from textiles and woolen materials are as important. The first part of this exercise will be concerned with hair and the second section will show you a simple technique for looking at the cross section of fibers.

Hair from any part of the body exhibits a range of characteristics, such as color, length, and diameter. Even hair from different parts of the same area, the crown, sides, and rear of the head, for example, will differ somewhat. It is, therefore, necessary for the forensic examiner to keep this in mind when collecting reference hairs and to obtain an adequate supply to compare with the suspect's hair. Usually, the collection of several dozen hairs from relevant parts of the body will suffice.

The parts of a hair that are easily seen by use of a microscope under magnification are the **medulla**, the **cortex**, and the **cuticle** as shown in Figure 17-1. Many animal hairs are easily distinguished from human hairs by the size and shape of their medullae and the patterns of their cuticle or scale structure. Synthetic fibers have no medulla or scale pattern and are therefore readily distinguishable from animal hair. Figure 17-2 shows several scale patterns.

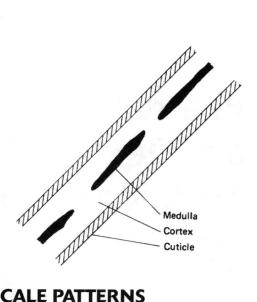

FIGURE 17–1   Structure of hair.

DEFINITION OF TERMS DESCRIBING SCALE PATTERNS

Coronal—scale structure characteristic of hairs of very fine diameter resembling a stack of paper cups. These scales are commonly encountered on small rodents and bats and only rarely in human hair.

Imbricate—overlapping scales with narrow margins. These scales are found on the hairs of humans and often of animals.

Spinous—triangular-shaped scales which frequently protrude from the hair shaft. These scales are never found in human hairs.

CRIME SCENE

Two persons are in an automobile involved in a one-car accident. Some property damage is sustained, and the car is badly damaged. This accident takes place in the evening with no witnesses present. The two persons in the automobile are only slightly bruised, neither sustaining any serious injury. Both persons do, however, suffer bumps on their heads, with some laceration of the skin and resultant bleeding. One person's head has come in contact with the windshield of the automobile, as evidenced by the windshield being cracked, a small amount of blood, and a few strands of hair stuck to the glass at the place of impact. This was on the passenger side of the automobile. Both persons are suspected of having been under the influence of alcohol, and each maintains that the other was driving the automobile at the time of the accident. The officers at the scene, in attempting to determine the identity of the driver, collected the blood and hairs from the impact point of the windshield. They have obtained sample hairs from the head of each of the two persons involved and have transferred all of these materials to a forensic laboratory.

The hair samples comprise the physical evidence that you will work with in this exercise. Be certain that you properly label your samples so that you do not lose their identity. You will find the gross samples labeled, "Person A" and "Person B," and "Scene." Attempt to identify the Scene samples with A or B. Hair should not be cleaned before it is examined. The adhering dust and impurities are sometimes of more evidential value than the hair itself.

EQUIPMENT

1 Beaker, 50 mL	1 Medicine dropper
1 Blade, razor, single edge	3 Microscope slides
24 Bottles, screw cap, 6 dram, for samples	1 Needle

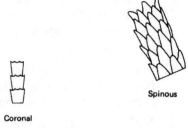

FIGURE 17–2   Scale patterns of several types of hair.

1 Compound microscope	1 Needle, dissecting
(100× is a good magnification)	1 pr Scissors
3 Cover glass	Tissue paper (Kleenex or some
1 Forceps	similar material)
1 pr Goggles, safety	

REAGENTS

Alcohol (ethyl or isopropyl)   Glycerine

Clear nail polish   Rubber cement

Canada balsam

Hair samples from various sources labeled Scene, A, and B; also animal hairs and synthetic fibers.

METHOD

PART A: GENERAL INTERNAL CHARACTERISTICS

This is a qualitative exercise in which you will try to determine characteristics of hair samples and attempt to match these hair samples with others.

1. Obtain a strand of human hair labeled **Scene** and place it on a glass microscopic slide.

2. Place a drop or two of glycerine on the hair in order to hold it in place, and put a cover slip over the hair. This is known as a **wet mount**.

3. Place the slide on the stage of the compound microscope, and adjust the magnification to 100×.

4. Locate the root end of the hair, if it has one. If the hair has been forcibly pulled out, you will see a bulb-shaped enlargement (pull out one of yours and examine it). This is the hair root, and adhering to it, you will see particles of matter composed of small pieces of flesh and tissues which surround the hair root.

5. Make a sketch of what you see in the proper place on the data sheet.

6. Scan along the length of the hair body. Note any foreign particles clinging to the hair. Is the medulla fragmental (that is, present in isolated spots), interrupted (long columns with open spaces now and then), or continuous (unbroken column)? Is it entirely absent?

7. Note the color, relative diameter, and pigment distribution of the hair. You may want to increase the magnification of your microscope to make these observations. Your instructor will explain how you can compare relative diameters of the hair samples.

8. Make a sketch of each type of medulla you observe as you examine different hair samples. At a magnification of 300× or greater, some hairs may show irregularly shaped air spaces, known as **cortical fuzi**, dispersed throughout the cortex. When present in abundant numbers, their size and distribution should be noted.

9. Examine the tip of the hair. This end can be determined by the gradual tapering of the hair. If the hair has been cut recently, you will see a square appearance at the end. Normally, hair tapers to a fine point as it grows. If hair has split ends it is normally due to artificial waving, bleaching, although repeated brushing may also produce this effect.

10. Repeat Part A for hair samples from A and B.

11. Record any differences you detect in the appearance of Scene A and B hairs on the data sheet.

12. Does A or B compare to the scene hair?

13. Repeat the previous steps for hairs obtained from known animals. Sketch the different types of medullae you observe as you examine different animal hairs.

PART B: SCALE PATTERNS

Scale patterns are of little value in human hair comparisons but can aid in distinguishing animal hairs. You will now attempt to examine the scale pattern of human and animal hairs.

1. Clean the strand of hair you intend to use by pulling it through a folded tissue moistened with alcohol to remove grease and oil from the hair surface.

2. Examine it briefly under the microscope to determine if cleaning has been effective.

   The pattern of cuticle scale is useful in determining the species origin of hair. In human hair, the scales overlap smoothly, whereas in other mammalian species they protrude in a rough, serrated form. Some examiners use a scale count per given distance to aid in making a comparison. It is difficult to examine the scales directly, so what is most often done is to prepare a cast of the scales. Proceed in the following manner.

3. Smear a glass slide with a thin layer of clear nail polish.

4. Before the clear nail polish dries, which takes place very quickly, place a strand of hair on the surface of the polish.

5. Before the polish has thoroughly dried, but after the surface becomes partially solidified, lift the strand of hair off of the slide. You should now see an imprint of the hair in the polish.

6. Place the slide on the stage of the microscope, focus, and observe the scale pattern of the hair.

7. Now try observing the scale pattern on a strand of hair placed on a slide. Which is more easily seen?

8. Record your observations on the data sheet.

9. Repeat the above, only use rubber cement and then Canada balsam.

10. Record your observations on the data sheet and tell which you like best.

11. Repeat this procedure for a hair from one of the samples obtained from an animal.

12. Make sketches of the scale patterns of the two different hairs you have used in this exercise.

PART C: HAIR COLOR

1. Try to obtain various colors of hair from other persons in the class: red, blonde, black, brown, etc.

2. Try to obtain an example of gray hair. If you are able to obtain this for examination, what do you notice that is different with respect to the other colors of hair you have examined?

3. Complete the data sheet and return all materials (cleaned) and the microscopes to the area designated by your laboratory instructor.

PART D: MAKING CROSS SECTIONS OF FIBERS (ADVANCED)

NOTE: This material was abstracted from "Practical Fiber Identification" by D. M. Hall, Auburn University Press, 1976.

Hair and fibers are not all round as they appear to the naked eye, but most have unique shapes when viewed in cross section. This characteristic can be used in many cases to aid the criminalist in the identification of a particular type of hair or fiber. Figure 17-3 shows the cross sections of several natural and synthetic fibers.

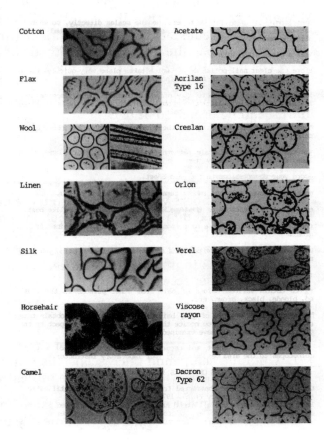

FIGURE 17–3 Cross sections of several natural and synthetic fibers. *Courtesy D.M. Hall, Practical Identification, Auburn Univ. Press, 1976.*

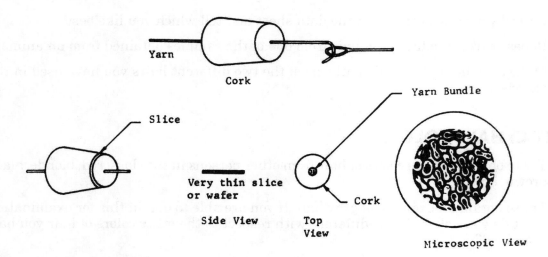

FIGURE 17-4 Razor blade and cork technique. *Courtesy D.M. Hall, Practical Identification, Auburn Univ. Press, 1976.*

For the best results, several fibers should be used, and should be thinly sliced so light from the microscope can be transmitted through them and be evenly cut so several can be in focus at the same time. Reflected light can be used, but it is not preferred. If, as in many criminal cases, only one or a few fibers are available, then they may be packed in the holder with several known fibers. There are several sectioning techniques described in the literature (see selected references), but only two of the easier methods will be described.

"The yarn or fiber bundle is threaded through a cork which holds the fibers intact through frictional forces (see Figure 17-4). A very thin slice is cut in order to have evenly cut fibers of the same length. The section is then viewed by transmitted or reflected light depending upon how thin the section was cut. This is a simple method, but cork is not always easy to cut smoothly. A way to insure an easier cut, but which requires a more complex apparatus is the metal plate method shown in Figure 17-5.

The plate, the size of a microscope slide and from 0.010 to 0.015 inches thick, is either of steel or brass. They are thin so the sections will be thin and more light can be transmitted. Many holes are drilled in the plate so several samples, including a variety of standards, can be prepared at once."

CRIME SCENE

A few clothing fibers were removed from the area around the headlight of a car suspected of being involved in a hit and run. Photography of the fender area using oblique lighting showed the outline of the weave pattern of the skirt worn by the victim, but is not as clear as desired. Another criminalist is examining a few of the fibers for color, type, and dye content. Your job is to match the cross section of the fibers on the victim's skirt with those found on the suspect vehicle.

METHOD

1. Obtain a compound microscope, place any object on a slide and adjust the illumination and focus with the 100× magnification.

2. If you are given more than a few fibers and they are together, separate them into individual fibers with a dissecting needle and lay them side by side on a clean paper.

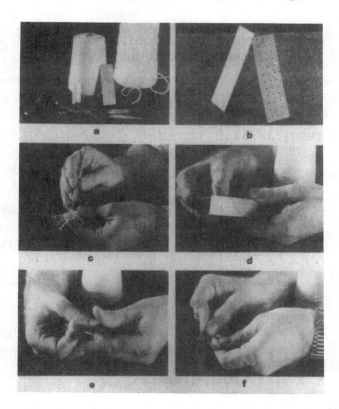

FIGURE 17–5 Metal plate for sectioning hair and fiber. *Courtesy D.M. Hall, Practical Identification, Auburn Univ. Press, 1976.*

3. Obtain a piece of small diameter wire or strong thread that will pass through the holes of the plate.

4. Pass the wire through one of the holes, loop it around a few fibers, and pass it back through the hole.

5. Draw the fibers nearly through the hole and hold them in place with your thumb. Before you do any cutting, make sure the fibers are firmly imbedded in the plate. If they are loose, repeat the process with either more fibers, or add fibers of known cross section to the sample before you pull them through.

6. Cut the fibers off on the short side with a slicing cut with a razor blade (not like a bulldozer).

7. Turn the plate over and repeat the process. Save the fibers for additional tests.

8. Place the plate under the lens, adjust the focus, and draw what you determine is the cross section of the fiber.

9. Repeat the process with the standards for comparison.

10. Clean out the holes by using a dissecting needle as a punch.

SELECTED SOURCES FOR ADDITIONAL INFORMATION

Andrasko, J., and Stocklassa, B., "Shampoo residue profiles in human head hair," *J. Forens. Sci.*, 36 (3), (1990), 569.

Barna, C.E., and Stoeffler, S.F., "A new method for cross sectioning single fibers," *J. Forens. Sci.*, 32 (3), (1987), 761.

Barnett, P.D., and Ogle, R.R., "Probabilities and human hair comparisons," *J. Forens. Sci.*, 27 (2), (1982), 272.

Benner, Bruce A., Goodpasture, J. V., Degrasse J. A., Tully, L. A., and Levin, B. C., "Characterization of surface organic components of human hair by on-line supercritical fluid extraction-gas chromatography/mass spectrometry: A feasibility study and comparison with human identification using mitochondrial DNA sequences," *J. Forens. Sci.,* 48 (3), (2003), 554.

Bresee, R.R., "Evaluation of textile fiber evidence: a review," *J. Forens. Sci.,* 32 (2), (1987), 510.

Bresee, R.R., and Annis, P.A., "Fiber transfer and the influence of fabric softener," *J. Forens. Sci.,* 36 (6), (1991), 1699.

Carroll, G.R., LaLonde, W.C., Gaudette, B.D., Hawley, S.L., and Hubert, R.S., "A computerized database for forensic textile fibers," *Can. Soc. Forens. Sci. J.,* 21, (1988), 1.

Chable, J., Roux, C., and Lennard, C., "Collection of fiber evidence using water soluble cellophane tape," *J. Forens. Sci.,* 39 (6), (1994), 1381.

Cook, R., and Norton, D., "An evolution of mounting media for use in forensic textile fibre examination," *J. Forens. Sci. Soc.,* 22, (1982), 57.

Cordiner, S.J., Stringer, P., and Wilson, P.D., "Fibre diameter and the transfer of wool fibres," *J. Forens. Sci. Soc.,* 25, (1985), 425.

Flinn, L.L., "Collection of fiber evidence using a roller device and adhesive lifts," *J. Forens. Sci.,* 37 (1), (1992), 106.

Fong, W., and Inami, S.H., "Simple, rapid, and unique hand technique for cross sectioning fibers and hair," *J. Forens. Sci.,* 33 (2), (1988), 305.

Fong, W., "Rapid microscopic identification of synthetic fibers in a single liquid mount," *J. Forens. Sci.,* 27 (2), (1982), 257.

Gaudette, B. D., "Probabilities and human pubic hair comparisons," *J. Forens. Sci.,* 21, (1976), 514.

Gaudette, B. D., "Some further thoughts on probabilities and human hair comparison," *J. Forens. Sci.,* 23, (1978), 758.

Gaudette, B. D., and Keeping, E.S. "An attempt at determining probabilities in human scalp hair comparison," *J. Forens. Sci.,* 19 (2), (1974), 599.

Gaudette, B. D., "A supplementary discussion of probabilities and human hair comparisons," *J. Forens. Sci.,* 27 (2), (1982), 279.

Goodpasture, John V., Drumheller, B. C., and Benner Jr., B. A., "Evaluation of extraction techniques for the forensic analysis of human scalp hair using gas chromatography/mass spectrometry (GC/MS)," *J. Forens. Sci.,* 48 (2), 2003, 299.

Grieve, M.C., and Kotowski, T.M., "An improved method of preparing fibre cross sections," *J. Forens. Sci. Soc.,* 26 (1), (1986), 29.

Grieve, M.C., "An index of textile fibers introduced during the last decade," *J. Forens. Sci. Soc.,* 32 (1), (1992), 35.

Grieve, M.C., and Dunlop, J., "A practical aspect of the Bayesian interpretation of fibre evidence," *J. Forens. Sci. Soc.,* 32 (2), (1992), 169.

Grieve, M.C. and Deck, S., "A new mounting medium for the forensic microscopy of textile fibres," *J. Forens. Sci. Soc.,* 35 (2), (1995), 109.

Grieve, M.C., "New man-made fibres under the microscope -Lyocell fibres and Nylon 6 block co-polymers," *Sci. & Just.,* 36 (2), (1996), 71.

Heuse, O., and Adolf, F.P., "Non-destructive identification of textile fibers by interference microscopy," *J. Forens. Sci. Soc.,* 22, (1982), 103.

Houck, M.M., and Buidowle, B., "Correlatioon of microscopic and mitrochondrial DNA hair comparisons," *J. Forens. Sci.,* 47 (5), (2002), 964.

Kempson, Ivan M., Skinner, W. M., and Kirkbride, P. K., "A method for the longitudinal sectioning of single hair samples," *J. Forens. Sci.,* 47 (4), (2002), 889.

Mann, M., "Hair transfer in sexual assault: a 6 year case study," *J. Forens. Sci.,* 35 (4), (1990), 951.

Miyake, B., and Seta, S., "Hair protein polymorphism and its application to forensic science hair comparison," *Forens. Sci. Rev. 2,* (1990), 25.

Petraco, N., "A microscopical method to aid in the identification of animal hair," *Microscope*, 35, (1987), 83.

Potsch, l., and Moeller, M.R., "On pathways for small molecules into and out of human hair fibers," *J. Forens. Sci.*, 41 (1), (1996), 121.

Prahlow, J.A., Lantz, P.E., Cox-Jones, K., Rao, P.N., and Pettenati, M.J., "Gender identification in human hair using fluorescence in situ hybridization," *J. Forens. Sci.*, 41 (6), (1996), 1035.

Robson, D., "Fibre surface imaging," *J. Forens. Sci. Soc.*, 34 (3), (1994), 187.

Roe, G.M., Cook, R., and North, C., "An evaluation of mountants for use in forensic hair examination," *J. Forens. Sci. Soc.*, 31 (1), (1991), 59.

Rosen, S. I., "Identification of primate hair," *J. Forens. Sci.*, 19 (1), (1974), 109.

Skopp, G., Potsch, L., and Aderjan, R., "Experimental investigations on hair fibers as diffusion bridges and opiates as solutes in solution," *J. Forens. Sci.*, 41 (2), (1996), 199.

Stoeffler, S.F.,"A flowchart system for the identification of common synthetic fibers by polarized light microscopy," *J. Forens. Sci.*, 41 (2), (1996), 297.

Swinton, S.F., "Construction of a roller device for the collection of hair and fiber evidence," *J. Forens. Sci.*, 44 (5), (1999), 1089.

Wickenheiser, R.A., and Hepworth, D.G., "Further evaluation of probabilities in human scalp hair comparisons," *J. Forens. Sci.*, 35 (6), (1990), 1323.

Wiggins, K.G., and Allard, J.E., "The evidential value of fabric car seats and car seat covers," *J. Forens. Sci. Soc.*, 27 (1), (1987), 93.

EXPERIMENT 17   Name _____

DATA SHEET   Date _____

EXAMINATION OF HAIR AND TEXTILE FIBERS BY MICROSCOPY

Part A: General Internal Characteristics

1. Observations from the examination of hair.

   a. Root

   b. External end

   c. Sketch of root and external end of hair

2. Note the color, relative diameter, and pigment distribution in the hairs examined.

   a. Scene

   b. Suspect A

   c. Suspect B

3. Sketch various forms of the medulla (label each with the form it represents).

4. Can you make a positive match, based on these notes, as to which person, A or B, was the driver of the automobile? Based upon your observations, which person, A or B, was the driver?

5. Sketch several animal hairs and synthetic fibers (label each).

Part B: Scale Patterns

1. Draw a scale pattern of human hair obtained with fingernail polish.

2. Draw scale patterns of the same hair obtained with rubber cement and/or Canada balsam.

3. Draw a scale pattern of hair from an animal (label).

Part C: Hair Color

1. List the similarities and differences between different colors of hair samples.
   Red

   Brown

Black

Blonde

Gray

PART D: MAKING CROSS SECTIONS OF FIBERS (ADVANCED)

1. Sketch the cross section of the sample fibers.

2. Sketch the cross sections of at least three known fibers.

3. Does the sample match any of the standards? If so, which ones?

Identification of Textile Fibers (Advanced)

NOTE: This is a lengthy experiment if all of the parts are done.

The need for the identification of textile fibers in forensic science is a common one. Many types of crimes, when investigated, yield fibers as physical evidence. Crimes in which fibers may be deposited at the scene are robbery, breaking and entering, homicide, rape, assault, and hit-and-run accidents involving a victim, to name a few.

In many cases, matching fibers from the scene with those from the clothing of a suspect or a victim is the required analysis. In others, the identification of the particular type of fiber is important. In the first instance, microscopy is the usual technique employed; in the second, chemical testing is necessary. There are numerous cases on recorded police files in which the conclusion as to guilt or innocence is based primarily on fiber analysis.

This exercise is concerned with the identification of textile fibers by chemical testing. We will not use a crime scene in this instance, as the purpose of the exercise is to investigate the proper procedure and to determine what techniques are required.

The chemical identification of fibers that will be done in this experiment consists of (1) dyeing the unknown with known stains to produce a color, (2) burning tests, and (3) solubility tests. These will be done on undyed known and unknown materials. As an optional experiment, you might want to see what you can do with a piece of dyed material and one that is a mixed fiber.

EQUIPMENT

6	Beakers, 30 mL	1	Hot plate
1	Beaker, 100 mL	1	Iron, pressing
14	Bottles, 4-oz, screw cap, sample	1	Microscope (preferably, stereoscopic)
1	Bottle, wash, 250 mL		Paper, pH
1	Cylinder, graduated, 10 mL	6	Rods, stirring, 10 cm
1 pr	Forceps	1	Test fabric
18	Glasses, watch, 10 cm	1	Thermometer, to 225° F
1 pr	Goggles, safety	2	Towels, cloth

REAGENTS

Acetic acid, 100%

Acetone, 100%

Ammonium hydroxide, 1%

Butyl carbitol, 15%

Calcium thiocyanate

Hydrogen peroxide, 3%

Monochlorobenzene

Nitric acid, concentrated

Phenol, 90%

Sodium hydrosulfite

Sodium hypochlorite, 5.25%

Sodium hypochlorite (acid)

Sodium hypochlorite (basic)

Chloroform

m-Cresol

Dimethylformamide, 55–60%

Formic acid, 90%

Hydrochloric acid, concentrated

Sodium hydroxide, 5%

Sodium hydroxide, 45%

Sulfuric acid, 60%

Sulfuric acid, 70%

TIS Formula I

TIS Formula II

Zinc chloride, 67%

The unknown samples are various types of textile fibers which have been placed in numbered containers. Try to identify the type of fiber, and report the identity along with the sample number.

METHOD

PART A: DYEING TESTS

The chemical nature of most fibers is usually sufficiently different so that when a common dye is used, each fiber type will produce a different color. Test Fabrics, Inc. (P.O. Drawer 0, 200 Blackford Avenue, Middlesex, N.J. 08846) produces several dyes that can be used to test various fabrics. Two of the more common dyes are TIS I and II. In addition, Test Fabrics make a fabric composed of 3/8 inch wide strips of 13 different fabrics placed side by side, which you can use as a reference standard. You will use these materials to learn how they function and then dye an unknown and see if you can identify it.

Test as many known fibers as time permits before determining the fiber content of the unknown fabric.

Formula I Test Fabric Identification Stain (TIS)

1. Place 20 mL of 1% TIS stain in a 30 mL beaker, and warm on a hot plate.

2. Wet the sample.

3. Heat the dye, and immerse the sample in the gently boiling solution for 3 to 5 minutes.

4. Rinse well in soft, cold water.

5. If the fabric is AATCC Multifiber Test Fabric Type I, press the sample with a warm iron to set the dye. Mount the sample.

Formula II Test Fabric Identification Stain (TIS)

1. Place 20 mL of 1% TIS stain in a beaker.

2. The test sample should be wetted and boiled off or stripped if colored. For stripping directions see Part C.

3. Bring the dye to a boil, add two drops of 10% solution of acetic acid and then add the fabric. Boil 5 minutes. Rinse at 120° F. Remove the fabric. Dry.

Cross Dyeing (Piece-Dye Method)

1. Place a piece of white union, blend, or mixture fabric in either formula I or formula II prepared dye solution, and boil 3 to 5 minutes. Rinse according to the formula-number specifications above; then press and mount the sample. Identify the fibers.

Xanthroproteic Protein Test (Wool, Silk)

1. With a stirring rod, drop 1 or 2 drops of nitric acid on the sample. (Use a slide or watch glass.) Nitric acid gives a yellow color due to the formation of xanthroproteic acid.

2. Add 1 or 2 drops of ammonium hydroxide. The color is intensified with ammonium hydroxide.

3. Note the color produced and the reactions. Only protein fibers react this way.

4. Test the protein fibers first and as many other fibers as time permits.

5. Report your fiber reactions.

Testing the Unknown

1. Repeat the foregoing tests on the unknown fabric, and make a preliminary identification.

2. Examine the fibers under a microscope to discern if multiple fiber types are present.

PART B: SOLUBILITY TESTS

1. 100% acetone (room temperature): applied to mixed fibers.
   Soluble: acetate, Arnel, Dynel, vinyon; and Verel at 104° C.

2. 100% acetic acid (boiling): acetate dissolves at room temperature.
   Soluble: acetate, Arnel, nylon (slowly).

3. m-Cresol (176–210° F): Arnel, vicose, silk, Orlon, nylon.
   Soluble: acetate, Fortisan, vinyon, Dynel lumps, Saran decomposes.

4. 90% phenol (room temperature).
   Soluble: acetate, Fortisan slowly, Arnel, Dynel, nylon; Dacron in warm phenol; vinyon and polyvinyl chloride (Rhovyl) in boiling phenol; viscose.

5. Calcium thiocyanate (hot).
   Soluble: Acrilan, Creslan, Orlon, Darvan.

6. Monochlorobenzene (boiling).
   Soluble: vinyon, Saran.

7. 5% sodium hydroxide (boiling).
   Soluble: cultivated silk, hairs, wool, Darvan.
   Partly soluble: tussah silk (wild), regenerated proteins, acetate, Arnel.

8. 45% sodium hydroxide (boiling).
   Soluble: cultivated silk, tussah silk, hairs, wool, Darvan, Arnel, acetate; Dacron in 40 minutes.
   Partly soluble: Orlon (Dynel and Saran melt).

9. 5.25% sodium hypochlorite (room temperature).
    Soluble: protein fibers, hair, silk, wool (Vicra about 50% discontinued).

10. 90% formic acid (room temperature).
    Soluble: acetate, Arnel, nylon at 100° F, Fortisan.

11. 1:1 hydrochloric acid (room temperature).
    Soluble: nylon.

12. Concentrated hydrochloric acid (room temperature): Fortisan.
    Soluble: pure silk, acetate, Arnel, nylon; cupra and viscose slowly.

13. Concentrated nitric acid (room temperature).
    Soluble: acetate, Acrilan, nylon, Arnel, vinyon, Zefran, Darvan, Creslan, Orlon.

14. 60% sulfuric acid: used mainly to separate viscose (soluble) from cotton.
    Soluble: cupra and viscose rayons, acetate, Arnel, silk and nylon.

15. 70% sulfuric acid (room temperature): Creslan.
    Soluble: cotton, linen, and all those fibers dissolving in 60% H_2SO_4.

16. 55–60% dimethylformamide (room temperature).
    Soluble: acetate, Arnel, Dacron, Darvan, nylon, vinyon, Saran, Acrilan, Orlon, Dynel, and Verel; breaks up.

17. Chloroform (room temperature).
    Soluble: Arnel, vinyon, acetate.

18. 67% zinc chloride (104–115° F)
    Soluble: cotton (not mercerized), viscose, acetate, Arnel, silk, Acrilan, Orlon, Creslan, and cupra.

PART C: STRIPPING A DYE

Many fibers contain dyes, fillers, softeners, brighteners, and antistatic agents that sometimes interfere with fabric tests and must be removed if good results are to be obtained.

Of all these fabric additives, dyes cause the most problems, so they must be removed. This is called **stripping**. The basic idea in stripping is to either reduce or oxidize the dye, causing it to lose its color.

Mild treatment is used initially, and if unsuccessful, a more rigorous treatment is applied. Most modern dyes are quite difficult to remove, as you will soon discover.

Several reagents for stripping are presented below.

1. Obtain a piece of fabric, and cut it into six small pieces about 1 cm².

2. Place a piece into each of six 30 mL beakers.

3. Add the following reagents to the beakers. Put one reagent in each beaker, and identify them so that they won't get mixed up.

Beaker 1. Two drops of 1% ammonium hydroxide and 0.5 g of sodium hydrosulfite in 10 mL of water. This is considered a neutral reduction.

Beaker 2. Add 10 mL of a solution containing 5% sodium hydrosulfite, 1% sodium hydroxide, and 15% butyl carbitol. This is a good general stripper, but will not work on cellulose acetate or animal fibers. It is a basic reducing agent.

Beaker 3. Add 10 mL of 5% acetic acid. This is an acid stripper and removes basic dyes from silk or wool.

Beaker 4. Add 10 mL of 1% ammonium hydroxide. This removes acid dyes from silk or wool and is considered a basic stripper.

Beaker 5. Add 10 mL of 0.1 N sodium hypochlorite, and adjust to pH 10–11 with sodium hydroxide. This is good for cellulose fibers and is a basic oxidizing agent.

Beaker 6. Add 10 mL of 2% sodium hypochlorite adjusted to pH 5 with acetic acid. If ClO_2 fumes begin to escape during heating, add a small amount of 3% hydrogen peroxide. This is used to strip black dyes.

4. Bring all of the solutions to a boil, and continue boiling gently until the dye is removed or it becomes obvious that no reaction is occurring.

5. Record your results on the data sheet.

6. Once the dye has been removed, proceed with the fiber identification as before.

7. What type of fiber do you have?

PART D: GENERAL IDENTIFICATION

There is no set procedure for fiber identification. The following is a suggested approach.

1. Use the burning test on fibers, yarns, and fabrics.

2. Use color tests on boiled off-white or stripped samples; including the xanthroproteic test.

3. Try fiber microscopy: longitudinal or cross sectional, or both.

4. Perform the applicable solubility tests. Use acetone first. Time, temperature, and reagent concentration are important, as well as the size of the fiber bunch, yarn, or fabric piece. Use the smallest sample possible in order to speed up the test results.

One flow chart which seems to work well is that developed by Rose Padget of Southern Illinois University and shown in Table 18-1. Obtain a piece of unknown fabric. Your job is to identify it by following this chart.

SELECTED SOURCES FOR ADDITIONAL INFORMATION

Beattie, B., Roberts, H., and Dudley, R.J., "The extraction and classification of dyes from cellulose acetate fibers," *J. Forens. Sci. Soc.*, 21, (1981), 233.

Causin, Valerio, Marega, C., Guzzini, G., and Margio, A., "The effect of exposure to the elements on the forensic characterization by infrared spectroscopy of poly(ethylene terephthalate) fibers," *J. Forens. Sci.*, 50 (4), (2005), 887.

Cheng, J., Wanogho, S.O., Watson, N.D. and Caddy, B., "The extraction and classification of dyes from cotton fibres using different solvent systems," *J. Forens. Sci. Soc.*, 31 (1), (1991), 31.

Cho, L., Reffner, J.A., Gatewood, B.M., and Wetzel, D.L., "A new method for fiber comparison using polarized infrared microspectroscopy," *J. Forens, Sci.*, 44 (2), (1999), 275.

Cho, L., Reffner, J.A., Gatewood, B.M., and Wetzel, D.L., "Forensic classification of polyester fibers by infrared dichroic ratio pattern recognition," *J. Forens. Sci.*, 44 (2), (1999), 283.

Choudry, M.Y., and Phil, M., "A novel technique for the collection and recovery of foreign fibers in forensic science caseworks," *J. Forens. Sci.*, 33 (1), (1988), 249.

Clayson, N.J., and Wiggins, K.G., Microfibers-a forensic perspective," *J. Forens. Sci.*, 42 (5), (1997), 842.

TABLE 18–1 Fiber Identification

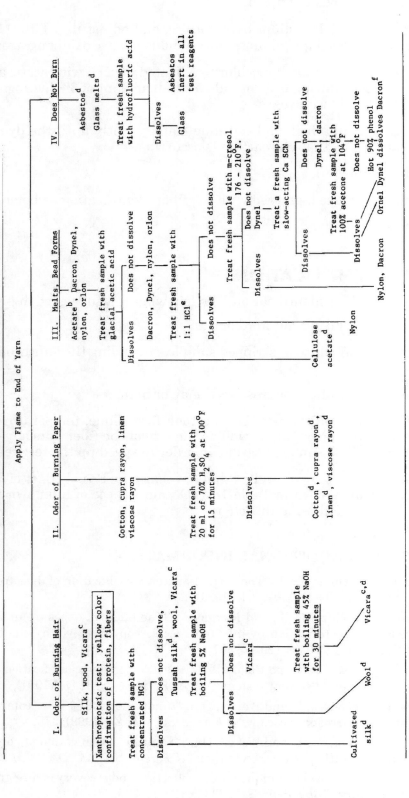

Apply Flame to End of Yarn

I. Odor of Burning Hair

Silk, wood, Vicara[c]

Xanthroproteic test: yellow color confirmation of protein, fibers

Treat fresh sample with concentrated HCl

Dissolves — Does not dissolve, Tussah silk[d], wool, Vicara[c]

Treat fresh sample with boiling 5% NaOH

Dissolves — Does not dissolve Vicara[c]

Treat fresh sample with boiling 45% NaOH for 30 minutes

Cultivated silk[d]   Wool[d]   Vicara[c,d]

II. Odor of Burning Paper

Cotton, cupra rayon, linen viscose rayon

Treat fresh sample with 20 ml of 70% H_2SO_4 at 100°F for 15 minutes

Dissolves

Cotton[d], cupra rayon[d], linen[d], viscose rayon[d]

III. Melts, Bead Forms

Acetate[b], Dacron, Dynel, nylon, orlon

Treat fresh sample with glacial acetic acid

Dissolves — Does not dissolve Dacron, Dynel, nylon, orlon

Treat fresh sample with 1:1 HCl[e]

Dissolves — Does not dissolve

Cellulose acetate[d]

Nylon

Treat fresh sample with m-cresol 176 – 210°F.

Does not dissolve Dynel

Dissolves

Treat a fresh sample with slow-acting Ca SCN

Dissolves — Does not dissolve Dynel, dacron

Treat fresh sample with 100% acetone at 104°F

Dissolves — Does not dissolve

Ornel Dynel dissolves Dacron[f]

Nylon, Dacron

Hot 90% phenol dissolves Dacron[f]

IV. Does Not Burn

Asbestos[d]
Glass melts[d]

Treat fresh sample with hydrofluoric acid

Dissolves — Glass
Asbestos inert in all test reagents

---

[a] All reagents are used at room temperature unless stated otherwise.

[b] Acetone dissolves vinyon, acetate, triacetate (15 minutes), Dynel slowly (104° – quickly), Verel.

[c] Discontinued.

[d] Identify microscopically.

[e] 1:1 HCl dissolves nylon only.

[f] Dacron decomposes in boiling 40% NaOH to form a milky suspension, which completely dissolves on diluting with H_2O to a clear solution. Acidification with HCl results in a precipitation of terephthalic acid. The acid is identified by its sublimation at about 300°C. Dacron dissolves in hot 90% phenol.

Courtesy of R. Padget, Southern Illinois University.

Fong, W., "Fiber evidence: laboratory methods and observations from casework," *J. Forens. Sci.*, 29 (1), (1984), 55.

Fong, W., "Analytical methods for developing fibers as forensic science proof: A review with comments," *J. Forens. Sci.*, 34 (2), (1989), 295.

Flynn, Kathryn, O'Leary, R. Roux, C., and Reedy, B. J., "Forensic analysis of biocomponent fibers using infrared chemical imaging," *J. Forens. Sci.*, 51 (3), (2006), 586.

Golding, G.M., and Kokot, S., "The selection of non-correlated thin layer chromatographic (TLC) solvent systems for the comparison of dyes extracted from transferred fabrics," *J. Forens, Sci.*, 34 (5), (1989), 1156.

Grieve, M.C., Dunlop, J. and Haddock, P., "An investigation of known blue, red, and black dyes used in the coloration of cotton fibres," *J. Forens. Sci.*, 35, (1990), 301.

Grieve, M.C., Dunlop, J., and Kotowski, T.M., "Bicomponent acrylic fibers, their characterization in the forensic laboratory," *J. Forens. Sci. Soc.*, 28, (1988), 179.

Grieve, M.C., "The role of fibers in forensic science examinations," *J. Forens. Sci.*, 28 (4), (1983), 877.

Grieve, M.C., and Kearns, J.A., "Preparing samples for the recording of infrared spectra from synthetic fibers," *J. Forens. Sci.*, 21 (2), (1976), 307.

Grieve, M.C., and Wiggins, K.G., "Fiber under fire: suggestions for improving their use to provide forensic evidence," *J. Forens. Sci.*, 46 (4), (2001), 835.

Grieve, M.C. and Biermann, T.W., "Wool fibres-transfer to vinyl and leather vehicle seats and some observations on their secondary transfer," *Sci. & Just.*, 37 (1), (1997), 31.

Grieve, M.C., "New manmade fibers under the microscope-Lyocell fibres and Nylon6 block copolymers," *Sci. & Just.*, 36 (2), (1996), 71.

Grieve, M.C., Bierman, T.W., and Davignon, M., "The evidential value of black cotton fibres," *Sci. & Just.*, 41 (4), (2001), 245.

Grieve, M.C., and Biermann, T., "The population of coloured textile fibres on outdoor surfaces," *Sci. & Just.*, 37 (4), (1997), 231.

Grieve, M.C., "A survey on the evidential value of fibers and on the interpretation of the findings in fibre transfer cases. Part I-fibre frequencies," *Sci. & Just.*, 40 (3), (2000), 189.

Grieve, M.C., "A survey on the evidential value of fibers and on the interpretation of the findings in fibre transfer cases. Part II-interpretation and reporting," *Sci. & Just.*, 40 (3), (2000), 201.

Grieve, M.C., "40 years of fibre examinations in forensic science," *Sci. & Just.*, 40 (2), (2000), 93.

Hartshorne, A.W., Wild, F.M., and Babb, N.L., "The discrimination of cellulose di- and tri-acetate fibres by solvent tests and melting point determination," *J. Forens. Sci. Soc.*, 31 (4), (1991), 457.

Huang, Min, Russo, R., Fookes, B. G., and Sigman, M. E., "Analysis of fiber dyes by liquid chromatography mass spectrometry (LC-MS) with electrospray ionization: Discriminating between dyes with indistinguishable UV-visible absorption spectra," *J. Forens. Sci.*, 50 (3), (2005), 526.

Koons, R.D., "Comparison of individual carpet fibers using energy dispersive x-ray fluorescence," *J. Forens. Sci.*, 41 (2), (1996), 199.

Massonnet, Genevieve, Buzzini, P., Jochem, G., Stauber, M., Coyle, T., Roux, C., Thomas, J., Leijenhorst, H., Van Zanten, Z., Wiggins, K., Russell, C., Chabli, S., and Rosengarten, A., "Evaluation of Raman spectroscopy for the analysis of colored fibers: A collaborative study," *J. Forens. Sci.*, 50 (5), (2005), 1028.

Palmer, R., "The retention and recovery of transferred fibers following the washing of recipient clothing," *J. Forens. Sci.*, 43 (3), (1998), 502.

Robertson, J., and Lloyd, A., "Observation on redistribution of textile fibers," *J. Forens. Sci. Soc.*, 24, (1984), 3.

Roux, C., and Margot, P., "The population of textile fibers on car seats," *Sci. & Just.*, 37 (1), (1997), 25.

Roux, C., and Margot, P., "An attempt to assess the relavence of textile fibres recovered from car seats," *Sci. & Just.*, 37 (4), (1997), 225.

Smalldon, K. W., "The identification of acrylic fibers by polymer composition as determined by infrared spectroscopy and physical characteristics," *J. Forens. Sci. Soc.*, 18, (1973), 69.

Stoeffler, S.F., "A flowchart system for the identification of common synthetic fibers by polarized light microscopy," *J. Forens. Sci.*, 41 (2), (1996), 297.

Suzuki, S., Suzuki, Y., Ohta, H., Sugita, R., and Marumo, Y., "Microspectrophotometric discrimination of single fibers dyed by indigo and its derivatives using ultraviolet-visible transmittance spectra," *Sci. & Just.*, 41 (2), (2001), 107.

Tungol, M., Bartick, E.G., and Montasar, A., "Analysis of single polymer fibers by FTIR: The results of case studies," *J. Forens. Sci.*, 36 (4), (1991), 1027.

Wiggins, K.G., Cook, R., and Turner, Y.J., "Dye batch variation in textile fibers," *J. Forens. Sci.*, 33 (4), (1988), 998.

Wiggins, K.G., "Forensic textile fiber examination across the USA and Europe," *J. Forens. Sci.*, 46 (6), (2001), 1303.

Wiggins, K.G., Turner, Y.J., and Miles, J.H., "The use of Foster & Freeman Fx5 Fibre Finder in forensic textile examinations," *Sci. & Just.*, 39 (1). (1999), 19.

Xu, X., Leijenhorst, H., Van den Hoven, P., De Koeijer, J.A., and Logtenberg, H., "Analysis of single textile fibers by sample-induced isotachophoresis-micellar electrokinetic capillary chromatography," *Sci. & Just.*, 41 (2), (2001), 93.

EXPERIMENT 18

DATA SHEET

Name _____

Date _____

IDENTIFICATION OF TEXTILE FIBERS

Part A: Dyeing Tests

1. Attach the fibers you test to this sheet.

Known Fibers TIS I	Unknown TIS I	Known Fibers TIS II	Unknown TIS II

2. Protein test

3. Cross dyeing with TIS I or II

4. Name the fiber content in the

    warp _____

    filling _____

Part B: Solubility Tests

Record any unusual or memorable events that occurred during the solubility tests.

1. 100% acetone

2. 100% acetic acid

3. m-Cresol

4. 90% phenol

5. Calcium thiocyanate

6. Monochlorobenzene

7. 5% sodium hydroxide

8. 45% sodium hydroxide

9. 5.25% sodium hypochlorite

10. 90% formic acid

11. 1:1 hydrochloric acid

12. Concentrated hydrochloric acid

13. Concentrated nitric acid

14. 60% sulfuric acid

15. 70% sulfuric acid

16. 55–60% dimethylformamide

17. Chloroform

18. 67% zinc chloride

Part C: Stripping a Dye

Describe the results of your stripping tests.

1. Neutral reduction

2. Boiling sodium hydrosulfite

3. Boiling acetic acid

4. Boiling 1% NH_3

5. Sodium hypochlorite (basic)

6. Sodium hypochlorite (acidic)

Part D: General Identification

1. Burning tests results

2. Solubility tests done and conclusions

3. Conclusions

A Qualitative Test for Marijuana*

Marijuana and hashish, along with some other related substances, belong to a class of substances termed *cannabis*. In recent years the smoking of marijuana by young people in North America has assumed epidemic proportions. Public interest in the long- and short-term effects of the drug has become intense. In 1964 the major active component tetrahydrocannabinol (THC), was isolated and its structure determined. The structural formula for this component, numbered by one of the accepted systems is:

Δ'-THC

One of the most commonly used qualitative tests for marijuana is the Duquenois-Negm test, developed in 1938. This test gives a purple color as a positive indication of the presence of marijuana. It lacks specificity however, in that other substances will also produce a purple color subjected to this test. The Levine modification of the Duquenois-Negm test makes it much more specific. In the modified procedure only the purple color due to marijuana is extracted into chloroform. Marijuana is one of a few substances that undergoes this color extraction, and in this form, the modified Duquenois test has been used by law enforcement agencies since 1941.

CRIME SCENE

The driver of a vehicle involved in a traffic accident is injured and transferred to a hospital. His personal possessions have been removed from his

---

*The instructor must have the proper Drug Enforcement Administration registration, as well as state and local authorization to conduct this experiment. It requires a Class I drug license to be in possession of marijuana. Permission can sometimes be obtained to have someone in the area that has a Class I license oversee this experiment. Law enforcement officers do not need a license, M.D.s and Druggists usually only have Class II licenses.

clothing, and one of these items is a pipe. The officer at the scene of the accident had detected what he thought was the odor of marijuana smoke in the injured person's car. The pipe has been sent to you in a criminalistics laboratory, where material from the inside of the pipe-bowl has been scraped away and the Duquenois-Levine test for marijuana is now to be performed.

In your supply area you will find the pipe bowl material labeled Sample A. Sample B is pipe tobacco. Sample C is made up of crushed leaves from a pipe that is known not to be marijuana. You will perform the modified Duquenois test on all three samples. This will give you a comparison between tobacco, weed, and the suspect material. Do the test carefully, as the results would be taken as evidence in a real situation.

EQUIPMENT

16	Bottles, screw cap, 2-oz	1	Microscope, stereoscopic
1	Brush, test tube	1	Mortar and pestle, small
6	Corks, to fit test tubes	1	Rack, test tube
1	Cylinder, graduated 10 mL	6	Rods, glass, stirring
1 pr	Goggles, safety	6	Tubes, test, 15 cm

REAGENTS

Chloroform

Coffee, various brands

Catnip

HCl, concentrated

Oregano

Cigars, cigarettes, pipe tobacco

Duquenois reagent, prepared as follows: 50 mL of ethanol (absolute), 1 g of vanillin, and 12 drops of acetaldehyde (fresh). Store in a refrigerator, or make fresh every 3 to 4 days.

Marijuana leaves or flowers, tobacco sample, weed leaves. (Caution: To do this test, the instructor must obtain a Class I drug license or have someone with a license agree to oversee the experiment.)

METHOD

PART A: MARIJUANA, WEEDS, AND TOBACCO

1. Obtain some of the pipe-bowl material from that suspected of being marijuana.

2. Obtain also a sample of tobacco and some leaves from the plant that is known not to be marijuana.

3. Crush the leaves, and place each sample in a separate 15-cm test tube. You will need approximately 1 cm of material in the tube.

4. Add 2 mL of the Duquenois reagent to each test tube, and stir to extract the residue.

5. Add 2 mL of concentrated hydrochloric acid, stir, and let stand for 10 minutes.

6. Note the color of the solution in each tube in the appropriate place on the data sheet.

7. Add 2 mL of chloroform to each tube, and shake to mix the contents.

8. Place the test tubes in a rack, and let stand to allow the liquids to separate. Note the color of the lower chloroform layer. A purple color is a positive test for the presence of marijuana.

9. Record all of your observations on the data sheet.

10. Wash all glassware, and return it to your supply area.

11. Complete the data sheet and the questions. Turn in these items to your laboratory instructor.

PART B: POSSIBLE COFFEE INTERFERENCES

It has been reported that some kinds of coffee give a positive test to the modified Duquenois test for marijuana. Specifically, Eight o'clock, Bokar, and Red Circle's coffee (all available from A&P) are reported to give a positive Duquenois test.

1. Collect small samples of different kinds of coffee, properly labeled and identified.

2. Perform the Duquenois test on each sample, and report your results.

3. Should you obtain a positive result for a sample, it might be well to check yourself by repeating the test.

PART C: MICROSCOPIC IDENTIFICATION

The identification of marijuana depends largely on identifying its botanical features. Marijuana is characterized by the presence of cystolithic hairs on one side of its leaf. These hairs are short in length and have a bear claw or thorn appearance. Further confirmation of marijuana's presence is made by the identification of longer nonglandular hairs on the opposite side of the leaf fragment.

In this experiment, 10 unknown vegetation mixtures have been set up in the laboratory. Place each under a stereoscopic microscope, and check each specimen for the presence or absence of marijuana. The specimens contain either marijuana, oregano, catnip, or any mixture thereof. Record your results.

SELECTED SOURCES FOR ADDITIONAL INFORMATION

Buchanan, B.E., and O'Connell, D., "Survey on cannabis resin and cannabis in unsmoked handrolled cigarettes seized in the Republic of Ireland," *Sci. & Just.*, 38 (4), (1998), 221.

Butler, W.P., "The Duquenois-Levine test for marijuana," *J. Assoc. Off. Agric. Chem.*, 45, (1962), 597.

Carew, D.P., "Microscopic, micro-chemical and T.L.C. study of marijuana grown or confiscated in Iowa," *J. Forens. Sci.*, 16 (1), (1971), 87.

Fochtman, F.W., and Winek, F.W., "A note on the Duquenois-Levine test for marijuana," *Clin. Tox.*, 4, (1971), 287.

Hauber, D.J., "Marijuana analysis with recording of botanical features present and without environmental pollutants of the Duquenois-Levine test," *J. Forens. Sci.*, 37 (6), (1992), 1656.

Hughes, R.B., and Warner, V.J., "A study of false positives in the chemical identification of marijuana," *J. Forens. Sci.*, 23 (2), (1978), 304.

Kintz, P., Cirimele, V., and Mangin, P., "Testing human hair for cannnabis II. Identification of THC-COOH by GC/MS/NCI as a unique proof," *J. Forens. Sci.*, 40 (4), (1995), 619.

Mason, A.P., and McBay, A.J., "*Cannabis*, pharmacology and interpretation of effects," *J. Forens. Sci.*, 30 (3), (1985), 615.

Moreland, J., Bugge, A., Skuterud, B., Steen, A., Wetthe, G.H., and Kieldsen, T., "Cannabinoids in blood and urine after passive inhalation of cannabis smoke," *J. Forens. Sci.*, 30 (4), (1985), 997.

Nakamura, G.R., and Thornton, J.I. "The forensic identification of marijuana: some questions and answers," *J. Pol. Sci. Admin.,* 1, (1973), 102.

Pitt, C.G., Hendrono, R., and Hsia, R.S., "The specificity of the Duquenois color test for marijuana and hashish," *J. Forens. Sci.,* 17 (3), (1972), 693.

Siniscalco Gigliano, G., "Identification of *Cannabis sativa* L. (Cannabaceae) using restriction profiles of the Internal Transcribed Spacer II (ITS2)," *Sci. & Just.,* 38 (4), (1998), 225.

Taylor, R., Lydon, J., and Anderson, J.D., "Anatomy and viability of cannabis sativa stem cuttings with and without adventitious roots," *J. Forens. Sci.,* 39 (3), (1994,) 769.

Thornton, J. I., "The identification of marijuana," *J. Forens. Sci. Soc.,* 12, (1972), 461.

Valentine, M.D., "Delta-9-tetrahydrocannabinol acetate from acetylation of cannabis oil," *Sci. & Just.,* 36 (3), (1996), 195.

EXPERIMENT 19

DATA SHEET

Name _____

Date _____

A QUALITATIVE TEST FOR MARIJUANA

Part A: Marijuana, Weeds, and Tobacco

1. Colors of solutions after the addition of HC1

   Bowl material   Tobacco   Other plants

2. Color of the chloroform layer.

   Bowl material   Tobacco   Other plants

3. Test positive or negative

   Bowl material   Tobacco   Other plants

Questions

1. Was the person involved in the traffic accident in possession of marijuana (regardless of the amount involved)?

2. Based on other tests that you have done which involve a production of color, could you make this test quantitative? If so, how might you do this?

3. Is it necessary to have a quantitative test for marijuana? Why or why not?

Part B: Possible Coffee Interferences

1. Colors of solutions after the addition of HC1

   Coffee 1   Coffee 2   Coffee 3

   Name _____ Name _____ Name _____

2. Color of the chloroform layer

   Coffee 1   Coffee 2   Coffee 3

3. Test positive or negative

   Coffee 1   Coffee 2   Coffee 3

Question

If a coffee were to give a positive test, can you envision a crime scene in which coffee would be present in a marijuana situation? Discuss.

Part C: Microscopic Identification (Advanced)

1. Sketch the "bear claw" hairs that you observed on an authentic sample of marijuana.

2. List the results of your microscopic examination of marijuana samples.

Specimen	Positive	Negative
1.		
2.		
3.		
4.		
5.		
6.		
7.		
8.		
9.		
10.		

Drug Analysis—Spot Tests for General Classes*

When a sample suspected of being a drug is brought into the laboratory, a series of spot tests are first made to see if the sample does indeed contain a drug and if so, what general class is involved. If a drug is present and a definite identification is desired, then a thin-layer separation may be performed, and this may be followed by obtaining an infrared spectrum. The spot tests most commonly done are:

1. Marquis reagent—usually turns violet in the presence of the opium alkaloids, such as heroin, morphine, and codeine. The amphetamines or "uppers," such as dextroamphetamine and methamphetamine, turn Marquis reagent red-brown.

2. Cobalt thiocyanate—for the coca alkaloids, cocaine in particular; a blue, flakey precipitate is formed.

3. p-Dimethylaminobenzaldehyde (p-DMAB)—forms a blue color with LSD.

4. Duquenois test—forms a purple color with marijuana. We will not do this test here since it was the subject of Experiment 19.

5. Dille-Koppanyi test—cobalt acetate and isopropylamine for the barbiturates. A red-violet color is formed by barbituric acid or its derivatives. These are the "downers." Examples are phenobarbital, secobarbital, amobarbital, and pentobarbital.

6. Mecke's reagent—selenous acid in sulfuric acid; an alternative test for the opium alkaloids that gives a distinct color-change sequence for each alkaloid, such as green for codeine.

EQUIPMENT

1 Beaker, 50 mL	4 Plates, spot, 3 × 4 hole
1 Beaker, 250 mL	1 Rack, dropping bottle
8 Bottles, dropping	6 Rods, glass stirring, 10 cm
1 pr Goggles, safety	3 Spatulas
1 Mortar and pestle, small	Disposable gloves

*Requires the same drug license requirements as Experiment 19. However, synthetic samples can be prepared by applying a few drops of the liquids obtained from the Gelman drug kits (600 Wagner Road, Ann Arbor, Mich.), which do not require a license. Drug standards exempt from Drug Enforcement Administration licensing requirements can also be obtained from Analabs, Inc. (North Haven, Conn.), Sigma Chemical Co., St. Louis, Mo, and Applied Science (State College, Pa).

REAGENTS

Alcoholic KOH: 5 g of KOH in 100 mL of EtOH

Chloroform

Cobalt acetate: 0.1 g of $Co(OAc)_2 \cdot 4H_2O$ in 100 mL of dry methanol, plus 0.2 mL of glacial acetic acid

Cobalt thiocyanate: 2 g/100 mL of H_2O

p-Dimethylaminobenzaldehyde: 2 g in 50 mL of 95% ethanol and 50 mL of concentrated hydrochloric acid

Drug standards: drug license possibly required

Isopropylamine: 5 mL plus 95 mL of dry methanol

Marquis reagent: 8–10 drops of 40% formaldehyde added to 10 mL of H_2SO_4; decays with age

Mecke's reagent: 0.25 g of H_2SeO_3 in 25 mL of H_2SO_4

Stannous chloride: 5 g of $SnCl_2$ in 10 mL of HCl, and dilute to 100 mL with H_2O

CRIME SCENE

Acting on the complaint of a neighbor, two police officers arrive at a house to quiet a disturbance. What they observe makes them suspect that drugs are being used. They obtain several samples from a "punch bowl" on a table in the room and bring them to the lab. Your job is to determine if these are drugs and, if so, what kind.

You will first run a set of knowns, and then do as many unknowns as your instructor gives you.

Laboratory Safety: Gloves and goggles should be worn routinely as good laboratory practice.

METHOD

Several habit-forming drugs can be obtained in doses too small to be harmful yet strong enough to give a positive test. The samples given you may be prepared from one of these drugs, or they may be actual street drugs. Your unknown may contain any of the drugs shown in Table 20-1. First, you will go through all of the tests with each drug listed; then you will do one or more unknowns.

1. Obtain one or more spot plates, and arrange them so that you can make the tests shown in Figure 20-1. You will need a total of 30 holes in a 6 by 5 arrangement.

2. Obtain knowns from your instructor such as:

   Opium alkaloids-Codeine   Coca alkaloids—Cocaine
   LSD—if available   Barbiturates—Nembutol
   Amphetamines—Dexadrine

3. Treat each as follows: Place a few crystals or drops of the drug into each of the five holes across the spot plate (holes 1 to 5: opium alkaloids; 6 to 10: coca alkaloids; 11 to 15: LSD; and so on), as shown in Figure 20-1.

4. Add a few drops of Marquis reagent to the first spot (1, 6, 11, 16, 21, 26). Stir, and observe the results. Record these on your data sheet. A violet color is considered a positive test for natural opium alkaloids.

5. To the second spot (2, 7, 12, 17, 22, 27) add 3 drops of cobalt thiocyanate, and wait a few minutes. If a blue precipitate forms, add 3 drops of $SnCl_2$ and stir. This is a test for cocaine-type drugs.

   Record your results. Cocaine will form a precipitate not soluble in $SnCl_2$, while novocaine is soluble.

TABLE 20-1 Color Tests for Screening Selected Drugs

Drug	Marquis Reagent	Cobalt Thiocyanate	Cobalt Acetate Isopropylamine	Selenious Acid	p-DMAB
Morphine	Violet				
Codeine	Red violet to blue violet			Green to blue-green	
Dihydrocodeine	Yellow to orange to brown to violet			Yellow to green	
Narcotine	Violet that fades				
Papaverine	Pink to blue			Green to blue	
Heroin	Violet				
Cocaine		Blue precipitate insoluble in $SnCl^2$			
Novocaine		Blue precipitate soluble in $SnCl^2$			
Demerol	Yellow to dark green				
Methadone	No color	Blue precipitate		Pink	
LSD					Blue
Nembutal			Red-violet		
Phenobarbital			Red-violet		
Sodium seconal			Red-violet		
D-amphetamine-SO_4	Red orange to brown				
Acetylsalicylic acid	Red in 15 minutes				

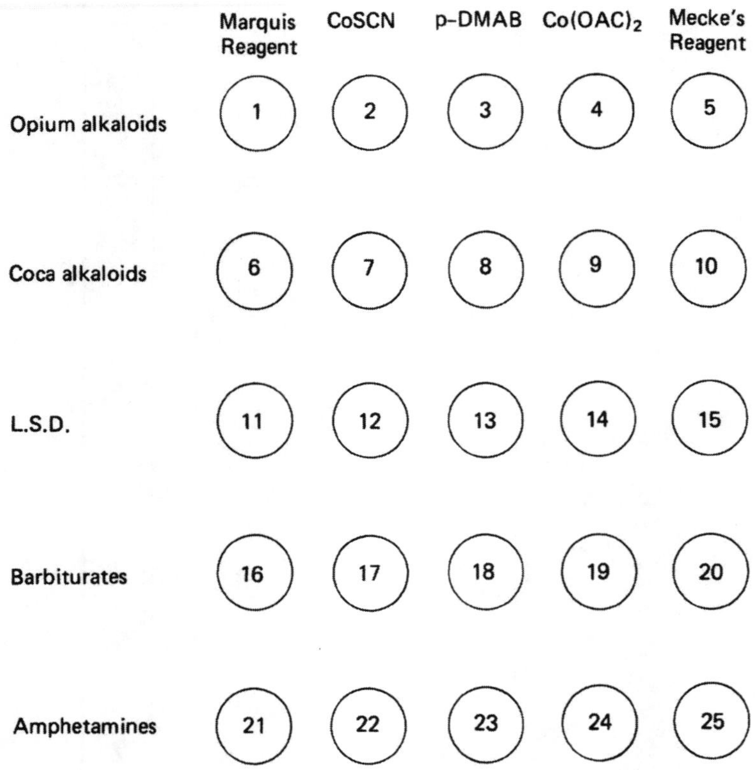

	Marquis Reagent	CoSCN	p–DMAB	Co(OAC)₂	Mecke's Reagent
Opium alkaloids	1	2	3	4	5
Coca alkaloids	6	7	8	9	10
L.S.D.	11	12	13	14	15
Barbiturates	16	17	18	19	20
Amphetamines	21	22	23	24	25

FIGURE 20–1 Spot plate arrangment for general tests.

6. To the third spot (3, 8, 13, 18, 23, 28) add 15 to 20 drops of H_2O if a solid. Add 10 drops of the p-DMAB solution. Formation of a blue color after 10 to 20 minutes is a positive test for LSD. Record your results.

7. To the fourth spot (4, 9, 14, 19, 24, 29) add 20 drops of cobalt acetate solution, and mix. Then add 10 drops of isopropylamine solution and mix. A red color is characteristic of barbiturates.

8. To the fifth spot (5, 10, 15, 20, 25, 30) add 10 drops of Mecke's reagent. This reagent produces different colors with each drug, and usually the colors change two, three, and even four times during the test. Watch carefully, and record all changes. Refer to Table 20-1.

9. Repeat all of the tests done above on your unknown drug samples. Make your decision, and record your data.

10. Clean up the equipment, and return it to its proper place.

SELECTED SOURCES FOR ADDITIONAL INFORMATION

Anastos, Nicole, McIntyre, I. M., Lynch, M. J., and Drummer, O. H., "Postmortem concentrations of citalopram," *J. Forens. Sci.,* 47 (4), (2002), 882.

Avelia, Joseph, and Lehrer, M., "Fatality due to methyl acetylene-propadiene (MAPP) inhalation," *J. Forens. Sci.,* 49 (6), (2004), 1361.

Baumgartner, W.A., Hill, V.A., and Blahd, W.H., "Hair analysis for drugs of abuse," *J. Forens. Sci.,* 34 (6), (1989), 1433.

Bravo, Dawn T., Harris, D. O., and Parsons, S. M., "Reliable, sensitive, rapid and quantitative enzyme-based assay for *Gamma*-hydroxybutyric acid (GHB)," *J. Forens. Sci.,* 49 (2), (2004), 379.

Burrows, David L., Hagardorn, A. N., Harlan, G. C., Wallen, E. D., and Ferslew, K. E., "A fatal drug interaction between oxycodone and clonazepan," *J. Forens. Sci.,* 48 (3), (2003), 683.

Caplain, Y.H., "Drug testing in urine," *J. Forens. Sci.*, 34 (6), (1989), 1417.

Couper, F.S., McIntyre, I.M., and Drummer, D.H., "Extraction of psychotropic drugs from human scalp hair," *J. Forens. Sci.*, 40 (1), (1995), 83.

Dasenbrock, Catherine O., Ciolino, L. A., Hatfield, C. L., and Jackson, D. S., "The determination of nicotine and sulfate in supermarket ground beef adulterated with Black Leaf 40," *J. Forens. Sci.,* 50 (5), (2005), 1134.

Defrancesco, James V., Witkowski, M. R., and Ciolino, L. A., "GHB free acid: 1. Solution formation studies and spectroscopic characterization by HNMR and FT-IR," *J. Forens. Sci.,* 51 (2), (2006), 321.

Elsohly, M.A., and Jones, A.B., "Morphine and codeine in biological fluids-approaches to source differentiation," *Forens. Sci. Rev.*, 1, (1989), 13.

Kalasinsky, Kathryn S., Hugel, J., and Kish, S. J., "Use of MDA (the "love drug") and methamphetamine in Toronto by unsuspecting users of Ecstasy (MDMA)," *J. Forens. Sci.,* 49 (5), (2004), 1106.

Kilmer, S.D., "The isolation and identification of lysergic acid diethylamide (LSD) from sugar cubes and a liquid substrate," *J. Forens. Sci.*, 39 (3), (1994), 860.

Kugelberg, Fredrik C., Holmgran, P., and Druid, H., "Codeine and morphine blood concentrations increase during blood loss," *J. Forens. Sci.,* 48 (3), (2003), 664.

McDermott, Sean D., and Power, J. D., "Drug smuggling using clothing impregnated with cocaine," *J. Forens. Sci.,* 50 (6), (2005), 1423.

McKibben, T., "Simple and rapid color screening tests for flunitrazepam (Rohypnol)," (Date rape drug. 3 methods, purple color) *J. Forens. Sci.*, 44 (2), (1999), 496.

Moore, C.M., "Solid phase cation exchange extraction of basic drugs from the urine of racing greyhounds," *J. Forens. Sci. Soc.,* 30 (3), (1990), 123.

Offidani, C., Carnevale, A., and Chiarotti, M., "Drugs in hair. A new extraction procedure," *Forens. Sci. Intl.,* 41, (1989), 35.

Wilson, W.L., "The identification and analysis of Canadian designer drugs," *J. Forens. Sci. Soc.*, 31 (2), (1991), 233.

Witkowski, Mark R., Ciolino, L. A., and Defrancesco, J. V., "GHB free acid: II. Isolation and spectroscopic characterization for forensic analysis," *J. Forens. Sci.,* 51 (2), (2006), 330.

Wolf, Barbara C., Lavezzi, W. A., Sullivan, L. M., Flannagan, L. M., "One hundred seventy two deaths involving the use of oxycodone in Palm Beach county," *J. Forens. Sci.,* 50 (1), (2005), 192.

EXPERIMENT 20   Name _____

DATA SHEET   Date _____

DRUG ANALYSIS—SPOT TESTS FOR GENERAL CLASSES

1. Opium alkaloid known   Observations

   Spot 1

   Spot 2

   Spot 3

   Spot 4

   Spot 5

   Test tube

2. Coca alkaloid known   Observations

   Spot 6

   Spot 7

   Spot 8

   Spot 9

   Spot 10

   Test tube

3. LSD known   Observations

    Spot 11

    Spot 12

    Spot 13

    Spot 14

    Spot 15

    Test tube

4. Barbiturate known   Observations

    Spot 16

    Spot 17

    Spot 18

    Spot 19

    Spot 20

5. Amphetamine known   Observations

    Spot 21

    Spot 22

    Spot 23

    Spot 24

    Spot 25

6. Opiate (synthetic opiums) known   Observations

    Spot 26

    Spot 27

    Spot 28

    Spot 29

    Spot 30

7. Unknown 1   Unknown 2

Identification of Drugs and Poisons by Infrared Spectroscopy (Advanced)

In previous experiments you have identified a single drug by a specific reagent, and have identified classes of drugs by spot tests. This experiment will show you one way to provide a positive identification of a drug and, if necessary, how to determine how much of the drug is present. The infrared (IR) spectrophotometer is used by the criminalist to determine drugs and organic poisons in powders, urine, and tablets. It measures the frequencies at which atoms and groups of atoms rotate and vibrate in a molecule and plots these on a sheet of paper. Each molecule has its own pattern, different from all other molecules. This pattern is called a **spectrum** (spectrum is singular, spectra is plural).

These are delicate instruments and quite expensive. They are called **instruments**, not **machines**. You mow the lawn with a **machine**, but you make measurements with an **instrument**. If you call it a machine you will treat it like a machine and it will not last very long. Treat it with tender loving care and it will reward you with accurate data and less down time.

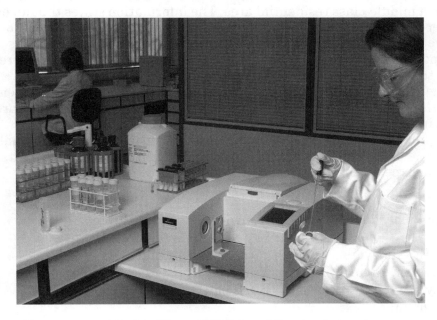

FIGURE 21–1   A Perkin-Elmer 1310 Infrared Spectrophotometer.
Courtesy of PerkinElmer Instruments, Norwalk, CT, USA.

There are many different manufacturers of IR spectrophotometers, and although they may look very different, the major components are the same and they all operate on the same principle. Therefore, if you learn the basic techniques on one instrument you will be able to work with almost any other instrument. Figure 21-1 shows a photograph of one IR instrument.

Most often in criminalistics, IR spectroscopy is used to determine what is present (qualitative analysis), not how much is there (quantitative analysis). Following the acquisition of the IR spectrum for the unknown sample, some preliminary work is done in the class determination, and then catalogs (or computer files) of reference spectra are consulted for comparison. When a match is found, a confirmatory spectrum is obtained on the same instrument for conclusive proof of identity.

The interpretation of IR spectra must be practiced before the analyst can become very certain of his conclusions. In this exercise, you are not expected to be, or to become, an expert or even a competent novice; you will, however, gain an insight into the methods and problems of an IR spectroscopist. If you are interested, you may do an extension of this exercise. You are going to be working with liquid samples. The analysis is often performed on solid and gaseous samples as well. If you wish to try solid samples yourself, see your laboratory instructor for the procedures.

Figure 21-2 shows the IR spectra of two compounds. Notice how different they are. Each drug has its own characteristic spectrum. In fact, no two pure chemical substances have exactly the same IR spectrum. For this reason an IR spectrum may be thought of as a *fingerprint* of a chemical compound.

Once we have a catalog of these spectra of known drugs and poisons, it is then a matter of matching the unknown with the standard in order to identify it. However, street drugs contain many compounds in addition to the drug, and preliminary extraction procedures are often necessary to obtain the drug in a form pure enough for identification.

CRIME SCENE

A law enforcement agency is alerted to the apparent sale of drugs by two persons living in a house located in a middle-class residential area. The information states that an excessively large number of persons have been visiting this house and that in one or two instances there have been sounds of violent arguments coming from within the house. The person requesting police investigation, a resident of the area, says that he is apprehensive of the violence that may result from these arguments.

After obtaining a search warrant, the law enforcement officials enter the premises and find only a bottle of liquid, which is not labeled. The occupants of the house profess ignorance of the identity of the bottle's contents.

The bottle of liquid has been transferred to the state forensic laboratory for analysis. You now have a sample of the contents of that bottle and will attempt to identify its contents by the following experiment.

EQUIPMENT

1 Calibration film, polystyrene	1 bx Kimwipes
1 Chart paper	1 Liquid sample cell or demountable
6 Corks, for the Erlenmeyers	cell with salt plate
6 Flasks, Erlenmeyer, 25 mL	6 Medicine droppers
1 pr Goggles, safety	1 Wash bottle
1 IR spectrophotometer	

REAGENTS

Acetone
5 liquid samples of known identity
1 liquid sample of unknown identity

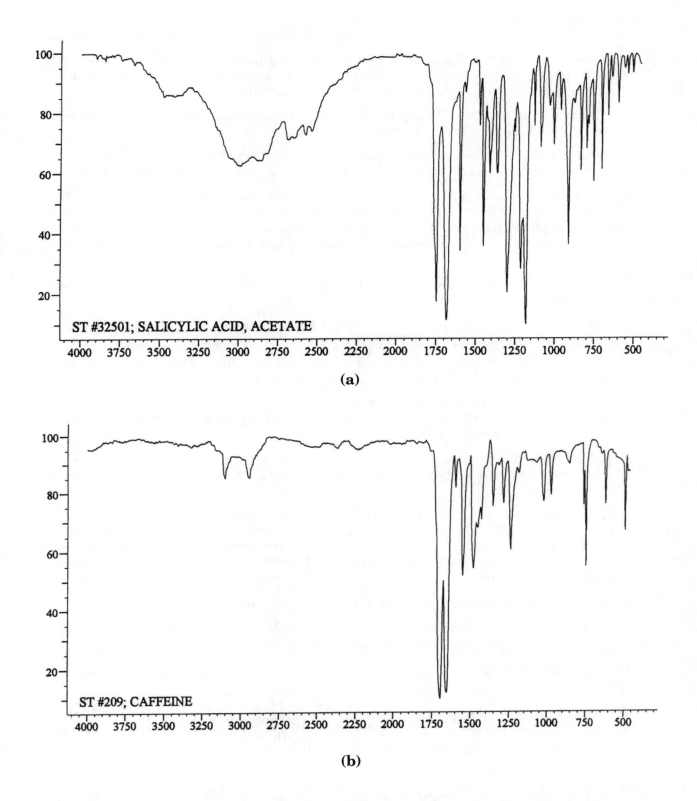

FIGURE 21–2 (a) Infrared spectrum of aspirin. (b) Infrared spectrum of caffeine. *Courtesy of ©BIO-RAD Laboratories, Sadtler Division, 1980, 1981–1999.*

METHOD

1. There are a number of manufacturers of IR spectrophotometers. Since the designs vary slightly, the operating instructions will also. See your laboratory instructor for instructions on the proper use of the instrument available to you.

2. Obtain a demountable IR sample cell from your laboratory instructor. Assemble it and fill it with your sample as follows.

3. Remove the knurled nuts from the bolts that hold the plate holder together. Steps 4 through 8 must be performed quickly. Read all of these steps before proceeding.

4. Obtain a salt plate from the desiccator. Be very careful not to touch the faces of the plates with your fingers, as the moisture on your skin will dissolve some of the salt from the plate and cause it to be cloudy and inaccurate. Place the salt plate on the cell plate with the bolts attached to it. Center the salt plate over the cell plate window.

5. Place the Teflon spacer on the salt plate and align the edges of the spacer and the salt plate.

6. Use a medicine dropper to transfer enough of your unknown sample to the cavity of the spacer to fill it completely. (This will require 3 or 4 drops.)

7. Place a second salt plate on top of the spacer and align the edges. Again be careful not to touch the faces of the salt plate with your fingers.

8. Place the metal plate with the holes in it over the bolts of the lower metal plate; replace the knurled nuts, and tighten them evenly and securely to hold the liquid sample in place between the salt plates.

9. Place the filled cell in the sample cell holder on the spectrophotometer and obtain the IR spectrum of your known liquid according to the operating instructions you were given earlier.

10. After you have obtained your spectrum, disassemble the cell and rinse both faces of each salt plate and both sides of the Teflon spacer with acetone, using a polystyrene squeeze bottle and holding the parts to be cleaned over a laboratory sink. **Never clean the salt plates with water, they will be ruined.** Take our word for it and don't try it for yourself.

11. Repeat steps 3 through 10 for each of the known compounds.

12. Look carefully at each spectrum you have just obtained, and notice that different groups of atoms produce specific bands in the spectra.

13. Repeat steps 3 through 10 for the unknown, and compare its spectrum with the spectra you have just obtained.

14. After you have finished the exercise, clean the salt plates and return them to the desiccator. Replace the desiccator cover. Turn the IR spectrophotometer off or leave it on standby, as directed by your laboratory instructor.

SELECTED SOURCES FOR ADDITIONAL INFORMATION

Cartier, J., Gueniat, O., and Cole, M.D. "Headspace analysis of solvents in cocaine and heroin samples," *Sci. & Just.*, 37 (3), (1997), 175.

Causin, Valerio, Marega, C., Guzzini, G., and Margio, A., "The effect of exposure to the elements on the forensic characterisation by infrared spectroscopy of poly(ethylene terephthalate) fibers," *J. Forens. Sci.*, 50 (4), (2005), 887.

Chappell, John S., Meyn, A. W., and Kangim K., "The extraction and infrared identification of *Gamma*-hydroxybutyric acid (GHB) from aqueous solutions," *J. Forens. Sci.,* 49 (1), (2004), 52.

Flanagan, R.J., Widdop, B., Ramsey, J.D., and Loveland, M., "Analytical toxicology," *Human Toxicology*, 7, (1988), 489.

Flynn, Katherine, O'Leary, R., Lennard, C., Roux, C., and Reedy, B. J., "Forensic application of infrared chemical imaging: Multi-layered paint chips," *J. Forens. Sci.,* 50 (4), (2005), 832.

Gorman, P. J., and Humphreys, I.J., "Identification of the major excipients in illicit tablets using infrared spectroscopy," *J. Forens. Sci. Soc.*, 15, (1975), 293.

Kohn, W.H., and Jeger, A.N., "Identification of drugs by their near infrared spectra," *J. Forens. Sci.*, 37 (1), (1992), 35.

Lopez-artiguiz, M., Camean, A., and Repetto, M., "Unequivocal identification of several common adulterants and solvents in street samples of cocaine by infrared spectroscopy," *J. Forens. Sci.*, 40 (4), (1995), 602.

Ravreby, M., and Gorski, A., "Variations in the IR spectra of heroin base," *J. Forens. Sci.*, 34 (4), (1989), 918.

Sakayanagi, Masataka, Konda, Y., Watanabe, Kunio, and Harigaya, Y., "Identification of pressure-sensitive adhesive polypropylene tape," *J. Forens. Sci.,* 48 (1), (2003), 68.

Stewart, R. D., and D. S. Erley, "Detection of toxic compounds in humans and animals by rapid infrared techniques," *J. Forens. Sci.*, 8 (1), (1963), 31.

Sugawara, Shigeru. "Comparison of near infrared light photograsphy and middle infrared light photography for deciphering obliterated writings," *J. Forens. Sci.,* 49 (6), (2004), 1349.

Suzuki, E.M., and Gresham, W.R., "Forensic science application and diffuse reflectance infrared Fourier transform spectroscopy (DRIFTS): I, principles, sampling, methods, and advantages," *J. Forens. Sci.*, 31 (3), (1986), 931.

Suzuki, E.M., and Gresham, W.R.,"Forensic science application and diffuse reflectance infrared Fourier transform spectroscopy (DRIFTS): II, direct analysis of some tablets, capsule powders, and powders," *J. Forens. Sci.*, 31(4), (1986), 1292.

Tahtouh, Mark, Kalman, J. R., Roux, C., Lennard, C., and Reedy, B. J., "The detection and enhancement of latent fingermarks using infrared chemical imaging," *J. Forens. Sci.,* 50 (1), (2005), 64.

Tweed, F.T., Cameron, R., Deak, J.S., and Rodgers, P.G., "The forensic microanalysis of paints, plastics, and other materials by an infrared diamond cell technique," *J. Forens. Sci. Soc.*, 14, (1974), 211.

Wielbo, D., and Tebbett, I.R., "The use of micro-Fourier transform infrared spectroscopy for the rapid determination of street drugs: Determination of interference by common diluents," *J. Forens. Sci. Soc.*, 33 (1), (1993), 25.

EXPERIMENT 21   Name _____

DATA SHEET   Date _____

IDENTIFICATION OF DRUGS AND POISONS
BY INFRARED SPECTROSCOPY (ADVANCED)

Fill in the data portion of your infrared spectrum chart paper. Give this spectrum, along with any others you have obtained, to your laboratory instructor.

Questions

1. What are the characteristic absorption peaks that classify your compound as to type? Below are listed some characteristic absorption ranges and peaks.

   Alkanes: $2900\text{-}3000\ cm^{-1}$

   Aromatics: $3000\text{-}3200\ cm^{-1}$ (maximum near $3030\ cm^{-1}$)

   Ethers: aliphatic, $1070\text{-}1150\ cm^{-1}$; aromatic, $1200\text{-}1270\ cm^{-1}$

   Alcohols: $3610\text{-}3640\ cm^{-1}$; also $1050\ cm^{-1}$

   Ketones: 1715 and $1100\ cm^{-1}$

   Aldehydes: 1725, 2820, and $2720\ cm^{-1}$

   Acids: 1760, 1710, and $2500\text{-}3000\ cm^{-1}$

   Esters: $1735\ cm^{-1}$; two between 1300 and $1050\ cm^{-1}$

2. What causes the length of the absorption peaks? How could you lengthen or shorten them?

3. Why would you have problems if you washed the salt plates with a liquid such as alcohol? What did you notice about the rate of evaporation of the acetone from the salt plates? How does this characteristic make the acetone useful as a washing liquid?

Salicylates in Blood by Visible Spectroscopy

Visible spectroscopy is the measurement of the amount of light absorbed by a solution, the amount absorbed being proportional to the concentration of the compounds in the solution. Each compound has a select few wavelengths that it will absorb in preference to other wavelengths. Therefore, by carefully selecting the wavelengths, it is often possible to measure the amount of one compound in the presence of several others.

Salicylates react with ferric salts (iron) to produce a violet color, which is proportional to the concentration of the salicylate. For the detection of salicylates we shall use the wavelength at 540 nm to measure light absorption. Because of the simplicity of this salicylate procedure, the assumption of salicylate poisoning may be verified within minutes, especially as severe poisoning produces a very strong and easily seen violet color with the color reagent.

There are many types of spectrophotometers on the market, one of which was shown in Figure 7-2. The light path and the major components were shown in Figure 7-3.

This experiment will consist of two parts. The first will involve developing the purple salicylate colors for several known solutions, preparing a calibration curve, and then determining an unknown. The second part will be to determine salicylate in a blood serum sample.

EQUIPMENT

1	Brush, test tube	1	Rack, test tube
1	Bulb, pipet	1	Spectrophotometer for operation
8	Cuvettes to fit the		in the visible range of the
	spectrophotometer		electromagnetic spectrum
1 pr	Goggles, safety	1	Sponge
1 bx	Kim Wipes	5	Tubes, test, 10 cm
2	Pipets, Mohr, 1.0 mL		
	and 0.1 mL		

REAGENTS

Ferric nitrate, 1%   Nitric acid, 0.07 M

Dilute ferric nitrate solution: 5 parts of 1% and 4 parts of 0.07 M HNO_3.

Nitric acid, 0.039 M: 5 parts of 0.07 M and 4 parts of distilled water.

Salicylic acid stock solution, 100 mg/dL (100 mg/100 mL): Transfer 1.16 g of sodium sali-cylate to a 1 liter flask, and dilute to 1 liter with distilled water. Add a few drops of chlo-roform as a preservative, then store the solution in a refrigerator. Discard the solution after 6 months. This solution is equivalent to 100 mg/dL of salicylic acid. The use of sal-icylic acid as a standard is not recommended.

Salicylic acid standard solution, 5.0 mg/dL: Transfer 5 mL of the salicylic acid stock solu-tion to 95 mL of water.

Solution of unknown salicylate concentration.

PART A: BASIC SPECTROPHOTOMETRY

1. Place seven spectrophotometer cuvettes in a small test tube rack.

2. Pipet the amounts of material into six cuvettes as shown in Table 22-1, and shake to mix thoroughly. Calculate the salicylate concentration in mg/dL for each known sal-icylate sample and record the value in the space provided in the data sheet at the end of this experiment. (Hint: Cuvette 2 has a salicylate concentration of 0.25 mg/dL).

3. The procedure described is written for use with the Bausch & Lomb Spectronic 20D spectro photometer shown in Experiment 7. Some minor changes may be required with other types of spectrophotometers.

4. Turn on the instrument by rotating the "power switch/zero" control clockwise until you hear a click. Allow the instrument to warm up for 15-20 minutes to stabilize the source and detector.

5. Adjust the wavelength to 540 mm.

6. Set the display mode to transmittance by pressing the "mode" control key until the LED beside "transmittance" is lit.

7. Adjust the 0% T with the "power switch/zero" control. Make sure the sample com-partment is empty and the cover is closed.

8. Insert the cuvette containing the blank all of the way down into the sample com-partment. Align the guide mark on the cuvette with the mark on the instrument. Make a mark on the side of the cuvette if ordinary test tubes are used.

9. Adjust the display to 100% T with the "transmittance/absorbance" control. Remove the cuvette from the compartment.

    NOTE: A flashing display indicates that the reading is out of range. Dilute the sam-ple.

10. Insert each of the known salicylic acid standards in the sample compartment, and obtain a transmittance reading for each sample. Record each reading on the data sheet.

11. Plot % transmittance (% T) on the vertical axis of a sheet of graph paper and the con-centration (C) in mg/dL along the horizontal axis for cuvettes 1 to 6. Draw the best straight line through these points. This is called a calibration curve.

12. Pipet 1.0 mL of the unknown solution into a cuvette, and mix with 1.0 mL of dilute ferric nitrate. Determine its absorbance.

13. From the calibration curve and the absorbance reading you obtained for the un-known, determine the concentration of salicylate in the unknown.

TABLE 22–1	Preparation of Salicylic Acid Standards			
	5.0 mg/dL Standard	Distilled H₂O	Dilute Ferric-Nitrate	0.039 M HNO₃
Cuvette 1 Blank	0.0	1.0	0.0	1.0
Cuvette 2	0.1	0.9	1.0	0.0
Cuvette 3	0.3	0.7	1.0	0.0
Cuvette 4	0.5	0.5	1.0	0.0
Cuvette 5	0.7	0.3	1.0	0.0
Cuvette 6	1.0	0.0	1.0	0.0

PART B: SALICYLATES IN BLOOD SERUM (ADVANCED)

CRIME SCENE

A police officer observes a car moving quite erratically down the highway, and, in fact, it even crosses over the centerline, forcing another vehicle off of the road. The officer stops the car, and the driver states that she had a severe headache and had taken some aspirin. She had trouble removing the safety cap on the bottle while driving, and this had caused the erratic driving. No aspirin container is found, the driver saying that she threw it away. The driver denies that she is under the influence of alcohol or other drugs. She is taken to a hospital, where she voluntarily provides blood for an alcohol and drug test. You now have a small sample of the blood serum and are to test it for the presence and/or concentration of aspirin.

METHOD

Perform this analysis in duplicate. (You will do the serum unknown and the 5.0 mg/dL standard twice each.)

1. Label two small cuvettes each for both the unknown sample and the 5.0 mg/dL standard.

2. The unknown sample cuvettes will be labeled "Test" and "Blank," and the standard sample cuvette will be labeled "Test" and "Blank."

3. Into each cuvette pipet 2.0 mL of distilled water.

TABLE 22–2	Contents of the various cuvettes
Standard (5.0 mg/dL)	**Serum unknown**
Blank	*Blank*
2.0 mL of distilled water	2.0 mL of distilled water
0.2 mL of 5.0 mg/dL standard	0.2 mL of serum
2.0 mL of 0.039 N nitric acid	2.0 mL of 0.039 N nitric acid
Test	*Test*
2.0 mL of distilled water	2.0 mL of distilled water
0.2 mL of 5.0 mg/dL standard	0.2 mL of serum
2.0 mL of dilute ferric nitrate	2.0 mL of dilute ferric nitrate

4. Into the cuvettes for the unknown sample, pipet 0.2 mL of serum.

5. Into the cuvette for the standard, pipet 0.2 mL of the 5.0 mg/dL standard.

6. Into the Blank tubes, pipet 2.0 mL of 0.039 N nitric acid.

7. Into the Test tubes, pipet 2.0 mL of dilute ferric nitrate solution.

8. Shake all tubes to mix the contents.

Table 22-2 lists each tube and its contents.

9. Let all tubes stand for 5 minutes.

10. Follow the directions given in Part A for the operation of the spectrophotometer, and obtain a reading for each cuvette. Record the absorbance reading on the data sheet.

SELECTED SOURCES FOR ADDITIONAL INFORMATION

Almog, Joseph, Cohen, Y., Azoury, M., and Hahn, T., "Cenipin-a novel fingerprint reagent with colorimetric and fluorogenic activity," *J. Forens. Sci.,* 49 (2), (2004), 255.

Berger, Charles, H., Dekneijer, J. A., Glas, W., and Madhuizen, H. T., "Color separation in forensic image processing," *J. Forens. Sci.,* 51 (1), (2006), 100.

DuBey, I.S. and Caplan, Y.H., "The storage of forensic drug specimens as dry stains: recovery and stability," *J. Forens. Sci.,* 41 (5), (1996), 845.

Exline, D. L., Wallace, C., Roux, C., Lennard, C., Nelson, M. P., and Treado, P. J., "Forensic application of chemical imaging: Latent fingerprint detection using visible absorption and luminescence," *J. Forens. Sci.,* 48 (5), (2003), 1047.

Koves, E.M., and Wells, J., "Evaluation of a photodiode array/HPLC based system for the detection and quantitation of basic drugs in postmortem blood," *J. Forens. Sci.,* 37 (1), (1992) 42.

Levinton-Shamuilov, Genyia, Cohen, Y., Azoury, M., Chaikovsky, A., and Almog, J., "Genipin, a novel fingerprint reagent with colorimetric and fluoregenic activity," *J. Forens. Sci.,* 50 (6), (2005), 1367.

Massonnet, G., and Stoecklein, W., "Identification of organic pigments in coatings: application to red automotive topcoats. Part I: Thin layer chromatography with direct visible microspectrophotometric detection," *Sci. & Just.,* 39 (2), (1999), 128.

Suzuki, S., Suzuki, Y., Ohta, H., Sugita, R., and Marumo, Y., "Microspectrophotometric discrimination of single fibers dyed by indigo and its derivatives using ultraviolet-visible transmittance spectra," *Sci. & Just.,* 41 (2), (2001), 107.

Vandenberg, Nicholas, and Van Oorschot, R. H., "The use of Polilight in the detection of seminal fluid, saliva, and bloodstains and comparison with conventional chemical-based screening tests," *J. Forens. Sci.,* 51 (2), (2006), 361.

Vogt, C., Becker, A., and Vogt, J., "Investigation of ball point pen inks by capillary electrophoresis (CE) with UV/vis absorbance and laser induced fluorescence detection and particle induced x-ray emission (PIXE)," *J. Forens. Sci.,* 44 (4), (1999), 819.

Voorhees, Jessica, Ferrance, J. P., and Landers, J. P., "Enhanced elution of sperm from cotton swabs via enzymatic digestion for rape kit analysis," *J. Forens. Sci.,* 51 (3), (2006), 574.

Whire, P.C., Etherington, A., and Catterick, T., "An HPLC method using absorbance ratioing for the identification of diamorphine in illicit heroin samples," *Forens. Sci. Intl.,* 37, (1988), 55.

William, L.A., "Drug identification using ultraviolet spectrophotometry," *J. Forens. Sci. Soc.,* 4, (1959), 492.

Wilson, Jeffrey D., Laporte, G. M., and Cantu, A. A., "Differentiation of black gel inks using optical and chemical techniques," *J. Forens. Sci.,* 49 (2), (2004), 364.

EXPERIMENT 22   Name _____

DATA SHEET   Date _____

SALICYLATES IN BLOOD BY VISIBLE SPECTROSCOPY

Part A: Basic Spectrophotometry

	Concentration of salicylate (mg/dL)	Absorbance
Cuvette 1		
Cuvette 2		
Cuvette 3		
Cuvette 4		
Cuvette 5		
Cuvette 6		

Absorbance of unknown _____

Concentration of unknown obtained from the graph: _____ mg/dL

Part B: Salicylates In Blood Serum (Advanced)

Standard 5.0 mg/mL	Absorbance	Absorbance
Standard blank		
Standard 5.0 mg/dL		
Unknown Blank		
Unknown		

Calculations

a. Use the relationship given below to determine the concentration of salicylate in the unknown sample.

$$\text{mg/mL} = \frac{\text{absorbance of unknown} - \text{absorbance of unknown blank}}{\text{absorbance of standard} - \text{absorbance of standard blank}} \times 50$$

b. Calculate each sample of the unknown separately, and average the results. If the individual results do not agree within 2 to 3 mg/dL, perform the analysis a third and a fourth time. Calculate and compare the results obtained before. Average the values which agree within 2 to 3 mg/dL of each other.

Questions

1. Do you suppose that there would normally be salicylate in human blood? Give reasons for your answer.

2. Why does the analyst perform the determination in duplicate?

3. Give an instance, other than the example cited, where this analysis might be applicable.

Salicylates in Blood by Fluorometry (Advanced)

Salicylate, in various forms, is the most widely used of all drugs. The determination of salicylate is important in toxicology. The accessibility of aspirin (acetylsalicylic acid) and oil of wintergreen (methyl salicylate) has led to frequent reported poisonings.

CRIME SCENE

A young woman confides to a friend of hers that she is very depressed. An argument with her fiancé has resulted in the breaking of their engagement. She says that she does not want to live if the problem cannot be resolved and the quarrel made up. Her friend offers what little consolation she can and says that she will call her later that evening. When she calls she cannot get an answer to the ringing of the telephone. She then calls the police, gives them the address, and someone is sent to investigate. On entering the distressed girl's apartment, the officers find her lying on the bed in a coma. An empty aspirin bottle is found in the bathroom. The girl is taken to a local hospital by ambulance and a sample of blood drawn from her arm. You now have that sample of blood to analyze for salicylate content.

This procedure measures salicylic acid and its conjugates (related compounds). Acetylsalicylic acid is readily, but incompletely, hydrolyzed to salicylic acid in the intestines and in the blood. The strongly alkaline conditions utilized in this experiment will largely complete the hydrolysis, yielding a substantially quantitative assay. The fate of oil of wintergreen is less certain. Such esters of salicylic acid are absorbed after hydrolysis. The procedure will detect ingestion with certainty, but the determined levels may be *low*.

Acetylsalicylic acid

Salicylic acid

EQUIPMENT

1 Beaker, 100 mL

2 Cuvettes to fit fluorometer

1 Cylinder, graduated, 100 mL

1 Flask, Erlenmeyer, 250 mL

1 Flask, volumetric, 10 mL

1 Flask, volumetric, 100 mL

1 Filter paper, 11.5-cm
    Whatman No. 40

1 pr Goggles, safety

1 bx Kimwipes

1 Pipet bulb

1 Pipet, Mohr, 10 mL

1 Plastic or glass funnels, 65 mm
    Stirring rods, glass

5 Test tubes, 22 × 150 mm

1 Test tube brush

1 Test tube rack

1 Turner model 110 or 111 fluorometer
    (or equivalent) fitted with the
    following items:
        Lamp No. 110-850 (standard)
        Filters: Primary, No. 110-811 (7-60)
        Secondary, No. 110-827 + No. 110-823

REAGENTS

Sodium tungstate, 10%: Dissolve 10 g of reagent-grade sodium tungstate, $Na_2WO_4.2H_2O$, in 100 mL of distilled water.

Sulfuric acid, 1/12 N: Add, cautiously, 2.3 mL of reagent-grade sulfuric acid to 1.0 L of distilled water.

Tungstic acid reagent: Mix 10 mL of the sodium tungstate solution and 80 mL of 1/12 N sulfuric acid. This reagent is stable for about 2 weeks. If it becomes turbid, it should be discarded.

Sodium hydroxide, 10 N: Carefully add 40 g of reagent-grade sodium hydroxide, NaOH, to 93 mL of water. Since this will become quite hot, solution should be effected by careful swirling in a borosilicate conical flask in a pan of cool water. After it has cooled to room temperature, it should be transferred to a polyethylene container for storage. Alternatively, 50% solutions (w/w) of reagent-grade sodium hydroxide are available. Mixing equal volumes of this and distilled water will produce, closely enough, a 10 M solution.

Salicylate stock standard, 100 mg/dL: (1 mg/dL = 1 mg/100 mL of solution). Dissolve 116.0 mg of reagent-grade sodium salicylate, $NaC_7H_5O_3$, in distilled water in a 100 mL volumetric flask, and dilute to the mark with distilled water. Invert several times to ensure thorough mixing. Store in the refrigerator.

Salicylate working standard, 10 mg/dL: Pipet 1.00 mL of the stock into a 10 mL volumetric flask, and dilute to the mark with tungstic acid reagent. Prepare fresh daily.

Blood samples containing known concentrations of salicylate ion (instructor prepared).

METHOD

NOTE: An older term, mg% (mg/100 mL of body fluid), is being replaced with mg/dL (also mg/100 mL). They both mean the same thing and the values are the same.

Salicylic acid is intensely fluorescent under alkaline conditions and can be measured directly in diluted serum or plasma, following precipitation of the proteins (see Note 1 at the end of this section). This procedure is based on the method of Saltzman (1948), wherein the proteins are precipitated with tungstic acid. Following the addition of concentrated sodium hydroxide, the sample fluorescence is compared with that of a standard solution. The values are expressed as salicylic acid in accordance with routine usage. As written, the procedure uses 0.5 mL of serum.

Blank values for plasma containing no salicylate are of the order of mg/dL and are not usually taken into account in the calculation of the results. If very low levels are of interest, it is recommended that an extraction procedure be used (see Note 1 below).

Convenient vessels for the following operations are test tubes of about 40 mL capacity (22×150 mm). Each unknown will require three such tubes. In addition, one tube each will be required for a standard and a blank. All volumes called for are measured and added by pipet.

1. To 0.5 mL of serum or plasma add 9.5 mL of tungstic acid reagent slowly and with stirring. Mix thoroughly, and let stand for 10 minutes.

2. Filter the solution through a small conical funnel (50 mm) using a medium retentive paper, such as Whatman No. 40. A clear filtrate is desirable, but a slight turbidity will not interfere.

3. Tubes are now set up for unknowns (U), standard (S), and blank (B).
   U: 5 mL of filtrate from step 2.
   S: 0.5 mL of salicylate working standard plus 4.5 mL of tungstic acid reagent.
   B: 5 mL of tungstic acid reagent.

4. Add 7 mL of 10 M sodium hydroxide to each tube and mix thoroughly.

5. The solutions are poured into 12×75 mm cuvettes and the fluorescence read any time within 30 minutes in a fluorometer which has been blanked with the dummy cuvette.

6. Clean all glassware well. The sodium hydroxide will leave a white residue, after drying, if this is not done. (Caution: Be sure to remove all of the NaOH from your hands; it can cause severe burns. Its presence is determined by a slippery feeling when the skin is rubbed.)

7. Repeat the procedure two more times, and average the results.

Calculations

Since the serum is diluted 20-fold whereas the standard is diluted only 10-fold, a factor of 2 must be used in computation (see Note 2 below). If the recommended working standard of 10 mg/dL is used, then

$$\text{mg/dL salicylate} = \frac{U - B}{S - B} \times 10 \times 2$$

Note 1: For the determination in tissues and other fluids, an extraction procedure is recommended.

Note 2: The procedure was arranged this way for convenience. The standard contains no protein, hence requires no filtration, and preparing it directly to the volume called for in Step 3 eliminates one pipetting operation. It could have been prepared from 0.25 mL of standard and 4.75 mL of tungstic acid reagent, eliminating the factor of 2 in calculation, but such volumes are difficult to read in graduated pipets.

SELECTED SOURCES FOR ADDITIONAL INFORMATION

Almog, Joseph, Cohen, Y., Azoury, M., and Hahn, T., "Cenipin-a novel fingerprint reagent with colorimetric and fluorogenic activity," *J. Forens. Sci.*, 49 (2), (2004), 255.

Almog, Joseph, Azoury, M., Elmaliah, Y., Berenstein, L., and Zaban, A., "Fingerprints third dimension: The depth and shape of fingerprints penetration into paper," *J. Forens. Sci.,* 49 (5), (2004), 981.

Gardner, Sarah, J., and Hewlett, D. F., "Optimization and initial evaluation of 1,2-indandione as a reagent for fingerprint detection," *J. Forens. Sci.,* 48 (6), (2003), 1288.

Kurata, Shoji, Hirano, H., and Nagai, M., "Determination of luminescent europium *B*-diketones used as tracers for shadowing pursuits," *J. Forens. Sci.,* 47 (4), (2002), 797.

Pretty, Iain A., Smith, P. W., Edgar, M., and Higham, S. M. "The use of quantitative light-induced fluorescence (QLF) to identify composite restorations in forensic examinations," *J. Forens. Sci.,* 47 (4), (2002), 831.

Procopio, J.R., Hernandez, P.H. and Hernandez, L.H., "Determination of lorazepam by fluorimetric and photochemical-fluorimetric methods," *Analyst,* 112, (1987), 79.

Saltzman, A., "Fluorometric method for the estimation of salicylate in blood," *J. Biol. Chem.,* 174, (1948), 399.

Turner Manual of Fluorometric Procedures, Turner Instruments Corporation.

Vogt, C., Becker, A., and Vogt, J., "Investigation of ball point pen inks by capillary electrophoresis (CE) with UV/vis absorbance and laser induced fluorescence detection and particle induced x-ray emission (PIXE)," *J. Forens. Sci.,* 44 (4), (1999), 819.

EXPERIMENT 23

Name _____

DATA SHEET

Date _____

SALICYLATES IN BLOOD BY FLUOROMETRY (ADVANCED)

1. Sample   Fluorometer dial reading:

   a. Blank (B)

   b. Standard (S)

   c. Unknown (   )

   d. Unknown (   )

   e. Unknown (   )

2. Calculation

$$\text{mg/dL salicylate} = \frac{U - B}{S - B} \times 10 \times 2$$

Calculate each sample of your unknown separately. Then average the three values for your unknown if they all agree closely. If one value for the unknown is very different from the other two (>20%), do not use that value and average the other two.

Unknown sample   mg/dL salicylate

c.

d.

e.

Average mg/dL salicylate in unknown = _____ mg/dL?

3. Do you suppose that there would normally be salicylate in human blood?

4. What precautions do you suppose one must observe when filtering the solutions in step 2 of the analysis?

5. Give an instance, other than the example cited, where fluorometric analysis might be applicable?

Quinine in Urine by Fluorometry (Advanced)

Fluorescence spectroscopy is an outgrowth of the observation that some materials will fluoresce or emit light when they are exposed to ultraviolet radiation. A characteristic property of any fluorescent compound is that it always absorbs and emits radiation at specific wavelengths. A fluorometer is an instrument designed to expose compounds to selected wavelengths of ultraviolet radiation and, at the same time, to measure the wavelengths of visible radiation they emit. Often, by utilizing a fluorometer, it is possible to detect and identify a fluorescing material that may be mixed in with other substances.

Quinine is a common adulterant of illicit heroin drug preparations. Hence, the finding of quinine in urine or blood is taken as an indication that heroin was used. If morphine is present as well, this assumption becomes very reasonable. Quinine may, however, be found in over-the-counter medications and in tonic water, and these may also be the cause of a positive test.

CRIME SCENE

A driver is stopped by a police officer for speeding and operating his vehicle in an erratic manner. The driver fails to respond properly to the balance and coordination tests administered by the arresting officer. Upon further questioning, the driver denies being under the influence of alcohol and agrees to take a breath test in a nearby police station. Within 30 minutes the suspect is driven to the station where the test is administered. The breath test results in a zero reading. However, the subject is observed to be sweating and drowsy. A urine specimen is requested and received from the driver for drug analysis. A short time later, a search of the driver's vehicle uncovers a syringe and other paraphernalia associated with the use of heroin. You now have the urine specimen, and as a preliminary test for the presence of heroin, you will analyze the specimen for quinine.

Quinine can be extracted out of a basic solution of urine with an organic solvent. Reextraction of the quinine into dilute acid produces a solution whose fluorescence spectrum can be used to identify the presence of quinine.

EQUIPMENT

A spectrofluorometer is set up at an excitation wavelength of 350 nm to record an emission spectrum at 445 nm. Since there are different models of fluorometers commercially available, your instructor will demonstrate the operation of the particular one being used in your laboratory. In 0.05 M sulfuric acid, quinine fluoresces at approximately 445 nm.

1	Bulb, for disposable pipets	1 pr	Goggles, safety
1	Bulb, pipet	1	Paper, pH
2	Cuvettes to fit the fluorometer	1	Pipet, Mohr, 5 mL
2	Cylinders, graduated 10 mL	3	Pipets, Pasteur
1	Cup, urine (get from hospital)	1	Rack, funnel
1	Flask, volumetric, 100 mL	1	Rack, test tube
2	Flasks, volumetric, 1 L	1	Stand, ring
5	Funnels, separatory, 125 mL		

REAGENTS

Chloroform

Potassium hydroxide, saturated aqueous solution

Quinine sulfate stock Solution: Dissolve 100 mg of quinine sulfate in 1 liter of distilled water.

Quinine sulfate reference solution: Dilute 1 mL of the quinine sulfate stock solution to 100 mL with distilled water.

Sulfuric acid, 0.05 M: Dilute 2.8 mL of concentrated sulfuric acid to 1 liter with distilled water.

Urine sample containing quinine (instructor prepared)

METHOD

1. Add a drop of saturated potassium hydroxide to 5.0 mL of urine. Test the specimen for alkalinity with pH paper. Add more potassium hydroxide, if necessary, until the pH is greater than 7. In the same manner, process 5.0 mL of quinine reference solution and 5.0 mL of water for a reagent blank.

2. Place the urine specimen in a separatory funnel, and extract with 10 mL of chloroform. Shake the funnel for at least 1 minute. Allow the solvent and aqueous phases to separate completely.

3. Carefully transfer the chloroform layer to a clean separatory funnel and re-extract the solvent with 6 mL of 0.1 N (0.05M) sulfuric acid.

4. Transfer the upper (aqueous) layer to a cuvette by means of a Pasteur Pipet and place the cuvette in the fluorometer.

5. To determine if quinine is present, excite the sample at 350 nm, and read the fluorescence at 445 nm.

6. Repeat the procedure for the quinine reference solution and the water blank.

   The fluorometer can also be used to measure the concentration of quinine in urine. This is done by comparing the intensity of the quinine fluorescence in the urine extract to the fluorescence of a quinine standard. These values were obtained in step 6.

Calculations

The concentration of the quinine sulfate reference solution is 0.1 mg/100 mL, or 0.1 mg/dL. Hence, the concentration of quinine in urine is found by applying the following equation:

$$\text{mg/dL quinine} = \frac{\text{fluorescence of urine extract} - \text{water blank}}{\text{fluorescence of quinine reference solution} - \text{water blank}} \times 0.1$$

SELECTED SOURCES FOR ADDITIONAL INFORMATION

Colbert, D.L., Sidki, A.M., Gallacher, G., and Landon, J., "Fluoroimmunoassay for cannabinoids in urine," *Analyst*, 112, (1987) 1483.

Goodpaster, J.V., Howerton, S.B., and McGuffin, V.L., "Forensic analysis of commercial petroleum products using selective fluorescence quenching," *J. Forens. Sci.*, 46 (6), (2001), 1358.

Kurata, S., Hirano, H., and Nagai, M., "Development of fluorescent markers using polycyclic aromatic hydrocarbons with vaseline," *J. Forens. Sci.*, 47 (2), (2002), 244.

Sunshine, I., *Methodology for Analytical Toxicology*. Cleveland, Ohio: CRC Press, Inc., 1975.

Vogt, C., Becker, A., and Vogt, J., "Investigation of ball point pen inks by capillary electrophoresis (CE) with UV/vis absorbance and laser induced fluorescence detection and particle induced x-ray emission (PIXE)," *J. Forens. Sci.*, 44 (4), (1999), 819.

EXPERIMENT 24

DATA SHEET

Name _____

Date _____

QUININE IN URINE BY FLUOROMETRY (ADVANCED)

1. Sample

   Blank

   Reference

   Unknown

   Fluorometer scale reading:

2. Calculation for unknown sample

   mg/dL quinine sulfate in urine = _____ mg/dL

Breath Alcohol by the Breathalyzer and Intoxilyzer

Each year thousands of motorists must be tested to determine whether or not they are operating a vehicle under the influence of alcohol. The most accurate method is to use a gas-liquid chromatograph and measure the alcohol directly in the blood. However, there is often a problem with violating a person's rights because a blood sample must be taken which requires penetrating the skin. A more popular way is to collect some breath from the suspect and determine its alcohol content. Two of the most convenient and popular procedures for administering such a test is the Breathalyzer and the Intoxilyzer. Basically, both take advantage of the fact that the ratio of alcohol in blood to alcohol in alveoli air (deep lung breath) is approximately 2100:1. The Breathalyzer is designed to capture alveolar breath and measure it for alcohol content by reacting the alcohol with potassium dichromate solution to produce a blue solution, which is then measured by an attached visible range spectrophotometer. The Intoxilyzer requires no chemical reaction, measuring the vibrational frequencies of the CH_2 and CH_3 groups in ethanol by infrared radiation.

PART A: THE BREATHALYZER

Figure 25-1 is a photograph of the Breathalyzer Model 900-A. Figure 25-2 shows a schematic diagram of the important components of this instrument.

FIGURE 25–1 Breathalyzer model 900-A. *Courtesy Draeger Safety, Inc., Breathalyzer Division.*

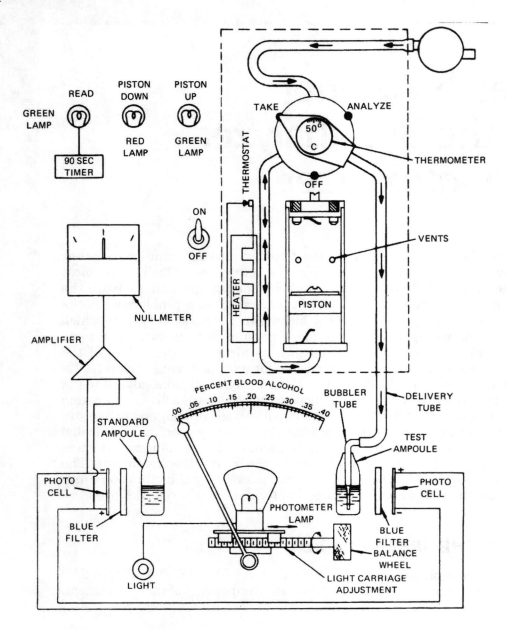

FIGURE 25–2   Schematic diagram of a breathalyzer. *Courtesy Draeger Safety, Inc., Breathalyzer Division.*

The operation of the Breathalyzer can be described in three steps.

1. A sample of deep lung breath (alveolar breath) is collected. The subject is asked to blow into a tube. The breath raises a piston to the top of its stroke above two vent holes. When the subject stops blowing, the piston settles to a predetermined position, trapping the last portion of breath, and covers the vent holes. The amount of breath captured is 56.5 mL.

2. The captured breath sample is passed into a test ampoule which consists of potassium dichromate, water, and sulfuric acid. After the breath sample has bubbled into the test ampoule, 90 seconds are allowed to complete the oxidation of any alcohol that may have been in the breath sample. The following chemical equation depicts the chemical reaction taking place in the ampoule:

$$2K_2Cr_2O_7 + 3C_2H_5OH + 8H_2SO_4 \rightarrow 2Cr_2(SO_4)_3 + 2K_2SO_4 + 3CH_3COOH + 11H_2O$$

| potassium dichromate + (orange) | ethyl alcohol + | sulfuric acid $\rightarrow$ | chromium sulfate + (green) | potassium sulfate + | acetic acid + | water |

The unused orange solution mixes with the green solution to form a blue solution.

3. The amount of potassium dichromate required to oxidize the alcohol is measured. This is done using a balanced electrical circuit with two photoelectric cells—one mounted behind the test ampoule, the other mounted behind a standard ampoule. A light source is located on a movable rack between both ampoules. Before the subject's breath enters the test ampoule, the light source is positioned between the two ampoules so that the same amount of light passes through both ampoules. When this position is reached, the instrument's null meter reads zero. After the subject's breath reacts with the contents of the test ampoule, the light source will be moved until the null meter returns to zero reading. The distance the light bulb moved is indicated on another dial, which is calibrated in figures that read directly in blood alcohol percentage.

CRIME SCENE

A man driving a motor vehicle in a reckless fashion is stopped by an officer who suspects him of driving under the influence of alcohol. After failing the balance and coordination tests, the driver is administered a Breathalyzer test, which he fails. A number of weeks later, the driver enters a plea of not guilty in court. His defense is that the Breathalyzer gave an abnormally high reading because he had earlier used an alcohol-containing mouthwash. The arresting officer counters by stating that 90 minutes had elapsed between the time of the arrest and the administration of the breath test. During this time nothing was seen entering the suspect's mouth. The officer claims that this was more than sufficient time for any alcohol residues present in the mouth to dissipate.

To determine who is telling the truth you will be asked to rinse your mouth with an alcohol-containing liquid. *Don't swallow it.* At 5, 10, 15, and 20 minute intervals, you'll test your breath with a Breathalyzer.

EQUIPMENT

1 Ampoule gauge	1 Bubble tube
1 Atomizer bulb	1 pr Goggles, safety
1 Breathalyzer	1 Mouthpiece

REAGENTS

Two Breathalyzer sealed ampoules   Alcohol-containing liquid

METHOD

1. Turn the Breathalyzer switch to the "on" position and wait until the thermometer shows a reading $50 \pm 3°$ C. This temperature indicates that the sample chamber and breath-carrying tubes are above body temperature. This prevents moisture condensation from the breath.

2. Gauge two sealed ampoules using the gauge provided. When the ampoule is in the gauge, the bottom of the meniscus should be level with the top of the gauge, or slightly above it. Remove the ampoule from the gauge.

3. Place a sealed ampoule in the left-hand compartment of the instrument.

4. Break the other ampoule seal, and place it in the right-hand compartment of the instrument. Connect a bubble tube to the rubber outlet tube on the instrument, and insert the bubbler into the ampoules

5. With the selector on the "take" position, pump air into the sample tube with an atomizer bulb for about 10 seconds. During this time the green light will go on, indicating that the chamber is full.

6. Turn the selector to the "analyze" position. This air will pass from the chamber and bubble into the test ampoule. The green light will go out as the piston leaves the top of its stroke. At the bottom of the stroke, an electrical contact will be made and a red light will come on. This should take about 25 to 35 seconds, but the time is not critical.

7. Ninety seconds after the red light appears, a green "read" lamp will go on. At this time, turn the light source on, and turn the balance wheel on the right side of the panel until the null-meter pointer is on the centerline.

8. Set the scale pointer on the zero position. In model 900 Breathalyzers, the knob on the pointer shaft must be pulled toward the operator to free the pointer.

9. Insert the mouthpiece into the plastic sample tube. This is a precaution to keep saliva or liquids from the instrument; without this precaution the piston could stick and cause a low reading.

10. Turn the selector to the "take" position, and blow into the mouthpiece. A deep breath is not necessary, but the subject should empty his lungs as completely as possible while giving a sample.

11. Repeat step 6.

12. After a 90-second wait from the time the red light comes on, adjust the balance wheel while the source light is on until the null meter needle is centered. The pointer will show the actual blood alcohol percentage. Record the answer.

13. Repeat steps 4 through 11, so that you blow into the Breathalyzer approximately 5, 10, 15, and 20 minutes after you have rinsed your mouth with alcohol. The same test ampoule can be used for each breath test.

14. At what time is alcohol no longer detectable in your breath?

PART B: THE INTOXILYZER

There are several models of the Intoxilyzer. All are based on the absorption of infrared radiation by alcohol in a suspects breath.

The Intoxilyzer measures ethanol (CH_3CH_2OH) in a person's breath based on infrared absorption spectroscopy. At present, interference filters isolate three wavelengths, 3.39, 3.48, and 3.80 μm to measure the ethanol and to correct for acetone and water. Originally it was thought, that while dozens of organic compounds have been detected in human breath, the total amount of these compounds was insignificant compared to the ethanol present after a person has consumed an alcoholic beverage. However, it was later found that if a person is diabetic that an excess of acetone ($CH_3C(O)CH_3$) may be present which produces a stronger CH_3 signal at 3.48 μm than ethanol alone. The Intoxilyzer measures the asymmetric stretching frequency at 3.39 μm of the CH_3 group, and the symmetric stretching frequency at 3.48 μm. A ratio of the intensity of the two frequencies is used to determine if ethanol alone is being measured. This ratio is adjusted close to 1.0. Water (H_2O) has a strong symmetrical stretching O-H band at 2.74 μm adjacent to the C-H bands and its shoulder overlaps the CH_3 group frequencies. This was originally

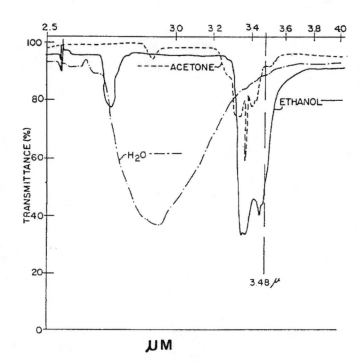

FIGURE 25–3 Infrared spectrum of ethanol, acetone, and water. *U.S. Patent 4,587,427, D. C. Talbot and J.L. Witler.*

thought not to interfere because a person's breath was saturated with water, and it was assumed that the shoulder absorption would be constant. This was found not to always be the case and a third filter was added to correct this, the one at 3.80 μm. Figure 25-3 shows transmission infrared spectra of ethanol, acetone, and water as presented in the instrument patent.

Figure 25-4 is a photograph of an Intoxilyzer 5000 and Figure 25-5 is a diagram of the optical path for this instrument.

CRIME SCENE

About 11:30 P.M. a van, going rather fast on a 2-way black top road, passed a parked police car. The police gave chase and the officer noticed that the van appeared to cross what he judged to be the center line (unmarked) several times. The driver stopped his car and got out. There was a high wind and he had trouble getting out of the car, but the officer decided to give the driver a roadside drunkenness test. The driver failed and was taken to the station. He was given a coordination test that was recorded on video and is to be given a breath test on the Intoxilyzer. You are to administer the test.

FIGURE 25–4 Photograph of an Intoxilyzer. *Courtesy of CMI Inc., Owensboro, KY.*

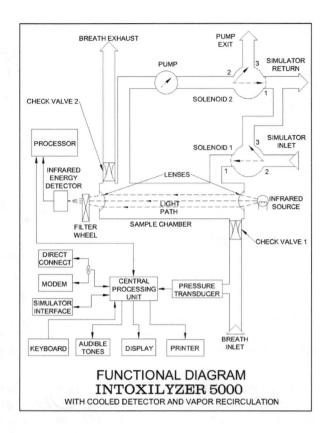

FUNCTIONAL DIAGRAM
INTOXILYZER 5000
WITH COOLED DETECTOR AND VAPOR RECIRCULATION

FIGURE 25–5   Optical diagram of the component partsof an Intoxilyzer Model 5000. *Courtesy of CMI Inc., Owensboro, KY.*

METHOD

NOTE: Material used in this section was obtained from the CMI Inc., operations manual and is for the model 5000.

The Intoxilyzer is quite easy to use. The problem in this class is having a suitable test subject. We cannot advocate that someone consume alcohol prior to coming to class, so have one member of the class rinse their mouth out with a mouth wash and perform the test on them. The Model 5000 will detect that this is not lung alcohol based upon its rapid disappearance and indicate so. However, this will serve to demonstrate the basic operation of the apparatus. This is a typical air blank-breath-air blank test.

	Display reads	Meaning
1.	"READY TO START"	Insert a new mouthpiece in the end of the breath tube. To start the test, push the "Start Test" button at any time.
2.	"INSERT CARD"	Insert an evidence card into the card slot (flashing) located on the front panel of the instrument. Make sure to insert the card face up with the top edge "in" according to the instructions printed on the card.
3.	"AIR BLANK"	
4.	"TIME ##HR ##MIN"	
5.	"DATE MM/DD/YY"	
6.	"AIR BLANK .000"	
7.	">..."	

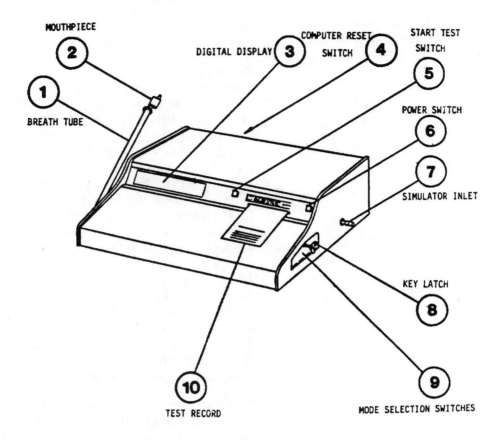

MOUTHPIECE
DIGITAL DISPLAY
COMPUTER RESET SWITCH
START TEST SWITCH
POWER SWITCH
BREATH TUBE
SIMULATOR INLET
KEY LATCH
TEST RECORD
MODE SELECTION SWITCHES

INTOXILYZER 5000 NOMENCLATURE AND FUNCTIONS

1. **Breath Tube** — A heated reinforced plastic tube through which the subject blows into the sample chamber.

2. **Mouthpiece** — A disposable, clear plastic trap which fits in the end of the breath tube, accepts the subject's breath, and prevents unwanted substances from entering the instrument.

3. **Digital Display** — A sixteen character alphanumeric readout that relates which operation the instrument is performing, alerts the operator to required actions, and expresses the Alcohol Concentration (AC).

4. **Computer Reset Switch** — A rocker switch, used to cancel a sequence, that returns the instrument to "Not Ready" and is followed by Internal Diagnostics.

5. **Start Test Switch** — A push button switch used to operate the instrument and initial control functions.

6. **Power Switch** — A push button switch used to apply AC power to the instrument.

7. **Simulator Inlet** — A plastic male adapter located on the side of the instrument, used for attaching a wet-bath simulator.

8. **Key Latch** — A hardened steel lock used for latching the hinged door covering the Mode Selection switches.

9. **Mode Selection Switches** — Dip, slide, and rotary switches located on the side of the instrument behind a lockable hinged door. The Mode Selection switches enable one to select a mode sequence, set the time and date, and perform diagnostic tests on several of the instrument's basic operations.

10. **Test Record** — A formatted multi-copy card that provides a printed record of the date, model and serial number of the instrument, test procedure, test results, and time of test.

CAUTION
TEN SECONDS MUST ELAPSE BETWEEN TURNING THE INSTRUMENT OFF AND ON.

---

8. "PLEASE BLOW INTO MOUTH PIECE UNTIL TONE STOPS; PLEASE BLOW

Request subject to blow into the mouthpiece until the tone stops; the subject has three minutes to provide (flashing) an adequate breath sample.

To insure delivery of a sufficient sample, the displayed command requests the subject to blow into the mouthpiece until the tone stops. The tone, however, does not actually stop until the subject stops blowing.

9. "PLEASE BLOW .###"
   followed by "PLEASE BLOW"
   "0.###"

In order to provide an adequate breath sample, a subject must blow for a minimum of 4 seconds.

As the subject blows into the mouthpiece, the instrument sounds a continuous tone and displays the message to the left: "PLEASE BLOW .###." The three-digit (optional two-digit) number is the subject's rising (falling, constant) blood alcohol concentration in percent weight by volume. The continuous tone tells you that the subject is blowing with sufficient pressure. When the zero appears before the BAC value (0.###), the subject has delivered an adequate breath sample. Do not, however, instruct the subject to stop blowing when the zero appears.

If S5 (Display During Test) is "off," the instrument will not display the blood alcohol concentration value until the subject stops blowing and has delivered a sufficient breath sample. The instrument will also not display the zero indicating when the subject has delivered an adequate breath sample.

If the subject stops blowing before providing a sufficient sample, "PLEASE BLOW" flashes on the display and a beep sounds every five seconds. If this occurs, request the subject to blow into the mouthpiece until the tone stops.

In the event that the subject fails to provide an adequate breath sample within three minutes, "DEFICIENT SAMPLE" appears on the display accompanied by a low-high tone sounding intermittently for five seconds. Next, the instrument displays "SUBJECT TEST .###" (the highest BAC value obtainable from the given breath samples), and completes the mode sequence. On the evidence card, the instrument indicates the highest obtainable BAC value by printing an asterisk (*) before 'SUBJECT TEST .###.' The asterisk (*) is a cross reference to the message printed at the bottom of the evidence card: "DEFICIENT SAMPLE—VALUE PRINTED WAS HIGHEST OBTAINED."

10. "SUBJECT TEST .###"

11. "AIR BLANK .###"

12. "TEST COMPLETE"   Remove evidence card after it is released by the instrument.

13. "READY TO START"

SELECTED ADDITIONAL SOURCES OF INFORMATION

Caldwell, J.P., and Kim. N.D., "The response of the Intoxilizer 5000 to five potential interfering substances," *J. Forens. Sci.*, 42 (6), (1997), 1080.

Coplano, Y.H., Yohman, D.T. , and Schaefer, J.A., "An in vitro study of the accuracy and precision of Breathalyzer Models, 900, 900-A, and 1000," *J. Forens. Sci.*, 30 (4), (1985), 1058.

Cowan, J.M. Jr, McCutchen. J.R., and Weatherman, A., "The response of the Intoxilizer 4011AS-A to a number of possible interfering substances," *J. Forens. Sci.*, 35 (4), (1990), 838.

Crockett, A.J., Rozee, M., Laslett, R., and Alpers, J.H., "Minimum lung function for breath alcohol testing using the Lion Alcolmeter SD-400," *Sci. & Just.*, 39 (3), (1999), 173.

Denney, R.C., "Solvent inhalation and 'apparent' alcohol studies on the Lion Intoximeter 3000," *J. Forens. Sci. Soc.*, 30 (6), (1990), 357.

Edwards, M.A., Giguire, W., Lewis, D., and Baselt, R.C., "Infrared absorption by Intoxilizer is nonspecific," *Drinking / Driving Law Letter*, 6, (5), (1987), 4-6

Edwards, M.A., Giguire, W., Lewis, D., and Baselt, R.C., "Intoxilizer interference by solvents," *J. Anal. Toxicol.*, 10, May/June (1986).

Fox, G.R., and Hayward, J.S., "Effects of hyperthermia on breath alcohol analysis," *J. Forens. Sci.*, 34 (4), (1989), 836.

Gainsford, Allan R., Fernando, D. M., Lea, R. A., Stowell, A. R., "A large scale study of the relationship between blood and breath alcohol concentrations in New Zealand.," *J. Forens. Sci.*, 51 (1), (2006), 173.

Gomm, P.J., Weston, S.I. and Osselton, M.D., " The effect of respiratory aerosol inhalers and nasal sprays on breath alcohol testing devices used in Great Britain," *Medicine Sci. and the Law*, 30, (1990), 203.

Gullberg, R.G., "Applying a data acquisition system to the analysis of breath alcohol profiles," *J. Forens. Sci. Soc.*, 29 (6), (1989), 397.

Gullberg, R.G., "Repeatability of replicate breath alcohol measurements collected in short time intervals," *Sci. & Just.*, 35 (1), (1995), 5.

Gullbereg, R.G., "Breath alcohol analysis in one subject with gastroesophageal reflux disease," *J. Forens. Sci.*, 46 (6), (2001, 1498.

Harding, P.M., Laessig, R.H., and Field, P.H., "Field performance of the Intoxilizer 5000: A comparison of blood and breath alcohol results in Wisconsin drivers," *J. Forens. Sci.*, 35 (5), (1990), 1022.

Jones, A.W., and Andersson, L., "Variability of the blood/breath alcohol concentration on the disappearance rate of alcohol from blood in drinking drivers," *J. Forens. Sci.*, 41 (6), (1996), 916.

Jones, A.W., "Ethanol distribution ratios between urine and capillary blood in controlled experiments and in apprehended drinking drivers," *J. Forens. Sci.*, 37 (1), (1992), 21.

Kechagias, S., Jonsson, K., Franzen, T., Andersson, L., and Jones, A.W., "Reliability of breath alcohol analysis in individuals with gastroesophageal reflux disease," *J. Forens. Sci.*, 44 (4), (1999), 814.

Lewis, M.J., "Blood alcohol—the concentration-time curve and retrospective estimation of level," *J. Forens. Sci. Soc.*, 26, (1986), 95.

Parker, K.M., and Green, J.L., "Delayed ethanol analysis of breath specimens: Long term field experience with commercial silica gel tubes and Breathalyzer collections," *J. Forens. Sci.*, 35 (6), (1990), 1353.

Smith, D.J., and Laslett, R., "Evaluation of the Drager Alccotest Model 7110 infrared breath alcohol analysing instrument," *J. Forens. Sci. Soc.*, 30 (6), (1990), 349.

Talbot, D.C., and Witler, J.L., "Breath Analyzer," U.S. Patent 4,587,427, May 6, (1986).

EXPERIMENT 25

Name _____

DATA SHEET

Date _____

BREATH ALCOHOL BY THE BREATHALYZER AND INTOXILYZER

Part A: The Breathalyzer

Time subject blows into Breathalyzer.   % Alcohol

  1.

  2.

  3.

  4.

  5.

Questions

  1. How will the following conditions affect the alcohol reading obtained on a Breathalyzer?
     The level of the liquid in the test ampoule is below the gauge.

     _____

     The operator fails to wait 90 seconds before reading the result.

     _____

     The subject does not blow properly into the mouthpiece.

     _____

     What will be the effect on the alcohol reading if the operator fails to warm it up to 50° C?

     _____

2. Can you think of any chemicals other than alcohol that will give a Breathalyzer reading?

Part B: The Intoxilyzer

1. Record what you see on the evidence card.

2. What was the effect of rinsing the mouth with mouthwash?

Questions

1. Molecules absorb radiation at (all, specific) wavelengths. Choose one.

2. The Intoxilyzer utilizes (infrared, visible) radiation. Choose one.

3. How is the Intoxilyzer set to the zero reference point?

4. Does the radiant energy striking the detector of the instrument increase or decrease as the amount of alcohol in the sample chamber increases? Why?

5. What are two sources of acetone in a subject's breath?

   1.   2.

6. How many times is each sample measured in the instrument?

7. What reagents are required for breath testing by this method?

8. How many attempts at producing a proper breath sample is a subject allowed?

9. What is the "implied consent" law?

10. How is the simulator solution used in this test?

Analysis of Blood Alcohol by Gas Chromatography Using a Thermal Conductivity Detector

Gas liquid chromatography (GLC) is a means of identifying and quantitating poisons, drugs, and alcohol in blood or urine samples. It is a rapid, simple, and specific procedure, assuming the availability of standard samples for comparison and quantitation. If the instrument is previously warmed up and ready to operate, the determination of alcohol can be performed in 6 to 8 minutes.

A sample (liquid or gaseous) is injected onto a heated column packed with a material capable of separating the components of a mixture into their individual parts. This packing material is determined by reference to the literature or by the analyst, who tries various materials and determines the best one for use by means of the separation data obtained.

Known and unknown samples are injected into the same column under identical conditions, and by comparing the time it takes for the peaks to emerge from the column (retention time), the components in the unknown are identified. Use of known concentrations of the standard samples will allow quantitation of the unknown by a comparison of sample peak areas or heights as shown on the strip-chart recorder paper.

Figure 26-1 shows a typical chromatogram. For sharp peaks the peak height is proportional to the concentration, whereas for broader peaks we find that the peak area gives a more accurate measure of the concentration.

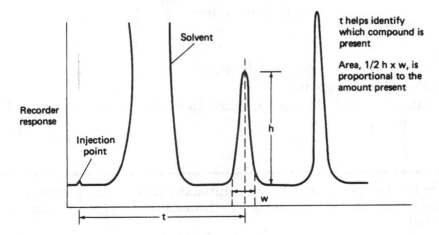

FIGURE 26–1   A typical gas chromatogram.

Operating instructions vary slightly, depending upon the particular instrument used; your instructor will explain how to use the gas chromatograph assigned to you.

Two procedures will be given, one which simulates the analysis of blood alcohol, employing an instrument with a thermal conductivity (TCD) detector, and the other, in the following experiment, which uses an instrument with the flame ionization detector (FID). In either case, the principle remains the same. This choice will allow schools which have either or both types of instruments to do the analysis and help students understand the principles involved. A working forensic laboratory would make use of the flame ionization detector because of its increased sensitivity and its lack of response to water.

CRIME SCENE

A law enforcement officer, in the routine performance of his duties, notices a car being operated in a rather erratic manner. The car, while not being driven excessively fast, swerves from one side of the street to the other, and the driver appears to be under the influence of alcohol or some other substance which impairs the safe operation of his vehicle. The officer stops the driver, and as he approaches, detects the odor of alcohol on the driver's breath. The officer requests that the driver accompany him to a nearby facility to take a blood alcohol test. The driver maintains that he is not under the influence of alcohol, but that he will submit to the test. He is taken to a hospital, where a sample of his blood is taken by a certified medical technologist and sent to a forensic laboratory for analysis of blood alcohol content. You now have that blood sample and will perform the analysis.

EQUIPMENT

1 Beaker, 10 mL	1 Pencil, grease
1 Beaker, 50 mL	1 Pipet, Mohr, 2 mL
1 Bulb, pipet	1 Pipet, Mohr, 10 mL
7 Corks	1 Razor blade, single edge
7 Flasks, Erlenmeyer 25 mL	1 Ruler, metric
1 Gas chromatograph equipped with a thermal conductivity detector and a column suitable for the separation of alcohols	1 Strip chart recorder compatible with the gas chromatograph used.
	1 Syringe, 10-microliter (μL)
1 pr Goggles, safety	6 Vials, 4 dram

REAGENTS

Absolute ethanol   n-Propanol
Unknown mixtures of ethanol in n-propanol
Suggested column: DC-200, 10% or Carbowax 20M, 10% on 60–80 mesh Chromosorb P

METHOD

The specific instructions for the operation of the gas chromatograph which you are to use will be given by your instructor. Be certain that you go through the instructions carefully before you begin your analysis.

This experiment will use a gas chromatograph with a thermal conductivity (TC) detector. This will require that we do a little "pretending" in this experiment. The instrument is not capable of detecting very low concentrations of compounds, which must be in the form of a gas, so the small amounts of alcohol in blood would not be useful for analysis.

Instead, your sample will be a mixture of two alcohols, one ethanol, and the other n-propanol. The n-propanol will be used as a comparison compound (internal standard), and the ethanol is the substance to be measured. The mixture is injected into the gas chromatograph, vaporized by the heated injection block, and then passed through the column. The components are separated by the column packing material and pass over the detector element. The interaction of the molecules with the filaments in the detector is converted to an electrical signal, passed to a recording device, and printed out as a peak on a moving chart paper. The height of the peak will be used as a representation of the quantity of substance detected, and therefore, present in the sample.

An example of one workable GC system is listed below for the typical Gow-Mac student gas chromatograph.

Flow rate: 60 mL/min; use helium or nitrogen carrier gas.

Filament current: 180 mA

Column temperature: 90° C

Column packing: 10% DC-200 on Chromosorb P

Attenuation: 4

Sample size: 5 μL

1. Inject 5 μL of ethanol. Once it has produced a peak, then inject 5 μL of n-propanol separately to determine their retention times and to determine what attenuation to use.

2. Prepare mixtures of ethanol and n-propanol in the following proportions, in 25 mL Erlenmeyer flasks. Be sure to cork each mixture to prevent evaporation.

    0.1 mL of ethanol + 1.9 mL of n-propanol
    0.2 mL of ethanol + 1.8 mL of n-propanol
    0.3 mL of ethanol + 1.7 mL of n-propanol
    0.4 mL of ethanol + 1.6 mL of n-propanol
    0.5 mL of ethanol + 1.5 mL of n-propanol

3. Inject these mixtures consecutively into the gas chromatograph, waiting for each to come through before the next is injected. Use a volume of the mixture that will keep the recorded peaks on scale on the chart paper. Injections are performed by use of a 10 μL syringe. Use the same volume for all your injections. The easiest way to determine this volume is to find the volume that keeps all peaks on scale for the mixture containing the greatest percentage of ethanol. Then use this volume for all of the other injections, including your unknown mixture. Do not change any of the instrumental settings after you begin your injections of the known mixtures.

4. After you have injected all of the known mixtures, obtain an unknown. Inject the unknown according to the previously given instructions.

5. Turn off or place the instrument in a standby mode, according to the directions of your laboratory instructor.

6. Tear off your chart paper and proceed as follows.

7. Measure the height of the ethanol peak for each of the known mixtures.

8. Calculate the percentage of ethanol in each mixture and prepare a calibration curve on graph paper of percentage ethanol versus peak height. Use the vertical axis for peak height and the horizontal axis for concentration.

9. Measure the ethanol peak height for your unknown, and determine the percentage ethanol from your calibration curve.

10. Report the value obtained for percentage ethanol in your sample on the data sheet.

11. Staple your calibration curve and the chart paper with your recorded peaks to the data sheet, answer all questions, and turn this material in to your laboratory instructor.

12. Clean and return all equipment and glassware to the designated locations. The actual procedure used for blood alcohol analysis differs from the one given here and is presented in Experiment 27.

SELECTED SOURCES FOR ADDITIONAL INFORMATION

Amick, G.D., and Habben, K.H., "Inhibition of ethanol production by Saccharomyces cerevisiae in human blood by NaF," *J. Forens. Sci.,* 42 (4), (1997), 690.

Barnes, Aisha, T., Dolan, J. A., Kuk, R. J., and Siegel, J. A., "Comparison of gasolines using gas chromatography-mass spectrometry and target ion response," *J. Forens. Sci.,* 49 (5), (2004), 1018.

DeVos, Betty-Jayne, Fronman, M., Rohwer, E., and Sutherland, D., "Detection of petrol (gasoline) in fire debris by gas chromatography/mass spectrometry/mass spectrometry (GC/MS/MS)," *J. Forens. Sci.,* 47 (4), (2002), 736.

Jones, A.W., "The precision and accuracy of a GC Intoximeter breath alcohol device, Part I - In vitro experiments," *J. Forens, Sci. Soc.,* 18, (1978), 75.

Jones, A.W., "The precision and accuracy of a GC Intoximeter breath alcohol device, Part II - In vivo experiments," *J. Forens, Sci. Soc.,* 18, (1978), 81.

Jones, A. W., and Holmgren, P., "Comparison of blood alcohol concentration in deaths attributed to acute alcohol poisoning and chronic alcoholism," *J. Forens. Sci.,* 48 (4), (2003), 874.

Jones, A.W., Jorfeldt, L., Hjertberg, H., and Jonsson, K.A., "Physiological variations in blood ethanol measurements during the post-absorptive state," *J. Forens. Sci. Soc.,* 30 (5), (1990), 273.

Jones, A.W., Jonsson, K., and Neri, A., "Peak blood-ethanol concentration and the time spent of its occurrence after rapid drinking on an empty stomach," *J. Forens. Sci.,* 36 (2), (1991), 376.

Neuteboom, W., and Jones, A.W., "Disappearance rate of alcohol from the blood of drunk drivers calculated from two consecutive samples—what do the results really mean?," *Forens. Sci. Intl.,* 45, (1990), 107.

Stowell, A.R., and Stowell, L.I., "Estimation of blood alcohol concentrations after social drinking," *J. Forens. Sci.,* 43 (1), (1998), 14.

EXPERIMENT 26   Name _____

DATA SHEET   Date _____

ANALYSIS OF BLOOD ALCOHOL BY GAS CHROMATOGRAPHY USING A THERMAL CONDUCTIVITY DETECTOR

1. Unknown sample number _____

2. Data for calibration curve

Mixture	% Ethanol (vol.)	Height of ethanol peak (cm)
1.		
2.		
3.		
4.		
5.		
Unknown		

3. Concentration of ethanol in unknown mixture (%).

4. Do the retention times of ethanol and n-propanol compare closely with these components in each mixture? Measure each component of each standard and the sample solution. List each retention time in the space below and compare them. Calculate the average retention time for each component and list them in question five.

5. What are the retention times of each component, expressed in centimeters?

    ethanol_____cm   n-propanol _____ cm

6. Is the plot of % ethanol by volume versus peak height linear? What might cause any deviation from linearity, if it exists? If the five points representing the five standards are not linear, draw the best straight line through the points, passing through as many points as possible and try to position the line in such a way as to have equal numbers of outliers above and below your line. DO NOT connect dot to dot.

7. How could you change the retention times of the components in the mixture to achieve better separation between them?

8. (Optional) Peak area versus concentration could also be used to prepare the calibration curve. Extra credit points will be awarded if you choose to use peak area to determine the percentage of ethanol in your mixture. What might cause any deviation from linearity, if it exists? If the five points representing the five standards are not linear, draw the best straight line through the points, passing through as many points as possible and try to position the line in such a way as to have equal numbers of outliers above and below your line. DO NOT connect dot to dot. How do the values compare for both calibration curve results?

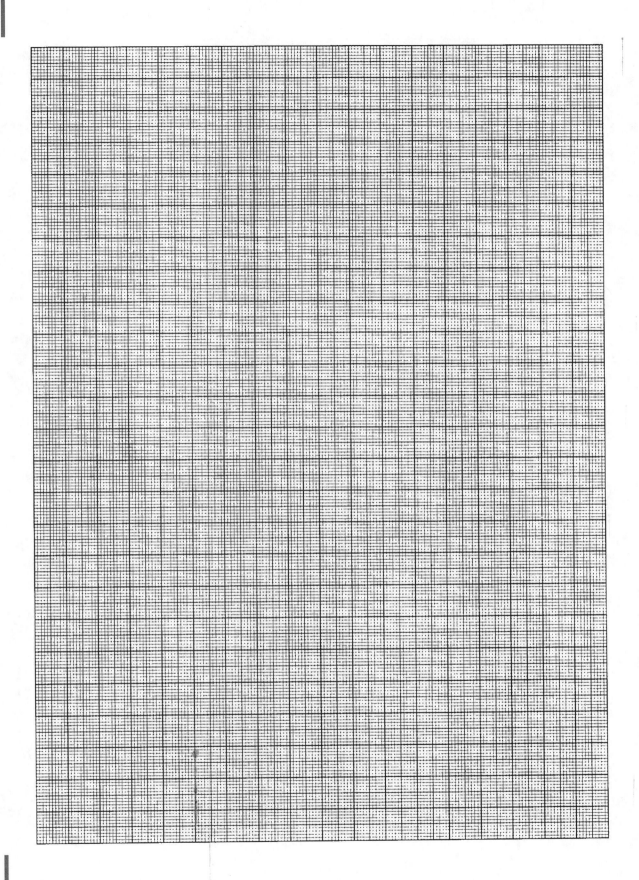

Analysis of Blood Alcohol by Gas-Liquid Chromatography Using a Flame Ionization Detector

The analysis given here is a standard method for determining the alcohol content by volume percentage in a blood or urine sample. This method, with maybe a few local variations, is routinely performed in laboratories associated with local police and state highway patrol law enforcement agencies in every state. The method is rapid, accurate, and reproducible.

This analysis is useful when a vehicle operator is suspected of being under the influence of alcohol. A typical example is cited in Experiment 26, and the student is referred to it for background information.

The gas chromatograph employed in this analysis is equipped with a flame ionization (FID) detector. This detector is very sensitive to small amounts of alcohol and other organic compounds, but is insensitive to water. This detector is about 100 times more sensitive than the TC detector. This makes the detector very useful for the analysis of alcohol or drugs in blood or urine samples. The method used here will be one of headspace analysis. This means that instead of a liquid sample being injected into the gas chromatograph, a sample of the vapor above the liquid sample, produced by incubating the sample in a constant temperature water bath at a slightly elevated temperature, is used for injection. This serves to eliminate extra peaks due to other substances in the blood or urine sample.

EQUIPMENT

1 Brush, test tube	1 Labels or glass marking pens
1 Flask, volumetric, 100 mL	2 Pipets, Mohr, 5 mL
1 Holder, test tube	1 Rack, test tube
1 bx Kimwipes	1 Ruler, metric

1 Gas chromatograph, equipped with an FID detector and column suitable for the separation of alcohols

1 Strip chart recorder compatible with the gas chromatograph used.

1 Syringe, Plastipak disposable syringe, 3 mL (Becton-Dickinson No. 5570)

7 Tubes, test, 10 cm, with rubber septum caps

1 Constant-temperature water bath, 50° C

7 Flasks, Erlenmeyer with rubber stoppers, 25 mL

REAGENTS

Blood samples containing varying percentages of ethanol.

Ethanol, stock solutions 1%; pipet 1.0 mL of absolute ethanol into a 100 mL volumetric flask and dilute to 100 mL with distilled water.

METHOD

The actual instructions for the operation of the gas chromatograph will vary slightly with the instrument used. These instructions will be provided by the person in charge of the laboratory and will not be dealt with here.

1. Prepare mixtures of the ethanol stock solution and distilled water in the following proportions in a 25 mL Erlenmeyer flask. Stopper the flask, shake vigorously, and transfer 4 mL to a stoppered test tube.

   1.0 mL of ethanol stock solution + 9.0 mL of water
   2.0 mL of ethanol stock solution + 8.0 mL of water
   3.0 mL of ethanol stock solution + 7.0 mL of water
   4.0 mL of ethanol stock solution + 6.0 mL of water
   5.0 mL of ethanol stock solution + 5.0 mL of water

2. Place the mixtures, in the septum-stoppered test tubes, in a 50° C constant temperature water bath for 10 minutes.

3. Obtain two blood samples.

4. Pipet 2 mL of your blood sample into a clean test tube, repeat with a second pipet, and pipet this sample into a second tube.

5. Be certain that you mark the tubes with the sample number, to avoid identification errors later.

6. Place the septum cap on each test tube, shake to mix the contents, and place both tubes in the 50° C constant-temperature water bath for 10 minutes.

7. Zero the recorder-gas chromatograph system as explained by your laboratory instructor.

8. Remove the known standard mixture containing the **highest percentage** of ethanol from the water bath.

9. Insert the gas-tight syringe needle through the septum cap completely, but do not allow the syringe needle to enter the liquid. We want a sample of the vapor above the liquid only.

10. Remove a 1.0 mL sample of the head-space vapor and inject it into the gas chromatograph. Set the controls of the gas chromatograph so that this sample will stay on the chart paper and give a complete peak for each component.

11. When this is accomplished, inject ethanol and n-propanol separately to determine the identity of each component by its retention time on the gas chromatograph column.

12. Return the mixture to the water bath, as you will need to sample this mixture again later.

13. Beginning with the sample mixture containing the lowest percentage of ethanol, inject each mixture in turn, taking care to only sample headspace vapor. Wait for both peaks to be recorded before injecting the next sample. Use 1.0 mL of sample in each injection.

14. Inject the headspace vapor of each of your unknowns in the same manner as the known mixtures.

15. Leave the gas chromatograph on standby or shut it down, as your laboratory instructor has indicated.

16. Tear off the chart paper and proceed as follows.

17. Measure the height of each ethanol peak in centimeters.

18. Calculate the percentage of ethanol in each mixture.

19. Prepare a calibration curve on graph paper of percentage ethanol (by volume) on the horizontal axis and peak height on the vertical axis.

20. Determine the percentage of ethanol in each of your blood unknowns by use of your calibration curve and the measured height of the ethanol peak in each unknown.

21. Record all data values on the data sheet.

22. Answer the questions, staple the chart paper with the recorded peaks and your calibration curve to the data sheet, and hand these in.

23. Clean all glassware and equipment. Return these items to their designated locations.

SELECTED SOURCES FOR ADDITIONAL INFORMATION

Booker, J.L., "End-position nystagmus as an indicator of ethanol intoxication," *Sci. & Just.*, 41 (2), (2001), 113.

Gullberg, Rod G., and Logan, B. K., "Results of a proposed breath alcohol proficiency test program," *J. Forens. Sci.,* 51 (1), (2006), 168.

Jones, A.W., "Concentration-time profiles of ethanol in capillary blood after ingestion of beer," *J. Forens. Sci. Soc.*, 31 (4), (1991), 429.

Jones, A.W., and Andersson, L., "Influence of age, gender, and blood-alcohol concentration on the disappearance rate of alcohol from blood in drinking drivers," *J. Forens. Sci.*, 41 (6), (1996), 922.

Jones, A.W., Jonsson, K., and Neri, A., "Peak blood-ethanol concentration and the time spent of its occurrence after rapid drinking on an empty stomach," *J. Forens. Sci.*, 36 (2), (1991), 376.

Luckey, M.J., "Headspace analysis for ethyl alcohol in blood, breath, and urine specimens using a specialized gas chromatograph," *J. Forens. Sci.*, 16 (1), (1971), 120.

Moore, Ronald L., and Guillen, J., "The effect of breath freshener strips on two types of breath alcohol testing instruments," *J. Forens. Sci.,* 49 (4), (2004), 829.

Stephens, A., and Franklin, S.D.A., "Level of lung function required to use the Camic Datamaster breath alcohol testing device," *Sci. & Just.*, 41 (1), (2001), 49.

Wilson, Christopher I., Ignacio, S. S., and Wilson, G. A., "An unusual form of fatal ethanol intoxication," *J. Forens. Sci.,* 50 (3), (2005), 676.

EXPERIMENT 27

Name _____

DATA SHEET

Date _____

ANALYSIS OF BLOOD ALCOHOL BY GAS CHROMATOGRAPHY USING A FLAME IONIZATION DETECTOR (ADVANCED)

1. Unkown sample number _____

   Unknown sample number _____

2. Data for calibration curve

Mixture	% Ethanol (vol.)	Height of ethanol peak (cm)
1.		
2.		
3.		
4.		
5.		

   Unknown no. _____

   Unknown no. _____

3. Concentration of ethanol (vol. %)

   Unknown no. _____   conc _____

   Unknown no. _____   conc _____

4. What are the retention times of each component, expressed in centimeters?

   Ethanol_____cm   n-Propanol _____ cm

5. Is the calibration curve linear with concentration of ethanol? How can you determine this?

6. How could you change the retention times of the components in a mixture to achieve better separation between them?

7. (Optional) Peak area versus concentration could also be used to prepare the calibration curve. Extra credit will be awarded if you choose to use your recorder peaks to determine the percentage of ethanol in your blood samples in this manner. How do the values compare for both calibration curve results?

Analysis of Ink by Paper Chromatography

Paper chromatography was developed in the early 1940s in England. The technique is based on the fact that paper contains a thin film of water around the cellulose fibers of the paper, called a **stationary phase**. A mixture of the compounds to be separated is placed in a small spot at one end of a strip of paper, and an organic solvent (**mobile phase**) is passed over the spot and across the paper. Since each compound present has a different size, shape, and distribution of electrical field, each compound will dissolve in the water and organic solvent to a different extent.

The net result is that if two compounds are started at the same place and solvent passed over them, one compound will move along the paper faster than the other. After a period of time the flow of the mobile phase is stopped. The paper is dried and then sprayed with a reagent that will produce colored spots if the compounds are not colored. The materials used in our experiments—lipsticks, gasoline, and inks—are already colored, so the latter step is not required.

Some years ago the color in inks was made of a single component substance. Therefore, when this ink was chromatographed, only one colored spot was evident. Inks manufactured in more recent times are more often multi-component materials, with the ink color due to a mixture of dyes. These inks, then, show a variety of colored spots when chromatographic separation is performed.

In this analysis we determine whether two different documents were written with the same ink, or at least with inks produced during the same period of manufacturing technology.

CRIME SCENE

Two documents are submitted to the document examination section of a forensic laboratory with the following explanation and request:

The patriarch of a very affluent family has written, in long hand, a statement giving one of his daughters permission to invest a substantial sum of money in a business venture. The second document is a statement that instructs the daughter to confer with other members of the family concerning investments before they are undertaken. Both have been written with a fountain pen containing black ink. The daughter maintains that the document was written at a much later time. You are to determine if the inks used are the same or different. Preparation for chromatographing the ink samples involves the determination of a proper developing solvent. Instructions are given for the accomplishment of this task.

EQUIPMENT

6 Clips, paper
6 Corks to fit test tubes, fitted with wire hooks
1 Cylinder, graduated, 50 mL
1 pr Goggles, safety
1 Holder, test tube
1 Paper, filter (Whatman No.1)

1 Rack, test tube
1 pr Scissors
1 Spotter (capillary melting tubes)
2 Tubes, test, 10 cm
6 Tubes, test, 20 cm

REAGENTS

Ammonium hydroxide, concentrated
Distilled H_2O
Ethanol (denatured)
Hydrochloric acid, 0.1 M

Methanol
Pyridine
Water-methanol, 50:50 (v/v)

METHOD

In order to chromatograph the inks on these documents you must get the ink back into solution.

1. Cut a small portion from the end of a written word contained in the original document and place it in a test tube. Add methanol dropwise; 2 or 3 drops may be sufficient. The methanol may extract the ink from the paper. Do this in a hood. If the ink does not dissolve, repeat this step using a small amount of pyridine (stench). Place a stopper over the top. This will be designated the **scene** ink.

2. Do this for both documents and properly label each extract. The second document will be designated **possible forgery**.

3. Place approximately 10 mL (depth of 2.5 cm) of one of the 6 solvents listed in the reagent section into each of six large test tubes. CARE: ammonium hydroxide is a strong irritant and pyridine smells horrible. Cover each test tube quickly with a stopper.

4. Obtain 6 strips of filter paper approximately 1 cm wide. They must hang suspended in the test tubes without touching the walls of the test tubes. Measure them for the proper length as shown in Figure 28-1 and attach them to the wire passing through the cork.

5. The scene ink is spotted on the paper 1 cm above the solvent level by just touching the top of one of the capillary tubes containing some of the dissolved ink. Use a small drop and allow it to dry before placing the strip in the test tube. Spot and dry 3 or 4 times to build up the concentration.

6. Attach 1 or 2 paper clips to the lower end of the strip to make the paper hang straight down and not curl.

7. Lower the strip into the solvent, but do not immerse the spot. Let the solvent come up over the spot by capillary action.

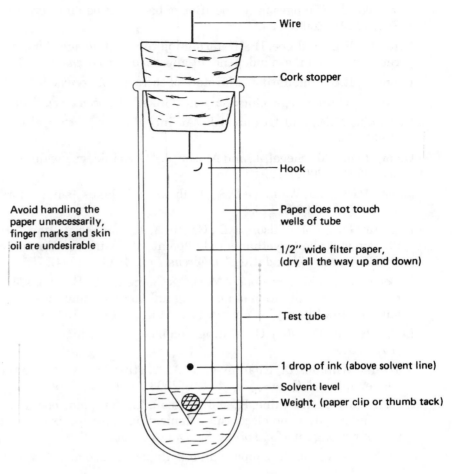

Wire

Cork stopper

Hook

Paper does not touch wells of tube

1/2" wide filter paper, (dry all the way up and down)

Test tube

1 drop of ink (above solvent line)

Solvent level

Weight, (paper clip or thumb tack)

Avoid handling the paper unnecessarily, finger marks and skin oil are undesirable

FIGURE 28–1 The ascending paper chromatographic system.

8. Allow the solvent to rise up the strip until it reaches a point 2.5 cm from the cork.

9. Remove the paper strip, mark the solvent front, and allow the strip to dry on a clean sheet of paper or suspended from a support.

10. Using the solvent which gave the best separation of the ink dyes, chromatograph the ink extract from the second **possible forgery** documents.

11. From the chromatograms determine the possibility of their having been written with the same type of ink by comparing the dye colors.

12. Attach all chromatograms to the back of the data sheet, and label each as to the solvent used.

13. Give the chromatograms to your laboratory instructor.

14. Clean all equipment and glassware before returning them. Dispose of all solvents in an appropriate waste container.

SELECTED SOURCES FOR ADDITIONAL INFORMATION

Abulafia, A., Brown, S., and Abramovich-Bar, S., "A fraudulent case involving novel ink eradicating methods," *J. Forens. Sci.*, 42 (1), (1997), 300.

Aginsky, V.A., "A microspectrophotometric method for dating ballpoint inks—a feasibility study," *J. Forens. Sci.*, 40 (3), (1995), 475.

Andrasko, J., "Changes in composition of ball point pen inks on aging in darkness," *J. Forens. Sci.*, 47 (2), (2002), 324.

Brunelle, R.L., and Lee, H., "Determining the relative age of ballpoint ink using a single solvent extraction mass independent approach," *J. Forens. Sci.*, 34 (5), (1989), 1166.

Brunelle, R.L., "Ink dating—the state of the art," *J. Forens. Sci.*, 37 (1), (1992), 113.

Doud, D., "Chromatographic analysis of inks," *J. Forens. Sci.*, 3 (1958), 486.

Gernandt, M.N., and Urlaub, J.J., "An introduction to the gel pen," *J. Forens. Sci.*, 41 (3), (1996), 503.

Grim, Donna, M., Siegel, J., and Allison, J., "Does ink age inside of a cartridge pen?," *J. Forens. Sci.,* 47 (6), (2002), 1294.

James, P.F.C., and Walker, J.D.S., "Ballpoint ink flakes as indicators of added entries," *Sci. & Just.*, 38 (2), (1998), 119.

Laporte, Gerald M., Wilson, J. D., Cantu, A. A., Mancke, A., and Fortunato, S. L., "The identification of 2-phenoxyethanol in ballpoint inks using gas chromatography/mass spectrometry-Relevance to ink dating," *J. Forens. Sci.,* 49 (1), (2004), 155.

Laporte, Gerald M., Arredondo, M. D., McConnell, T. S., Stephens, J. C., Cantu, A. A., and Shaffer, D. K., "An evaluation of matching unknown writing inks with the United States International Ink Library," *J. Forens. Sci.,* 51 (3), (2006), 689.

Len, N.K., and Ghosh, P.C., "Dating iron base ink writings on documents," *J. Forens. Sci.*, 16 (1971), 511.

Mazzella, Williams D., Khanmy-vital, A., "A study to investigate the evidential value of blue gel pen inks," *J. Forens. Sci.,* 48 (2), (2003), 419.

Ng, Lay-Keow, Lafontaine, P., and Brazeau, L., "Ballpoint pen inks characterization by positive and negative ion-electrospray ionization mass spectrometry for the forensic examination of writing inks," *J. Forens. Sci.,* 47 (6), (2002), 1238.

Throckmorton, G.J., "Disappearing ink: its use, abuse and detection," *J. Forens. Sci.*, 35 (1), (1990), 199.

Vogt, C., Becker, A., and Vogt, J., "Investigation of ball point pen inks by capillary electrophoresis (CE) with UV/vis absorbance and laser induced fluorescence detection and particle induced x-ray emission (PIXE)," *J. Forens. Sci.*, 44 (4), (1999), 819.

Wilson, Jeffrey D., Laporte, G. M., and Cantu, A. A., "Differentiation of black gel inks using optical and chemical techniques," *J. Forens. Sci.,* 49 (2), (2004), 364.

EXPERIMENT 27

Name _____

DATA SHEET

Date _____

ANALYSIS OF INK BY PAPER CHROMATOGRAPHY

1. Which solvent gave the best separation of the components in the ink?

2. Is the order of colors on the strips the same in every case of solvent used?

3. What is the maximum number of different colors that you see on a chromatogram? What are these colors?

4. Is this black ink really "black"?

5. In your opinion, were the two documents written with the same ink? Why or why not?

Separation of Ink Dyes Using Thin Layer Chromatography

This experiment will demonstrate a technique that forensic scientists have developed for identifying the colored pigments in pen inks. The need for differentiating inks arises when people prepare fraudulent documents. For example, someone may alter a document long after it was originally written.

Similarly, a person intent on cheating the government may backdate a record or receipt to substantiate a false tax claim. The ability to distinguish inks will often permit the forensic scientist to determine how many inks or pens were used to prepare a document and the year(s) of manufacture for the inks used.

The actual identification of inks is made by various procedures, one of which is thin layer chromatography (TLC). Modern day inks are actually comprised of a mixture of colored dyes. These dyes can be separated by TLC.

Thin layer chromatography utilizes a thin film of silica gel or alumina coated onto a glass or plastic strip. As in paper chromatography, this thin film is called the **stationary phase**. A mixture of the compounds to be separated is placed in a small spot at one end of a strip, and a liquid organic solvent (**mobile phase**) is passed over the spot. As the solvent moves up the strip, it carries with it the various components in the spot. Because each compound present has a different size, shape, and distribution of electrical field, each compound will adhere to the stationary phase and dissolve in the solvent to a different extent. Thus, if two compounds are started at the same place and solvent is passed over them, one compound will move along the strip faster than the other. After a period of time the flow of the mobile phase is stopped; the strip is dried and then sprayed with a reagent that will produce colored spots, if the compounds are not colored. The distance the compound moves relative to the distance the mobile phase moves is a characteristic of that compound and is known as the R_f value.

Modern inks are a mixture of different dye components. These dyes can often be separated by thin-layer chromatography, and the resultant separation pattern provides a useful characteristic for comparing one ink to another.

The chromatography sheets that may be used come in a variety of types. Silica gel and Eastman Kodak Chromatogram sheets are equally

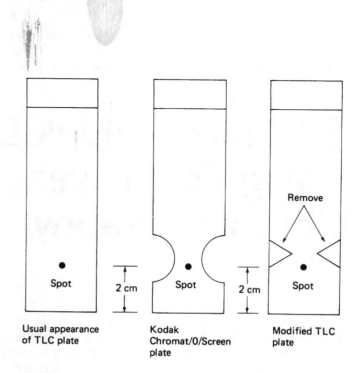

FIGURE 29–1   Notching techniques.

suitable. The TLC plates may be notched as shown in the accompanying diagram (Figure 29-1). This notching permits all of the solvent to move through a narrow space, with the result that the dyes will appear as thin bands of color, well separated in most instances, rather than as a gradient of unresolved, colored spots.

If the plates used in this experiment are glass or aluminum backed, they may be difficult to notch. To produce the same effect, the TLC plate coating is removed from the portion of the plate shown in Figure 29-1. This is easily accomplished by the use of a single-edged razor blade, a scalpel, or some similar sharp instrument.

This type of analysis is useful for the chromatographing of ballpoint pen inks and water-base inks, such as those used in fountain and felt-tip pens. The ball-point pen inks, because of their intensity of color and their high viscosity, are best diluted with an organic solvent, such as ethyl or methyl alcohol. One can also cut or punch the ink out of a written line with a squared-off syringe needle, dissolve it in a suitable solvent, and chromatograph the extract by this method. This affords a means of comparison between written lines, which may or may not have come from a single pen.

The chromatographic developing chamber for this analysis is quite small. Capped bottles, 4 oz or smaller in size, are used. They must have a wide mouth to facilitate the introduction and removal of a TLC plate approximately 10 to 12 cm long and 2 to 3 cm wide. In most instances, this length of plate gives adequate separation in a rather short period of time. Vials fitted with corks will work very well if bottles are not available.

CRIME SCENE

A woman repeatedly receives notes of an obscene nature through the mail. This continues for a period of time, during which the woman hopes her tormentor will tire of such activity, but to no avail. The woman informs the police. She suspects a former admirer with whom she has severed all communications under quite antagonistic circumstances. The police officers call upon the man in question. He of course denies any involvement in the note-writing harassment. The officers obtain the necessary papers to search his living quarters and find some pens and some stationary samples similar to those on which the notes were written. These articles are sent to a forensic laboratory for analysis and comparison with those of the notes, both for ink and paper comparisons. The analysis you will perform in this exercise will be that of the ink comparison.

EQUIPMENT

1 Beaker, 100 mL
1 Beaker, 400 mL
   Bottles, 16-oz, sample holders
1 Bulb, pipet
1 Burner, Bunsen
1 Capillary melting-point tubes
1 Cover, metal, steam bath type
1 Cylinder, graduated, 10 mL
1 pr Forceps
1 Gauze, wire
1 pr Goggles. safety
2 Holders, test tube
1 bx Matches
2 Medicine droppers or disposable pipets
1 Rack, test tube
1 Razor blade, single-edged scalpel, or
     other sharp-edged instrument

6 Bottles, wide mouthed, 4-oz
1 Bottle, wash, 250 mL
1 Brush, test tube
1 Ring, iron, 10 cm
4 Rods, glass, stirring
1 Ruler, metric
1 pr Scissors
6 Silica gel TLC plates, cut into
     strips to fit the bottles
1 Spatula
1 Stand, ring
1 Tape, masking
6 Tubes, test, 10 cm
1 Tubing, burner, 1 meter
   Stoppers, small

REAGENTS

n-Butanol
Distilled water
Isopropanol
Methanol

Paper with notes written on it by an admirer
5 Pens, ballpoint, different brands, same color
Pyridine

METHOD

1. Obtain a sample of the letter upon which is written a message in ink.

2. Using scissors, cut out small portions of a few words.

3. Place the pieces of paper in a 10 cm test tube.

4. Add 1 or 2 drops of methanol to the test tube, and let it stand to extract the ink from the paper into the methanol. If the ink does not dissolve, repeat this step with pyridine in a stoppered test tube.

5. Make a heavy mark on a piece of paper with each of the test pens.

6. Cut out each mark and treat it in the same way as you did the suspect letter.

7. Prepare a mixture of 10 mL of n-butanol, 5 mL of isopropanol, and 5 mL of distilled water to use as a solvent or mobile phase in your chromatographing of the ink samples. Use a 10 mL graduated cylinder, and pour the reagents into a 100 mL beaker to mix them.

8. Into each of the small bottles to be used as developing chambers, place enough of the developing solvent so that its depth is approximately 0.5 cm.

9. Cap or cork the bottles, and let them stand until you are ready to use them.

10. Prepare a strip of the TLC plate for each of the inks to be chromatographed. This is done as indicated in the discussion section at the beginning of this experiment and

as shown in Figure 29-1, where the modified TLC plate is shown. Alternately, use a 5 cm × 10 cm TLC plate and place all of the samples on the same plate. Be sure the spots are separated.

11. Remove the inked test papers from the small test tubes.

12. Place the tubes in a steam bath, and evaporate the solvent to 1 or 2 drops. If it becomes dry, don't worry. Just add 1 drop of methanol and shake gently. You may omit this step if you added the methanol dropwise initially.

13. Apply the extracted ink in methanol solvent to the TLC plate, at a point 1 cm from the bottom of the plate, just below the constricted areas of the coating material. Use a capillary melting-point tube for application. Apply a very small spot of extract, let dry, then apply a small spot again in the same place. Let dry thoroughly.

14. Hold the spotted plate along the side of the bottle containing the solvent. Make certain that the level of solvent in the bottle will be below the applied sample on the strip when placed inside the bottle, but close to it. If it is at too high a level, remove some solvent with a medicine dropper.

15. Place the TLC plates in the bottles of solvent. Be certain that they are properly identified. Cap or cork the bottles, and let them stand until the solvent front has moved up about 5 cm from the sample spot.

16. Remove them, and mark the solvent front.

17. Let them dry, and compare the colored bands which have appeared.

18. Measure the distance each band moved from the point of application to the front of the band.

19. Measure the distance the solvent front moved from the point of application of the spot.

20. Calculate the R_f value for each band by use of the relationship

$$R_f = \frac{\text{distance of sample band front to application point}}{\text{distance of solvent front to application point}}$$

21. Compare the known ink chromatograms with that of the ink from the note.

22. Do any of the inks have a common origin? Which ones?

23. Can you determine conclusively that the inks are the same, or only that they could have come from the same manufacturer?

24. Attach your TLC plates to the data sheet using transparent tape.

25. Answer all questions, and turn in the data sheet and questions to the laboratory instructor.

26. Clean all equipment used, and return it to its proper place. Dispose of all solvents in an appropriate waste container.

SELECTED SOURCES FOR ADDITIONAL INFORMATION

Aginshy, V.N., "Forensic examination of 'slightly soluble' ink pigments using TLC," *J. Forens. Sci.*, 38 (5), (1993), 1131.

Brunelle, R.L., and Pro, M.J., "A systematic approach to identification," *J. Assoc. Anal. Chem.*, 55 (1972), 823.

Claybourn, M., and Ansell, M., "Using Raman spectroscopy to solve crime: inks, questioned documents and fraud," *Sci & Just.*, 40 (4), (2000), 261.

Fanali, S., and Schudel, M. "Some separations of black and red water-soluble fibre-tip pen inks by capillary zone electrophoresis and thin layer chromatography," *J. Forens, Sci.*, 36 (4), (1992), 1192.

Gernandt, M.N., and Urlaub, J.J., "An introduction to the gel pen," *J. Forens. Sci.*, 41 (3), (1996), 503.

Gillis, Trevor, D., Kubic, Thomas A., De Forest, P. R., "An alternative method to screen for pepper spray residue," *J. Forens. Sci.,* 48 (1), (2003), 111.

Harris, J., "Developments in the analysis of writing inks on questioned documents," *J. Forens. Sci.*, 37 (2), (1992), 6712.

Hilton, O., " Distinctive qualities of today's pens," *J. Forsens. Sci. Soc.*, 24 (1984), 157.

Horton, R.A., and Nelson, L.K., "An evaluation of the use of laser induced infrared luminescence to differentiate writing inks," *J. Forens. Sci.*, 36 (3), (1991), 838.

Jasuja, O.P., Singla, A.K., and Chattopadhyay, P.K., "A simple method for determining the sequence of intersecting ball point lines," *J. Forens. Sci.*, 27 (1), (1987), 227.

Kato, N., and Ogamo, A., "A TLC visualization for dimethylamphetamine and other abused tertiary amines," *Sci. & Just.*, 41 (4), (2001), 239.

Kaur, N., Jasuja, O.P., and Singla, A.K., "Thin layer chromatography of computer ribbon inks," *Forens. Sci. Intl.*, 53 (1992), 51.

Lewis, J.A., "Thin layer chromatography of writing inks-quality control considerations." *J. Forens. Sci.*, 41 (5), (1996), 874.

Lofgren, A., and Andraska, J., "HPLC analysis of printing inks," *J. Forens. Sci.*, 38 (5), (1993), 1151.

Radley, R., "Determination of sequence of intersecting ESDA impressions and porous tip, fibre tip and roller ball point pen inks," *Sci. & Just.*, 35 (4), (1995), 267.

Throckmorton, G.T.," Erasable ink. Its ease of erasability and its performance," *J. Forens. Sci.*, 30 (2), (1985), 526.

Wiggins, Kenneth K., Holness, J., and March, B.M., "The importance of thin layer chromatography and UV microspectrophotometry in the analysis of reactive dyes released from wool and cotton fibers," *J. Forens. Sci.*, 50 (2), (2005), 364.

Wilson, Jeffrey D., Laporte, G.M., and Canta, A.A., "Differentiation of black gel inks using optical and chemical techniques," *J. Forens. Sci.*, 49 (2), (2004), 364.

EXPERIMENT 29

Name _____

DATA SHEET

Date _____

SEPARATION OF INK DYES USING THIN LAYER CHROMATOGRAPHY

1. Attach the plates to the data sheet.

2. R_f values obtained with test pen _____

    R_f values obtained for the unknown pen____

    Band 1

    Band 2

    Band 3

    Band 4

    Band 5

3. Comparison of R_f values and conclusions concerning similarity or difference of inks.

4. Do you think a different mobile phase would improve the separation of the ink dyes?

5. How does the analyst select the mobile phase to be used?

6. Would this method work for the separation of dyes in waterproof ink?

7. The smaller the spot applied to the TLC plate, the better the separation obtained. Why do you think this would be true?

Seminal Stains by Human Prostatic Acid Phosphate

Acid phosphatase is an enzyme secreted by the prostate gland into seminal fluid. Since its concentrations in seminal fluid are up to 400 times greater than those found in any other body fluid, forensic scientists use its presence to characterize human seminal stains. However, the fact that other body organs do produce this enzyme means that its presence is not a totally specific test for seminal stains. For example, female vaginal secretions may, in fact, contain this enzyme.

Forensic scientists have long been searching for a technique that will distinguish acid phosphatase originating from the prostate gland as opposed to other sources. One approach used in the past stemmed from the belief that the chemical reactivity of human seminal acid phosphatase was specifically inhibited by L-tartaric acid. Thus, the presence of such inhibition was taken as proof of sexual relations. However, recent evidence has disproved this theory. It seems that a significant percentage of the female population also produces in vaginal secretions acid phosphatase that is inhibited by L-tartaric acid. What this test now shows is that a very high level of acid phosphatase is evidence of sexual relations and that inhibition is probably only of value if you can be sure there is no vaginal secretion contamination.

The term **acid phosphatase** is applied to enzymes, regardless of source, which can hydrolyze certain organic phosphates in slightly acid media. The substrate in the method we use in this experiment is alpha naphthylphosphate. This is incubated with suspected prostatic acid phosphatase at a pH of 4.9. The enzyme, if present, splits away the phosphate radical, liberating the alpha-naphthyl group, which in turn reacts with an added dye (naphthanil diazo blue B) to give a violet-colored complex.

CRIME SCENE

A young woman phones the police station to say that she has just been raped and that she knows the identity of the rapist. The police arrive on the scene within a few minutes. The police officer who listens to her explanation is experienced and knows that she should obtain proof of rape as soon as possible. She takes the woman to a hospital, and a doctor obtains swabs from around the genital area as well as swabs from the vagina. In addition, her skirt is kept as evidence. You have been given the swabs and the skirt, and your job is to tell the police officer if the woman has in fact had recent sexual relations or is merely telling a story to get the fellow in trouble.

EQUIPMENT

6 Bottles, 4-oz	1 Pencil, grease
2 Bottles, wide mouth, 16-oz (samples)	1 pH meter
1 Brush, test tube, small	1 Pipet, Mohr, 1 mL
1 Cylinder, graduated, 100 mL	1 Pipet, Mohr, 5 mL
1 Cylinder, graduated, 10 mL	1 Rack, test tube
Disposable gloves	1 Rod, glass, stirring, 15 cm
1 Flask, Dewar, 0.5 L	1 pr Scissors
1 Flask, Erlenmeyer, 125 mL	1 Stopper, rubber, solid, No. 13
1 Forceps	1 Stopper, rubber, solid, No. 6
1 pr Goggles, safety	Swabs (Q-tips)
1 Lamp, UV	6 Tubes, test, 10 cm
2 Medicine droppers	

REAGENTS

Glacial acetic acid, reagent-grade

Sodium acetate, reagent-grade

Liquid Nitrogen, 1 pt

Sodium chloride, reagent-grade

Normal saline solution, 0.9%

Sodium hydroxide solution, 1 M

Seminal fluid: Usually several mL can be obtained from a hospital or clinic if they have a few weeks notice. They get it from patients who have had vasectomies and are being checked for sperm. Store it in a refrigerator.

Alpha-naphthyl phosphate, calcium salt, Cat. No. 5547, Dajac Laboratories (Borden, Inc., Philadelphia, Pa. 19124), or Aldrich Chemical Company Naphthanil diazo blue B, Cat. No. 4741, K & K Laboratories (121 Express S Plainview, N. Y. 11803).

Acetate buffer solution: Using a laboratory balance, add 23.0 g of NaCl, 2.0 g of $NaC_2H_3O_2$, and 0.5 mL of glacial acetic acid to about 90 mL of deionized water in a graduated 150 mL beaker. Stir with a glass stirring rod until the solids dissolve. Adjust the pH to 4.9. Add additional water to make the final volume about 100 mL, place in a glass-stoppered 125 Erlenmeyer flask, and store in a refrigerator.

Alpha-naphthyl phosphate solution: Weigh 0.30 g of alpha-naphthyl phosphate calcium salt, on an analytical balance. Place in a 30-mL dropping bottle and add 20 mL of acetate buffer solution. Swirl and suspend the powder, and store in a refrigerator. This should be prepared fresh about every 2 months.

Dye solution: Weigh 0.30 g of naphthanil diazo blue B on an analytical balance. Add it to a 30 mL dropping bottle containing 20 mL of normal saline. This suspension should be kept in a refrigerator and prepared fresh about every 2 months.

Inhibitor solution: Weigh 3.0 g of L-tartaric acid on an analytical balance. Add to some deionized water and 35 mL of 1 M NaOH in a graduated 150 mL beaker, and stir until dissolved. Adjust the pH to 4.9 by adding 1 M NaOH if too low and L-tartaric acid if too high. Add deionized water to make 100 mL, and store in a refrigerator. Fresh solution should be made every 2 months.

METHOD

Laboratory safety: Gloves and goggles should be worn routinely as good laboratory practice.

PART A: SUSPECTED STAINS ON CLOTHING OR BEDDING

1. Cut a 1×1 cm piece of the material including or containing the suspected seminal stain. Place it in a 10 cm test tube with 3 mL of deionized water. Label this T for test.

2. Cut a 1×1 cm piece from an unstained area and place it in a 10 cm test tube with 3 mL of deionized water. Label the tube C for control.

3. After 15 minutes, prepare four additional 10 cm test tubes as follows:

T (test)	3 drops of phosphate solution
TI (test inhibitor)	3 drops of phosphate solution
	3 drops of inhibitor solution
C (control)	3 drops of phosphate solution
CI (control inhibitor)	3 drops of phosphate solution
	3 drops of inhibitor solution

   Swirl each tube to mix the contents.

4. Transfer 0.5 mL from the test solution prepared in step 1 to each of the T and TI tubes prepared in step 3. Swirl to mix.

5. Transfer 0.5 mL from the control solution prepared in step 2 to each of the C and CI tubes prepared in step 3. Swirl to mix.

6. Add 3 drops of the dye solution to each of the T, TI, C, and CI tubes. Swirl to mix.

7. If the T tube turns reddish-brown to violet in less than 30 seconds, while the TI tube remains clear to a pale yellow, the test is positive. The C and CI tubes, however, must also remain clear to pale yellow, or the result is suspect. Another control portion should be prepared and run to determine if a seminal stain was included in "control" or if one or more of the reagents has deteriorated.

8. If T turns reddish-brown to purple in 30 seconds or less, and no purple color is imparted to TI, C, or CI, report the test as positive for acid phosphatase.

PART B: EXAMINATION OF SWABS

1. Place the swab in a 10 cm test tube containing 3 mL of deionized water, label it T for "test" and proceed as in Part A. Use deionized water as control or blank.

PART C: VAGINAL WASHINGS

1. Place 3 drops of wash in each of two 10 cm test tubes containing 0.5 mL of deionized water. Label one tube T and the other TI. Add 3 drops of phosphate solution to T and 3 drops of phosphate solution plus 3 drops of inhibitor to TI. Use deionized water for the control. Add 3 drops of the dye solution to each tube. Swirl to mix.

2. If the wash sample contains too much acid phosphatase it may exceed the inhibiting capacity of the L-tartrate solution. Both T and TI would turn purple. To eliminate this possibility, repeat the test using only 1 drop of aspirate or some further dilution made in deionized water.

PART D: LOCATION OF SEMINAL STAINS BY THEIR PHOSPHORESCENCE (ADVANCED)

1. Obtain a half-liter Dewar flask and fill it with liquid nitrogen. (Caution: The temperature of liquid nitrogen is −320° F, and it freezes fingers quickly! You may wish to wear insulated gloves.)

2. Hold a piece of the suspect stain with a forceps, carefully lower it into the solution, and hold it there until rapid bubbling ceases.

3. Turn out the lights or go into a dark room and direct the rays from a UV lamp on the stain. A seminal stain should glow. Record what you see.

4. Repeat the procedure with a blank piece of cloth.

SELECTED SOURCES FOR ADDITIONAL INFORMATION

Allard, J.E., "The collection of data from findings in cases of sexual assault and the significance of spermatozoa on viginal, anal and oral swabs," *Sci. & Just.*, 37 (2), (1997), 99.

Allery, J., Telmun, N., Mieusset, R., Blanc, A., and Rouge, D., "Cytological detection of spermatozoa comparisons of three staining methods," *J. Forens. Sci.*, 46 (2), (2001), 288.

Banerjee, P.K., "Identification of spermatozoa through fluorescent microscopy," *Medicine Sci. and the Law*, 27 (1987), 51.

Berti, Andrea, Virgill, A., D'Errico, G. Vespi, G., Lago, G., and Cavazzana, A., "Expression of seminal vesicle specific antigen in serum of lung tumor patients," *J. Forens. Sci.*, 50 (5), (2005), 1114.

Bryson, C.K., Garlo, A.M., and Piner, S.C., "Vaginal swabs: endogenous and postcoital components," *J. Forens. Sci. Soc.*, 29 (3), (1989), 157.

Chapman, R.L., Brown, N.M., and Keating, S.M., "The isolation of spermatozoa from sexual assault swabs using proteinase K," *J. Forens. Sci. Soc.*, 29 (3), (1989), 207.

Chen, J., Kobilinsky, L., Wolosiu, D., Shaler, R., and Baum, H., "A physical method for separating spermatozoa from epithelial cells in sexual assault evidence," *J. Forens. Sci.*, 43 (1), (1998), 114.

Harada, A., Umetsu, K., Yuasa, I., Ikeda, N., and Suzuki, T., "Detection of orosomucoid 1 phenotype in semen and semen stains," *J. Forens. Sci.*, 34 (3), (1989), 665.

Honma, M., Yoshi, T., Ishiyama, I., Mitani, K., Kominami, R., and Muramatsu, M., "Individual identification from semen by the deoxyribonucleic acid (DNA) fingerprint technique," *J. Forens. Sci.*, 34 (1), (1989), 222.

Hooft, P.J., and Van de Voorde, H.P., "The zinc test as an alternative for acid phosphatase spot tests in the primary identification of seminal traces," *Forens. Sci. Intl.*, 47, (1990), 269.

Iwasaki, M., Kubo, S., Ogata, M., and Nakasono, I., "A demonstration of spermatozoa on vaginal swabs after complete destruction of the vaginal cell deposits," *J. Forens. Sci.*, 34 (3), (1989), 659.

Johnson, E.D., and Kotowski, T.M., "Detection of prostrate specific antigen by ELISA," *J. Forens. Sci.*, 38 (2), (1993), 250.

Keating, S.M., and Higgs, D.F., "The detection of amylase on swabs from sexual assault cases," *J. Forens. Sci. Soc.*, 34 (2), (1994), 89.

Khaldi, Nadia, Miras, A., Botti, K., Benali, L., and Gromb, S., "Evaluation of three rapid detection methods for the forensic identification of seminal fluid in rape cases," *J. Forens. Sci.,* 49 (4), (2004), 754.

King, S.J., Kelly, R.W., and Sutton, J.G., "The development of an enzyme-linked immunosorbent assay for 19-OH PG F1alpha/F2alpha," *Forens. Sci. Intl.*, 40 (1989), 211.

King, S.J., and Sutton, J.G., "A survey of the concentration of the 19-OH F1alpha/F2alpha prostaglandins in the semen of fertile, infertile, and vasectomized men and their stability in both liquid semen and semen stains," *Forens. Sci. Intl.*, 40 (1989), 217.

Kobus, Hilton, J., Silenieks, E., and Schamberg, J., "Improving the effectiveness of fluorescence for the detection of semen stains on fabrics," *J. Forens. Sci.,* 47 (4), (2002), 819.

Kobus, H.J., Silenieks, E., and Scharnberg, J., "Improving the effectiveness of fluorescence for the detection of semen stains on fabrics," *J. Forens. Sci.,* 47 (4), (2002), 950.

Montagna, C.P., "The recovery of seminal components and DNA from the vagina of a homicide victim 34 days after postmortem," *J. Forens. Sci.,* 41 (4), (1996), 700.

Rutter, E.R., Kind, S.S., and Smalldon, K.W., "Estimation of time since intercourse from acid phosphatase/UV270 absorbance ratios," *J. Forens. Sci. Soc.*, 20 (1980), 271.

Sarada, A., and Ramasastri, B.V., "A simple TLC identification of choline in human semen," *J. Forens. Sci. Soc.*, 23 (1983), 241.

Schiff, A. F., "Reliability of the acid phosphatase test for the identification of seminal stains," *J. Forens. Sci.*, 23 (4), (1978), 833.

Standefer, J.C., and Street, E.W., "Postmortem stability of prostatic acid phosphatase," *J. Forens. Sci.*, 22 (1), (1977), 165.

Still, A., "Police enquiries in sexual offenses," *J. Forens. Sci. Soc.*, 15 (1975), 183.

Stoilovic, M., "Determination of semen and blood stains using Polilight as a light source," *Forens. Sci. Intl.*, 51 (1991), 289.

EXPERIMENT 30

DATA SHEET

Name _____

Date _____

SEMINAL STAINS BY HUMAN PROSTATICACID PHOSPHATASE

Part A: Suspected Stains on Clothing or Bedding

Record your observations for each tube here.

Tube T   Tube C

Tube TI   Tube CI

Conclusions

Part B: Examination of Swabs

Tube T   Tube C

Tube TI   Tube CI

Conclusions

Part C: Vaginal Washings

Tube T   Tube C

Tube TI   Tube CI

Conclusions

Part D: Location of Seminal Stains by Their Phosphorescence (Advanced)

Observations with   Observations with
stained material   blank material

Question

1. How do you think you could use this test to determine the order of deposition of overlapping seminal and blood stains?

Arson Detection—
The Recovery
of Flammable Liquids

Fires generally burn from the point of origin upward and outward; therefore, if a liquid accelerant has been used to start a fire, some of it will probably have soaked downward and not have been entirely consumed. The fire investigator attempts to trace the fire to its point or points of origin and then digs down and collects samples. To prevent the evaporation and loss of volatile liquids, samples must be placed in air-tight containers. Frequently, new quart or gallon paint cans are used as are quart fruit jars.

Once the samples arrive at the laboratory, the forensic chemist may use any of a number of procedures to recover and identify the accelerants from the collected debris. One popular method is the headspace technique, introduced in Experiment 27. Here a portion of the debris is placed in a glass jar or empty paint can which has had a small hole punched in the lid. This hole is covered with a silicone septum glued on with Super-glue. When the container is heated, any volatile residue present in the debris will be driven off and trapped in the container's enclosed air space. A few milliliters of the vapor is removed with a syringe and analyzed by gas chromatography. This procedure will be followed in Part A. A recent modification involves adding a charcoal trap. This technique will be explained in Part B. An older technique involves the use of an immiscible solvent distillation with toluene and water and collecting any volatile materials in the toluene layer. Again, gas chromatography is used to analyze the recovered liquid. Gas chromatography (GC) will be used to identify the recovered accelerant as to general type, such as gasoline, kerosene, etc.

CRIME SCENE

The fire department is called to put out a fire in a furniture warehouse. The fire appears to have started in one of the large wooden storage containers. A check of the storage records indicates that nothing spontaneously combustible was in the container, so the fire chief suspects foul play. He has collected some of the charred wood from where the fire appears to have started and a few partially burned rags lying nearby. You have one of these samples, and your job is to determine if gasoline, kerosene, lighter fluid, or some similar material was present.

EQUIPMENT

1	Beaker, 250 mL	1	Hot plate
1	Brush, test tube, small	1	Pipet, 1 mL
1	Gas chromatograph, equipped	1	Pipet, Pasteur
	preferably with a FI detector	1	Rack, test tube
1 pr	Goggles, safety	1	Syringe, 10 μL
1	Holder, test tube		

1 Syringe, gas tight, 5 mL, or Plastipak disposable syringe, 3 mL (Becton-Dickinson No. 5570)

4 Test tubes with rubber septum caps, 20 × 150 mm (a quart fruit jar or gallon paint can is preferred). If they are available, then a drying oven is necessary, but the hot plate and test tubes indicated are not needed.

1 Tube, test, 50 mm

REAGENTS

Accelerants (kerosene, gasoline, lighter fluid)

Activated charcoal, 50–200 mesh (Fisher Scientific)

Carbon disulfide (Fisher Scientific)

Copper wire, 22 ga. × 4 cm., flattened on one end for a distance of 5 mm.

Samples of burned fabric or wood with accelerants on them.

SE-30, 3% on Chromosorb W, 60-80 mesh, TC detector or 10% DC-200 on Chromosorb P

SE-30, 10%, on Chromosorb P, 60-80 mesh, FI detector

Sodium silicate solution (Fisher Scientific)

METHOD

PART A: HEADSPACE ANALYSIS

We will assume you do not have glass jars or clean metal cans.

1. Obtain a sample from your instructor.

2. Place a portion of your sample into the bottom third of a test tube. Place a septum cap on the test tube.

3. Fill a 250 mL beaker with water and heat it to boiling on a hot plate. Place the test tube in the hot water for 3 to 5 minutes, holding it steady with the aid of a test tube holder.

4. Remove the tube from the water, and insert the syringe needle through the septum cap to obtain a sample of vapor.

5. Remove 1 mL of vapor, and inject it into the gas chromatograph. Obtain directions on the use of the gas chromatograph from your instructor.

6. Pipet 1 mL of each accelerant into separate test tubes. Cover each with a septum cap, and at room temperature remove 1 mL of vapor from each tube for analysis.

7. Compare the general profile of each accelerant to that obtained in step 5 to identify the accelerant present in the debris. Table 31-1 shows one set of GC conditions.

   Figure 31-1 shows the results obtained for gasoline.

TABLE 31–1	Conditions for Using the Gow-Mac Gas Chromatograph
Flow rate	60 mL/min, N$_2$)
Column	10% DC-200 on Chromosorb P, 4 ft.
Temperature	85° C
Filament current	180 mA
Attenuation	4
Sample size	5 µL

PART B: VAPOR CONCENTRATION ON CHARCOAL (ADVANCED) *

Often headspace analysis is not sufficiently sensitive to detect minute traces of flammable hydrocarbons that may be present in debris collected at the scene of a suspected arson. One approach for enhancing the sensitivity of detecting small quantities of flammable residues is to improve the collection process so that a significant quantity of flammable hydrocarbons can be removed from the debris for analysis by gas chromatography. For this purpose the use of absorbent materials for trapping hydrocarbons has achieved wide use in the crime laboratory. Commonly, activated charcoal is used as an absorbent.

Activated charcoal particles readily absorb hydrocarbons and when they are exposed to hydrocarbon vapor, they are able to trap a large quantity of material on a small number of charcoal particles. The trapped hydrocarbon molecules can then be recovered by washing them off of the charcoal with a solvent, carbon disulfide (CS$_2$).

METHOD

1. Obtain a piece of copper wire from your instructor and flatten one end with a hammer if it is not already flattened.

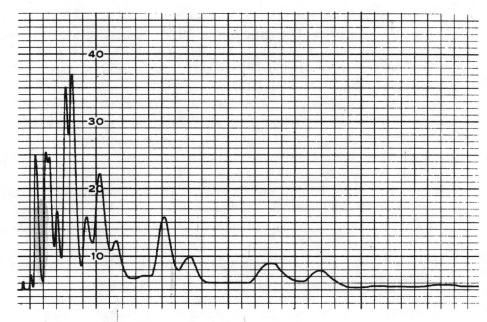

FIGURE 31–1 A gas chromatogram of one brand of regular gasoline.

*This method is based on a procedure developed by John A. Juhala, Ph.D. and published in Arson Analysis Newsletter, Vol. 6, No. 2, 1982.

2. Dip the flattened end of the wire in sodium silicate solution and then into activated charcoal. Dry the wire in an oven at 70° C for 15 minutes.

3. Insert the coated wire into the air space of a test tube containing a small quantity of a volatile hydrocarbon. Insert the wire through a hole placed in the septum cap of the test tube.

4. Fill a 250 mL beaker with water and heat it to 70–80° C on a hot plate. Place the test tube in the hot water and hold it steady for 10–15 minutes with a test tube holder.

5. Remove the tube from the water and carefully remove the coated wire.

6. Wash the coated wire with 3–5 drops of carbon disulfide using a Pasteur pipet. Collect the washings in a 50 mm test tube.

7. Your instructor will assist you in injecting 1–2 μL of the carbon disulfide washings into a gas chromatograph.

8. Compare the profile of your chromatogram to results obtained in Part A of this experiment.

SELECTED SOURCES FOR ADDITIONAL INFORMATION

Almirall, J.R., Bruna, J., and Furton, K.G., "The recovery of accelerants in aqueous samples from fire debris using solid-phase microextraction," *Sci. & Just.*, 36 (4), (1996), 283.

Armstrong, Andrew, Babrauskas, V., Holmes, D. L., Martin, C., Powell, R., Riggs, S., and Young, L. D., "The evaluation of the extent of transporting or "tracking" an identifiable ignitable liquid (gasoline) throughout fire scenes during the investigative process," *J. Forens. Sci.*, 49 (4), (2004), 741.

Barshick, S., "Analysis of accelerants and fire debris using aroma detection technology," *J. Forens. Sci.*, 43 (2), (1998), 284.

Berrett, R.R., and Candy, C.F., "The training of fire investigators in the UK," *Sci. & Just.*, 38 (3), (1998), 195.

Caddy, B., and Smith, F.P., "Methods of fire debris preparation for detection of accelerants," *Forens. Sci. Rev.*, 3 (1991), 57.

Coulombe, R., "Chemical markers in weathered gasoline," *J. Forens. Sci.*, 40 (5), (1995), 867.

Dhole, V.R., Kurhekar, M.P., and Ambade, K.A., "Detection of petroleum accelerant residues on partially burnt objects in burning/arson offences," *Sci. & Just.*, 35 (3), (1995), 217.

Dietz, W.R., "Improved charcoal packaging for accelerant recovery by passive diffusion," *J. Forens. Sci.*, 36 (1), (1991), 111.

Fernandes, M.S., Lau, C.M., and Wong, W.C., "The effect of volatile residues in burnt household items on the detection of fire accelerants," *Sci. & Just.*, 42 (1), (2002), 7.

Frenkel, M., Tsaroom, S., Aizenstadt, Z., Kraus, S., and Daphna, D., "Enhanced sensitivity in analysis of arson residues: an adsorption tube/gas chromatograph method," *J. Forens. Sci.*, 29 (3), (1984), 723.

Furton, K.G., Almirall, J.R., and Bruna, J.C., "A novel method for the analysis of gasoline from fire debris using headspace solid-phase microextraction," *J. Forens. Sci.*, 41 (1), (1996), 12.

Hirz, R., "Gasoline brand identification and individualization of gasoline lots," *J. Forens. Sci. Soc.*, 29 (2), (1989), 91.

Holleyhead, R., "Ignition of flammable gases and liquids by cigarettes: a review," *Sci. & Just.*, 36 (4), (1996), 257.

Karkkainen, M., Seppala, I., and Himberg, K., "Detection of trace levels of gasoline in arson cases by GC/MS with an automatic on-line thermal desorber," *J. Forens. Sci.*, 39 (1), (1994), 186.

Kinard, W.D., and Midkiff, C.R., "Arson evidence container evaluation: "new generation" ka-pak bags," *J. Forens. Sci.*, 36 (6), (1991), 1714.

Kurz, M.E., Schultz, S., Griffith, J., Broadus, K., Sparks, J., Dabdour, G., and Brock, J., "Effect of background interference on accelerant detection by canines," *J. Forens. Sci.*, 41 (5), (1996), 868.

Lennard, C.J., Tristan Rochaix, V., Margot, P. and Huber, K., "A GC-MS data base of target compound chromatograms for the identification of arson accelerants," *Sci. & Just.*, 35 (1), 19.

Lewis, R.J., Denieul, S.E., Chem, C., Langford, A.M., and Okley, M., "The analysis of fire debris for the presence of propan-2-ol using dynamic head space concentration and gas chromatography with flame ionization detection," *J. Forens. Sci.*, 44 (5), (1999), 1061.

Lloyd, Julie A., and Edmiston, P. L., "Preferential extraction of hydrocarbons from fire debris samples by solid phase microextraction," *J. Forens. Sci.,* 48 (1), (2003), 130.

McGee, E., Dip, N., and Lang, T.L., "A study of the effects of a micelle encapsulation fire suppression agent on dynamic head space analysis of fire debris samples," *J. Forens. Sci.*, 47 (2), (2002), 267.

Newman, R., Dietz, W.R., and Lothridge, K., "The use of activated charcoal strips for fire debris extractions by passive diffusion. Part I: The effects of time, temperature, strip size, and sample concentration," *J. Forens. Sci.*, 41 (3), (1996), 361.

Phelps, J.L., Chasteen, C.E., and Render, M.M., "Extraction and analysis of low molecular weight alcohols and acetone from fire debris using passive head space analysis," *J .Forens. Sci.*, 39 (1), (1994), 194.

Reeve, V., Jeffrey, J., Weiks, D., and Jennings, W., "Developments in arson analysis: a comparison of charcoal adsorption and direct headspace injection techniques using fused silica capillary gas chromatography," *J. Forens. Sci.*, 31 (2), (1986), 479.

Ren, Q., and Bertsch, W., "A comprehensive sample preparation scheme for accelerants in suspect arson cases," *J. Forens. Sci.*, 44 (3), (1999), 504.

Russell, L.W., "The concentration and analysis of volatile hydrocarbons in fire debris using Tenax GC," *J. Forens. Sci. Soc.*, 21 (1981), 317.

Saferstein, R., and Park, S.A., "Applications of dynamic headspace analysis to laboratory and field arson investigation," J. Forens. Sci., 27 (3), (1982), 484.

Stackhouse, C.C., and Gray, C.I., "Alternative methods for processing arson samples in polyester bags," *J. Forens. Sci.*, 33 (3), (1988), 515.

Tantarskir, R.E., "Using absorbents to collect hydrocarbon accelerants from concrete," *J. Forens. Sci.*, 30 (4), (1985), 1230.

Tranthim-Fryer, D.J., "The application of a simple and inexpensive modified carbon wire adsorption/solvent extraction technique to the analysis of accelerants and volatile organic compounds in arson debris," *J. Forens. Sci.*, 35 (2), (1990), 271.

Trimpe, M.A., "Turpentine in arson analysis," *J. Forens. Sci.*, 36 (4), (1991) 1059.

Waters, L.V., and Palmer, L.A., "Multiple analysis of fire debris samples using passive headspace concentration," *J. Forens. Sci.*, 38 (1), (1993), 165.

EXPERIMENT 31   Name _____

DATA SHEET   Date _____

ARSON DETECTION—THE RECOVERY OF FLAMMABLE LIQUIDS

Record all instrumental settings (parameters) on your chromatograms. Be sure also to record the column packing material. These are to be turned in to your instructor along with the identity of the accelerant used in starting the fire, if you have determined that one was present.

Identity of accelerant (if present) _____

Questions

1. A suspect is apprehended, and his lawyer questions your results. She says that what you found was a cleaning rag used on a forklift and no arson was committed. How could you go about verifying the truth or fiction of her statement?

2. Suppose you determine that the fire started on a cement pad. How might you get a sample out of the cement without destroying the pad?

3. Why might there still be accelerant present on materials found at the base of the fire even though the building was almost entirely burned down?

4. How might one determine the physical location of the origin of the fire, so that he might know where to look for evidence of accelerants?

Spot Tests for Explosives and Explosive Residues*

The detonation of a bomb leaves in its wake a large number of fragments and a lot of debris, not only from the bomb, but from the surrounding area. In order for an investigation to proceed, the basic components of the bomb must be reconstructed. One of these components is the type of explosive used, and that is what will interest us here.

Microscopic particles are usually found on many pieces of debris. The difficulty is in discovering which pieces of debris contain particles from explosives and which are just debris. This experiment presents several spot tests that can help determine which pieces of debris are worthy of further analysis. (Note: After a bombing, there is considerable milling around and sightseers come by the hundreds, so it is important to remove the valuable debris as soon as possible.)

HANDLING OF DEBRIS

According to Hoffman and Byall (1974):

> The location of the bomb at detonation must be found and loose soil or other debris from the interior of the blast site should be scraped out, packaged, and labeled since the debris from the blast site is most likely to contain traces of the undetonated explosive. Other good sources of explosive residue are the objects located near the device on detonation. Wood, insulation, rubber, or other soft materials which are readily penetrated often collect traces of the explosive. Even metal objects in close proximity to the bomb should be collected since explosive residues have been found on these surfaces in many cases. A portion of the device itself is an excellent source for recovering traces of the explosive. In pipe bombs, for example, particles of the explosive are frequently found adhering to the pipe cap or to the pipe threads, either by being impacted into the metal by the force of the explosion or by being deposited in the threads during the construction of the bomb.
>
> The samples should be packaged in containers of appropriate size. Soil and other soft, loose material can be stored in plastic bags with suitable closures. Metal or other objects with sharp edges should be wrapped in plastic after

---

*This experiment is based almost entirely on Parker et al. (1975b), with excerpts from Beveridge et al. (1975), Hoffman and Byall (1974), and Parker et al. (1975a); see the Selected Sources at the end of this experiment.

placing some protective material such as cardboard around the sharp edges to prevent them from piercing the plastic wrapper. It is important to properly wrap metal or other objects with hard, smooth, surfaces since explosive residues clinging to these surfaces are often dislodged in transmitting the package to the laboratory. Loose particles can be recovered from the packing material if the container has remained tightly sealed.

TYPES OF EXPLOSIVES

There are many ways to classify explosives, some of which are: military, civilian, high-order, or low-order. Few bombings involve military explosives (e.g, PETN, RDX, TNT) because their availability is severely restricted. The most commonly used explosives are dynamite and homemade bombs made from black powder, smokeless powder, or chlorate and sugar. More recently, ammonium nitrate and fuel oil have become popular. Table 32-1 lists several explosives and their common abbreviations.

DYNAMITE

Dynamite is by far the most commonly encountered high-order explosive used in destructive devices associated with criminal acts in this country. There are a number of types of dynamites, including straight dynamite, ammonia dynamite, blasting gelatin, ammonia gelatin, and nitrostarch dynamite. The color of these explosive compounds vary widely—from off-white to nearly black.

While there are a variety of dynamite formulations, only a few components need to be identified to confirm the presence of dynamite residues in bomb debris. These components are sulfur, ammonium nitrate, sodium nitrate, and the explosive oils [nitroglycerin (NG) and ethylene glycol dinitrite (EGDN)] absorbed on the binder, or dope, which makes up the bulk of the dynamite compounds.

Not all of these components will be present in every type of dynamite and, hence, not in the debris from every dynamite bomb. Even dynamites of the same type differ in their composition. For example, straight dynamite of up to 30% strength contains about 2% sulfur, while higher-strength dynamites usually do not contain this component.

Most dynamites contain sodium nitrate, but only ammonia dynamite contains ammonium nitrate. All commercial dynamites, with the exception of nitrostarch dynamite, contain explosive oils in their binders. A comprehensive discussion of the specific compositions of the various types of dynamites is a very involved subject, and it is not our purpose here to do more than indicate the variability of their compositions with respect to certain compounds.

TABLE 32–1	Abbreviations of Common Explosives
2,4-DNT	2,4-dinitrotoluene
2,6-DNT	2,6-dinitrotoluene
EGDN	Ethyleneglycol dinitrate
MMAN	Monomethylamine nitrate
NC	Nitrocellulose
NG	Nitroglycerin
NS	Nitrostarch
PETN	Pentaerythityl tetranitrate
PDX	Cyclotrimethylene trinitramine
TETRYL	2,4,6-trinitrophenyl methylnitramine
TNT	2,4,6-trinitrotoluene

The identification of dynamite in bomb debris is based on the detection of the explosive oils (NG and EGDN) and one or more of the inorganic components.

IMPROVIZED MIXTURES

Low-order explosive mixtures made from commonly available chemicals have been termed **improvised mixtures**. The majority of the improvised mixtures used in criminal bombings in this country fall into two categories: homemade black powders and homemade flash powders. These mixtures are usually confined in some container such as a section of capped pipe, and initiated with an external burning pyrotechnic or homemade fuse. Homemade black powder is a mixture of potassium nitrate, sulfur, and charcoal. It is usually poorly made, and unconsumed particles are abundant in the bomb debris. The components of this mixture can be chemically identified using techniques described previously.

Homemade flash powder mixtures have a variety of formulations. They usually contain finely divided aluminum or magnesium metal and an oxidizing agent, such as ammonium chlorate, potassium chlorate, or potassium perchlorate, with possible additions of sulfur and/or sawdust.

CRIME SCENE

A bomb exploded about half an hour ago outside the marine recruiting station. A huge crowd gathered immediately, and they destroyed nearly as much as the bomb. A detective managed to gather up several pieces of debris and put them in a box. These have been delivered to you, and your job is to determine which pieces of debris have explosive residues on them.

EQUIPMENT

5	Beakers, 10 mL	1 bx	Matches
3	Beakers, 250 mL (for reagents)	5	Medicine droppers
16	Bottles, 2-oz, dropping	2	Plates, spot, black
1	Bottle, wash	4	Plates spot, white
1	Brush, test tube	1	Rack, test tube
1	Burner, Bunsen	5	Rods, glass, stirring, 10 cm
1	Cylinder, graduated, 100 mL	1	Spatula
1 pr	Goggles, safety		Swabs, cotton-tipped
1	Holder, test tube	3 ft	Tubing, rubber, burner, 1 m
1	Lamp, UV	10	Tubes, test, 10 cm
1	Magnifying glass		Disposable gloves

REAGENTS

Aniline sulfate reagent: Dissolve 0.1 g of aniline sulfate (Eastman Organic Chemicals) in 100 mL of concentrated sulfuric acid.

Barium chloride reagent: Dissolve 5 g of barium chloride in 100 mL of distilled water.

Brucine reagent: Dissolve 5 g of brucine sulfate (NF grade, Union Carbide) in 100 mL of concentrated sulfuric acid.

Cupric tetrapyridine reagent: Dissolve about 5 g of cupric nitrate trihydrate in 40 mL of distilled water; add 80 mL of pyridine.

Diphenylamine reagent: Dissolve 1 g of diphenylamine in 100 mL of concentrated sulfuric acid.

Griess reagent:

Solution 1: Dissolve 1 g of sulfanilic acid in 100 mL of 30% acetic acid.

Solution 2: Dissolve 0.1 g N-2-naphthyl-ethylenediamine dihydrochloride (Fischer Scientific) in 230 mL of boiling distilled water. Cool. Decant the colorless supernatant liquid, and mix with 100 mL of glacial acetic acid. Store the excess reagent in a refrigerator. Do not keep over 2 months.

J-Acid reagent: Dissolve 1 g of 6-amino-l-naphthol-3-sulfonic acid (technical grade, Eastman Kodak Company) in 100 mL of concentrated sulfuric acid.

Methylene blue reagent:

Solution 1: Mix 0.1 mL of 1.6% aqueous solution of methylene blue (USP) with 25 mL of 50% aqueous solution of zinc sulfate.

Solution 2: Dissolve 40 g of potassium nitrate in 100 mL of distilled water.

Nessler reagent: Stir 10 g of mercuric iodide into a thin paste with a little distilled water. Add 5 g of potassium iodide, forming a solution. Dissolve 20 g of sodium hydroxide in 80 mL of distilled water, add to above solution, and bring to 100 mL. Let the solution stand for several days. Decant and store the supernatant liquid in a brown bottle.

Nitron reagent: Dissolve 1 g of nitron reagent (Eastman Kodak Company) in 20 mL of 88% formic acid. Use a black spot plate with this reagent.

Potassium test paper: Potassium test paper is manufactured by Macherey, Nagel & Company, Duren, West Germany, and distributed by Gallard-Schlesinger Chemical Manufacturing Corporation, Carle Place, N.Y.

Silver nitrate reagent: Dissolve 5 g of silver nitrate in 100 mL of distilled water.

Sodium test reagent:

Solution A: Dissolve 10 g of uranyl acetate in 50 mL of distilled water.

Solution B: Stir 30 g of zinc acetate with 3 g of 30% acetic acid. Dilute to 50 mL with distilled water. Warm solutions A and B, and mix them while warm. This must result in a clear solution. Add a trace of sodium chloride, stopper, and let stand for 24 hours. Filter off the precipitated sodium zinc uranyl acetate, and discard. Store the filtrate in a glass-stoppered bottle. This reagent keeps indefinitely.

Sulfuric acid reagent: Add 1 drop of concentrated sulfuric acid to the sample (use caution!).

Acetone	HNO_3, 1:10
Black powder	Pyridine
Carbon disulfide	Smokeless powder, double-base
Chlorate/sugar mixture	Smokeless powder, single-base
Dynamite fragments	NaOH, 2 M

One stick of dynamite (cost $0.70 + $5.00 bookkeeping fee) is sufficient to make dozens of samples. Flush the unused stick down the drain or you have to maintain a storage record. The powders can be obtained from most sporting goods stores.

METHOD

GENERAL INFORMATION

An initial extraction is done with acetone. This has a dual advantage in that it extracts sufficient inorganic ions and explosive organic compounds to perform the spot tests and to use for TLC and IR follow up measurements. (Of the organic compounds used in this study, nitroglycerin, ethyleneglycol dinitrate, cyclotrimethylenetrinitramine (RDX), pentaerythritol tetranitrate (PETN), tetryl, and the nitrotoluenes are all soluble in acetone to a sufficient degree to give good tests. The least soluble is RDX, where 1 g dissolves in approximately 25 mL of acetone. While nitrocellulose and nitrostarch are not truly soluble in acetone, they are completely dispersed in it to form colloidal "solutions." The acetone solution is then filtered if necessary. This extract is allowed to evaporate to dryness without heating in a hood. Some explosives, for example, nitroglycerine, are extremely temperature sensitive and may decompose upon excessive heating. The residue may be scraped from the evaporating dish and spot tests run on the solid, or, as it is often more convenient, it may be taken up in a small amount of acetone. For spot tests, 1 to 2 drops of this solution are placed on a spot plate and allowed to evaporate to dryness. The test reagent is added and the results noted.

If necessary, a water extraction is performed to obtain possibly stronger tests for the inorganic ions. The extract is filtered, if necessary, and evaporated to less than 1 mL. One to 2 drops of this concentrated solution are placed on a spot plate and the test reagent added.

Unfortunately, the acetone extraction also carries with it extraneous material which may interfere with the spot tests. This is particularly true for those reagents in a concentrated sulfuric acid solution. The acid tends to char any organic materials present, thereby obscuring the tests. In these instances, a methanol or ether extraction, or both, may be performed instead of the acetone extraction. Alternatively, the dried acetone extract may be taken up in methanol or diethylether rather than acetone. This presents fewer interferences or less masking of the spot test. However, it has the disadvantage that many explosives are less soluble in methanol and ether than in acetone.

Unless otherwise specified, the procedure for each test consists of adding 1 drop of reagent to the sample in a white spot plate. If 2 reagents are needed for the test, 1 drop of each is used. Color development is observed and compared with knowns. Table 32-2 shows the results of positive tests. If a black spot plate is specified, then the type and color of precipitate is noted.

1. Arrange 4 white and 2 black spot plates as shown in the data sheet.

2. Obtain from the instructor a small piece of dynamite, break it into smaller pieces, and place a small fragment into each of the top 12 spots.

    (It will not explode in your hands. It is like brown sugar and crumbles easily.)

3. Repeat step 2 for black powder, the single-base and double-base smoke powders, and a chlorate/sugar mixture.

4. If the instructor has another known explosive, such as TNT, substitute this for debris unknown No. 1 of the unknown debris.

5. Obtain five pieces of debris from the instructor, and examine each carefully with a magnifying glass. Record any observations, and compare the crystal structure and appearance of what you see with the samples of known explosives.

6. Dip a cotton-tipped swab into acetone and carefully swab one-half of the surface you judge to contain possible explosive residues. (The other half is saved for any additional tests you might want to make.)

7. Place the swab into a 10 mL beaker (mark No. 1), and repeat the process with another swab, going over the same area as before.

8. Repeat steps 6 and 7 for the other pieces of debris. Be sure to mark each beaker clearly.

9. Use a wash bottle filled with acetone and wash off the swabs into the beaker. Use a gentle stream of acetone, 4 to 5 mL in total. Let the acetone evaporate to about 1 to 1.5 mL.

TABLE 32–2	Spot Plate Arrangement to Test for Explosives and Explosive Residues

	Greiss Reagent	Aniline Sulfate	Brucine	Cupric Tetrapyridine	Diphenylamine	J-Acid	Nessler	Metaylene Blue	Barium Chloride	Nitron	Silver Nitrate	Sulfuric Acid
Dynamite, known	○	○	○	○	○	○	○	○	○	○	○	○
Black powder, known	○	○	○	○	○	○	○	○	○	○	○	○
Smokeless powder single base, known	○	○	○	○	○	○	○	○	○	○	○	○
Smokeless powder double base, known	○	○	○	○	○	○	○	○	○	○	○	○
Chlorate/sugar known	○	○	○	○	○	○	○	○	○	○	○	○
Debris unknown No. 1	○	○	○	○	○	○	○	○	○	○	○	○
Debris unknown No. 2	○	○	○	○	○	○	○	○	○	○	○	○
Debris unknown No. 3	○	○	○	○	○	○	○	○	○	○	○	○
Debris unknown No. 4	○	○	○	○	○	○	○	○	○	○	○	○
Debris unknown No. 5	○	○	○	○	○	○	○	○	○	○	○	○
	White				White				Black			

10. Use a medicine dropper, and place 1–2 drops of the acetone concentrate in each of the 12 spots for debris sample No. 1. Do not wash out the beakers. You will need a few more drops later on.

11. Repeat step 10 (fresh medicine droppers) for the other pieces of debris.

Individual tests

Laboratory safety: Many of the reagents used in this laboratory are corrosive to the skin. Wear goggles and gloves.

The Greiss reagent is probably the best single reagent to use and should be used first, particularly if only a small amount of residue is available so that other tests cannot be made.

1. Add 1 drop of Greiss reagent to the first spot for each of the samples. Record your observations (briefly) directly on the data sheet on the spot provided.

The appearance of a pink to a red color indicates the presence of WEAK inorganic nitrites. The appearance of a red color fading immediately to a yellow color indicates the presence of STRONG inorganic nitrites. If no color develops immediately, add a few milligrams of zinc dust. The rapid development of a pink to red color indicates the presence of inorganic nitrites or some organic nitro compounds. The mixed reagents will turn pink upon setting and drying out, especially as solution No. 2 ages.

2. Repeat step 1 using aniline sulfate; this test is primarily for Br and I contaminants, but also as a confirmatory test for chlorate.

3. Repeat step 1 using Brucine reagent.

4. Repeat step 1 using cupric tetrapyridine reagent. This reagent requires 1 to 2 minutes to develop a precipitate. It is primarily for the perchlorate ion.

5. Repeat step 1 using diphenylamine.

6. Repeat step 1 using J-acid.

7. Repeat step 1 using Nessler's reagent.

8. Repeat step 1 using the methylene blue reagent.

9. Repeat step 1 using the barium chloride reagent. This should be the first spot on the black plates.

10. Repeat step 1 using the nitron reagent.

11. Repeat step 1 using the silver nitrate reagent. (*Caution:* This will turn your skin black wherever it touches once it gets in the sunlight. Wash any $AgNO_3$ off immediately.)

12. Repeat step 1 using sulfuric acid.

13. Add 3 to 4 drops of acetone to the residue on the beaker from the debris No. 1 extract. Slowly roll the beaker to dissolve the residue. Moisten the end of a stirring rod with this liquid, and touch this end to a piece of potassium test paper.

    Apply 1 drop of the neutral solution to be tested to the paper. Apply 1 to 2 drops of dilute nitric acid (1:10) to the same spot. The paper turns yellow, whereas the spot with the solution containing potassium remains orange. Check the manufacturer's instructions for possible interferences.

14. Repeat step 13 for all of the samples including the knowns. Record your observations on the data sheet, part 3.

15. Repeat the first part of step 13.

16. Add 1 or 2 drops of sodium reagent to the sample in a white spot plate. Place the spot plate under a UV lamp. Long wavelength UV gives better sensitivity than short wavelength. A bright fluorescence indicates the presence of sodium. A very concentrated potassium solution may also fluoresce, but more weakly. Record your observations on the data sheet, part 4.

17. Sulfur test: Use a very small fragment (approximately one-quarter to one-half the size of a pinhead) of the suspected sulfur in a small test tube. Add approximately 1 mL (20 drops) of pyridine. Gently warm the tube. Remove the heat, and add 2 drops of 2 M NaOH. Depending upon the concentration of sulfur, a blue to red-brown color is developed in the pyridine layer.

    If the sample must be extracted, carbon disulfide may be used. Completely evaporate the carbon disulfide over gentle heat (for example, a steam bath) and take up the remaining residue in pyridine. Carbon disulfide is quite flammable. Use care if using an open flame. If there are any traces of carbon disulfide remaining, a false positive may result. Traces of aluminum metal interfere and inhibit color formation. Thus, explosives like flash powder must be extracted first before the test for sulfur is made.

18. Clean up the spot plates, and put all the reagents back where they belong.

19. Add your conclusions to the data sheet.

SELECTED SOURCES FOR ADDITIONAL INFORMATION

Almog, Joseph, Klein, A., Yamirl, T., Shloosh, Y., and Abramovich-bar, S., "A field diagnostic test for the improvised explosive urea nitrate," *J. Forens. Sci.,* 50 (3), (2005), 582.

Bellamy, A.J., "Triacetone triperoxide: its chemical destruction," *J. Forens. Sci.*, 44 (3), (1999), 603.

Beveridge, A.D., Payton, S.F., Audette, R.J., Lambertus, A.J., and Shaddick, R.C., "Systematic analysis of explosive residues," *J. Forens. Sci.*, 20 (3), (1975), 431.

Brown, Ilayley, Kirkbride, K. P., Pigou, P. E., and Walker, G. S., "New developments in SPMER part 2: Analysis of ammonium nitrate-based explosives," *J. Forens. Sci.,* 49 (2), (2004), 215.

Burnett, B., and Golubous, P., "The first mail bomb (1833)," *J. Forens. Sci.*, 45 (5), (2000), 1090.

Calderara, Stephane, Gardebas, D., Martinez, F., and Khong, S., "Organic explosives analysis using on column-ion trap EI/NICI GC-MS with an external source," *J. Forens. Sci.,* 49 (5), (2004), 1005.

Cassamento, Sonia, Kwok, R., Roux, C., Dawson, M., and Doble, P., "Optimization of the separation of organic explosives by capillary electrophoresis with artificial neural networks.," *J. Forens. Sci.,* 48 (5), (2003), 1075.

Davies, J.P., Blackwood, L.G., Davis, S.G., Goodrich, L.D., and Larson, R.A., "Design and calibration of pulse vapor generators for 2,4,6-trinitrotoluene, 1,3,5-trimethylene-2,4,6-trinitramine and pentaerythritol tetranitrate," *Analyt. Chemist*, 65 (1993), 3004.

Furton, K., Wu, K., and Almaril, J.R., "Optimization of solid phase micro extraction (SPME) for the recovery of explosives from aqueous and post-explosion debris followed by gas and liquid chromatic analysis," *J. Forens. Sci.*, 45 (4), (2000), 857.

Goodpasture, J. V., and Keto, R. O., "Identification of ascorbic acid and its degradation products in black powder substitutes," *J. Forens. Sci.,* 49 (3), (2004), 523.

Hayes, T.S., "A systematic procedure for the identification of post explosion samples of commercial blasting explosives," *J. Forens. Sci. Soc.*, 21, (1981), 307.

Hiley, R.W., "Investigations of thin layer chromatographic techniques used for forensic explosive analysis in the early 1970s," *J. Forens. Sci.*, 38 (4), (1993), 864.

Kamyshny, A., Magdassi, S., Avissar, Y., and Almog, J., "Water soaked evidence: Detectability of explosive traces after immersion in water," *J. Forens. Sci.,* 48 (2), (2003), 312.

Kee, T.G., Holmes, D.M., Doolan, K., Hamill, J.A., and Griffin R.M.E., "The identification of individual propellant particles," *J. Forens. Sci. Soc.*, 30 (5), (1990), 285.

Kirkbride, K.P., and Kobus, H.J., "The explosive reaction between swimming pool chlorine and brake fluid," *J. Forens. Sci.*, 36 (3), (1991), 902.

Kirkbride, K.P., Klass, G., and Pigou, P.E., "Application of solid phase microextraction to the recovery of organic explosives," *J. Forens. Sci.*, 43 (1), (1998), 67.

Kolla, P., and Sprunkel, A., "Identification of dynamite explosives in post explosion residues," *J. Forens. Sci.*, 40 (3), (1995), 406.

Lloyd, J.B.F., and King, R.M., "One pot processing of swabs for organic explosives and firearms residue traces," *J. Forens. Sci.*, 35 (4), (1994), 956.

MacCrennan, W.A., and Reardon, M.R., "A qualitative comparison of smokeless powder measurements," *J. Forens. Sci.*, 47 (5), (2002), 996.

Mahoney, R.J., Thornton, J.I., and Crim, D., "Color tests for diphenylamine stabilizer and related compounds in smokeless gunpowder," *J. Forens. Sci.*, 27 (2), (1982), 318.

McKeown, W.J., and Speers, S.J., "Automated method for the analysis of organic explosive residues by HPLC with a pendant mercury drop electrode detector," *Sci. & Just.*, 36 (1), (1996), 15.

McKeown, W.J., and Speers, S.J., "Automated method for the analysis of organic explosive residure by HPLC with a pendant mercury drop electrode detector," *Sci. & Just.*, 36 (1), (1996), 15.

Monsfield, A.M., Marshall, M., Walker, C.L., and Hubbard, P., "Physical and chemical evidence remaining after the explosion of large improvised bombs. Part 3: firings of calcium carbonate ammonium nitrate/sugar," *J. Forens. Sci.*, 46 (3), (2001), 535.

Oxley, Jimmie C., Smith, J. L., Resende, E., Pearce, E. and Chamberlain, T., "Trends in explosive contamination," *J. Forens. Sci.*, 48 (2), (2003), 334.

Oxley, Jimmie C., Smith, J. L., Resende, E., and Pearce, E., "Quantification and aging of the post-blast residue of TNT landmines," *J. Forens. Sci.*, 48 (4), (2003), 742.

Oxley, Jimmie C., Smith, J. L., Kirschenbaum, L. J., Shinde, K. P., and Marimganti, S., "Accumulation of explosives in hair," *J. Forens. Sci.*, 50 (4), (2005), 826.

Oxley, J.C., Smith, J.L., Resende, E., Rogers, E., Strobel, R.A., and Bender, E.C., "Improved explosive devices: pipe bombs," *J. Forens. Sci.*, 46 (3), (2001), 510.

Parker, R.G., McOwen, J. M., and Cherolis, J. A., "Analysis of explosives and explosive particles, Part 2: Thin-layer chromatography," *J. Forens. Sci.*, 20 (2), (1975a), 254.

Parker, R.G., Stephenson, M.O., McOwen, J.M., and Cherolis, J. A., "Analysis of explosives and explosive residues, Part 1: Chemical tests," *J. Forens. Sci.*, 20 (1), (1975b), 133.

Paull, Brett, Roux, C., Dawson, M., and Doble, P., "Rapid screening of selected organic explosives by high performance liquid chromatography using reversed phase monolithic columns," *J. Forens. Sci.*, 49 (6), (2004), 1181.

Phillips, S.A., and Hiley, R., "Workshop on explosives trace analysis methods," *Sci, & Just.*, 39 (4), (1999), 261.

Reardon, Michelle R., and Bender, E., "Differentiation of composition C-4 based on the analysis of the process oil," *J. Forens. Sci.*, 50 (3), (2005), 564.

Smith, K.D., McCord, B.R., MacCrehan, W.A., Moont, K., and Rowe, W.F., "Detection of smokeless powder residue on pipe bombs by micellular electrokinetic capillary electrophoresis," *J. Forens. Sci.*, 44 (4), (1999), 789.

Thompson, R.Q., Fetterhoff, D.D., Miller, M.L., and Mothershean, R.F., "Aqueous recovery from cotton swabs of organic explosives residue followed by solid phase extraction," *J. Forens. Sci.*, 44 (4), (1999), 795.

Walker, C., Cullum, H., and Hiley, R., "An environmental survey relating to improvised and emulsion/gel explosives," *J. Forens. Sci.*, 46 (2), (2001), 254.

Wallace, J.S., and McKeown, W.J., "Sampling procedures for firearms and/or explosives residues," *J. Forens. Sci. Soc.*, 33 (2), (1993), 107.

Walsh, Graham A., Inal, O. T., and Romero, V. D., "A potential metallographic technique for the investigation of pipe bombings," *J. Forens. Sci.*, 48 (5), (2003), 945.

Warren, D., Hiley, R.W., Phillips, S.A., and Ritchie, K., "Novel technique for the combined recovery, extraction and clean-up of forensic organic and inorganic trace explosives," *Sci. & Just.*, 39 (1), (1999), 11.

Substance Tested	(2) Aniline Sulfate	(9) Barium Chloride	(3) Brucine	(4) Cupric Tetrapyridine	(5) Diphenylamine	(1) Griess	(6) J-Acid	(7) Nessler	(10) Nitron	(8) Methylene Blue	(11) Silver Nitrate	(12) Sulfuric Acid
Bromide	Yellow to yellow-orange	NR	Yellow to orange	NR	Yellow[a] NR[b]	NR	Dirty orange[a] NR[b]	NCD	NR	Light purple[a] NR[b]	Creamy white precipitate	Yellow to yellow-orange
Carbonate	NCD	White precipitate	NCD	NCD	NCD	NCD	NCD	NCD	NR	NCD	Creamy white precipitate	NCD
Chlorate	Yellow to orange	NR	Orange to red	NR	Blue to blue-black	NCD	Orange-brown	NR	Dirty white precipitate	NR	NR	Yellow
Chloride	NCD	NR	NR	NR	NR	NR	NCD	NR	NR	NR	White precipitate	NCD
Iodide	Brown to purple to black	NR	Brown to purple to black	Brown precipitate	Purple	NR	Brown to purple	NR	Dirty white precipitate	Purple	Yellow precipitate	Brown to purple to black
Nitrate	Light yellow to yellow	NR	Orange to yellow	NR	Blue to blue-black	Pink to red	Orange-brown	NR	White precipitate	NR	NR	NR
Nitrite	NR[a] yellow[b]	NR	Orange to red	Green	Blue-black	Red to yellow	NR[a] Brown-orange[b]	NR	Dirty white precipitate	NR	White precipitate	NR
Nitrocellulose	NR	NR	Orange to red	NR	Blue-black	Pink	Orange-brown	NR	NR	NR	NR	NR
Nitroglycerin	NR	NR	Orange to red	NR	Blue to blue-black	Pink to red	Orange-brown	NR	Light, dirty white precipitate	NR	NR	NR
Nitrostarch	NR	NR	Orange to red	NR	Blue-black	Pink	Orange-brown	NR	NR	NR	NR	NR
Perchlorate	NR	NR	NR	Purple crystalline precipitate	NR	NR	NR	NR	White turns gray-white	Purple to purple precipitate	NR	NR
PETN	NR	NR	Orange to red	NR	Blue	Pink to red	Orange-brown to red	NR	NR	NR	NR	NR
RDX	NR	NR	Orange to red	NR	NR	Pink to red	Orange-brown	NR	NR	NR	NR	NR
Sulfate	NR	White precipitate	NR	NR	NR	NR	NR	NR	NR	NR	NR	NR
Tetryl	NR	NR	Orange-Red	NR	Blue	Pink to red	Yellow to orange-brown	NR	NR	Orange to red	NR	NR
TNT;2,4-DNT; 2,6-DNT	NR	NR	NR	NR	NR	NR	Yellow to orange-brown	NR	NR	NR	NR	NR
MHMX	Dirty light yellow	NR	Deep red, turns orange	NR	Deep blue	Red	Green turns brown	White precipitate	White precipitate	NR	NR	NR

NR, no reaction; NCD, no color development.

[a] Solid.
[b] Aqueous.

B. G. Parker, M. O. Stephenson, J. M. McOwen, and J. A. Cherolis, "Analysis of explosives and explosive residues. Part I: Chemical Tests," J. Forens Sci., 20 (1975), 133.

Source: Reprinted by permission of the American Society for testing and materials.

EXPERIMENT 32

DATA SHEET

Name _____

Date _____

SPOT TESTS FOR EXPLOSIVES AND EXPLOSIVE RESIDUES

1. Refer to Figure 32-1. Use a magnifying glass if needed, and record your spot tests observations.

   Debris No. 1

   Debris No. 2

   Debris No. 3

   Debris No. 4

   Debris No. 5

2. Potassium test paper results

   Dynamite   Debris No. 1

   Black   Debris No. 2

   Smokeless powder (SB)   Debris No. 3

   Smokeless powder (DB)   Debris No. 4

   Chlorate/sugar   Debris No. 5

3. Sodium test results

   Dynamite   Debris No. 1

   Black   Debris No. 2

   Smokeless powder (SB)   Debris No. 3

   Smokeless powder (DB)   Debris No. 4

   Chlorate/sugar   Debris No. 5

4. Conclusions

  a. What individual components (if any) did you find on the debris?

  b. What type of explosive do you believe was used?

Metal Residues on Hands from Guns, Knives, and Other Metal Weapons*

There are many crimes committed in which hand guns are not used, and with more strict gun laws in force, the possibility of weapons other than guns being used is greater. What is needed is a simple, inexpensive test to determine whether a subject has recently handled a metallic object.

Such a test was proposed in 1970, in which the reagent 8-hydroxyquinoline is used to chelate with any trace metallic fragments left on the palm of the hand when a metal object was handled. These chelates fluoresce when exposed to UV radiation and often indicate the imprint of the object handled. There are many variables, however, such as how tightly the object was held, how old it was, whether it was oiled, how sweaty the suspect's hand was, and the kinds of metals involved. Our own success with this approach has been excellent. Other investigators have had good success also. The interpretation of the imprint requires a great deal of experience and a large file of photographs of known objects in order to draw definite conclusions. Nonetheless, we will have you perform the test so that you will know it exists. We believe that the potential for this test is better than the results you will obtain.

In 1976 a new reagent, ferrozine, was suggested as a better test for weapons containing iron. You will experiment with this reagent in Part B.

PART A: THE 8-HYDROXYQUINOLINE METHOD

Basically this procedure involves applying a 0.1 to 0.2% solution of 8-hydroxyquinoline (oxine) in alcohol to the subject's hands, either by immersion or by spraying from an entirely metal-free system, and allowing them to air dry. The 8-hydroxyquinoline undergoes a chelating reaction with various metallic ions present on the skin's surface to form oxine complexes. When viewed under short wavelength UV radiation, these complexes either emit various fluorescent colors or cause a quenching of the light yellow background fluorescence imparted to treated areas of the skin by the solution. The fluorescent color observed depends upon the particular metal present, with different metals producing different colors.

---

*Based on Goldman and Thornton (1976) and National Institute of Law Enforcement and Criminal Justice (1970).

When viewed under UV radiation, any metallic residue left on the hands after handling a particular object would appear as various colored patterns outlining those areas of the hand which were in contact with the object. Each of the various objects, held in the usual manner for its intended use, would produce a distinctive pattern which could be recognized and identified by the observer, once he had gained sufficient experience in observing such patterns. The color of the pattern gives information concerning the metallic composition of the object, with the position, shape, and extent of the pattern indicating the shape of the object.

CRIME SCENE

A highway patrolman is called by a CB operator to the scene of a roadside beating. The victim has apparently been struck by a heavy object, possibly a jack handle or a tire iron. The CB operator states that from a distance he thought he saw a semi-trailer pull away, but he can't be sure. The highway patrolman calls the local forensic lab. You have been rushed out to a truck stop just outside of town accompanied by the sheriff. All of the truck drivers deny knowing anything about the crime. They may be telling the truth, and admittedly it is a long shot, but you decide to test their hands for metal particles, which you do according to the following procedure.

EQUIPMENT

1 pr Goggles, safety	1 Towel, cloth
1 Hair dryer	1 Viewing box or darkened room
1 Jar, wide mouth, gallon size	Several metal test objects, such as a jack
1 Lamp, UV, 6 watt preferred	handle, pipe wrench, scissors, knife, etc.

REAGENTS

8-hydroxyquinoline, 0.15% in isopropanol. Prepare 2 L in a widemouthed plastic bottle. It is good for 40 to 50 immersions, or until pronounced discoloration occurs. Store in a dark plastic bottle.

3-(2-pyridyl)-5,6-diphenyl-1,2,4-triazine-p-p'-disulfonic acid, disodium salt trihydrate, also known as PDT or ferrozine, is capable of detecting 0.090 mg of iron.

METHOD

Prior to this experiment the lab instructor will take 4 or 5 students into another room and have one of them hold a metal object and strike a surface with it 2 or 3 times. When the group comes back, you will test all the suspects to see if you can tell which one handled the weapon.

1. Place each hand of the first suspect into the jar containing the 8-hydroxyquinoline in isopropanol for a period of 3 to 5 seconds.

2. Dry the suspect's hands with a hair dryer.

3. Take the suspect into a dark room, or place his/her hands in a UV viewing box and examine them under a UV lamp (a 6 watt UV lamp works best). Record what you see.

4. Repeat this procedure with each of the suspects, and record what you see. Can you identify which one handled the weapon?

5. Have 3 or 4 students who have not touched a metal object today (including door handles) each handle a specific "weapon" just as they might if they were to use it in a

crime. You must grip the weapon extra tight to be realistic. A person involved in a crime is under tension, so they grip the weapon tightly; and they usually sweat, so good contact is made.

6. Test each student and see if you can (1) see any metal evidence at all, and (2) distinguish any pattern related to the weapon.

7. If you have good results and are in fact able to detect metal residuals, then have the person wet his/her hands and repeat the test. Record your results.

8. Clean up the area, and replace the lid tightly on the reagent solution container.

PART B: THE FERROZINE METHOD

METHOD

1. The reagent (1 mg/mL of methanol) is sprayed over the hands of the subject.

2. Follow the steps listed in Part A.

SELECTED SOURCES FOR ADDITIONAL INFORMATION

Almog, J., and Glattstein, B., "Detection of firearms imprints on hands of suspects. Study of the PDT based field test," *J. Forens. Sci.*, 42 (6), (1997), 993. (Forms a magenta color with submicrograms of Fe.)

Basu, S., Boone, C.E., Denio, D.S., and Miazga, R.A., "Fundamental studies of gunshot residue deposition by glue-lift," *J. Forens. Sci.*, 42 (4), (1997), 571.

Collins, Peter, Coumbaros, L., Horsley, G., Lynch, B., Kirkbride, K. P., Skinner, W., and Klass G., "Glass containing gunshot residue particles: A new type of highly characteristic particle?," *J. Forens. Sci.,* 48 (3), (2003), 538.

Glassr S.W., and Grasi, N.J., "A new trace metal detection reagent," *J. Forens. Sci.*, 24 (1), (1979), 247.

Goldman, G.L., and Thornton, J.I., "A new trace ferrous metal detection reagent," *J. Forens. Sci.*, 21 (3), (1976), 625.

Jalanti, T., Henchoz, P., Gallusser, A., and Bonfanti, M.S., "The persistence of gunshot residue on shooter's hands," *Sci. & Just.*, 39 (1), (1999), 48.

Lee, C.W., "The determination of iron traces on hands by ferrozine sprays. A report on the sensitivity and interferences of the method and recommended procedure in forensic science investigation," *J. Forens. Sci.*, 31 (3), (1986), 920.

Leifer, A., Avissar, Y., Berger, S., Wax, H., Donchin, Y., and Almog, J., "Detection of firearm imprints on the hands of suspects—effectiveness of PDT reaction," *J. Forens. Sci.*, 46 (6), (2001), 1442. (Better than 8-hydroxy-)

McDermont, S.D., "Metal particles as evidence in criminal cases," *J. Forens. Sci.*, 39 (6), (1994), 1552.

Meng, H., and Caddy, B., "Gunshot residue analysis—a review," *J. Forens. Sci.*, 42 (4), (1997), 553.

Migeot, Gerard and De Kinder, J., "Gunshot residue deposits on the gas pistons of assault rifles," *J. Forens. Sci.,* 47 (4), (2002), 808.

Reardon, M.R., and MacCrehan, W.A., "Developing a quantitative extraction technique for determining the organic additives in smokeless hand gun powder," *J. Forens. Sci.*, 46 (4), (2001), 802.

Reis, E. I., T., Souza Sarkis, J. E., Neto, O. N., Rodrigues, C., Kakazu, M. H., and Viebig, S., "A net method for collection and identification of gunshot residues from the hands of shooters," *J. Forens. Sci.,* 48 (6), (2003), 1269.

Schyma, C., and Placidl, P., "The accelerated polyvinyl alcohol-alcohol method for GSR collection-PVAL 2.0," *J. Forens. Sci.,* 45 (6), (2000), 1303.

Stahling, S., and Karlsson, T., "A method for collection of gunshot residues from skin and other surfaces," *J. Forens. Sci.,* 45 (6), (2000), 1299.

Stahling, S., "Modified sheet printing method (MSPM) for the detection of lead in determination of shooting distance," *J. Forens. Sci.,* 44 (1), (1999), 179.

Stevens, J. M., and Messler, H., "The trace metal detection technique (TMDT): A report outlining a procedure for photographing results in color, and some factors influencing the results in controlled laboratory tests," *J. Forens. Sci.,* 19 (3), (1974), 496.

Wallace, J.S., "Discharge residue from mercury fulminate-primed ammunition," *Sci. & Just.,* 38 (1), (1998), 7.

Zeichner, Arie and Eldar, B., "A novel method for extraction and analysis of gunpowder residues on double side adhesive coated stubs," *J. Forens. Sci.,* 49 (6), (2004), 1194.

Zeichner, A., Eldar, B., Glattstein, B., Koffman, A., Tamiri, T., and Muller, D., "Vacuum collection of gunpowder residues from clothing worn by shooting suspects and their analysis by GC/TEA, IMS, and GC/MS," *J. Forens. Sci.,* 48 (5), (2003), 961.

EXPERIMENT 33

DATA SHEET

Name _____

Date _____

METAL RESIDUES ON HANDS FROM GUNS, KNIVES, AND OTHER METAL WEAPONS

Part A: The 8-Hydroxyquinoline Method

Record your observations below by both a brief description of colors and a sketch of any patterns.

Suspect 1

Suspect 2

Suspect 3

Suspect 4

Suspect 5

Part B: The Ferrozine Method

Record your observations below by both a brief description of colors and a sketch of any patterns.

Suspect 1

Suspect 2

Suspect 3

Suspect 4

Suspect 5

Can you tell who handled the weapon? If so, on what do you base your conclusions?

Sketch any weapon patterns that you detect and indicate the colors involved.

The Emission Spectrum of Elements

Often criminalists are asked to identify materials by the chemical elements of which they are composed. For example, in the identification of poisons or the analysis of coins, weapons, or tools. In addition, most man-made and natural materials contain small quantities of elements known as trace elements. Often, by comparing the trace elements contained within physical evidence it is possible to successfully link evidence to a particular source or location. The analytical techniques used for the identification of elements can be quite lengthy and often involve the application of sophisticated and expensive equipment. In this experiment we will make no attempt to utilize such instrumentation; instead, our objective will be to have you learn about the underlying principles of one important technique, **emission spectroscopy**.

We will shortly see that elements emit radiation when they are heated to high temperatures, as in a flare. All elements are composed of atoms. Each atom has electrons in orbit around a central nucleus, a situation analogous to the planets in orbit around the sun. When heat is applied to an element, many of its atoms will become **excited**; that is, their electrons will jump into higher-energy orbitals. These electrons will stay in these higher orbitals for only a very short time. When the excited electrons fall back to a lower level, energy is emitted in the form of radiation. This radiation, called **light**, if our eye is sensitive to it, when analyzed, will show a characteristic spectrum consisting of discrete lines of differing wavelengths. The simplest instrument used to separate light into its component wavelengths is known as a **spectroscope**. What makes this technique so valuable to the criminalist is the fact that no two elements emit the same combination of wavelengths; in essence, the emission spectrum of an element is a **fingerprint**. In the following exercise we will study the colors and wavelengths of visible radiation (light) that different elements emit when they are heated. You will also learn to use a simple spectroscope.

EQUIPMENT

1 Beaker, 25 mL	Wire, nichrome
1 Burner, Bunsen	1 Tube, helium discharge
1 pr Goggles, safety	1 Tube, hydrogen discharge
1 Spectroscope	

REAGENTS

Barium chloride

Calcium chloride

Hydrochloric acid

Potassium chloride

Sodium chloride

Strontium chloride

PART A: OBTAINING FLAME EMISSIONS

METHOD

1. Place a small quantity of sodium chloride on a loop of Nichrome wire, and hold it in the flame of a Bunsen burner. Record the color you see on your data sheet.

2. Clean the wire by heating it in the flame until the color imparted to the flame by sodium disappears. If this color does not disappear after the wire becomes red hot, allow it to cool for 10 seconds and immerse it in a beaker of concentrated hydrochloric acid. Then return the wire to the flame. Repeat until the wire no longer imparts a color to the flame.

3. Next, repeat steps 1 and 2 with each of the following substances: potassium chloride, calcium chloride, strontium chloride, and barium chloride. Record the colors you see on the data sheet.

PART B: THE SPECTROSCOPE

In Part A you found that some elements are easy to distinguish by the colors they emit in a hot flame, but many elements are not so easily identified. We need a way to separate the mixed colors that elements emit so that we can notice slight differences in the color emissions of elements. This can be accomplished by spreading out the various colors of emitted light in a way similar to the formation of a rainbow. This spread of colors is called a spectrum. As noted earlier, the instrument used for separating the colors of light is called a spectroscope; it contains a prism or grating to separate light into its component wavelengths.

Radiation from the excited atoms enters the spectroscope through a narrow slit and passes through the prism or grating, where it is separated into various colors; the radiation then passes through a tube and into the viewer's eye. Your instructor will show you the parts of your spectroscope and how to operate it.

Your spectroscope may contain a scale for measuring the wavelengths of the separated light. The numbers on the scale are arbitrary and do not correspond to any particular wavelength. Therefore, it is necessary to calibrate the spectroscope against a known standard, in this case, helium. The purpose of the calibration is to relate the numbers of your scale to the wavelength values of helium.

METHOD

1. Place a helium discharge tube directly in front of the spectroscope's slit. Make sure that the slit is very nearly closed; if not, the helium lines will not be well separated.

2. Focus the spectroscope, and adjust the width of the slit so that you can see the first red line on the left side of the spectrum. Record on your data sheet the scale reading for this line.

3. Moving from left to right along the spectrum, record the scale readings for each of the 5 or 6 additional colored lines in the helium spectrum. You will notice that the known wavelengths of each helium line are recorded in a Table on the data sheet.

4. Draw a graph with wavelengths in nanometers as the abscissa and with the scale reading as the ordinate for the lines of the helium spectrum. The smooth curve so obtained is the calibration curve of the instrument. This curve is obtained by plotting the scale readings of each of the known lines of an element against the corresponding wavelength. From this curve the wavelength of the lines observed in other spectra may be calculated.

5. Substitute a hydrogen discharge tube for the helium source, and record the scale readings for the observed lines. Record these readings along with the line colors on your data sheet. From your calibration curve identify the wavelength for each scale reading.

6. Look at the radiation from an ordinary tungsten bulb through your spectroscope. What difference do you observe between this source of radiation and that of helium and hydrogen?

PART C: THE EMISSION SPECTRA OF ELEMENTS

In this portion of the experiment you will examine the emission spectra of various elements.

1. Place a lighted Bunsen burner in front of the slit of the spectroscope, but far enough away so that the flame will not damage the instrument.

2. Clean the Nichrome wire as described in Part A.

3. Individually introduce each of the following materials into the flame: sodium chloride, potassium chloride, calcium chloride, strontium chloride, and barium chloride. It may be necessary to add the powder to the flame several times to observe all the spectral lines.

4. Record the number of lines and colors that you observe for each material. If your spectroscope has a scale reading, you may want to record the reading for each line observed. Your instructor may ask you to determine the emission wavelengths for some of these elements.

5. Your instructor may issue you an unknown containing one or more elements for you to identify.

SELECTED SOURCES FOR ADDITIONAL INFORMATION

Almarall, J.R., Cole, M.D., Gettinnby, G., and Furton, K.G., "Discrimination of glass sources using elemental composition and refractive index: development of predictive models," *Sci. & Just.*, 38 (3), (1998), 93.

Curran, J.M., Triggs, C.M., Almarall, J.R., Buckleton, J.S., and Walsh, K.A.J., "The interpretation of elemental composition measurements from forensic glass evidence: I," *Sci. & Just.* 37 (4), (1997), 241.

Curran, J.M., Triggs, C.M., Almarall, J.R., Buckleton, J.S., and Walsh, K.A.J., "The interpretation of elemental composition measurements from forensic glass evidence: II," *Sci. & Just.* 37 (4), (1997), 245.

Kasamatsu, Masaaki, Suzuki, Y., Sugita, R., and Suzuki, S., "Forensic determination of match heads by elemental analysis with inductively coupled plasma-atomic emission spectrometry," *J. Forens. Sci.,* 50 (4), (2005), 883.

Kinoshita, Hiroshi, Ameno, K., Sumi, Y., Kumihashi, M., Ijiri, J., Ameno, S., Kubota, A., and Hishida, S., "Evidence of hexavalent chromium ingestion," *J. Forens. Sci.,* 48 (3), (2003), 633.

Koons, R. D., and Grant, D., "Compositional variation in bullet lead manufacture," *J. Forens. Sci.,* 47 (5), (2002), 950.

Koons, Robert D., and Buscaglia, J., "Forensic significance of bullet lead compositions," *J. Forens. Sci.,* 50 (2), (2005), 352.

McDermont, S.D., "Metal particles as evidence in criminal cases," *J. Forens. Sci.*, 39 (6), (1994), 1552.

Poolman, D.G., and Pistorius, P.C., "The possibility of using elemental analysis to identify debris from the cutting of mild steel," *J. Forens. Sci.*, 41 (6), (1996), 998.

EXPERIMENT 34   Name _____

DATA SHEET   Date _____

THE EMISSION SPECTRUM OF ELEMENTS

Part A: Obtaining Flame Emissions

Compound   Color observed

Sodium chloride

Potassium chloride

Calcium chloride

Strontium chloride

Barium chloride

Part B: The Spectroscope

Helium spectrum:

Color	Wavelength (nm)	Scale reading
Red	668	
Yellow	588	
Green	502	
Green	492	
Blue-green	471	
Blue-violet	447	
Violet	403	

Hydrogen spectrum:

Color	Scale reading	Calculated wavelength (nm)

Part C: The Emission Spectra of Elements

List the elements examined, along with the color of each of their spectral lines. You may also be asked to record the scale readings of each line and to find its wavelength from the calibration curve prepared in Part B.

Element	Color of line	Scale reading	Calculated wavelength (nm)

1. Unknown Number _____

   Element(s) present in the unknown _____

2. Does the chlorine have any effect on the spectra of the compounds analyzed?

Heavy Metal Poisons by Atomic Absorption Spectroscopy (Advanced)

Poisonous plants were recognized by prehistoric man, and ancient writings indicate that the early Indians and Egyptians knew of a certain number of poisons. Peach and apricot kernels contain the substance amygdalin, which is converted to HCN in the body, and the "penalty of the peach" was often used. The early Greeks put snake venom on their arrow tips, and an extract of hemlock (2-propyl-piperidine) was used to poison Socrates in 339 B.C.

From 1400 to 1800 poisoning was almost a fact of life. One woman, Madame Toffane, ran a professional organization that is reported to have used arsenic to kill nearly 600 people in 1709 alone. The reason poisoning was so effective was that many poisoning symptoms looked like death from any one of several diseases prevalent in those times. In addition, the chemistry of detecting poisons was simply not known.

The first major breakthrough came in 1836, when James Marsh devised a highly sensitive test for arsenic. In 1839, Joseph Orfila extracted arsenic from human organs. By 1850, Jean Stas and Robert Otto extracted alkaloids from cadavers.

The chemistry of recovering and detecting poisons is now at a level where the forensic scientist can detect all known poisons present in a human body down to the part-per-million (ppm) range and many even lower.

The gas chromatograph, mass spectrometer, and the high-pressure liquid chromatograph are used for the organic poisons, and the atomic absorption spectrophotometer, emission spectrograph, and inductively coupled plasma are the usual instruments used for detecting the heavy metal poisons.

There are many possibilities for accidental as well as intentional metal poisonings. Copper arsenate (Paris green) was a green coloring pigment in fancy wallpaper for years before it was learned that the vapors were toxic. Lead arsenate has long been used for spraying fruit trees. Thallium sulfate is an excellent rodent and coyote poison. Cadmium poisoning occurred a few years back when refrigerator racks were being used on outdoor grills. Lead in paints, both as a coloring pigment and as a drying agent, has caused considerable problems with small children in old tenement houses because the children eat the paint chips. Lead is used to

EXPERIMENT 35

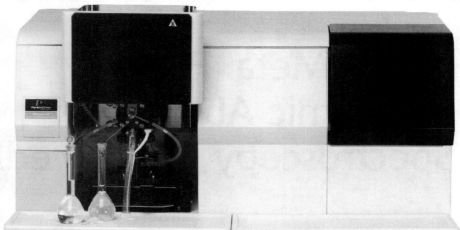

FIGURE 35–1   A photo of an Analyst 300 atomic absorption spectrometer. *Courtesy of PerkinElmer Instruments, Norwalk, CT, USA.*

glaze pottery and dishes, but if they are not heated sufficiently, the lead can be leached out by the weak acids in fruits. A grapefruit half, turned upside down on a saucer and placed in a refrigerator for storage, can leach several milligrams of lead out of a poor-quality saucer overnight.

Figure 35-1 shows a photo of one model of an atomic absorption spectrophotometer.

CRIME SCENE

A child becomes quite ill and is taken to a hospital. It is found that the child is suffering from lead poisoning. A forensic laboratory is contacted and asked if it can determine the source of the lead which the child has ingested. No crime has been committed, per se, but the source must be eliminated to prevent future danger to the child. Paint samples from a number of objects with which the child has repeated contact are collected. Paint on the child's crib, paint from his toys, and paint from the child's swing, to name a few, are sent to the laboratory. These are the three unknowns you will work with.

You now have these samples, which have been dissolved in a suitable solvent, and you must determine the lead concentration in each. The dissolving of the samples has been done for you to save time, and to eliminate problems that might result from the use of techniques with which you are not familiar.

With some variations in the instrumental parameters, this same method can be used for the determination of the concentration of nearly any metal atom of interest. A few such atoms might be arsenic, mercury copper, zinc, or antimony. Any of these metals are toxic if ingested in sufficient quantity.

EQUIPMENT

Atomic absorption spectrometer, with hollow cathode lamp for lead analysis

Recorder, potentiometer, variable range input

Bottle, wash, 250 mL   Beaker, 10 mL

REAGENTS

Standard solutions of lead ion, 2.5, 5.0, 7.5, 10.0, 25.0, and 50.0 ppm (milligram per kilogram of solution)

Unknown solutions of lead ion

Distilled water

METHOD

To save time, the atomic absorption spectrophotometer will be warmed up and optimized by your laboratory instructor. If you are interested, you may return at a later time and learn how this is done. Your laboratory instructor will explain the proper method of operation of the instrument in performing this analysis, as it varies to some extent from one instrument to another. After this has been done, proceed as follows:

1. Beginning with the standard of lowest lead concentration, aspirate each standard in turn. Record the absorbance value for each standard, or other meter reading, depending on the instrument you are using. Allow sufficient aspiration time for the pen to reach maximum deflection and trace a flat-topped peak. Following aspiration of each standard, place the aspirator tube in a beaker of distilled water and wait for the recorder pen to return to the baseline and the absorbance digital readout to come to 0.000.

2. When you have completed the aspiration of all of the standard solutions, aspirate your lead unknowns in the same manner, recording the absorbance values as before. Aspirate the distilled water until the readout again returns to 0.000.

3. Shut down the instrument according to the instructions of your laboratory instructor.

Treatment of the Data

1. Make a plot of the absorbance values for each standard lead solution *versus* the concentration of lead in that standard on linear graph paper. Connect all of the points. Determine the lead concentration in your unknowns by drawing a line from the absorbance value of your unknown to the calibration curve on your graph. Draw a second line from the intersection of the absorbance line with the curve to the concentration axis of your graph. This will resemble the graph shown in Figure 35-2. The calibration curve must pass through the intersection of the two axes of the plot, as zero concentration would have zero absorbance. For instruments that do not have an absorbance mode of readout, plot the meter needle deflections *versus* concentration to produce the same result.

2. Make a second plot of the peak height for each standard lead solution *versus* concentration, and find the concentration of your unknown solution from its peak height.

3. Report both concentration values for your unknowns on the data sheet. Include your graphs with the data sheet and answered questions when you hand in your experiment.

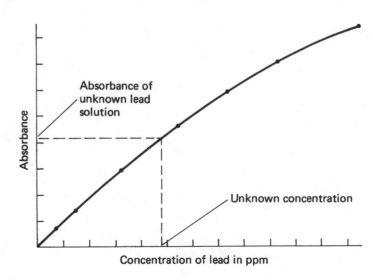

FIGURE 35–2 Example of how the data is plotted.

SELECTED SOURCES FOR ADDITIONAL INFORMATION

Espinoza, E.O., Mann, M.S., Bleasdell, R., Dekorte, S., and Cox, M., "Toxic metals in selected traditional Chinese medicinals," *J. Forens. Sci.*, 41 (3), (1996), 453.

Fulton, B.A., Meloan, C.E., and Finnegan, M., "Reassembling scattered and mixed human bones by trace element ratios," *J. Forens. Sci.*, 31 (4), (1986), 1455.

Hickman, D.A., "Glass types identified by chemical analysis," *For. Sci. Intl.*, 33 (1987), 23.

Hunsaker, Donna M., Spiller, H. A., and Williams, D., "Acute selenium poisoning suicide by ingestion," *J. Forens. Sci.*, 50 (4), (2005), 942.

Koons, R.D., Havekost, D.G., and Peters, C.A., "Analysis of gunshot primer residue collection swabs using flameless atomic absorption spectrophotometry: a reexamination of extraction and instrument procedures," *J. Forens. Sci.*, 32 (4), (1987), 846.

Koons, R.D., Havekost, D.G., and Peters, C.A., "Determination of barium in gunshot residue collection swabs using inductively coupled plasma atomic absorption spectrometry," *J. Forens. Sci.*, 33 (1), (1988), 35.

Koons, R.D., Havekost, D.G., and Peters, C.A., "Analysis of gunshot primer residue collection swabs using flameless atomic absorption and inductively coupled plasma-atomic emission spectroscopy—effects of a modified extraction procedure and storage of standards," *J. Forens. Sci.*, 34 (1), (1989), 218.

Koons, R.D., and Grant, D.M., "Compositional variation in bullet lead manufacturers," *J. Forens. Sci.*, 47 (5), (2002), 950.

Koons, R.D., Peters, C.A., and Merrill, R.A., "Forensic comparison of household aluminum foils using elemental composition by ICP-AE spectroscopy," *J. Forens. Sci.*, 38 (2,) (1993), 302.

Oommen, Zachariah, and Pierce, S. M., "Lead-free primer residues: A qualitative characterization of Winchester Win Clean, Remington/UMC leadless, Federal BallisticClean, and Speer Lawman clean fire, handgun ammunition," *J. Forens. Sci.*, 51 (3), (2006), 509.

Person, Eric C., Meyer, J. A., and Vyvyan, J. R., "Structural determination of the principal byproduct of the lithium-ammonium reduction method of methamphetamine manufacture," *J. Forens. Sci.*, 50 (1), (2005), 87.

Rogers, C., Bernstein, G., Nakamura, R., Indohl, G., and Bhoapat, T., "Vaginal fluid zinc concentration as a marker for intercourse," *J. Forens. Sci.*, 33 (1), (1988), 77.

Zeichner, A., Schecter, B., and Brener, R., "Antimony enrichment on the bullet's surfaces and the possibility of finding it in gunshot residue (GDR) of the ammunition having antimony free primers," *J. Forens. Sci.*, 43 (3), (1998), 493.

EXPERIMENT 35   Name _____

DATA SHEET   Date _____

HEAVY METAL POISONS BY ATOMIC ABSORPTION SPECTROSCOPY

Concentration of lead standard solutions, ppm	Absorbance	Deflection
2.5		
5.0		
7.5		
10.0		
15.0		
25.0		
50.0		
Unknown 1		
Unknown 2		
Unknown 3		

Value of lead ion concentrations in the unknowns

a. From a plot of absorbance *versus* concentration

Unknown 1

Unknown 2

Unknown 3

b. From a plot of peak height *versus* concentration

Unknown 1

Unknown 2

Unknown 3

Questions

1. Is the plot of absorbance *versus* concentration linear for all concentration of standards? Why or why not?

2. Is the plot of peak height *versus* concentration linear for all concentrations of standards? Why or why not?

3. Did the blue flame change color as the lead solutions were introduced into it? If so, what color did it become?

4. What was absorbed in the flame, and what caused this absorption?

5. What relationship do you notice about the concentration of the standard lead solutions and their absorbances? Where does this relationship fail to exist?

6. Which of the samples could have been the source of the lead that caused the child to become ill?

Determination of Blood Spatter Angles of Impact*

The solution of crimes of violence can often be aided by the determination of certain aspects of the commission of the crime. Two of these aspects are the relationship of the victim and the perpetrator with respect to each other and the location of the victim at the time of occurrence. Was he/she standing, sitting or reclining? Some of these questions perhaps may be answered by the application of the procedure that you are about to follow. Maybe the pattern of blood spots and their shape can be of help. It has been found that when a drop of blood strikes a surface it tends to spread out, longer in the direction of impact. If you measure the width of the spot and compare it to the length, making a ratio, you can determine the angle that the drop of blood was traveling at the moment of impact. Ratios are used to eliminate the effect of different sizes of drops. It has been suggested that the average height of a drop of blood falling from either a wounded person or a person carrying a wounded person would be about 42 inches. Large differences in height can make a difference since the blood tends to cool and start to coagulate shortly after exposure to air, thus altering the pattern.

According to Webster's dictionary there is not much difference between the definitions of the words "spatter" and "splatter." In fact, to see the definition of "splatter" one is referred to the definition of "spatter." This is defined as "to scatter by splashing; to sprinkle around." Also, "to spurt forth in drops." The latter definition best suits our purpose here. You will make some careful measurements of blood spatters on a surface at various angles. These measurements, when properly applied, can be used to determine the angle at which the spatter struck the surface. This angle can be used to determine a very close approximation of the location in three-dimensional space where the blood spatters originated. This would be valuable information for the crime scene analyst.

CRIME SCENE

A person has been found in the living room of his home. The person has been determined to be dead, apparently of wounds sustained from a severe beating. There is evidence of blood on the floor, walls, and ceiling

*Adapted from material authored by Terry Laber and Bart Epstein, Minnesota Bureau of Criminal Apprehension Laboratory. Used with permission.

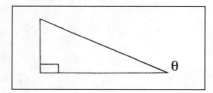

FIGURE 36-1   Right angle with angle θ being the angle of impact, measured from the horizontal (floor) side.

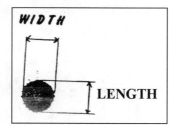

FIGURE 36-2

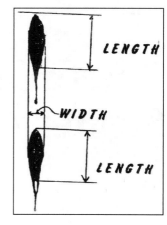

FIGURE 36-3

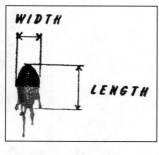

FIGURE 36-4

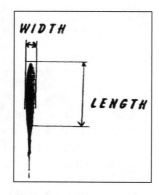

FIGURE 36-5

of the room. It is the task of the crime scene investigator, in this case you, to determine a variety of factors. Information pertaining to the position of the victim when the beating occurred, the location in the room of the victim when beating was initiated and subsequent movements of the victim during the beating. These questions may be, all or in part, answered by the measurements that you will learn to make in this experiment. The scene described above will be used in both this and the succeeding experiment. In this one it will be used only as a basis for the necessity of making the determinations with which you will be involved.

EQUIPMENT

1 Table of trigonometric Sine values
1 Ruler
4-6 Rectangles of tag board (poster board)
1 Medicine dropper

1 Protective paper to place under tag board
1 Protractor
1 Meter stick or yard stick approximately 6″ × 6″
1 Scissors or razor blade.

CHEMICALS

Blood or simulated blood (made from honey diluted with water)
Red food coloring
Dry milk powder (optional)
Glue

METHOD

Your course instructor may have provided surfaces upon which you will find dried blood spatters. If so, proceed to part B of this experiment. If not, you will make your own spatters and you will begin with part A. The first item needed to accomplish this production of your own will be either bovine blood or simulated blood. Human blood is not used due to the risk of exposure to certain health hazards contained in the blood. Among these hazards are hepatitis, and the immune destroying factor, HIV. The experiment can be conducted through the use of "make believe" blood, such as honey diluted with water and food coloring added to make a viscosity similar to that of real blood. Another preparation could use red food coloring, water, and dry milk powder to produce a liquid with a viscosity similar to that of blood. The viscosity is important in trying to reproduce the spatter patterns of human blood. If you are to produce your own blood spatters, using a simulation or bovine blood, you will need to use a protractor to measure angles. You will find a drawing of a large protractor on a page at the end of this experiment. Tear out that page and glue the drawing to a piece of cardboard or tag board to give it some rigidity. Cut out the protractor and use it in the following steps. You will need the protractor in the next experiment also so do not lose it. Try not to bend the protractor. When you have the liquid that you are going to use in the experiment you are ready for the next step. You will need to perform the following steps with a partner or in small groups of students.

PART A: OBTAINING BLOOD SPATTERS

1 Obtain six pieces of precut tag board, approximately 6 inches × 8 inches.

2. Your partner, or one person in your group, will place the tag board on the protective paper at an angle of 0 degrees with the floor—in other words, lying flat on the floor. Be sure to place some protective paper under the tag board to avoid getting stains on the floor.

3. Draw some of the liquid being used into your medicine dropper. Be careful not to expel any of the liquid before you are ready to do so. It may stain cloth so be aware of this possibility.

4. Place one end of the meter stick vertically on the floor next to the tag board. Place your hand holding the medicine dropper at some distance on the meter stick that is near the full length of the stick. Remember what this distance is for later reference. Incline the meter stick slightly so that the opening of the medicine dropper will be over the center portion of the tag board.

5. Very carefully squeeze the bulb of the medicine dropper to expel a single drop of the fluid. It will strike the tag board and produce a "blood" spatter.

6. Very carefully move the tag board aside and replace it with another piece. One person will hold this piece of tag board at an angle of 30 degrees to the floor, with the 6-inch edge on the floor, as determined through the use of the protractor.

7. Repeat the expulsion of a drop of the liquid on to the surface of this piece of tag board. If you desire, you may expel more that one drop of liquid on each tag board, but you must move your hand slightly, so that each drop will strike the tag board in a different place, not on top of each other. Separate them completely. The height at which the medicine dropper is held should remain as constant as possible.

8. Repeat steps 6 and 7 with other pieces of tag board, changing the angle of the tag board to 45°, 60°, and 75°.

9. Allow all of the spatters to dry thoroughly before proceeding. If your course instructor has provided you with previously prepared blood spatters, this is where you will begin the experiment—at part B on the next page.

PART B: MESURING ANGLES OF IMPACT

10. All of your measurements must be made as accurately as possible, given the tools that you are working with. You will notice that, with the exception of the spatter made when the tag board was lying flat on the floor, all of the spatters have an elliptical shape. The ellipse becomes more pronounced as the angle of the target with the floor becomes greater. You must complete the ellipse before making your measurement of the length of the spatter. See the illustration on page 306, labeled Figures 36-2, 36-3, 36-4, and 36-5. Measure the length of each spatter, omitting from this measurement the 'tail' of the spatter, if one is present. See the illustrations shown on page 306. Record this measurement in the proper column on the data sheet at the end of this experiment.

11. Carefully measure the width of the spatter at its widest point. This is shown on page 306. Record this measurement in the proper space on the data sheet.

12. Repeat these measurements for each of the spatters which you have prepared, or which you have been provided. You only need to measure one spatter on each piece of tag board, but if you are interested you can measure others also.

Now it is time for an explanation of a trigonometric function. These functions give the relationships between the sides and angles of right triangles; that is, a triangle with one 90° angle contained in it. In our case, this is the angle made by the junction of the meter stick with the floor. In a crime scene, this would be the vertical distance from the point of origin of the blood of the victim to the surface upon which that victim is standing, sitting, or lying. The angle of impact is the angle at which the blood spatter strikes the surface upon which it comes to rest. In this case it is the angle between the floor and the edge of the piece of tag board. You can make the extension to the situation of the crime scene. The "sine" of the angle of impact is the function that we are interested in. This is illustrated in Table 36-1 on the following page. To determine the angle of impact from its sine you may use your calculator or the table of sine values given on a succeeding page. Your course instructor has probably given you an explanation of this procedure. This may serve as a reminder. Now we will go back to work.

13. Determine the sine of the angle of impact for each of the cards that you are working with. The use of your calculator will make the next step a little more accurate, but the table of sine values given will also give good results. However, the results will only be as good as your measurement of the spatters.

14. Look in the table for the value that is the closest to your calculated result. If you are using your calculator for this step, you must use the second function button and then the "arc sin" button. This will provide you with the angle that has that value as its sin(e).

15. Record the value of the angles in the table on the data sheet. Compare it with the value that the angle was supposed to have, either from the use of the protractor or from the data provided by your instructor for each of the cards you are using.

SELECTED SOURCES FOR ADDITIONAL INFORMATION

Burnett, B.R., Orantes, J.M., and Pierson, M.L., "An unusual bloodstain case," *J. Forens. Sci.*, 42 (3), (1997), 519.

Raymond, M.A., Smith, E.R., and Liesegang, J., "Oscillating blood droplets—implications for crime scene reconstruction," *Sci. & Just.*, 36 (3), (1996), 161.

TABLE 36–1	*Impact Angle Determinations*

One of the methods of determining the impact angle of a blood drop was based on the trigonometric relationship:

$$\frac{\text{Width of Stain}}{\text{Length of Stain}} = \text{Sine of the impact angle}$$

Thus, by locating the width-to-length ratio of the blood stain in the following sine table, the angle of impact of the drop causing the stain can be obtained directly.

Degs.	Sine	Degs.	Sine	Degs.	Sine	Degs.	Sine	Degs.	Sine
0	0.00	19	0.33	37	0.60	55	0.82	73	0.956
1	0.02	20	0.34	38	0.62	56	0.83	74	0.961
2	0.03	21	0.36	39	0.63	57	0.84	75	0.966
3	0.05	22	0.37	40	0.64	58	0.85	76	0.970
4	0.07	23	0.39	41	0.66	59	0.86	77	0.974
5	0.09	24	0.41	42	0.67	60	0.87	78	0.978
6	0.10	25	0.42	43	0.68	61	0.87	79	0.982
7	0.12	26	0.44	44	0.69	62	0.88	80	0.985
8	0.14	27	0.45	45	0.71	63	0.89	81	0.988
9	0.16	28	0.47	46	0.72	64	0.90	82	0.990
10	0.17	29	0.48	47	0.73	65	0.91	83	0.993
11	0.19	30	0.50	48	0.74	66	0.914	84	0.995
12	0.21	31	0.52	49	0.75	67	0.921	85	0.996
13	0.23	32	0.53	50	0.77	68	0.927	86	0.997
14	0.24	33	0.54	51	0.78	69	0.934	87	0.998
15	0.26	34	0.56	52	0.79	70	0.940	88	0.9994
16	0.28	35	0.57	53	0.80	71	0.946	89	0.9998
17	0.29	36	0.59	54	0.81	72	0.951	90	1.00
18	0.31								

EXPERIMENT 36

DATA SHEET

Name _____

Date _____

DETERMINATION OF BLOOD SPATTER ANGLES OF IMPACT

Target in the table below will be defined as the piece of tag board used in this experiment.

Angle of target in degrees	Width of spatter in mm	Length of spatter in mm	Width/length ratio	Impact angle from the sine table
0				
30				
45				
60				
75				

Questions

1. How closely to the known values of the angles of impact compare with those that you determined from the use of the sine function?

2. What is the most likely cause of any difference between the two values which you compared in question 1, above?

3. Do you think that the height of the medicine dropper above the target tag board has anything to do with the ratio calculated from the width/length ratio of the spatter? Why or why not?

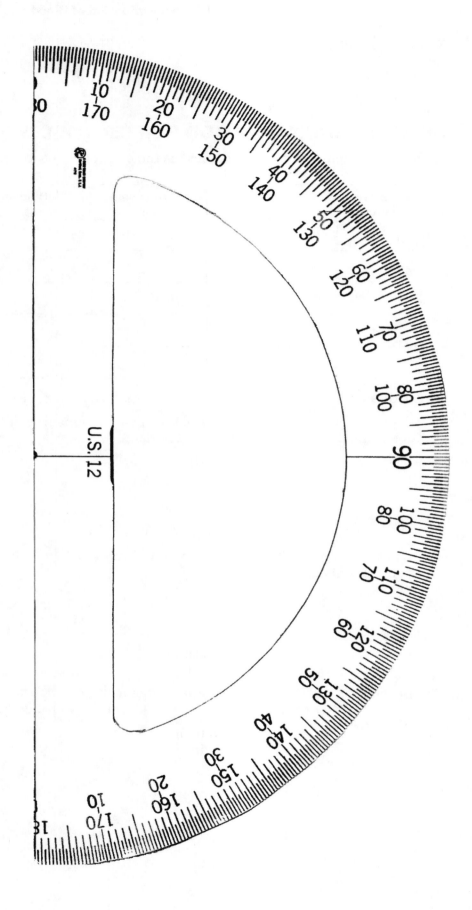

FIGURE 36–6

Determining the Origin of Blood Spatters*

This experiment will use the crime scene described in the Determination of Blood Spatter Angles of Impact in this manual. In this work we will use the method learned in that experiment and add a few steps to it. We can then determine the location in three- dimensional space within a very small area where the blood spatters originated. This can provide valuable information to the crime scene investigator in trying to reconstruct the series of events occurring during the commission of the crime. Very careful measurements will aid in the obtaining of a good result. Refer to Figure 38-1 on page 315 to see how this is done.

EQUIPMENT

1 Ruler   1 Meter stick or yardstick
1 Protractor   Balls of string or yarn (several colors will be best)
1 Tall ring stand or some vertical pole that string can be tied to.
Paper or other surface containing blood spatters

METHOD

Your course instructor will have prepared for you a large piece of paper or tag board upon which you will see a number of blood spatters. These spatters will be used to determine the location in space of their origin. If you make very careful measurements of the blood spatter lengths and widths you will find that you can make this determination with a high degree of accuracy. You will use the following steps to determine the angle of impact of a number of different spatters. It is best to work in a team of students and assign certain spatters to each team member. The work will progress much more quickly and efficiently in this manner. You must also determine the point of convergence of the blood spatters. This will give the location of the victim at the time the crime was committed. Remember that during a beating, which is what we are apparently dealing with in

*Adapted from material authored by Terry Laber and Bart Epstein, Minnesota Bureau of Criminal Apprehension Laboratory. Used with their permission.

this experiment, the victim may move around quite a bit. We are going to stylize this situation slightly, and assume one location, but perhaps a number of positions, such as standing, bending over, sitting, etc. You are going to determine the point of convergence, so perhaps we should look at that first. The blood spatters all display an elliptical shape when they strike a surface at an angle of impact of less than 90° and more than 0°. In many cases you will see a sort of "tail" on the spatter. This tail always points in the direction of travel of the spatter. In other words, the spatter was moving in the direction of the tail of the spatter. You will need to place your ruler or meter stick along the longest axis of the spatter and draw a line on the surface of the paper or tag board from the trailing end of the spatter back along the ruler. See the illustration of this step on the next page of this manual. You will need to perform this step for a number of the blood spatters and you will see that the extensions of the lines through their length will all meet within a very small area on your paper or tag board.

1. You need to place a vertical object, such as a ring stand, at the point of convergence of the lines drawn on your spatter surface. Be sure that the vertical rod is as nearly at the point where the lines meet as you can. Your succeeding determinations depend upon very careful measurement and placement.

2. Now measure the widths and lengths of a number of blood spatters on your assigned paper or tag board. Record these measurements on the data sheet at the end of this experiment. Calculate the sine of the angle of impact for each spatter, as you did in the previous experiment, and record these values in the proper column on the data sheet. Determine the angle of impact for each spatter and record this also. You may find that not all of the values agree with each other. That is because the victim may have changed position at various times during the beating. The location may be nearly the same, but the position can vary considerably, due to falling while being beaten, etc.

3. Choose a particular color of string for a set of values for the angle of impact that agree very closely with each other. Tape one end of the string to the surface upon which the spatter is seen, at the edge of the spatter closest to the point of convergence. Use your protractor to elevate the string to the angle of impact determined for that spatter. Fasten the string to the vertical support, located at the point of convergence, by tying or by the use of tape. Continue these steps for all of the spatters that display the same, or nearly the same, angles of impact. Try to use a different color of string for each of the sets of angles that closely agree with each other. You will end up with strings meeting the vertical support at heights that show the position of the victim during the progress of the crime. Do not expect that the strings will meet the vertical support at exactly the same place. The body of a person has mass and volume, so the strings will meet in an *area* of that body, not a single point. A bullet wound, producing spatters, will meet in a much tighter area that those produced by being struck with a large blunt object, such as a baseball bat.

4. Leave your string experiment assembled so that your laboratory instructor can evaluate it. Answer the questions at the end of this experiment and hand in your data sheet(s) and question pages for scoring. This type of experiment can be very instructive and a lot of fun when performed in a simulated crime scene setting. Perhaps you will have the opportunity to do this as part of a final laboratory exam near the end of this course. Sometimes this is done as a means of drawing together all that you have learned during the course of the semester.

NOTE: If in the future you are at the scene of a crime, DO NOT clean up the mess or let anyone else do it just because it looks horrible. Let the police get their photos first and wait until they give the all clear - which may be days away.

SELECTED SOURCES FOR ADDITIONAL INFORMATION

Burnett, B.R., Orantes, J.M., and Pierson, M.L., "An unusual bloodstain case," *J. Forens. Sci.*, 42 (3), (1997), 519.

Hulse-Smith, L., Mehdizadeh, N. Z., and Chandra, S., "Deducing drop size and impact velocity from circular bloodstains," *J. Forens. Sci.*, 50 (1), (2005), 54.

Raymond, M.A., Smith, E.R., and Liesegang, J., "Oscillating blood droplets—implications for crime scene reconstruction," *Sci. & Just.*, 36 (3), (1996), 161.

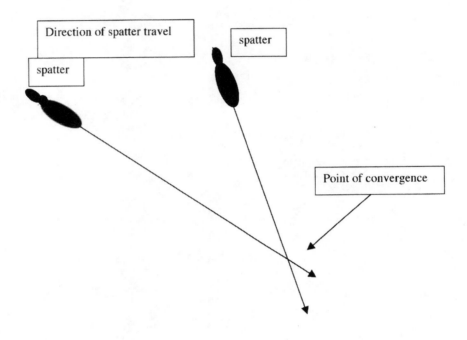

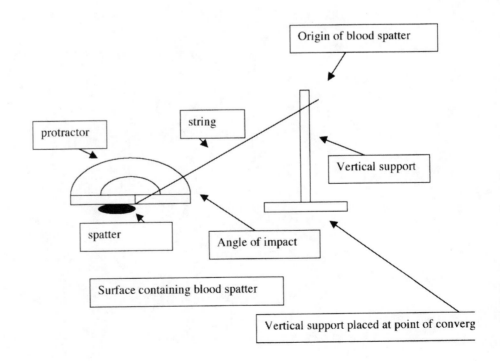

FIGURE 37–1

EXPERIMENT 37

Name _____

DATA SHEET

Date _____

DETERMINING THE ORIGIN OF BLOOD SPATTERS

Record your measurements for the blood spatters in the following table. Referring to Table 36-1, page 309, calculate the sine of the angle of impact and determine the angle of impact of the blood spatter from those values. Record all data in the proper columns.

Width of spatter	Length of spatter	Sine of angle of impact	Angle of impact in degrees	Color of string used for angle of impact

Questions

1. What is a possible major source of error in the determination of the sine of the angle of impact?

2. What does "completing the ellipse" mean in connection with the angle of impact of a blood spatter?

3. What purpose does the use of different colors of string serve in this experiment?

Electrophoretic Analysis of Blood for Human Origin (Advanced)

Experiments 38, 40, and 41 involve a technique called electrophoresis. Experiment 38 involves solution electrophoresis, while experiments 40 and 41 involve gel electrophoresis. Experiment 38 is concerned with the determination of whether or not a stain is human blood as opposed to animal blood or something that just looks like blood. Experiment 39 extends this further to introduce you to the technique of obtaining DNA and Experiments 40 and 41 introduces you to several uses of DNA typing.

It was found by Arne Tiselius in the mid-1930s that if ions of similar charge were placed in solution between two oppositely charged electrodes as shown in Figure 38-1 that the smaller ions of the same charge move (migrate) toward the electrode of opposite charge faster than the larger ions. He also found that if ions of different charge were placed in the solution, that the more highly charged ions migrate faster than the lower charged ions.

When these factors are combined, a separation is possible. Modern techniques pass the compounds through a gel on a piece of plastic or paper because it is easier to stain and measure them later on.

When a stain is analyzed in the laboratory and found to be a bloodstain, the forensic analyst will have to determine whether the stain is of human origin. For this purpose the standard test used is the **precipitin test**.

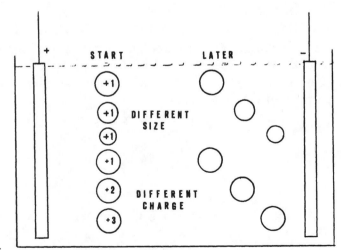

FIGURE 38–1 Diagram of electrophoretic migration.

Precipitin tests are based on the fact that when animals (usually rabbits) are injected with human blood, antibodies are formed that react with the invading blood to neutralize its presence. The animal's serum can be recovered and marketed commercially as human antiserum. This experiment sets forth a practical, rapid, inexpensive, and sensitive electrophoretic method for confirming the fact that a bloodstain is of human origin.

The technique that we shall use in this experiment is known as **counter immuno-electrophoresis** or **crossover electrophoresis**. It takes advantage of the fact that human blood is antigenic; that is, its presence in the body of animals such as rabbits will cause the production of antibodies. In crossover electrophoresis an agar mixture is poured onto a microscope slide and allowed to harden. Then a set of holes is punched into the gel where the antigen solution (bloodstain) and the commercial human antiserum are placed. Under the influence of an electrical field, the antigens and antibodies move toward each other across the gel. If the blood is of human origin, a line of precipitation will form midway between the two holes (see Figure 38-2).

CRIME SCENE

A suspect was arrested based on a man's charge of assault and robbery. In the preliminary hearing the defense lawyer challenged the results of the blood typing test, asserting that the blood was not of human origin. The prosecution has requested the laboratory to do a crossover electrophoresis test in order to determine human origin. You have a portion of the suspect stain to do the following experiment.

EQUIPMENT

1 Beaker, 25 mL
1 Bulb to fit the Pasteur pipets
1 Burner, Bunsen
1 Constant voltage power source; only up to 100 volts needed
1 pr Goggles, safety
1 Paper, filter, Whatman #2
1 Pipet, 1.0 mL

1 Pipet, Pasteur
Slides, microscope, 5 × 8 cm
1 Syringe, 10 μL
1 Tank, electrophoresis, to hold microscope slides in shoulders (shoulders should be placed less than 7 cm apart)
1 Tube, test, 10 × 75 mm

REAGENTS

Agarose (K & K Laboratories, Plainview, N.Y.)

Anti-human serum (Cappel Laboratories, Inc., Conchranville, Pa. 19350)

Gel buffer solution (pH 8.6); barbituric acid, 0.55 g, sodium barbitone, 3.5 g, calcium lactate, 0.51 g, distilled water to 500 mL.

Tank buffer solution (pH 8.6): barbituric acid, 1.38 g. sodium barbitone, 8.76 g, calcium lactate, 0.38 g, distilled water to 1 L.

Antigen and antibody are added to their respective wells

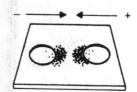

Antigen and antibody are being moved toward each other

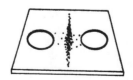

Antigen and antibody have formed a visible precipitin line in the gel between the wells

FIGURE 38-2 The sequence of events on the microscope slide.

METHOD

If you look at Figures 38-2 and 38-3 before you read the following directions the directions will be easier to understand.

1. Cut a 1×1 cm piece of the material containing a suspected human blood stain. Place this in a test tube with 1 mL of gel buffer. Label this "T" for "test." Allow the material to soak for 5 to 10 minutes. The ideal extract will appear as a pale straw color.

2. Cut a 1×1 cm piece from an unstained area and place it in a test tube with 1 mL of gel buffer. Label the tube "C" for "control."

3. Cut a 1×1 cm piece of material containing a known human bloodstain. Treat as in Step 1. Label the test tube "K" for "known."

4. Weigh 0.1 g of agarose and add it to 5 mL of distilled water; add an equal volume of gel buffer and heat the mixture in a boiling water bath until the agarose dissolves.

5. Pour the agarose mixture onto a leveled 5×8 cm microscope slide. Allow it to gel at least 15 minutes, scraping off any excess gel from the edges.

6. Once the gel hardens, punch three pairs of holes in the gel with a Pasteur pipet (with suction). Position the holes about midway up the slide. The holes should be about 1.5 mm in diameter and separated from each other by about 1.5–2.0 mm. Note: A well-punching kit is commercially available.

7. Holding the coated plate lengthwise, with a Pasteur pipet place the test solution, known, and control extracts in the right set of holes. Place the human anti-serum into the left set of holes. The wells should be filled to their tops, but not overflowing.

8. Place 50 mL of the tank buffer in each side of the electrophoresis tank. Saturate 22×4 cm strips of filter paper and place them on each side of the tank.

9. Invert the plate into the filter papers so that the antiserum wells are closest to the anode (+ electrode) and the stain extracts nearest to the cathode (- electrode) as shown in Figure 38-2.

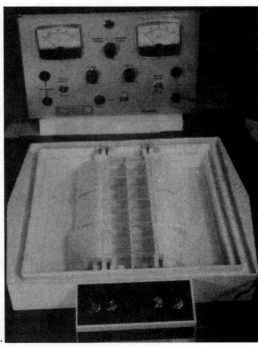

FIGURE 38–3   Position of the gel side in the electrophoresis.

10. Electrophoresis is carried out at 100 to 150 volts for 10 to 20 minutes.

11. A fine line of white precipitate between holes of a pair represents a positive reaction.

SELECTED SOURCES FOR ADDITIONAL INFORMATION

Buel, E., LaFountain, M., Schwartz, M., and Walkinshaw, M., "Evaluation of capillary electrophoresis performance through resolution measurements," *J. Forens. Sci.*, 46 (2), (2001), 341.

Calliford, B.J., "The examination and typing of bloodstains in the crime laboratory," Washington, D.C.: U.S. Government Printing Offices, 1971.

Klapec, D.J., and Ng, D., "The use of capillary electrophoresis in the detection of monomethylamine and benzoate ions in the forensic examination of explosive residues," *J. Forens. Sci.*, 46 (5), (2001), 1168.

Moretti, T.R., Baumstark, A.L., Defenbaugh, D.A., Keys, K.M., Brown, A.L., and Budowle, B., "Validation of STR typing by capillary electrophoresis," *J. Forens. Sci.*, 46 (3), (2001), 661.

Quarino, L., Samples, M., San Pietro, D., Shaler, R., Orta, A., and Jack, D., "Haptoglobin typing of bloodstains using horizontal discontinuous polyacrylamine gel electrophoresis," *Sci. & Just.*, 35 (3), (1995), 213.

Stowell, L.I., Thomson, D.G., Vintiner, S.K., and Dick, G.L., "Behavior of animal blood in blood typing systems. Isoelectric focusing of erythrocyte acid phosphatases and phosphoglucomutase," *J. Forens. Sci.*, 34 (5), (1989), 1095.

Thomas, A.S., "The evaluation of five electrophoretic phenotyping systems for routine screening of bloodstains," *J. Forens. Sci. Soc.*, 29 (4), (1989), 243.

EXPERIMENT 38

DATA SHEET

Name _____

Date _____

ELECTROPHORETIC ANALYSIS OF BLOOD FOR HUMAN ORIGIN (ADVANCED)

1. Attach your slide to this sheet.

2. What is agar and what is its purpose in this experiment?

3. A person suspected of just robbing a meat market was apprehended and found to have several bills in his pockets. His explanation was that he was shooting craps in the alley and picked up the money and ran when the "cops" came. The police detective asked the lab people if they could tell if the bills had been in a meat market. They said they could if given a little time. How could they do this using "Experiment 38"?

Nuclear DNA Extraction*

DNA evidence is used whenever possible in criminal investigations. The next several experiments involve DNA in various situations. It is therefore desirous to learn how DNA can be obtained and in a situation safer than using human blood. This procedure can be used to isolate chromosomal DNA from a variety of sources such as *E. coli*, peas, onion and other vegetable sources.

All organisms are composed of cells. Some organisms such as bacteria and yeast are single-celled organisms. Others, such as humans, are made of trillions of specialized cells. Cells are composed of proteins, lipids, carbohydrates, and nucleic acids. DNA (deoxyribonucleic acid) is the hereditary material found in all cells. It is the genetic material that directs the development and function of all organisms.

* Courtesy of Laura Anne Roselli, Biotechnology Department, Burlington County College, Mt Laurel, New Jersey 08054

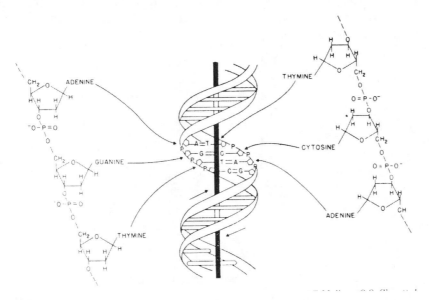

FIGURE 39–1 A diagram of the double helix DNA module. Courtesy M.F. Mallette, C.O. Clagett, A.T. Phillips, and R.L. McCarl, *Introductory Biochemistry*, Williams and Wilkens Co. (1971).

One of DNA's most important functions is to direct the synthesis of proteins. Genes are long segments of DNA which encode proteins. Genes contained on one strand of DNA make up a chromosome. Humans have twenty-three pairs of chromosomes, one maternal set and one paternal set. If the DNA from one human cell was stretched end to end, it would be 7 feet long. Before DNA can be amplified via polymerase chain reaction or analyzed through genetic fingerprinting, the DNA must be extracted from the cell. We will review several procedures which can accomplish this goal.

In the following procedures we are going to complete three basic steps: 1. Lyse (break open) the cells; 2. Separate DNA from other cellular components; 3. Stain DNA for visualization. The procedures vary slightly due to the differing cellular composition between cell types. In the first procedure, you will isolate the chromosome of a rod-shaped prokaryotic bacterium called *Escherichia coli* (*E. coli*). Prokaryotic cells do not enclose their chromosomal DNA in a nuclear membrane. These include bacteria. In the second procedure, you will be working with eukaryotic plant cells. Eukaryotic cells have a nuclear membrane around the chromosomes. Plants and animals are eukaryotic organisms. Plant cells, in particular, have walls which need further enzymatic digestion for cell lysis to occur. This is shown in diagram form in Figure 39-2.

In the first step we will lyse the cells using a detergent. Lysing the cells refers to breaking the outer plasma membrane of the cell, thus releasing the internal components of the cell. This can be accomplished with dishwashing liquid, shampoo, as well as some laundry detergents. The cell (plasma) membrane is composed of lipids. Detergents have a similar structure to these membrane lipids. The molecules of detergent integrate into the cell membrane and cause it to dissociate. This is shown in diagram form in Figure 39-3.

In the second step we separate the DNA from other cellular components through alcohol extraction. When the ethanol is added, two phases form in your tube, the aqueous and alcohol phases. The DNA will separate from the other two phases and precipitate at the interphase (thin layer between the aqueous and alcohol layers).

For those eukaryotic sources of DNA, an additional step of protein digestion is included. This is necessary because eukaryotic DNA is wrapped around protein molecules called *histones*. Meat tenderizers contain enzymes which will remove these proteins. The enzymes also aid in digestion of the **cell** wall.

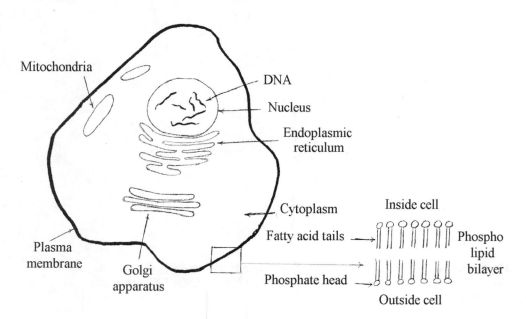

FIGURE 39–2   Eukarotic cell, detailing the plasma membrane. The membrane is composed of phospholipid molecules.

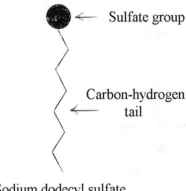

Sulfate group

Carbon-hydrogen
tail

Sodium dodecyl sulfate
(Detergent)

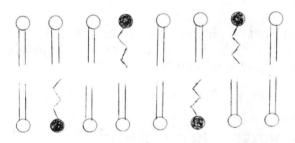

Detergent integrating
into the plasma membrane

FIGURE 39–3 Diagram illustrating how a detergent disrupts the cell membrane.

Lastly, the DNA can be removed from the interphase by gently moving a rod through the two phases repeatedly. The white precipitate which begins to spool is chromosomal DNA. DNA can be visualized at higher magnification under a microscope, with the use of methylene blue, a stain which dyes DNA.

CRIME SCENE

It has been found, although in limited experiments, that plant DNA is as unique as animal DNA. This was first shown by demonstrating that trees have unique DNA. A young woman was found murdered under a group of trees. The police located a suspect who denied even being in the area. The police noticed some seed pods in the back of his pickup truck that looked just like those on the trees where the body was found. Would the DNA of these seeds match the tree over the body and be different from the adjacent trees? In order to give you some practice in obtaining plant DNA before you test the evidence you are going to experiment with the basic techniques involved.

PART A: ISOLATION OF CHROMOSOMAL DNA FROM *E. COLI*

EQUIPMENT

5-6 Wooden stir rods
    (can use the wooden end of cotton swabs)
 1 Water bath set at 65°C.
 1 Medicine dropper

1 Pipet, Mohr, 10 mL
1 Test tube, 10 mL capacity.
1 Test tube holder

CHEMICAL

7 mL *E.coli* (actively growing culture 24 hrs)
4 mL Ethanol (or isopropyl alcohol)
3 mL Detergent or shampoo

METHOD

1. Make 5 mL of a 50% dilution of detergent in water.

2. Add 5 mL of 50% detergent directly to the *E. coli* culture.

3. Heat the tube for 15 minutes at 65°C.

4. Cool the bacteria to room temperature.

5. Tilt the test tube slightly and add 4 mL of cold ethanol dropwise down the side to the bacterial tube. Do not mix the two layers.

6. Move a stirring rod back and forth through the two phases. Do not move the rod entirely to the bottom of your broth tube. Moving the rod slightly into the aqueous phase and then slightly back into the alcohol phase will suffice.

7. Twirl the wooden rod. DNA should begin to spool around it.

PART B: ISOLATION OF DNA FROM VEGETABLE SOURCES

EQUIPMENT

4-5 Wooden stir rods	1 Beaker, 250 mL
1 Waterbath	1 Graduated cylinder, 50 or 100 mL
1 Blender	1 Pipet, Mohr, 10 mL
Cheese cloth, approximately 6″ × 6″	4-5 Test tubes, 10 mL capacity
	1 Test tube rack

CHEMICALS

DNA source (i.e., Peas, Onions)
Salt
Water
Ethanol
Detergent or shampoo
Meat tenderizer

METHOD

1. Combine 1/2 cup (or 118 mL) of your vegetable with 1 cup (236 mL) of water.

2. Blend on high or homogenize until liquid.

3. Strain through cheese cloth and catch the filtrate in a 250 mL beaker.

4. Place 4 mL aliquots of the liquid into each of 4-5 test tubes.

5. Add 3 mL of 50% detergent to a test tube containing strained vegetable liquid.

6. Add a pinch of meat tenderizer (contains an enzyme).

7. Tilt the test tube slightly and add 3 mL of cold ethanol dropwise down the side to the tube. Do not mix the two layers.

8. Move stirring rod back and forth through the two phases. Do not move the rod entirely to the bottom of your sample tube. Moving the rod slightly into the aqueous phase and then slightly back into the alcohol phase will suffice.

9. Twirl the wooden rod. DNA should begin to spool.

PART C: STAINING OF DNA FOR VISUALIZATION (CAN BE USED SUBSEQUENT TO PART A OR PART B)

EQUIPMENT

2-3 Coverslips	1 Medicine dropper
2-3 Microscope slides	2-3 Toothpicks
1 Compound microscope	

CHEMICALS

Methylene blue indicator solution.

METHOD

1. Remove the isolated DNA from the wooden rod with a toothpick and place it on a glass slide.

2. Place 2 drops of methylene blue directly on the DNA.

3. Place a coverslip over the stained DNA.

4. View under a compound microscope. Look under 2 magnifications: 40X and 100X

ALTERNATE EXPERIMENTS

1. Use a laundry detergent vs. dishwashing detergent to compare the differences in the amounts of DNA isolated from the same vegetable source.

2. Try isolating DNA from different vegetable sources. How do the yields of DNA compare in peas vs. onions, carrots?

3. Using baker's yeast and athletic shoe cleaner, yeast genomic DNA can be isolated. See reference 2 below.

SELECTED SOURCES FOR ADDITIONAL INFORMATION

http://vslc.genetics.utah.edu/units/activities/extractionZ

Kelly, K.F., Rankin, J.J., and Wink, R.C., "Method and application of DNA fingerprinting: a guide for the non-scientist," *Criminal Law Review* (1987), 105.

Kimber, C., "Interpretation of mitochondrial DNA sequencing," *Sci. & Just.*, 40 (3), (2000), 217.

Montpetit, Shawn A., Fitch, I. T., and O'Donnell, P. T., "A simple automated instrument for DNA extraction in forensic casework," *J. Forens. Sci.*, 50 (3), (2005), 555.

EXPERIMENT 39   Name _____

DATA SHEET   Date _____

NUCLEAR DNA EXTRACTION

1. Describe the appearance of the DNA that you have isolated on the wooden rod. Illustrate below.

2. Describe the appearance of the DNA as viewed under the microscope. Illustrate below.

3. After the addition of ethanol, two phases develop in your tube. Which phase is on top? Why does this phase sit on the top rather than the bottom?

4. Why is the addition of detergent necessary to isolate DNA?

5. How would your results differ in Part B if you omitted the meat tenderizer?

DNA Fingerprinting I
EDVO-Kit # 109

EXPERIMENT COMPONENTS

ELECTROPHORESIS SAMPLES

- Ready-to-Load™ DNA samples

  A DNA from crime scene cut with Enzyme 1
  B DNA from crime scene cut with Enzyme 2
  C DNA from Suspect 1 cut with Enzyme 1
  D DNA from Suspect 1 cut with Enzyme 2
  E DNA from Suspect 2 cut with Enzyme 1
  F DNA from Suspect 2 cut with Enzyme 2

REAGENTS & SUPPLIES

- Practice Gel Loading Solution
- UltraSpec-Agarose™ powder
- Concentrated electrophoresis buffer
- InstaStain® Methylene Blue
- Methylene Blue Plus™
- 1 ml pipet
- 100 ml graduated cylinder (packaging for samples)
- Microtipped Transfer Pipets

  THIS EXPERIMENT DOES NOT CONTAIN HUMAN DNA.

REQUIREMENTS

- Horizontal gel electrophoresis apparatus
- D.C. power supply
- Automatic micropipets with tips
- Balance
- Microwave, hot plate or burner
- Pipet pump
- 250 ml flasks or beakers

- Hot gloves
- Safety goggles and disposable laboratory gloves
- Small plastic trays or large weigh boats (for gel destaining)
- DNA visualization system (white light)
- Distilled or deionized water

INTRODUCTION TO DNA FINGERPRINTING

DNA typing (also called DNA profile analysis or DNA fingerprinting) is the process whereby the genomic DNA of an organism is analyzed by examining several specific, variable DNA sequences located throughout the genome. In humans, DNA fingerprinting is now used routinely for identification purposes.

Human DNA fingerprinting was pioneered by Dr. Alex Jeffreys at the University of Leicester in 1984. His analytical method led to the apprehension of a murderer in the first DNA fingerprinting conviction in September 1987 in the UK. Two months later, the first U.S. conviction based on DNA fingerprinting occured in Orlando, Florida. Since then, the use of DNA fingerprinting has led to thousands of criminal convictions, as well as dozens of exonerations.

In contrast to earlier methodologies, such as blood typing which can only exclude a suspect, DNA fingerprinting can provide positive identification with great accuracy. In addition to criminal identification cases, DNA fingerprinting is now used routinely in paternity determinations and for the identification of genetic disease "markers". It is also used for the identification of human remains, such as in war casualties, and was used extensively to identify victims of the September 11, 2001 terrorist attacks on the World Trade Center and Pentagon.

Human cells contain two types of DNA. The first type is cellular chromosomal DNA, which is packaged in 23 sets of chromosomes in the nucleus of the cell. This DNA, obtained from both parents, reflects the combined parental genetic inheritance of an individual. DNA fingerprinting utilizing cellular DNA involves analysis of the sequence of two alleles for a particular gene.

The second type of DNA is different from cellular DNA and is present only in the mitochondria, which are the energy-producing organelles of the cell. Mitochondrial DNA is inherited maternally by both males and females and is extremely useful in the analysis of specific cases where fraternal linkages are important to determine. For example, a brother, sister, half brother or half sister who share the same mother would inherit the same mitochondrial DNA. Identification is determined by sequencing certain regions within mitochondrial DNA, which is a single circular chromosome composed of 16,569 base pairs and 37 genes identified.

The DNA fingerprinting methods developed by Dr. Jeffreys utilizes cellular chromosomal DNA, which is submitted to restriction enzyme digestion, followed by Southern blot analysis. When human DNA is digested by a restriction enzyme, a very large number of DNA fragments are generated. When separated by agarose gel electrophoresis, the numerous DNA fragments appear as a "smear" on the gel. Labeled probes are used to detect Restriction Fragment Length Polymorphic (RFLP) regions within DNA, which will be described later in greater detail. The RFLP method is statistically very accurate but requires relatively large amounts of DNA and takes several weeks to perform.

In recent years, the method utilizing Polymerase Chain Reaction (PCR) has subsequently superceded the RFLP method because of two important advantages. The first is the sensitivity of the PCR method, which allows for DNA fingerprinting identification using much smaller amounts of DNA. This is because the PCR method is able to amplify DNA to facilitate analysis. A second advantage is the speed of PCR analysis, which allows critical questions to be answered more quickly compared to Southern Blot analysis.

In the biotechnology teaching classroom, many important concepts, theories and the practice of molecular biology can be conveyed in the context of the various DNA Fingerprinting methods. In this experiment, emphasis is placed on concepts related to the RFLP method. The experiment activities focus on the identification of DNA by analyzing restriction fragmentation patterns separated by agarose gel electrophoresis.

Use of Restriction Enzymes In DNA Fingperprinting

DNA fingerprinting involves the electrophoretic analysis of DNA fragment sizes generated by restriction enzymes. Restriction enzymes are endonucleases which catalyze the cleavage of phosphodiester bonds within both strands of DNA. The points of cleavage occur in or near very specific palindromic sequences of bases called recognition sites, which are generally 4 to 8 base pairs in length.

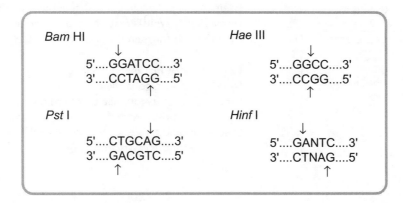

The two most commonly used restriction enzymes for DNA profile analysis are *Hae* III and *Hinf* I, which are 4-base and 5-base cutting enzymes. The examples in the figure above show recognition sites for various restriction enzymes.

The size of the DNA fragments generated depends on the distance between the recognition sites. In general, the longer the DNA molecule, the greater the probability that a given recognition site will occur. Human DNA is very large and contains approximately three billion base pairs. A restriction enzyme having a 6-base pair recognition site, such as *Eco* RI, would be expected to cut human DNA into approximately 750,000 different fragments.

DNA is highly polymorphic—that is, no two individuals have exactly the same pattern of restriction enzyme recognition sites in their DNAs. A large number of alleles exist in the population. Alleles, which are alternate forms of a gene, result in alternative expressions of genetic traits which can be dominant or recessive.

Chromosomes occur in matching pairs, one of maternal and the other of paternal origin. The two copies of a gene (alleles) at a given chromosomal locus represent a composite of the parental genes constituting an individual's unique genotype. It follows that alleles have differences in their base sequences which consequently creates differences in the distribution and frequencies of restriction enzyme recognition sites. Other differences in base sequences between individuals can occur because of mutations and deletions. Such changes can also create or eliminate a recognition site.

Polymorphic DNA refers to chromosomal regions that vary widely from individual to individual. By examining several of these regions within the genomic DNA obtained from an individual, one may obtain a "DNA fingerprint" for that individual. The most commonly used polymorphisms are those which vary in length; these are known as Fragment Length Polymorphisms (FLPs). There are two main reasons for the occurrence of FLPs. Restriction Fragment Length Polymorphisms (RFLPs) are the result of variations in length of a given segment of genomic DNA between two restriction endonuclease recognition sites among individuals of the same species. RFLPs are the result of an altered restriction enzyme cut site that may be the result of a mutation of a restriction enzyme recognition site.

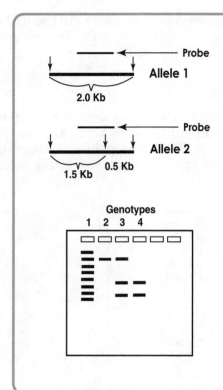

RFLP as Determined in Southern Blot analysis

An allele is recognized by a probe that spans over the internal restriction enzyme site which is present in certain alleles. In Allele 1, the internal restriction enzyme site is missing. In Allele 2, the internal restriction enzyme is present resulting in two fragments. Upon separation by agarose gel electrophoresis of the digested Allele 2, two fragments are generated. Probes will bind to the 2.0 Kb allele as well as the two smaller fragments (1.5 Kb and 0.5 Kb) generated by the restriction enzyme digestion because the probe spans over the two fragments as well as the intact allele.

Lane 1   DNA Marker
Lane 2   Homozygous allele
Lane 3   Heterozygous alleles where one can be cut
              with the restriction enzyme
Lane 4   Homozygous alleles where both are cut
              with the restriction enzyme

A second major type of FLP occurs mainly in "intergenic" or noncoding regions of DNA and is known as Variable Number of Tandem Repeats (VNTRs). In this case, segments of DNA that contain sequences from 2 to 40 bases in length repeat in tandem manner many times. The number of segments or "core units" repeats varies among individuals of the same species. The restriction enzyme cut sites are not altered. VNTR loci are very polymorphic. There are potentially hundreds of alleles at a single locus and therefore they are very useful in DNA fingerprinting. Ten to fifteen percent of mammalian DNA consists of sets of repeated, short sequences of bases that are tandemly arranged in arrays. The length of these arrays (the amount of repeated sets) varies between individuals at different chromosomal loci.

TGTTTA | TGTTTA | TGTTTA | ....variable number

When these arrays are flanked by recognition sites, the length of the repeat will determine the size of the restriction enzyme fragment generated. There are several types of these short, repetitive sequences and they have been cloned and purified.

The DNA Fingerprinting Process

Agarose gel electrophoresis is a procedure used to analyze DNA fragments generated by restriction enzymes. The agarose gel consists of microscopic pores that act as a molecular sieve. Samples of DNA are loaded into wells made in the gel during casting. Since DNA has a negative charge at neutral pH, it migrates through the gel towards the positive electrode during electrophoresis. DNA fragments are separated by the gel according to their size. The smaller the fragment the faster it migrates. After electrophoresis, the DNA can be visualized by staining the gel with dyes. Restriction enzyme cleavage of relatively small DNA molecules, such as plasmids and viral DNAs, usually results in discrete banding patterns of the DNA fragments after electrophoresis. However, cleavage of large and complex DNA, such as human chromosomal DNA, generates so many differently sized fragments that the resolving capacity of the gel is

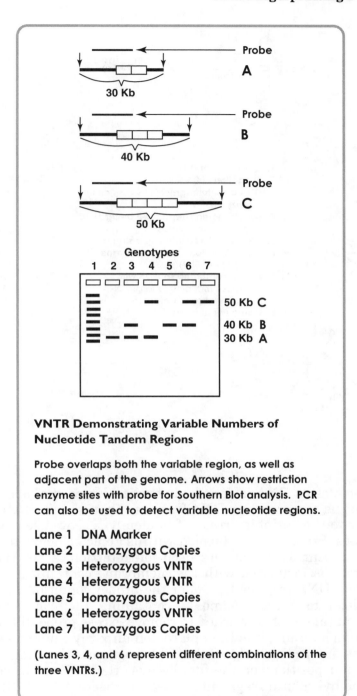

VNTR Demonstrating Variable Numbers of Nucleotide Tandem Regions

Probe overlaps both the variable region, as well as adjacent part of the genome. Arrows show restriction enzyme sites with probe for Southern Blot analysis. PCR can also be used to detect variable nucleotide regions.

Lane 1 DNA Marker
Lane 2 Homozygous Copies
Lane 3 Heterozygous VNTR
Lane 4 Heterozygous VNTR
Lane 5 Homozygous Copies
Lane 6 Heterozygous VNTR
Lane 7 Homozygous Copies

(Lanes 3, 4, and 6 represent different combinations of the three VNTRs.)

exceeded. Consequently, the cleaved DNA is visualized as a smear after staining and has no obvious banding patterns.

RFLP analysis of genomic DNA is facilitated by Southern Blot analysis. After electrophoresis, the DNA fragments in the gel are denatured by soaking in an alkali solution. This causes double-stranded DNA fragments to be converted into single-stranded form (no longer base-paired in a double helix). A replica of the electrophoretic pattern of DNA fragments in the gel is made by transferring (blotting) them to a sheet of nylon membrane. This is done by placing the membrane on the gel after electrophoresis and transferring the fragments to the membrane by capillary action or suction by vacuum. The DNA, which is not visible, becomes permanently adsorbed to the membrane, which can be manipulated much more easily than gels.

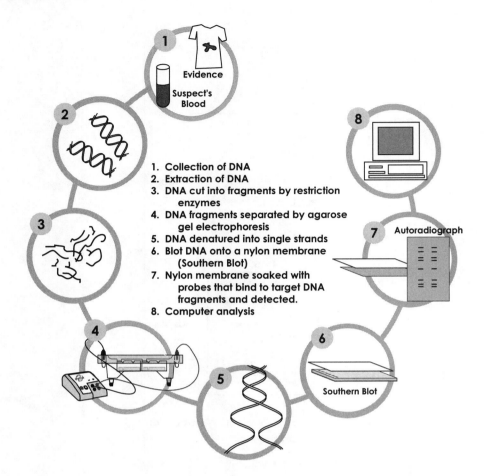

1. Collection of DNA
2. Extraction of DNA
3. DNA cut into fragments by restriction enzymes
4. DNA fragments separated by agarose gel electrophoresis
5. DNA denatured into single strands
6. Blot DNA onto a nylon membrane (Southern Blot)
7. Nylon membrane soaked with probes that bind to target DNA fragments and detected.
8. Computer analysis

Analysis of the blotted DNA is done by hybridization with a labeled DNA probe. In forensic RFLP analysis, the probe is a DNA fragment that contains base sequences which are complementary to the variable arrays of tandemly repeated sequences found in the human chromosomes. Probes can be labeled with isotopic or nonisotopic reporter molecules, such as fluorescent dyes, that are used for detection. A solution containing the single-stranded probe is incubated with the membrane containing the blotted, single-stranded (denatured) DNA fragments. Under the proper conditions, the probe will only base pair (hybridize) to those fragments containing the complementary repeated sequences. The membrane is then washed to remove excess probe. If the probe is isotopically labeled to the membrane, it is then placed on an x-ray film for several hours. This process is known as autoradiography. Only DNA fragments that have hybridized to the probe will reveal their positions on the film because the localized areas of radioactivity cause exposure. The hybridized fragments appear as discrete bands (fingerprint) on the film and are in the same relative positions as they were in the agarose gel after electrophoresis. Only specific DNA fragments, of the hundreds of thousands of fragments present, will hybridize with the probe because of the selective nature of the hybridization (base pairing) process. Since autoradiography is an extremely sensitive technique, only small amounts of DNA samples are required.

In forensic cases, DNA samples can be extracted and purified from small specimens of skin, blood, semen, or hair roots collected at the crime scene. DNA that is suitable for analysis can even be obtained from dried stains of semen and blood. The RFLP analyses performed on these samples is then compared to those performed on samples obtained from the suspect. If the RFLP patterns match, it is then beyond reasonable doubt that the suspect was at the crime scene. In practice, several different probes containing different types of repetitive sequences are used in the hybridizations in order to satisfy certain statistical criteria for absolute, positive identification. The use of different restriction enzymes allow for accuracies in positive identifications of greater than one in 100 million.

The Polymerase Chain Reaction (PCR) method amplifies target sequences of DNA, which are referred to as AMRFLPs. PCR has made it possible for very small amounts of DNA found at crime scenes to be amplified for DNA fingerprinting analysis. Using specific probes to prime DNA polymerase, many copies of the targeted areas of DNA can be synthesized *in vitro* and subsequently analyzed.

In this experiment, DNAs have been cut by restriction enzymes and the fragmentation patterns serve as the individual fingerprint. The DNA fragmentation patterns are simple enough to analyze directly in the stained agarose gel, which eliminates the need for a Southern blot. In this hypothetical case, DNA obtained from two suspects are cleaved with two restriction enzymes in separate reactions. The objective is to analyze and match the DNA fragmentation patterns after agarose gel electrophoresis and determine if Suspect 1 or Suspect 2 was at the crime scene.

THIS EXPERIMENT DOES NOT CONTAIN HUMAN DNA.

EXPERIMENT OVERVIEW

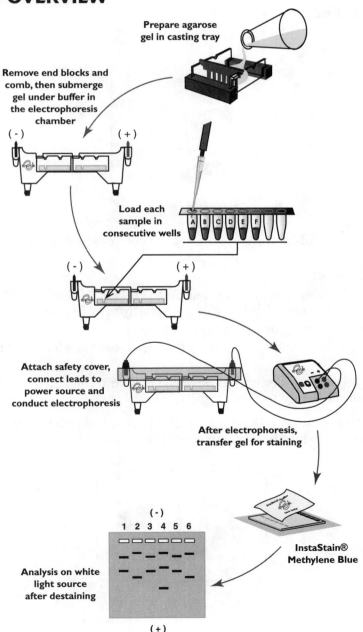

Prepare agarose gel in casting tray

Remove end blocks and comb, then submerge gel under buffer in the electrophoresis chamber

(-)   (+)

Load each sample in consecutive wells

A B C D E F

(-)   (+)

Attach safety cover, connect leads to power source and conduct electrophoresis

After electrophoresis, transfer gel for staining

InstaStain® Methylene Blue

(-)

1 2 3 4 5 6

Analysis on white light source after destaining

(+)

Experiment Objective:

The objective of this experiment is to develop a basic understanding of DNA fingerprinting. You will analyze variations in restriction enzyme cleavage patterns obtained from different DNA molecules and identify the possible perpetrator of a crime using the logic of DNA fingerprinting.

Gel Requirements

* Recommended gel tray size: 7 × 7 cm or 7 × 15 cm
* Number of sample wells required: 6
* Placement of well-former template: first set of notches
* Agarose gel concentration required: 0.8%

AGAROSE GEL PREPARATION

Preparing the Gel Bed

1. Close off the open ends of a clean and dry gel bed (casting tray) by using rubber dams or tape.
   A. Using Rubber dams:
      * Place a rubber dam on each end of the bed. Make sure the rubber dam fits firmly in contact with the sides and bottom of the bed.
   B. Taping with labeling or masking tape:
      * With 3/4 inch wide tape, extend the tape over the sides and bottom edge of the bed.
      * Fold the extended edges of the tape back onto the sides and bottom. Press contact points firmly to form a good seal.

2. Place a well-former template (comb) in the first set of notches at the end of the bed. Make sure the comb sits firmly and evenly across the bed.

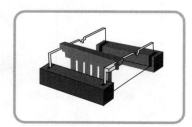

Casting Agarose Gels

3. Use a 250 ml flask to prepare the gel solution. Add the following components to the flask as specified for your experiment (refer to Table A).
    *   Buffer concentrate
    *   Distilled water
    *   Agarose powder

TABLE A	Individual 0.8% UltraSpec-Agarose™ Gel DNA Staining with InstaStain® MetBlue				
Size of EDVOTEK Casting Tray (cm)	Amt of Agarose (g)	+	Concentrated Buffer (50x) (ml)	+	Distilled Water (ml)	=	Total Volume (ml)
7 × 7	0.24		0.6		29.4		30
7 × 15	0.48		1.2		58.8		60

4. Swirl the mixture to disperse clumps of agarose powder.

5. With a marking pen, indicate the level of the solution volume on the outside of the flask.

6. Heat the mixture to dissolve the agarose powder. The final solution should appear clear (like water) without any undissolved particles.
    A. Microwave method:
        *   Cover the flask with plastic wrap to minimize evaporation.
        *   Heat the mixture on High for 1 minute.
        *   Swirl the mixture and heat on High in bursts of 25 seconds until all the agarose is completely dissolved.
    B. Hot plate method:
        *   Cover the flask with aluminum foil to prevent excess evaporation.
        *   Heat the mixture to boiling over a burner with occasional swirling. Boil until all the agarose is completely dissolved.

Check the solution carefully. If you see "crystal" particles, the agarose is not completely dissolved.

At high altitudes, it is recommended to use a microwave oven to reach boiling temperatures.

7. Cool the agarose solution to 55°C with careful swirling to promote even dissipation of heat. If detectable evaporation has occurred, add distilled water to bring the solution up to the original volume as marked on the flask in step 5.

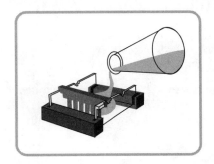

After the gel is cooled to 55°C:
If you are using rubber dams, go to step 9.
If you are using tape, continue with step 8.

8. Seal the interface of the gel bed and tape to prevent the agarose solution from leaking.
   - Use a transfer pipet to deposit a small amount of cooled agarose to both inside ends of the bed.
   - Wait approximately 1 minute for the agarose to solidify.

9. Pour the cooled agarose solution into the bed. Make sure the bed is on a level surface.

10. Allow the gel to completely solidify. It will become firm and cool to the touch after approximately 20 minutes.

Preparing the Gel for Electrophoresis

11. After the gel is completely solidified, carefully and slowly remove the rubber dams or tape from the gel bed.

Be especially careful not to damage or tear the gel wells when removing the rubber dams. A thin plastic knife, spatula or pipet tip can be inserted between the gel and the dams to break possible surface tension.

12. Remove the comb by slowly pulling straight up. Do this carefully and evenly to prevent tearing the sample wells.

13. Place the gel (on its bed) into the electrophoresis chamber, properly oriented, centered and level on the platform.

14. Fill the electrophoresis apparatus chamber with the required volume of diluted buffer for the specific unit you are using (see guidelines in Table B).

For DNA analysis, the same EDVOTEK 50x Electrophoresis Buffer is used for preparing both the agarose gel buffer and the chamber buffer. The formula for diluting EDVOTEK (50x) concentrated buffer is 1 volume of buffer concentrate to every 49 volumes of distilled or deionized water.

TABLE B	Dilution of Electrophoresis (Chamber) Buffer				
EDVOTEK Model #	Concentrated Buffer (50x) (ml)	+	Distilled Water (ml)	=	Total Volume (ml)
M6+	6		294		300
M12	8		392		400
M36 (blue)	10		490		500
M36 (clear)	20		980		1000

The electrophoresis (chamber) buffer recommended is Trisacetate-EDTA (20 mM Tris, 6 mM sodium acetate, 1 mM disodium ethylenediamine tetraacetic acid) pH 7.8. Prepare the buffer as required for your electrophoresis apparatus.

15. Make sure the gel is completely covered with buffer.

16. Proceed to loading the samples and conducting electrophoresis.

SAMPLE DELIVERY (GEL LOADING)

Practice Gel Loading

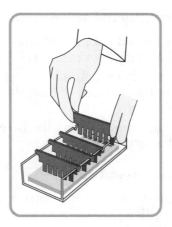

Accurate sample delivery technique ensures the best possible gel results. Pipeting mistakes can cause the sample to become diluted with buffer, or cause damage to the wells with the pipet tip while loading the gel.

If you are unfamiliar with loading samples in agarose gels, it is recommended that you practice sample delivery techniques before conducting the actual experiment. EDVOTEK electrophoresis experiments contain a tube of practice gel loading solution for this purpose. Casting of a separate practice gel is highly recommended. One suggested activity is outlined below:

1. Cast a gel with the maximum number of wells possible.

2. After the gel solidifies, place it under buffer in an electrophoresis apparatus chamber. Alternatively, your teacher may have cut the gel into sections between the rows of wells. Place a gel section with wells into a small, shallow tray and submerge it under buffer or water.

   Note: The agarose gel is sometimes called a "submarine gel" because it is submerged under buffer for sample loading and electrophoretic separation.

3. Practice delivering the practice gel loading solution to the sample wells. Take care not to damage or puncture the wells with the pipet tip.
   • For electrophoresis of DNA to be stained with InstaStain®b Methylene Blue, load the sample well with 35-38 microliters of sample.
   • If using transfer pipets for sample delivery, load each sample well until it is full.

4. If you need more practice, remove the practice gel loading solution by squirting buffer into the wells with a transfer pipet.

5. Replace the practice gel with a fresh gel for the actual experiment.

   Note: If practice gel loading is performed in the electrophoresis chamber, the practice gel loading solution will become diluted in the buffer in the apparatus. A small amount of practice gel loading solution (filling up to 12 wells) will not interfere with the experiment, so it is not necessary to prepare fresh buffer.

CONDUCTING AGAROSE GEL ELECTROPHORESIS

Electrophoresis Samples

Samples in EDVOTEK Series 100 and Sci-On® Series electrophoresis experiments are packaged in one of two different formats:

- Pre-aliquoted QuickStrip™ connected tubes (new format)
  or
- Individual 1.5 ml or 0.5 ml microtest tubes

Pre-aliquoted QuickStrip™ connected tubes

- Each set of QuickStrip™ connected tubes contains pre-aliquoted ready-to-load samples for one gel. A protective overlay covers the strip of QuickStrip™ sample tubes.
- Check the sample volume. Sometimes a small amount of sample will cling to the walls of the tubes. Make sure the entire volume of sample is at the the bottom of the tubes before starting to load the gel.
- Tap the overlay cover on top of the strip, or tap the entire QuickStrip™ on the table to make samples fall to the bottom of the tubes

Individual 1.5 ml or 0.5 ml microtest tubes

- Your instructor may have aliquoted samples into a set of tubes for each lab group. Alternatively, you may be required to withdraw the appropriate amount of sample from the experiment stock tubes.
- Check the sample volume. Sometimes a small amount of sample will cling to the walls of the tubes. Make sure the entire volume of sample is at the the bottom of the tubes before starting to load the gel.
- Briefly centrifuge the sample tubes, or tap each tube on the tabletop to get all the sample to the bottom of the tube.

QuickStrip™ Samples

Successful Pipetting with Micropipets

1. Do not disturb the samples in the QuickStrip™. Gently tap the QuickStrip™ tubes on the lab bench to ensure that samples are at the bottom of the tubes.

2. Stabilize the QuickStrip™ by firmly anchoring it on the lab bench.

3. Gently pierce the printed protective overlay with the pipet tip attached to a micropipet. Depress the micropipet plunger to the first stop before the tip is placed in contact with the sample.

4. With the pipet plunger depressed to the first stop, insert the tip into the sample.

5. Raise the plunger of the micropipet to withdraw the sample.

6. Load the sample into the appropriate well of the gel. Discard the tip.

7. Repeat steps 3-6 for each sample.

Delivering QuickStrip™ Samples with Transfer Pipets:
If using disposable transfer pipets for sample delivery, pierce the protective overlay with a paper clip before inserting the transfer pipet to withdraw the sample.

*If a sample becomes displaced while inserting the pipet tip in the tube, gently tap the QuickStrip™ on the lab bench to concentrate the sample to the bottom of the tube. With the pipet plunger depressed to the first stop, re-insert the tip into the sample and raise the micropipet plunger to withdraw the sample.

Load the Samples

For either QuickStrip™ or individual microtest tube format, samples should be loaded into the wells of the gel in consecutive order.

Load the DNA samples in tubes A - F into the wells in consecutive order. The amount of sample that should be loaded is 35-38 µl.

A DNA from crime scene cut with Enzyme 1
B DNA from crime scene cut with Enzyme 2
C DNA from Suspect 1 cut with Enzyme 1
D DNA from Suspect 1 cut with Enzyme 2
E DNA from Suspect 2 cut with Enzyme 1
F DNA from Suspect 2 cut with Enzyme 2

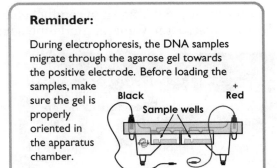

Reminder:

During electrophoresis, the DNA samples migrate through the agarose gel towards the positive electrode. Before loading the samples, make sure the gel is properly oriented in the apparatus chamber.

Black   Red

Sample wells

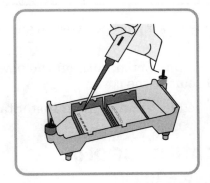

Running the Gel

1. After the DNA samples are loaded, carefully snap the cover down onto the electrode terminals.

   Make sure that the negative and positive color-coded indicators on the cover and apparatus chamber are properly oriented.

2. Insert the plug of the black wire into the black input of the power source (negative input). Insert the plug of the red wire into the red input of the power source (positive input).

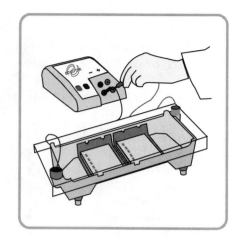

3. Set the power source at the required voltage and conduct electrophoresis for the length of time determined by your instructor. General guidelines are presented in Table C.

TABLE C	Time and Voltage Electrophoresis of DNA	
	Recommended Time	
Volts	**Minimum**	**Maximum**
125	30 min	40 min
70	40 min	75 min
50	60 min	100 min

4. Check to see that current is flowing properly—you should see bubbles forming on the two platinum electrodes.

5. After the electrophoresis is completed, turn off the power, unplug the power source, disconnect the leads and remove the cover.

6. Remove the gel from the bed for staining with InstaStain® Methylene Blue.

STAINING & VISUALIZATION OF DNA: INSTASTAIN® METHYLENE BLUE

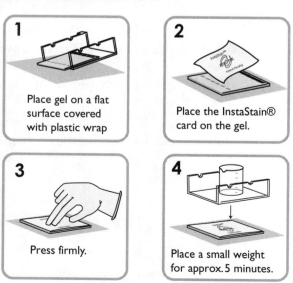

1 Place gel on a flat surface covered with plastic wrap

2 Place the InstaStain® card on the gel.

3 Press firmly.

4 Place a small weight for approx. 5 minutes.

Staining Of DNA

1. After electrophoresis, place the agarose gel on a flat surface covered with plastic wrap.

2. Wearing gloves, place the blue dye side of the InstaStain® Methylene Blue card on the gel.

3. Firmly run your fingers several times over the entire surface of the InstaStain® card to establish good contact between the InstaStain® card and the gel.

4. To ensure continuous contact between the gel and the InstaStain® card, place a gel casting tray and weight, such as a small empty beaker, on top of the InstaStain® card.

5. Allow the InstaStain® Methylene Blue to sit on the gel for 5 to 10 minutes.

6. After staining, remove the InstaStain® card.
   If the color of the gel appears very light, wet the gel surface with buffer or distilled water and place the InstaStain® card back on the gel for an additional 5 minutes.

Destaining and Visualization of DNA

7. Transfer the gel to a large weigh boat or small plastic container.

8. Destain with distilled water.*
   • Add approximately 100 ml of distilled water to cover the gel.
   • Repeat destaining by changing the distilled water as needed.

The larger DNA bands will initially be visible as dark blue bands against a lighter blue background. When the gel is completely destained, the larger DNA bands will become sharper and the smaller bands will be visible. With additional destaining, the entire background will become uniformly light blue.

* Destaining Notes
• Warmed distilled water at 37°C will accelerate destaining. Destaining will take longer with room temperature water.
• DO NOT EXCEED 37°C! Warmer temperatures will soften the gel and may cause it to break.

*InstaStain is a registered trademark of EDVOTEK, Inc. Patents Pending.

- The volume of distilled water for destaining depends upon the size of the tray. Use the smallest tray available that will accommodate the gel. The gel should be completely submerged during destaining.
- Do not exceed 3 changes of water for destaining. Excessive destaining will cause the bands to be very light.

9. Carefully remove the gel from the destain solution and examine the gel on a Visible Light Gel Visualization System. To optimize visibility, use the amber filter provided with EDVOTEK equipment.

10. If the gel is too light and bands are difficult to see, repeat the staining and destaining procedures.

Easy One-Step Staining and Destaining Overnight with Instastain® Metblue

Agarose gels can be stained overnight with InstaStain™ Methylene Blue cards in one easy step. This one-step method is an excellent alternative if time does not permit staining during a regular class session. Instructions for staining a 7 × 7 cm gel after electrophoresis follow.

1. Remove the 7 × 7 cm agarose gel from its bed and totally submerse the gel in a small, clean tray containing 75 ml of distilled or deionized water, or used electrophoresis buffer. The agarose gel should be completely covered with liquid.

   Do not stain gel(s) in the electrophoresis apparatus.

2. Gently float a 7 × 7 cm card of InstaStain® MetBlue with the stain side (blue) facing the liquid.

3. Let the gel soak undisturbed in the liquid overnight. The gel will be stained, destained and ready for photography the next day.

Examples of small trays include large weigh boats, or small plastic food containers.

Storage and Disposal of Instastain® Methylene Blue Cards and Gels

- Stained gels may be stored in the refrigerator for several weeks. Place the gel in a sealable plastic bag with destaining liquid.

  DO NOT FREEZE AGAROSE GELS!

- Used InstaStain® cards and destained gels can be discarded in solid waste disposal.
- Destaining solutions can be disposed down the drain.

STAINING & VISUALIZATION OF DNA: METHYLENE BLUE PLUS™ LIQUID STAINING

Liquid Staining and Destaining of DNA

1. Remove each agarose gel from its bed and totally submerse up to 6 gels in a tray containing 600 ml of diluted Methylene Blue Plus™ stain. Do not stain gel(s) in the electrophoresis apparatus.
   Each group should mark their gel, such as removing a small slice, or making a small hole in a designated corner, to facilitate identification after staining and destaining.

2. Stain gel(s) for a minimum of 30 minutes, with occasional agitation.

3. Destain in 600 ml of distilled water that has been warmed to 37°C.
   - Completely submerse the gel(s) in 600 ml of 37°C distilled water for 15 minutes with occasional agitation. Then discard the destaining solution
   - Change the distilled water for a second destain for another 15 minutes with occasional agitation.

   Bands will become visible after the second destain. You may also leave the gel(s) in destain overnight.

4. Carefully remove the gel from the destain solution and examine on a Visible Light Gel Visualization System. To optimize visibility, use the amber filter provided with EDVOTEK equipment.

5. If the gel is too light and bands are difficult to see, repeat the staining and destaining procedures.

Storage and Disposal Methylene Blue Plus™ Stain and Gel

- Gels stained with Methylene Blue Plus™ may be stored in the refrigerator for several weeks. Place the gel in a sealable plastic bag with destaining liquid.

  DO NOT FREEZE AGAROSE GELS.

- Stained gels which are not kept can be discarded in solid waste disposal.
- Methylene Blue Plus™ stain and destaining solutions can be disposed down the drain.

EXPERIMENT RESULTS AND STUDY QUESTIONS

Laboratory Notebook Recordings:

Address and record the following in your laboratory notebook or on a separate worksheet.

Before starting the experiment:
- Write a hypothesis that reflects the experiment.
- Predict experimental outcomes.

During the Experiment:
- Record (draw) your observations, or photograph the results.

Following the Experiment:
- Formulate an explanation from the results.
- Determine what could be changed in the experiment if the experiment were repeated.
- Write a hypothesis that would reflect this change.

Study Questions

Answer the following study questions in your laboratory notebook or on a separate worksheet.

1. Define FLP's and give their significance.
2. What is the most likely cause of Restriction Fragment Length Polymorphisms?
3. What are Variable Number of Tandem Repeats (VNTRs)?
4. Who are the only individuals possessing the same DNA fingerprints?

5. List the steps involved in DNA fingerprinting from extraction of DNA through the matching of a suspect to a crime scene sample.

6. What type of human cells can be utilized for this technique?

SELECTED SOURCES FOR ADDITIONAL INFORMATION

Esslinger, Kelly J., Siegel, J. A., Spillane H., and Stallworth, S., "Using STR analysis to detect human DNA from exploded pipe bomb devices," *J. Forens. Sci.,* 49 (3), (2004), 481.

Melton, Terry, Dimick, G., Higgins, B., Lindstrom, L., and Nelson, K., "Forensic mitochondrial DNA analysis of 691 casework hairs," *J. Forens. Sci.,* 50 (1), (2005), 73.

Montpetit, Shawn A., Fitch, I. T., and O'Donnell, P. T., "A simple automated instrument for DNA extraction in forensic casework," *J. Forens. Sci.,* 50 (3), (2005), 555.

Nakazono, Takehiko, Kashimura, S., Hayashiba, Y., Hara, K., and Miyoshi, A., "Successful DNA typing of urine stains using a DNA purification kit following dialfiltration," *J. Forens. Sci.,* 50 (4), (2005), 860.

Rankin, D.R., Narveson, S.D., Birkby, W.H., and Lai, J., "Restriction fragment length polymorphism (RFLP) analysis on DNA from human compact bone," *J. Forens. Sci.,* 41 (1), (1996), 40.

Smith, Steve, and Morin, P. A., "Optimal storage conditions for highly dilute DNA samples: A role for Trehalose as a preserving agent," *J. Forens. Sci.,* 50 (5), (2005), 1101.

Thompson, William C., Taroni, F., and Aitken, C. G. G., "How the probability of a false positive affects the value of DNA evidence," *J. Forens. Sci.,* 48 (1), (2003), 47.

PCR Amplification of DNA for Fingerprinting EDVO-Kit # 130

EXPERIMENT COMPONENTS

ELECTROPHORESIS SAMPLES

- Ready-to-Load™ DNA samples

    A DNA Standard marker
    B Crime scene PCR reaction
    C Suspect 1 PCR reaction
    D Suspect 2 PCR reaction
    E Suspect 3 PCR reaction

REAGENTS & SUPPLIES

- Practice Gel Loading Solution
- UltraSpec-Agarose™ powder
- Concentrated electrophoresis buffer
- InstaStain® Methylene Blue
- Methylene Blue Plus™
- 1 ml pipet
- 100 ml graduated cylinder (packaging for samples)
- Microtipped Transfer Pipets

    THIS EXPERIMENT DOES NOT CONTAIN HUMAN DNA.

REQUIREMENTS

- Horizontal gel electrophoresis apparatus
- D.C. power supply
- Automatic micropipets with tips
- Balance
- Microwave, hot plate or burner
- Pipet pump
- 250 ml flasks or beakers

- Hot gloves
- Safety goggles and disposable laboratory gloves
- Small plastic trays or large weigh boats (for gel destaining)
- DNA visualization system (white light)
- Distilled or deionized water

DNA FINGERPRINTING

Deoxyribonucleic acid (DNA), present in the nucleus of every living cell, is the genetic material that acts as a blueprint for all of the proteins synthesized by cells. In mammals, a large fraction of the total DNA does not encode for proteins. Polymorphic DNA refers to chromosomal regions that vary widely from individual to individual. By examining several of these regions within the genomic DNA obtained from an individual, one may determine a "DNA Fingerprint" for that individual. DNA polymorphisms are now widely used for determining paternity/maternity, kinship, identification of human remains, and the genetic basis of various diseases. The most widely used and far-reaching application, however, has been to the field of criminal forensics. DNA from both crime victims and offenders can now be definitively matched to crime scenes, often affecting the outcome of criminal and civil trials.

The beginning of DNA fingerprinting occurred in the United Kingdom in 1984, following the pioneering work of Dr. Alex Jeffreys at the University of Leicester. Analysis by Jeffreys led to the apprehension of a murderer in the first DNA fingerprinting case in September 1987. The first U.S. conviction occurred on November 6, 1987 in Orlando, FL. Since then, DNA analysis has been used in thousands of convictions. Additionally, over 70 convicted prison inmates have been exonerated from their crimes, including eight death row inmates.

In 1990, the Federal Bureau of Investigation (FBI) established the Combined DNA Index System (CODIS), a system which allows comparison of crime scene DNA to DNA profiles in a convicted offender and a forensic (crime scene) index. A match of crime scene DNA to a profile in the convicted offender index indicates a suspect for the crime, whereas a match of crime scene DNA to the forensic index indicates a serial offender. CODIS has now been used to solve dozens of cases where authorities had no suspect for the crime under investigation.

The first step in forensic DNA fingerprinting is the collection of blood or tissue samples from the crime scene or victim (Figure 1). A blood sample, often present as a stain, is treated with detergent to rupture cell membranes and obtain DNA for further analysis. The early method, called restriction fragment length polymorphism (RFLP) analysis, involves digesting the DNA with restriction enzymes, separation on an agarose gel, transferring the DNA to a membrane, and hybridizing the DNA on the membrane with probes to polymorphic regions. This method requires relatively large amounts of DNA and takes several weeks to complete.

More recently, the polymerase chain reaction (PCR) has been used in forensics to analyze DNA (Figure 2). This technique requires about 500- fold DNA than RFLP analysis and is less time-consuming. PCR amplification (Figure 2) uses an enzyme known as *Taq* polymerase. This enzyme, originally purified from a bacterium that inhabits hot springs, is stable at very high (near boiling) temperatures. Also included in the PCR reaction mixture are two synthetic oligonucleotides known as "primers" and the extracted DNA. The region of DNA to be amplified is known as the "target".

In the first step of the PCR reaction, the template complementary DNA strands are separated (denatured) from each other at 94°C, while the *Taq* polymerase remains stable. In the second step, known as annealing, the sample is cooled to an intermediate temperature, usually 40°–65°C, to allow hybridization of the two primers, one to each of the two strands of the template DNA. In the third step, known as extension, the temperature is raised to 72°C and the *Taq* polymerase adds nucleotides to the primers to complete the synthesis of the new complementary strands. These three steps—denaturation, annealing, and extension—constitute one PCR "cycle". This process is typically repeated for 20-40 cycles, amplifying the target sequence within DNA exponentially (Figure 2). PCR is performed in a thermal cycler, an instrument that is programmed to rapidly heat, cool and maintain samples at designated temperatures for varying amounts of time.

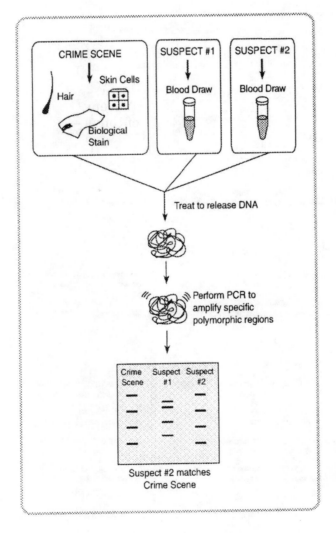

Figure 1:
Comparison of crime scene DNA to DNA from suspects.

In forensics, PCR is used to amplify and examine highly variable (polymorphic) DNA regions. These are regions that vary in length from individual to individual and fall into two categories: 1) variable number of tandem repeats (VNTR) and 2) STR (short tandem repeats). A VNTR is a region that is variably composed of a 15-70 base pair sequence, typically repeated 5-100 times. An STR is similar to a VNTR except that the repeated unit is only 2-4 nucleotides in length. By examining several different VNTRs or STRs from the same individual, investigators obtain a unique DNA profile for that individual which is unlike that of any other person (except for identical twins).

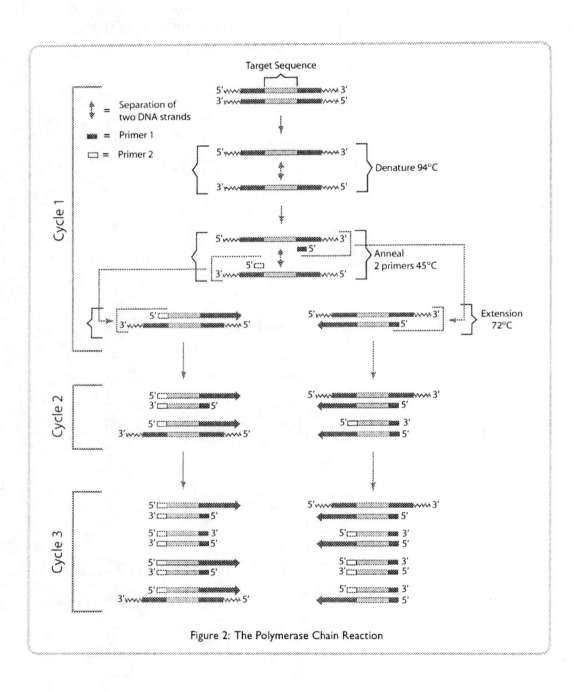

Figure 2: The Polymerase Chain Reaction

EXPERIMENT OVERVIEW

Experiment Brief Description

This experiment demonstrates a PCR reaction that has been performed on hair obtained from a murder scene. Students will separate this DNA sample by agarose gel electrophoresis and compare the preamplified DNA from two possible suspects to determine if either suspect was present at the crime scene.

Experiment Objective:

The objective of this experiment is to develop a basic understanding of DNA Fingerprinting. Students will analyze PCR reactions obtained from different suspects and compare them to a crime scene sample.

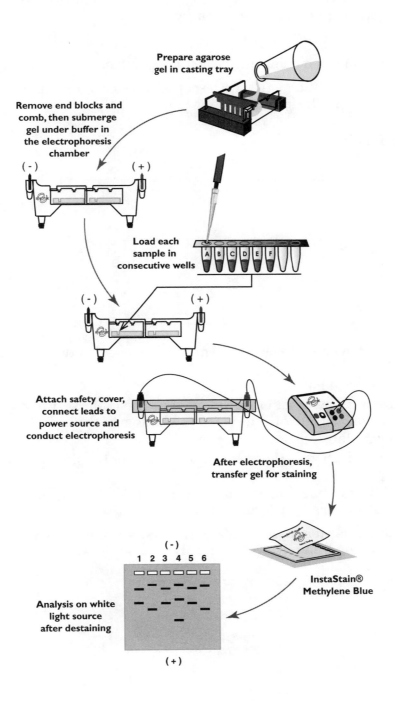

Gel Requirements

- Recommended gel tray size: 7 x 7 cm or 7 x 15 cm
- Number of sample wells required: 5
- Placement of well-former template: first set of notches
- Agarose gel concentration required: 0.8%

AGAROSE GEL PREPARATION

Laboratory Safety

1. Gloves and goggles should be worn routinely as good laboratory practice.

2. Exercise extreme caution when working with equipment that is used in conjunction with the heating and/or melting of reagents.

3. DO NOT MOUTH PIPET REAGENTS—USE PIPET PUMPS.

4. Exercise caution when using any electrical equipment in the laboratory.

5. Always wash hands thoroughly with soap and water after handling reagents or biological materials in the laboratory.

Preparing the Gel Bed

1. Close off the open ends of a clean and dry gel bed (casting tray) by using rubber dams or tape.
   A. Using Rubber dams:
      - Place a rubber dam on each end of the bed. Make sure the rubber dam fits firmly in contact with the sides and bottom of the bed.
   B. Taping with labeling or masking tape:
      - With 3/4 inch wide tape, extend the tape over the sides and bottom edge of the bed.
      - Fold the extended edges of the tape back onto the sides and bottom. Press contact points firmly to form a good seal.

2. Place a well-former template (comb) in the first set of notches at the end of the bed. Make sure the comb sits firmly and evenly across the bed.

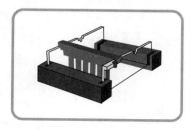

Casting Agarose Gels

3. Use a 250 ml flask to prepare the gel solution. Add the following components to the flask as specified for your experiment (refer to Table A).
   • Buffer concentrate
   • Distilled water
   • Agarose powder

TABLE A	Individual 0.8% UltraSpec-Agarose™ Gel DNA Staining with InstaStain® MetBlue			
Size of EDVOTEK Casting Tray (cm)	Amt of Agarose (g) +	Concentrated Buffer (50x) (ml) +	Distilled Water (ml) =	Total Volume (ml)
7 × 7	0.24	0.6	29.4	30
7 × 15	0.48	1.2	58.8	60

4. Swirl the mixture to disperse clumps of agarose powder.

5. With a marking pen, indicate the level of the solution volume on the outside of the flask.

6. Heat the mixture to dissolve the agarose powder. The final solution should appear clear (like water) without any undissolved particles.
   A. Microwave method:
      • Cover the flask with plastic wrap to minimize evaporation.
      • Heat the mixture on High for 1 minute.
      • Swirl the mixture and heat on High in bursts of 25 seconds until all the agarose is completely dissolved.
   B. Hot plate method:
      • Cover the flask with aluminum foil to prevent excess evaporation.
      • Heat the mixture to boiling over a burner with occasional swirling. Boil until all the agarose is completely dissolved.

Check the solution carefully. If you see "crystal" particles, the agarose is not completely dissolved.

At high altitudes, it is recommended to use a microwave oven to reach boiling temperatures.

7. Cool the agarose solution to 55°C with careful swirling to promote even dissipation of heat. If detectable evaporation has occurred, add distilled water to bring the solution up to the original volume as marked on the flask in step 5.

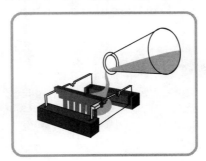

After the gel is cooled to 55°C:
If you are using rubber dams, go to step 9.
If you are using tape, continue with step 8.

8. Seal the interface of the gel bed and tape to prevent the agarose solution from leaking.
   - Use a transfer pipet to deposit a small amount of cooled agarose to both inside ends of the bed.
   - Wait approximately 1 minute for the agarose to solidify.

9. Pour the cooled agarose solution into the bed. Make sure the bed is on a level surface.

10. Allow the gel to completely solidify. It will become firm and cool to the touch after approximately 20 minutes.

Preparing the Gel for Electrophoresis

11. After the gel is completely solidified, carefully and slowly remove the rubber dams or tape from the gel bed.

Be especially careful not to damage or tear the gel wells when removing the rubber dams. A thin plastic knife, spatula or pipet tip can be inserted between the gel and the dams to break possible surface tension.

12. Remove the comb by slowly pulling straight up. Do this carefully and evenly to prevent tearing the sample wells.

13. Place the gel (on its bed) into the electrophoresis chamber, properly oriented, centered and level on the platform.

14. Fill the electrophoresis apparatus chamber with the required volume of diluted buffer for the specific unit you are using (see guidelines in Table B).

For DNA analysis, the same EDVOTEK 50x Electrophoresis Buffer is used for preparing both the agarose gel buffer and the chamber buffer. The formula for diluting EDVOTEK (50x) concentrated buffer is 1 volume of buffer concentrate to every 49 volumes of distilled or deionized water.

TABLE B	Dilution of Electrophoresis (Chamber) Buffer				
EDVOTEK Model #	Concentrated Buffer (50x) (ml)	+	Distilled Water (ml)	=	Total Volume (ml)
M6+	6		294		300
M12	8		392		400
M36 (blue)	10		490		500
M36 (clear)	20		980		1000

The electrophoresis (chamber) buffer recommended is Trisacetate-EDTA (20 mM Tris, 6 mM sodium acetate, 1 mM disodium ethylenediamine tetraacetic acid) pH 7.8. Prepare the buffer as required for your electrophoresis apparatus.

15. Make sure the gel is completely covered with buffer.

16. Proceed to loading the samples and conducting electrophoresis.

SAMPLE DELIVERY (GEL LOADING)

Practice Gel Loading

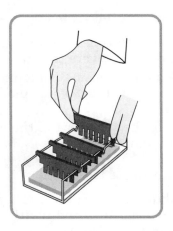

Accurate sample delivery technique ensures the best possible gel results. Pipeting mistakes can cause the sample to become diluted with buffer, or cause damage to the wells with the pipet tip while loading the gel.

If you are unfamiliar with loading samples in agarose gels, it is recommended that you practice sample delivery techniques before conducting the actual experiment. EDVOTEK electrophoresis experiments contain a tube of practice gel loading solution for this purpose. Casting of a separate practice gel is highly recommended. One suggested activity is outlined below:

1. Cast a gel with the maximum number of wells possible.

2. After the gel solidifies, place it under buffer in an electrophoresis apparatus chamber. Alternatively, your teacher may have cut the gel into sections between the rows of wells. Place a gel section with wells into a small, shallow tray and submerge it under buffer or water.

   Note: The agarose gel is sometimes called a "submarine gel" because it is submerged under buffer for sample loading and electrophoretic separation.

3. Practice delivering the practice gel loading solution to the sample wells. Take care not to damage or puncture the wells with the pipet tip.
   • For electrophoresis of DNA to be stained with InstaStain®b Methylene Blue, load the sample well with 35-38 microliters of sample.
   • If using transfer pipets for sample delivery, load each sample well until it is full.

4. If you need more practice, remove the practice gel loading solution by squirting buffer into the wells with a transfer pipet.

5. Replace the practice gel with a fresh gel for the actual experiment.

   Note: If practice gel loading is performed in the electrophoresis chamber, the practice gel loading solution will become diluted in the buffer in the apparatus. A small amount of practice gel loading solution (filling up to 12 wells) will not interfere with the experiment, so it is not necessary to prepare fresh buffer.

CONDUCTING AGAROSE GEL ELECTROPHORESIS

Electrophoresis Samples

Samples in EDVOTEK Series 100 and Sci-On® Series electrophoresis experiments are packaged in one of two different formats:

- Pre-aliquoted QuickStrip™ connected tubes (new format)
  or
- Individual 1.5 ml or 0.5 ml microtest tubes

Pre-aliquoted QuickStrip™ connected tubes

- Each set of QuickStrip™ connected tubes contains pre-aliquoted ready-to-load samples for one gel. A protective overlay covers the strip of QuickStrip™ sample tubes.
- Check the sample volume. Sometimes a small amount of sample will cling to the walls of the tubes. Make sure the entire volume of sample is at the the bottom of the tubes before starting to load the gel.
- Tap the overlay cover on top of the strip, or tap the entire QuickStrip™ on the table to make samples fall to the bottom of the tubes

Individual 1.5 ml or 0.5 ml microtest tubes

- Your instructor may have aliquoted samples into a set of tubes for each lab group. Alternatively, you may be required to withdraw the appropriate amount of sample from the experiment stock tubes.
- Check the sample volume. Sometimes a small amount of sample will cling to the walls of the tubes. Make sure the entire volume of sample is at the the bottom of the tubes before starting to load the gel.
- Briefly centrifuge the sample tubes, or tap each tube on the tabletop to get all the sample to the bottom of the tube.

QuickStrip™ Samples

Successful Pipetting with Micropipets

1. Do not disturb the samples in the QuickStrip™. Gently tap the QuickStrip™ tubes on the lab bench to ensure that samples are at the bottom of the tubes.
2. Stabilize the QuickStrip™ by firmly anchoring it on the lab bench.
3. Gently pierce the printed protective overlay with the pipet tip attached to a micropipet. Depress the micropipet plunger to the first stop before the tip is placed in contact with the sample.
4. With the pipet plunger depressed to the first stop, insert the tip into the sample.
5. Raise the plunger of the micropipet to withdraw the sample.
6. Load the sample into the appropriate well of the gel. Discard the tip.
7. Repeat steps 3-6 for each sample.

Delivering QuickStrip™ Samples with Transfer Pipets:
If using disposable transfer pipets for sample delivery, pierce the protective overlay with a paper clip before inserting the transfer pipet to withdraw the sample.

*If a sample becomes displaced while inserting the pipet tip in the tube, gently tap the QuickStrip™ on the lab bench to concentrate the sample to the bottom of the tube. With the pipet plunger depressed to the first stop, re-insert the tip into the sample and raise the micropipet plunger to withdraw the sample.

Load the Samples

For either QuickStrip™ or individual microtest tube format, samples should be loaded into the wells of the gel in consecutive order.

Load the DNA samples in tubes A - E into the wells in consecutive order. The amount of sample that should be loaded is 35-38 µl.

- A   DNA Standard marker
- B   Crime scene PCR reaction
- C   Suspect 1 PCR reaction
- D   Suspect 2 PCR reaction
- E   Suspect 3 PCR reaction

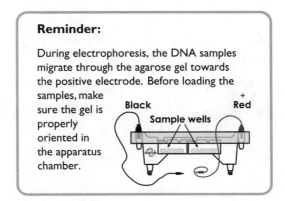

Reminder:

During electrophoresis, the DNA samples migrate through the agarose gel towards the positive electrode. Before loading the samples, make sure the gel is properly oriented in the apparatus chamber.

Black   + Red

Sample wells

Running the Gel

1. After the DNA samples are loaded, carefully snap the cover down onto the electrode terminals.

   Make sure that the negative and positive color-coded indicators on the cover and apparatus chamber are properly oriented.

2. Insert the plug of the black wire into the black input of the power source (negative input). Insert the plug of the red wire into the red input of the power source (positive input).

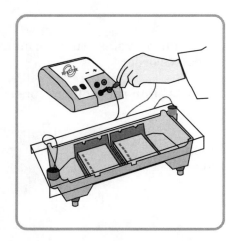

3. Set the power source at the required voltage and conduct electrophoresis for the length of time determined by your instructor. General guidelines are presented in Table C.

TABLE C	Time and Voltage Electrophoresis of DNA	
	Recommended Time	
Volts	**Minimum**	**Maximum**
125	30 min	40 min
70	40 min	75 min
50	60 min	100 min

4. Check to see that current is flowing properly—you should see bubbles forming on the two platinum electrodes.

5. After the electrophoresis is completed, turn off the power, unplug the power source, disconnect the leads and remove the cover.

6. Remove the gel from the bed for staining with InstaStain® Methylene Blue.

STAINING & VISUALIZATION OF DNA: INSTASTAIN® METHYLENE BLUE

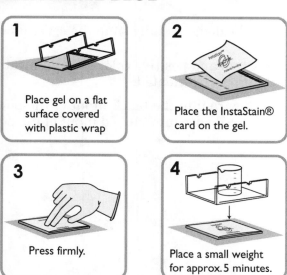

1 Place gel on a flat surface covered with plastic wrap

2 Place the InstaStain® card on the gel.

3 Press firmly.

4 Place a small weight for approx. 5 minutes.

Staining Of DNA

1. After electrophoresis, place the agarose gel on a flat surface covered with plastic wrap.

2. Wearing gloves, place the blue dye side of the InstaStain® Methylene Blue card on the gel.

3. Firmly run your fingers several times over the entire surface of the InstaStain® card to establish good contact between the InstaStain® card and the gel.

4. To ensure continuous contact between the gel and the InstaStain® card, place a gel casting tray and weight, such as a small empty beaker, on top of the InstaStain® card.

5. Allow the InstaStain® Methylene Blue to sit on the gel for 5 to 10 minutes.

6. After staining, remove the InstaStain® card.
   If the color of the gel appears very light, wet the gel surface with buffer or distilled water and place the InstaStain® card back on the gel for an additional 5 minutes.

Destaining and Visualization of DNA

7. Transfer the gel to a large weigh boat or small plastic container.

5
Transfer to a small tray for destaining.

8. Destain with distilled water.*
   • Add approximately 100 ml of distilled water to cover the gel.
   • Repeat destaining by changing the distilled water as needed.

6
Destain with 37°C distilled water

The larger DNA bands will initially be visible as dark blue bands against a lighter blue background. When the gel is completely destained, the larger DNA bands will become sharper and the smaller bands will be visible. With additional destaining, the entire background will become uniformly light blue.

* Destaining Notes

• Warmed distilled water at 37°C will accelerate destaining. Destaining will take longer with room temperature water.

• DO NOT EXCEED 37°C! Warmer temperatures will soften the gel and may cause it to break.

*InstaStain is a registered trademark of EDVOTEK, Inc. Patents Pending.

- The volume of distilled water for destaining depends upon the size of the tray. Use the smallest tray available that will accommodate the gel. The gel should be completely submerged during destaining.

- Do not exceed 3 changes of water for destaining. Excessive destaining will cause the bands to be very light.

9. Carefully remove the gel from the destain solution and examine the gel on a Visible Light Gel Visualization System. To optimize visibility, use the amber filter provided with EDVOTEK equipment.

10. If the gel is too light and bands are difficult to see, repeat the staining and destaining procedures.

Easy One-Step Staining and Destaining Overnight with Instastain® Metblue

Agarose gels can be stained overnight with InstaStain™ Methylene Blue cards in one easy step. This one-step method is an excellent alternative if time does not permit staining during a regular class session. Instructions for staining a 7 × 7 cm gel after electrophoresis follow.

1. Remove the 7 × 7 cm agarose gel from its bed and totally submerse the gel in a small, clean tray containing 75 ml of distilled or deionized water, or used electrophoresis buffer. The agarose gel should be completely covered with liquid.

   Do not stain gel(s) in the electrophoresis apparatus.

2. Gently float a 7 × 7 cm card of InstaStain® MetBlue with the stain side (blue) facing the liquid.

3. Let the gel soak undisturbed in the liquid overnight. The gel will be stained, destained and ready for photography the next day.

Examples of small trays include large weigh boats, or small plastic food containers.

Storage and Disposal of Instastain® Methylene Blue Cards and Gels

- Stained gels may be stored in the refrigerator for several weeks. Place the gel in a sealable plastic bag with destaining liquid.

  DO NOT FREEZE AGAROSE GELS!

- Used InstaStain® cards and destained gels can be discarded in solid waste disposal.
- Destaining solutions can be disposed down the drain.

STAINING & VISUALIZATION OF DNA: METHYLENE BLUE PLUS™ LIQUID STAINING

Liquid Staining and Destaining of DNA

1. Remove each agarose gel from its bed and totally submerse up to 6 gels in a tray containing 600 ml of diluted Methylene Blue Plus™ stain. Do not stain gel(s) in the electrophoresis apparatus.
   Each group should mark their gel, such as removing a small slice, or making a small hole in a designated corner, to facilitate identification after staining and destaining.

2. Stain gel(s) for a minimum of 30 minutes, with occasional agitation.

3. Destain in 600 ml of distilled water that has been warmed to 37°C.
   - Completely submerse the gel(s) in 600 ml of 37°C distilled water for 15 minutes with occasional agitation. Then discard the destaining solution
   - Change the distilled water for a second destain for another 15 minutes with occasional agitation.

   Bands will become visible after the second destain. You may also leave the gel(s) in destain overnight.

4. Carefully remove the gel from the destain solution and examine on a Visible Light Gel Visualization System. To optimize visibility, use the amber filter provided with EDVOTEK equipment.

5. If the gel is too light and bands are difficult to see, repeat the staining and destaining procedures.

Storage and Disposal Methylene Blue Plus™ Stain and Gel

- Gels stained with Methylene Blue Plus™ may be stored in the refrigerator for several weeks. Place the gel in a sealable plastic bag with destaining liquid.

  DO NOT FREEZE AGAROSE GELS.

- Stained gels which are not kept can be discarded in solid waste disposal.
- Methylene Blue Plus™ stain and destaining solutions can be disposed down the drain.

EXPERIMENT RESULTS AND STUDY QUESTIONS

Laboratory Notebook Recordings:

Address and record the following in your laboratory notebook or on a separate worksheet.

Before starting the experiment:
- Write a hypothesis that reflects the experiment.
- Predict experimental outcomes.

During the Experiment:
- Record (draw) your observations, or photograph the results.

Following the Experiment:
- Formulate an explanation from the results.
- Determine what could be changed in the experiment if the experiment were repeated.
- Write a hypothesis that would reflect this change.

Study Questions

Answer the following study questions in your laboratory notebook or on a separate worksheet.

1. What is polymorphic DNA? How is it used for identification purposes?
2. What is CODIS? How is it used to solve crimes?
3. What is an STR? A VNTR? Which (STR or VNTR) is predominantly now used in law enforcement? Why?

The Comparison Microscope

The comparison microscope is one of the most valuable instruments of the forensic scientist. It first came to public attention during the Sacco-Vanzetti trial of the 1920s, when the markings on a bullet obtained from the victim matched the markings made by a gun owned by the suspects.

A photo of one type of professional comparison microscope is shown in Figure 42-1. Basically, this microscope permits the forensic examiner to simultaneously view and compare two specimens side by side. The unique feature of this microscope is an optical bridge consisting of a number of mirrors and lenses. This bridge joins two separate objective lenses into a single eyepiece lens.

When looking through the eyepiece lens of a comparison microscope, a specimen mounted under the left objective is seen in the left half of the field, while the specimen mounted under the right objective is seen in the right half of the field.

To illustrate some of its capabilities you will compare toolmarks, bullets, and shell cases in this experiment.

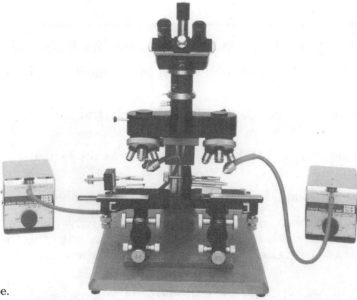

FIGURE 42-1
A comparison microscope.

EQUIPMENT

1 Aluminum sheet	1 Hand magnifying glass
1 Balance, ±0.001 g	1 Micrometer
Bullets and bullet casings	2 Microscopes
Camera attachments	3 Screwdrivers
1 Comparison bridge, including 10× eyepieces and eyepiece holder (see p. 370)	

PART A: COMPARISON OF TOOLMARK SCRATCHES

The scrapings of a tool against a softer surface at a crime scene will frequently leave scratch marks that are unique to that tool and no other. These scratch markings will arise from imperfections present on the tool's edge. Once a suspect tool is seized, the forensic examiner will attempt to duplicate the suspect scratch markings by scraping the tool against a soft metal, of the same type if possible, at various angles and pressures. The test and suspect markings are compared under the comparison microscope. A sufficient number of similarities between the two will ultimately lead to the conclusion that the suspect tool did indeed produce the markings found at the crime scene.

CRIME SCENE

A sporting goods store has been broken into. Entry was gained through an aluminum panel skylight in the back of the store. The detective at the scene examined the frame and suspected the tool used might possibly be a screwdriver or something similar. It is apparent that the tool must have slipped once because there are scratch marks on the window frame. The next day a suspect is apprehended. He has two screwdrivers in his tool chest. The detective has obtained that portion of the frame that has the scratch marks on it and has given it to you, as well as the two screwdrivers. Your job is to see if the marks on the frame could have been made by either of the screwdrivers.

METHOD

1. Obtain a small piece of aluminum, and place it on a flat surface.

2. Take one of the screwdrivers, and with a pencil, mark one side of the blade 1 and the other side 2.

3. Hold the screwdriver at about a 30 to 45° angle and make about a 2-cm-long scrape on the aluminum sheet.

4. Turn the blade over, and make a second scrape about 1 cm away from the first scrape. Label these.

5. Repeat steps 2 through 4 with the other screwdriver, labeling the blade sides 3 and 4.

6. Examine the scratches on the frame with a magnifying glass to see if there is any obvious pattern of scratch marks. Then do the same with the first scratches to see if there appears to be a side that might match or if there are sides that can readily be discounted.

7. Place the frame metal under the lens of the left microscope. Pull the halving-line control to the right. Turn on the left light and focus the lowest-power optics. Turn the frame so that the scratches are horizontal with your viewing direction.

8. Place the most likely test scratch portion under the right microscope. Push the halving-line control knob to the left. Turn on the right light and focus with the lowest power lens.

9. Move the halving line to the middle of the field of view.

10. Sharpen the focus if necessary with the halving-line focus knob.

11. Slowly and carefully move one set of scratch marks to see if it is possible to line up an adjacent series of scratch marks. If you believe you have a match, record what you see.

12. Repeat steps 7 through 11 with each blade side. Record any match on the data sheet.

13. Turn off the lights, and clean up the area.

PART B: COMPARISON OF SHELL CASES AND SLUGS

There is no way that this experiment will make you an expert on ballistics; that takes many years of experience. What we hope to do is show you the general areas that are examined.

1. Obtain three casings from the instructor, two of which are from the same weapon and the third of the same caliber, but from a different weapon.

2. Weigh each casing to the nearest milligram.

3. Using a micrometer, measure the length of the casings and their diameter.

4. Examine the head of each casing with a magnifying glass, and sketch the markings you see.

5. Look at the rim of the head, noticing any extractor or ejector marks. The extractor pulls the casing out of the breech, and the ejector throws the casings out of the weapon if the weapon is a rifle or an automatic pistol.

6. Mount each casing on a ball of clay so that the head end is up and flat. Focus on the head with low power.

7. Repeat step 6 with a second casing. Orient this casing so that it is turned in the same manner as the other casing.

8. Move the halving line to the center. Turn the casings so that it appears that only one head is in view.

9. When a gun is fired, the head of the shell is forced back against the breech block, and imprints of the breech block are pressed onto the back of the casing. Slowly turn the two casings to see if any marks on the heads match up.

10. Try different combinations of casings to see if you find any scratch and firing-pin identification matchups.

11. Remove the casings from the microscope stage.

12. Obtain three slugs from the instructor, two of which are from the same weapon and a third from a different weapon.

13. Repeat step 2.

14. Repeat step 3.

15. Repeat step 4, if the slugs are not too distorted, and record any manufacturer's mark.

16. Examine the sides of the slugs with a magnifying glass, and record the gross general characteristics, such as the number of lands and grooves.

17. If your comparison microscope does not have slug rotators, the slugs must be turned by hand. Place the slugs on a small block of wood with a half circle groove cut into its surface, just slightly larger than the object. Between the wood block and the slug, place a long, narrow piece of tissue paper. When this paper is gently pulled, the slug will rotate, and can be used to rotate the slug without any danger of putting additional scratches on it.

18. Place a slug on each stage of the microscope, and center the halving line. Focus each with the lowest power.

19. Slowly rotate one of the slugs to see if a match can be made. Look carefully at the fine structure because these are the critical markings. Record any matchups you see.

20. Return all casings and slugs to your instructors and clean up the microscope.

PART C: PHOTOMICROGRAPHS

Figure 42-2 shows a camera attachment mounted on a comparison microscope. In addition, Figure 42-2 shows an attachment that can be obtained from Nikon Optical to couple two regular microscopes together to make a comparison microscope. If you have a photographic attachment on your microscope, take a photograph of what you believe is a matchup. Obtain the exposure times and camera settings from your instructor. Attach any clear photos to your data sheet.

SELECTED SOURCES FOR ADDITIONAL INFORMATION

Bonfanti, M.S., and DeKinder, J., "The influence of manufacturing processes on the identification of bullets and cartridge cases," *Sci. & Just.*, 39 (1), (1999), 3.

Cain, S., and Winand, J.E., "Striation evidence in counterfeits cases," *J. Forens. Sci.*, 28 (2), (1983), 360.

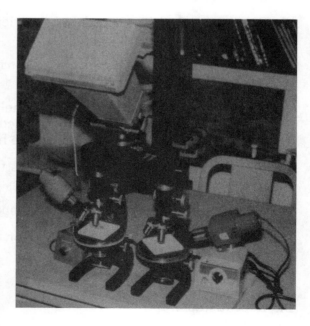

FIGURE 42–2   An inexpensive camera attachment for a microscope.

Diaz, A.A., Boehm, A.F., and Rowe, W.F., "Comparison of fingernail ridge patterns of monozygotic twins," *J. Forens. Sci.*, 35 (1), (1990), 97.

Kempton, J.B., Sirignano, A., DeGaetano, D.H., and Rowe, W.F., "Comparison of fingernail striation patterns in identical twins," *J. Forens. Sci.*, 37 (6), (1992), 1534.

Krone, C.S., "Examination of random weld bead flow patterns on welding slag and comparison of these patterns to the flow patterns present on welded surfaces," *J. Forens. Sci.*, 38 (4), (1993), 1131.

Petraco, N., and Gale, F., "A rapid method for cross sectioning multilayered paint chips," *J. Forens. Sci.*, 29 (2), (1984), 597.

Von Bremen, U.G, and Blunt, L.K.R., "Physical comparison of plastic garbage bags and sandwich bags," *J. Forens. Sci.*, 28 (3), (1983), 644.

Warlow, T.A., "Ballistics examination of British citizens from Waco siege," *Sci. & Just.*, 38 (4), (1998), 255.

EXPERIMENT 42

DATA SHEET

Name _____

Date _____

THE COMPARISON MICROSCOPE

Part A: Comparison of Toolmark Scratches

1. Sketch what you believe to be a match. If no match was found with any of the blades, so indicate.

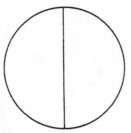

2. Conclusions

3. Suppose that the screwdriver had not slipped. Do you believe that you could make a comparison from the impression material?

Part B: Comparison of Shell Cases and Slugs

Weight of shell	Length of shell	Diameter of shell
Case 1	Case 1	Case 1
Case 2	Case 2	Case 2
Case 3	Case 3	Case 3

Shell case base markings

Case 1   Case 2   Case 3

   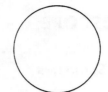   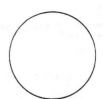

Shell case comparison matchup

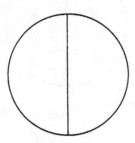

Weight of shell   Length of shell   Diameter of shell

Shell 1   Shell 1   Shell 1

Shell 2   Shell 2   Shell 2

Shell 3   Shell 3   Shell 3

Base markings

Side markings on the slugs

  Slug 1   Slug 2   Slug 3

Comparison view of fine structure

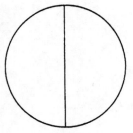

Conclusions

Burglaries and Murders— The Final Exam

Previously, you have concentrated on only one type of evidence. Now you will be allowed to examine a crime scene and you will decide what evidence to collect and how to measure it. We will provide you with a brief introduction and then present some different crimes. Your instructor may choose one of these or think up something else.

The names of all persons and the crime situation themselves, presented below, are fictitious and any similarity to persons living or dead is purely coincidental.

PART A: A BUNGLED BURGLARY

We are confronted with a crime in which there is evidence of a physical nature that will strongly link one of two suspects with the crime scene, and show that the other suspect could not have been present at the scene.

The type of crime perpetrated is a burglary—the breaking and entering of a suburban home. A window is broken, and one can see the fragments of glass strewn about. The soil below the window is damp, and it is likely that the person committing the crime transported some of this soil away from the scene on his shoes or clothing. During the course of breaking the window glass, or in reaching inside to unlock the window sash, the burglar was cut quite badly. There are blood stains on some of the glass fragments and also on a piece of cloth that was picked up inside the house, apparently in an attempt to stem the flow of blood from the wound.

A powdered material is found scattered about the floor, apparently left by the burglar. Perhaps he had a box of some sort of pills with him, and in removing the handkerchief to stop the flow of blood from his cut, he dropped the box of pills on the floor. Some of the pills apparently broke on impact, and he did not completely remove this powder.

A locked drawer has been pried open with some sort of tool which had been covered with a protective coat of paint. Small flakes of paint are found adhering to the drawer and on the carpet immediately below this drawer. These flakes have been dissolved in an appropriate solvent and are now ready for the analysis. In the cars of both suspects, tools suitable for the purpose of prying open a drawer have been found. Both are painted, and both have chips or flakes of paint missing. Samples from both tool paints have been removed.

It is thought that this burglary may have been for the purposes of financing the purchase of drugs of abuse. Some powdered material was found on the carpet of the cars of both suspects. This has been dissolved in a suitable solvent for gas chromatographic analysis. The solvent used is methanol, and the suspected drug is phenobarbital. Standard solutions of various drugs in methanol are available for comparison by this means.

A number of analyses can be performed in an effort to link one of the two possible suspects with the scene of the crime. Both suspects are employed in work that could involve contact with glass fragments, and both claim to have cut themselves on their hands while working.

It is the task of the laboratory personnel to perform the analysis of the physical evidence collected. The matching of the glass fragments can be quite easily done by measurement of their density or refractive index. While the results cannot be conclusive, they may contribute toward a final decision.

Matching of the soil samples also serves only to supply rare data upon which to base a conclusion; in itself, such evidence is not conclusive.

There may be stains at the scene that were not associated with the crime at all, such as spilled coffee, shoe polish, and the like. It may be well to test any apparent bloodstains first to make certain they are blood before any attempt is made to establish the blood group of the stain. Blood typing may help to eliminate one of the suspects, if the blood type does not belong to the same group as the bloodstains found at the scene. It will not prove a suspect guilty, as many persons have the same general blood type.

The paint samples may also help link the suspect to the scene, as will the analysis of the spilled powders. If the spilled powder proves to be aspirin, or some other common medicinal tablet, perhaps the suspect is a habitual user of aspirin. If this is the case, then a blood sample will perhaps yield this information. The powdered material found in the cars of the suspects may be analyzed by infrared spectrophotometry and by gas chromatography to establish its identity.

Hair samples found at the scene of the crime may be used to aid in the case presented against a suspect, but as noted earlier, this is not conclusive in itself.

The goal is to establish with as much certainty as possible that one of the suspects was involved in the perpetration of this crime and that the other could not have been present at the crime scene.

You do not have to work on these analyses during your regularly scheduled laboratory period. You have two weeks to get everything done. You must write up your analyses in a clear, readable fashion, with a summary of your findings presented at the end. All data obtained in the laboratory must be included. Each analysis will involve three samples: suspect A, suspect B, and the physical evidence found at the scene of the crime.

PART B: CAMPSITE CRIME

The circumstances surrounding the crime to which you will be assigned as analysts are as follows:

County law enforcement officers were summoned to a state owned and operated campground. They were notified of an apparent homicide by the Park Ranger. The slain woman had been discovered by persons camping at a nearby site. The time of discovery was approximately 9:15 A.M. Plans had been made the evening before to go on a morning nature hike. When the victim and her friends did not meet at the designated time, the members of the other party went to the campsite to awaken them. It was presumed that they had overslept. There was no answer to their wake-up calls, so one of the women in the party entered the victim's tent. There she found the deceased, fully clothed, as if all ready for the outing, lying on the floor of the tent. She was obviously dead, lying in a stained area of what appeared at first glance to be blood. What appeared to be stab wounds were seen on the neck and chest area of the body. The hikers immediately notified the Park Ranger of what they had found.

Crime scene investigators were called to the campground. They sealed off the scene to preserve any physical evidence which might yield clues as to the cause of death and the identity of any person or persons who might have been involved in the perpetration of the crime.

An extensive, careful search of the interior of the tent was conducted after the body of the victim was photographed and removed to the County Medical Examiner's morgue for a post-mortem examination.

Campers occupying neighboring sites were questioned by the investigating officers. The following information was compiled. There had been three women occupying the tent the evening previous to the slaying. It was not definitely known if all of the women were actually camping together, or whether some of them were only there for a campfire visit and meant to return home that same night. The nature hike invitation had been extended to whoever might be interested in accompanying the other groups of campers.

The tent search showed the contents to be the following: One sleeping bag, two unopened packages of Marlboro Lights filter-tip cigarettes, another pack of the same brand with only three cigarettes remaining. A stainless steel fork and spoon, a hairbrush, a cotton handkerchief, one fountain pen, one ballpoint pen, a tube of lipstick, a small bottle of aspirin which contained three tablets, and coins whose sum totaled $0.82. All of the above items were contained in a small overnight case. In addition, the tent inventory included a small can of green paint, a one-half inch wide nylon bristle paint brush, used but uncleaned, and a small amount of a white powdered substance, found beneath the edge of the sleeping bag. The crime scene investigators properly packaged and labeled all of the above list items for transport to the State Crime Laboratory for analysis. The tent and the sleeping bag were also included for a more careful search at the lab.

The campsite area in front of the tent contained the following: ashes of a smouldering campfire, three pieces of unburned firewood, one small hand axe, a folding wire grill, a green painted folding campstool, a length of one-quarter-inch diameter rope, 7 feet 2 inches long, a waterproof match container with 9 matches inside and a 24-quart Thermos brand portable cooler, in which were various foodstuffs. A 4/5 quart bottle of a popular brand of bourbon, containing approximately one-fourth of the original contents, was also found along with 2 unused paper cups.

The area immediately behind the tent contained 2 empty 2-liter disposable plastic carbonated beverage containers.

The campsite was also found to contain—in locations surrounding the tent site—11 burned, filter-tip cigarette stubs. Four of the cigarettes had been Marlboro Lights brand; the others were Eve brand filter-tip cigarettes. All of these stubs were collected, packaged, labeled as to their location and included in the items sent to the laboratory.

The rest of the materials contained in the immediate vicinity of the tent area were of natural origin and not of evidential value in the opinion of the scene investigators.

A grid search of the wooded area surrounding the site led to the discovery of a stainless steel table knife of a design which matched that of the fork and spoon found in the dead woman's tent. The blade of the knife was seen to be stained with what appeared to be blood of human or animal origin, not definable at the site. It was packaged for analysis of blood type, blood species, fingerprints, and comparison of manufacture with the utensils found in the tent. The dead woman's car was also impounded, sealed, and transported to the laboratory to be searched for physical evidence which might aid in the investigation.

The following day the Coroner's office reported to the Sheriff's Department that the woman died of multiple stab wounds to the neck and chest area, producing massive hemorrhage and a blood clot in the brain. Her clothes were transferred to the crime laboratory, along with some strands of hair caught under her fingernails. Her shirt was stained with blood and what at first glance appeared to be lipstick. Samples of her own hair, different in color from that found under her fingernails were also taken to the lab.

The crime laboratory analysts, in working with the physical evidence from the crime scene and the body of the victim, have compiled the following information. The blood of the deceased was Type B, the bloodstains found on the edge of the victim's sleeping bag were found to be of Type O in some cases and of Type B in others. The bloodstains on the tent floor were of Type B. A more thorough search of the tent interior produced a small wad of paper, which, when unfolded, contained an inked name of the campground where the murder occurred. Analysis of the extracted ink has shown that it was not written with either of the pens found in the tent contents. Comparison of hairs from the head of the slain woman and of those found under her fingernails did not produce a match. Although this comparison is never conclusive, there were distinct differences between the two, primarily in color. Analysis of the shirt of the dead woman, with regard to the stain identified as lipstick and the contents of the tube of lipstick found in her tent, showed them to be dissimilar.

A search of the victim's car produced a small purse in the glove compartment. The driver's license showed the identity of the victim to be Ms. Inez Montego. Letters also found in the glove compartment were responses from two women, Ms. Prunella Pruitt and Ms. Hortense Hochstedtler, accepting invitations to a weekend of camping with the murdered woman for the same campground and the same weekend during which the crime was committed. The former invited guest will be called suspect A and the latter suspect B during the remainder of this narrative and for purposes of your cataloging evidence results.

Return addresses on the envelopes found in the slain woman's car enabled the Sheriff's deputies to locate the two women, presumed to be suspects in the case. Both women were brought to the Sheriff's office for questioning. These are the stories which they gave as statements.

Suspect A, Ms. Prunella Pruitt, stated that she had not been at the campsite of the victim the previous evening. She was shocked to learn of the death of her friend, Ms. Montego. Ms. Pruitt said that she had known the deceased for approximately 4 years, had been good friends and had gone camping with her many times. She stated that she had intended to meet her friend at the campground, but that she had remembered a previous commitment and had not been able to go camping. She said that she had been alone the previous evening, preparing some papers which were due at her office the following morning. The investigating officer requested that she give a blood sample to be analyzed as to type and content of foreign substances. She was fingerprinted and photographed. Various items in her possession were impounded for comparative analysis at the crime laboratory. Lipsticks, writing pens, some samples of her hair, and some white medication tablets found in her purse were also collected. A search warrant was issued and a search of her home produced a pair of jeans, stained with what appeared to be blood. The suspect, when asked about the jeans, said that she had cut her hand on her garage door the day before and had gotten some blood on her clothing. The search unit also noticed paint stains on the suspect's jeans. She said that she was an amateur furniture refinisher and had been working on a project the day before, prior to remembering the office work which she had to complete. Investigators did find a partially refinished small table in the kitchen of the suspect's home. It was newly painted, with what had been subsequently analyzed to be lead-free green paint. Ms. Pruitt was released, but informed that she was to remain available for further questioning, if needed in the future.

Sheriff's Department officials also located the other woman whose name appeared on the letters found in the car of the murdered woman. Ms. Hochstedtler stated, in response to questioning, that she had indeed been invited on the campout. She had accepted the invitation and then had changed her plans at the last minute. She had informed Ms. Montego that she would not be able to stay the night. She had indeed gone to the campground that evening, but had left just after another women, whom she described as Ms. Pruitt, had also gone home. She apparently was the last person to see the slain woman alive. The investigating officers collected the same samples and items from Ms. Hochstedtler as they did from Ms. Pruitt. A legal search of suspect B's home produced a pair of slacks containing apparent blood and paint stains. The suspect could offer no explanation for their presence, saying she had not noticed the stains and had no idea as to where she might have gotten them.

The descriptions of the two women who were with the slain woman, as given by the persons at the campground, were sufficiently vague, due to poor lighting conditions, as to be applicable to any number of persons.

You are the crime lab analyst. It is your task to analyze the physical evidence which has been collected, or which you will collect from the simulated crime scene, in some instances. Maintain an unbiased viewpoint throughout your laboratory work. Do not consciously try to make the results come out in favor of either of the suspects. Impersonal, honest, analytical work is essential if the data are to be useful in exonerating or implicating the innocent or the guilty. You are not the attorney or the judge. Your assistance to the Sheriff's Department will include a percent certainty of the connection between the crime and each of the two suspects, based upon your laboratory results.

PART C: A PARKING RAMP RUMBLE

Police authorities were called to a public parking ramp where the body of a young woman had been found beside a parked car. She had apparently met her death by stab wounds to the neck and chest areas of her body. Signs of a struggle were evident, her clothing was torn, and the contents of her purse strewn about. The driver's door of the car was open and there were bloodstains on the seat of the car on the driver's side. The victim was found in a position which suggested that she may have fallen from the car when attempting to reach for her keys. The keys were found to be just under the body of the vehicle, on the parking ramp floor.

Investigators found the following physical evidence associated with the scene of the crime: The window glass in the left front door of the vehicle had been broken. There were pieces of glass found on the floor of the parking ramp and left in the window itself. Perhaps the woman's assailant may have carried some of this glass away from the scene, lodged in clothing or soles of shoes. There were found to be some small chips of paint on the floor near the door of the vehicle. The paint apparently was chipped from the vehicle door, as there was a dented area with paint missing, freshly removed, and no rust or dirt was found on this location. The remainder of the vehicle was quite dirty and did not appear to have been washed recently.

A careful search of the vehicle and the parking ramp produced a knife, believed to be the murder weapon. It was found to have stains on the blade which might be blood. The knife was transmitted to the crime lab for fingerprint examination.

Among the articles from the victim's purse was a small scrap of paper upon which was written a telephone number. This was sent to the lab for ink analysis.

The body of the deceased was taken to the medical examiner's office for autopsy. During the course of his postmortem examination of the victim, the coroner found hair and small bits of skin under the victim's fingernails. The victim's blood was determined to be Type A.

The medical examiner found stains on the shirt of the deceased which he determined to be smears of lipstick. Perhaps they came from her attacker during the struggle which took place before her death.

An examination of the victim's purse contents produced a small vial of a powdered material. Analysis shows this to be a drug cut with a substance of rather unusual composition.

Analysis of the victim's blood shows no presence of alcohol or any drug.

An address book in the purse contents contained a number of names, but only two of these were women. Due to the presence of the lipstick stains on the victim's shirt, these two women were questioned by police investigators.

The following information was obtained and evidence collected. Ms. Franc Dorant, hereafter called suspect A, denied being at the parking ramp at any time. She stated that she was acquainted with the murdered girl, but had not seen her for some time. At the time of her interrogation, Ms. Dorant seemed slightly disoriented. She said that she had not been feeling well, due to having attended a party the evening before and had drank too heavily. She was suffering from a headache and had slept only a short time before the police arrived at her apartment. She was taken to police headquarters for fingerprinting, a blood specimen collected for typing, and alcohol and drug analyses. Police collected an article of clothing from her apartment containing bloodstains. The woman stated that she had gone fishing with a friend a few days before and in cleaning the catch had gotten blood on her clothes. Two tubes of lipstick were also taken to the lab, of a color appearing to be similar to the stains on the victims shirt. A white, powdered material found in a bathroom cabinet was also sent to the lab. The vial container was similar to that found in the dead woman's possession. Some pens with ink similar in color to that on the paper in the victim's purse were found.

The other woman, Ms. Abigail Adamson, denoted suspect B, was not home when authorities called on her, but returned to her apartment later in the day. She said she had stayed at the home of a friend the evening before and was not in the vicinity of the parking ramp the previous night. Her friend, upon questioning, said that Ms. Adamson had come to see her late on the night in question and, after having been there for a time, seemed quite upset. She asked if she might stay at her friend's home that night as she did not feel like being alone. Her friend agreed. Police found an article of bloodstained clothing in Ms. Adamson's apartment. She said she had been working on an art project and had cut herself on the hand. The blood had stained her clothing and she had not had time to wash it. Other articles collected include lipstick, ink pens and a powdered substance, claimed to be an antacid by Ms. Adamson. Blood samples for analysis and fingerprints were taken from this suspect.

A thorough search of the suspect's shoes showed both had small bits of glass and paint in the soles and heels of one pair. This could be picked up at many locations and simply in the course of walking on the sidewalk. Analysis may show some similarities to that found at the crime scene.

Hair from each suspect had been collected and compared to that found under the victim's fingernails.

The crime lab has extracted the ink from the note and from the suspect pens. The note and ballpoint pens are also available to some analysts.

The note, if written by someone other than the victim, may contain fingerprints which could be very useful evidence, if legible.

You have the evidence from this crime scene and from the suspects available to you. It is your task to attempt to implicate or exonerate either or both of the suspects, based upon this evidence. The evidence, by itself, may not convict, but could provide the basis for further investigation. Do the best you can. Careful work is a must.

PART D: A HOUSEHOLD HOMICIDE

Law enforcement authorities were summoned to the scene of a crime. The victim, a young woman, was found lying on a floor in her home. Signs of a struggle were evident. Some articles of furniture were overturned. A lamp with a decorative glass base, was found broken on a table. A candy dish, its contents scattered, was found broken on the floor, apparently having fallen from a small stand during the assault. The police investigators proceeded to search the premises for physical evidence which might be useful in identifying the victim's assailants. This is what was found and what you have to work with.

The victim apparently met her death through stab wounds in her chest and neck. A knife was found under a couch which shows evidence of stains, thought to be blood. A postmortem examination has confirmed the cause of death as massive internal hemorrhaging, compounded with wounds to the lungs which would have resulted in their collapse. Due to the placement of wounds and the appearance of the room in which the victim was found, police investigators feel that she died at the hand of an assailant, and suicide is ruled out of the question.

Interrogation of persons having known or lived near the deceased has established her identity as Ms. Ann Holbook. She was 23 years of age, Caucasian, lived alone, and was employed by a pharmacy. She was known to have a large circle of friends and was the hostess of a number of social gatherings, some of which became quite bothersome to her neighbors. Raucousness, loud music, and sounds of physical combat had resulted in complaints which had caused law enforcement authorities to be called to the home on a few occasions. None of the victim's neighbors had known her very well, but were able to describe two other women who had been seen to visit her quite frequently. These two women were questioned that same morning and released pending further investigation. Both of these persons' homes were also searched by the police, following the acquisition of warrants obtained from the proper agency.

The remainder of this report is concerned with the physical evidence found in the victim's home and those of the two women, the only two suspects in the case thus far. Some suggestions as to possible analyses which the forensic laboratory might perform on this evidence will also be included. You are employed by the laboratory as an analyst and it will be your findings which may lead to conviction or exoneration of the persons being investigated.

The knife, which evidently was the weapon in the crime—now suspected of being homicide—is to be examined. The stains must be identified as being blood, if possible, and if positive results are obtained, the blood type determined. The victim's blood type was O. Ms. Alice Vick, one of the suspects, and the other woman being investigated, Ms. Marthe Malcomb, have submitted to blood samples being taken for typing. This will be done by the crime lab. Both of the suspects' living quarters have yielded articles of apparel exhibiting stains thought to be blood. Both women involved have logical explanations for the stains on their clothing. If the stains were indeed blood, and of the suspect's own type, they mean nothing. If of the victim's blood type and different from their own, they could be significant. Many persons, however, possess blood of Type O. By itself, the blood type of the stains is not conclusive.

Fragments of glass were found lodged in the cuffs of slacks belonging to both suspects. Perhaps they match shards from either the candy dish or lamp. Find out, if you can.

The County Medical Examiner has fixed the time of the victim's death as somewhere between midnight and 4:00 A.M. The suspects, when questioned in their homes the following day, both appeared to be recovering from the effects of either liquor or drugs. They were not totally coherent and explained this saying they had been alone the evening before, had passed the time watching television, had a few drinks, had awakened with headaches and had take aspirin to relieve the pain associated with it. Perhaps incoherence may be attributed to drowsiness caused by a high concentration of blood salicylate. Perhaps the headache was due to stress caused by the perpetration of the crime. They submitted to blood samples being taken for both alcohol and drug analysis by the crime lab. The blood samples have been prepared for both of these procedures and are available to you.

A small amount of white, powdered material was found on the carpet of the room in which the deceased was found. This material, if identified as a drug of abuse, may establish the victim as a supplier, something which her employment would make possible. Perhaps one of the suspects is a user, and in the course of an argument over drugs and in an alcoholic rage, caused the demise of Ms. Holbrook.

The knife, suspected of being the murder weapon, must be dusted for fingerprints. One must be careful not to touch the handle since this is an area of primary interest. Both suspects' inked prints are available for comparison with any latent prints which might be found. Remember, since both suspects have been known visitors of the victim, they may have plausible explanations for the prints on the knife, if found. However, the position of the prints with respect to the knife point may be useful in reconstructing the crime. Make note of this when "lifting" any prints which you find on the weapon.

A scrap of paper was found on the floor of the room in which the victim was found. A phone number was written in ink on the paper. Perhaps ink analysis will show similarities between the written number and pens taken from the purses of each of the suspects.

The ink samples have been prepared for analysis and are available for chromatographic separation of the dyes.

The paper, in addition to being utilized for ink analysis, may also contain latent prints of the person who murdered Ms. Holbook. The paper is available and one may use a variety of methods for print development.

The victim's shirt was found to have some stained areas which appear to be lipstick smears. Perhaps they came from a lipstick belonging to the victim herself, but equally probable, they may have come from the lips of the assailant during the assault. The police have collected, as evidence, tubes of lipstick from each of the suspects, as well as some from the victim's purse and makeup table. A possible match would be quite useful in preparing a case against one of the suspects.

The County Coroner, in conducting the examination of the victim's body found several strands of hair lodged under the fingernails. These have been determined to have not come from the head of the deceased. Hair samples have been collected from both suspects for comparison with those from the victim's fingernails.

A small painted table was found overturned in the room where the victim was murdered. Some small chips of paint were also found caught in the fibers of the suspects' clothing. Paint fragments can be picked up on one's clothing in a variety of ways, but if the possible lead content of the paint from the scene table and that of either of the suspects' clothing are the same, this will help in the prosecution building a case against one or the other of the suspects.

A small amount of soil was found on the carpet of the room in which the deceased was found. Soil was collected from shoes belonging to each of the suspects and is available for comparison. This is not very conclusive evidence in itself, but added to other findings, may be of considerable importance.

This constitutes the report of the crime and the evidence that has been found associated with it. You will be awarded additional points, beyond those given for the analyses results, by writing a reconstruction of the crime from your analyses, should you find that either or both of the suspects are implicated. This reconstruction is not required.

PART E: A LOVE TRIANGLE?

The body of a young woman was found in her apartment. The circumstances which led to this event were as follows. A young woman (Ms. Marquette) had confided to her friend that she was worried about a circumstance which had recently occurred. She was dating a man (Mr. Strand) who was in the process of obtaining a divorce. The man's estranged wife did not want this divorce and was trying to reconcile with her former husband. The man intended to marry Ms. Marquette when the divorce was finalized. Ms. Marquette told her friend that the man's former wife had called her a number of times and pleaded with her to break off her relationship with Strand. Strand's wife felt that this would aid in the reconciliation. Ms. Marquette refused to do this. Mrs. Strand had made vague threats to Marquette over the phone, but had not attempted to harm her, as yet. Mrs. Strand had mentioned that she could get help in persuading Marquette, if necessary.

Ms. Marquette's friend was concerned and invited her to lunch one day. The agreement was made and the meeting place decided. At the appointed time, Ms. Marquette failed to appear. Her friend called her apartment, but no one answered the phone. Marquette's friend went to her apartment later in the day, but could not get an answer to her knock. She called the police. The police gained entrance to the apartment and found the body of the woman on the floor of the living room. Death had apparently occurred sometime the previous evening. Crime scene investigators were called in and evidence was gathered to be forwarded to the crime lab for analysis.

The victim apparently was involved in a struggle before her death. Furniture was out of place and a lamp was broken on the floor. Fragments of the lamp were collected as evidence. The victim met her death through multiple stab wounds to the neck and chest area.

A bloodstained knife was found wrapped in a towel in a waste basket in the kitchen. This was sent to the crime lab for fingerprinting.

The post mortem examination of the victim by the medical examiner yielded the following: Hair was found under the fingernails of the deceased. This could have come from the head of her assailant during the struggle. The victim's blouse was found to have stains on it which were determined to be lipstick. The blood type of the victim was Type A. Some of the stains were identified as paint. The victim was known to be an amateur furniture refinisher, and a partially completed project was seen in the kitchen. A paint brush was found containing dried paint of the same color as those on the victim's clothing.

A careful search of the deceased woman's apartment resulted in the investigators discovering a note, upon which was written a phone number. The ink from this number was extracted by crime lab analysts. Investigators identified the phone number as belonging to a Ms. Mockridge. Questioning of this person resulted in her giving this statement. She did indeed know Mrs. Strand and was aware of her impending divorce. She stated, however, that although she had heard of Ms. Marquette, she was not personally acquainted with her. On the evening when Ms. Marquette was killed, Ms. Mockridge had been attending a community education course in art. She had returned from this class with a headache, had taken some aspirin, and retired for the night. She had not seen Mrs. Strand for some time, she insisted. Ms. Mockridge could not give the name of any persons who had seen her since she left the class building and so could not substantiate her whereabouts.

Police investigators also visited Mrs. Strand who stated that she had not seen the victim in person and had not spoken with her for some time. She did admit, however, to a phone conversation with the deceased during which she had asked her not to see her husband anymore. On the evening that Ms. Marquette was killed, she had not left her apartment. She said she had not been feeling well and had decided to stay home and take care of some correspondence.

Questioning of the murdered woman's neighbors in her apartment building revealed one person who had seen two women talking with the victim in front of the building at approximately 10:30 P.M. on the night she was killed. This person said that it appeared that an argument was taking place with loud voices and some agitation. The apartment building was of new construction so there was no lawn as yet and only a few boards for walking.

Law officers returned to the homes of both Mrs. Strand and Ms. Mockridge and asked them to come to the police station for further questioning, and a search of both homes was conducted after warrants were issued. The following items were found and taken to the crime laboratory.

Both women had shoes in their possession which had soil adhering to the soles. Both had pens containing ink of a similar color to that in the note in the victim's apartment. Tubes of lipstick were collected from both women for comparison. Small fragments of glass were found in the cuffs of slacks in their soiled laundry, as well as stains which appeared to be either paint or blood. Both women's clothing had smudges of a white, powdered substance which could be from many sources and may be insignificant.

Both women were fingerprinted and samples of their blood were taken for analysis. Samples of their hair were collected as well. Both women are now under suspicion of murder. Ms. Mockridge will be called Suspect A and Mrs. Strand will be Suspect B.

You are working as analysts in the crime lab and your task will be to determine similarities or differences between the scene samples and those belonging to each suspect. Some of the evidence may serve to implicate one or the other of these two women; some may not be useful at all. After completing the work, summarize your findings and state the certainty upon which you base your conclusion, if you can make one.

I hope you will enjoy this exercise and that you will find it a worthwhile conclusion to the work which you have done this term.

R. E. James

C. E. Meloan

R. Saferstein